# THE HISTORY OF THE VIOLIN
## *Its Ancestors and Collateral Instruments*

# THE
# HISTORY OF THE VIOLIN

*Its Ancestors and Collateral Instruments*

## FROM EARLIEST TIMES
## TO THE PRESENT DAY

*by*

## E. VAN DER STRAETEN

*Author of "The History of the Violoncello, etc."*
*"The Romance of the Fiddle," "The Revival of the Viols," etc.*

*With 48 Plates and numerous illustrations in text*

## VOL. II

*CASSELL*
*and Company, Ltd.*
*London, Toronto, Melbourne*
*and Sydney*

First Published . . . . *1933*

PRINTED IN GREAT BRITAIN
BY BUTLER AND TANNER LTD., FROME AND LONDON
F7.5.833

# Contents: Vol. II

## PART II

### HISTORY OF THE VIOLIN FROM 1700 TO 1800—*continued*

#### VIOLINISTS OF THE PERIOD

## PART III

### HISTORY OF THE VIOLIN FROM 1800 TO THE PRESENT DAY

#### VIOLINISTS OF THE PERIOD

# Contents

vi

# List of Illustrations

vii

# List of Illustrations

# List of Illustrations

# PART II
# HISTORY OF THE VIOLIN FROM
## 1700 TO 1800—*continued*

GIUSEPPE TARTINI

CARLO TESSARINI
From an engraving in the possession of
Messrs W. E. Hill & Sons.

# CHAPTER 33

## *Italy: to 1725*

AT the head of this epoch stands the Grandmaster Archangelo Corelli. His first four books of sonatas are testimony to his mastery of the sonata form, but they are really trio sonatas with an organ or harpsichord in which all parts are co-ordinated. In his sonatas, op. V, published in 1700, he gives us the first *real* solo sonatas, although Uccellini had already written sonatas for violin solo and bass, and Torelli a concertino for violin and violoncello, and capriccios for violin and viola or archlute, but neither can be compared with Corelli's sonatas either in point of invention, form, or violinistic treatment, in which they surpass all that has gone before of their kind, and this applies also to his Concerti grossi, op. VI. The latter served as models for Handel's similar works, and laid the foundation for the later style of writing for the orchestra. Corelli fixed the clear and firm structure, the outlines of sonata form, the final detailed development whereof was reserved to the German masters of the second half of the 18th century. In his slow movements Corelli shows a breadth and nobility of thought which are of a spiritual, almost ascetic, character in accordance with the nature of the church sonata. The more emotional and individual melody, showing a greater variety of expression, found in the works of later composers, was alien to the style of the church sonata which followed different aims and ideals. In his chamber sonatas the dance forms are reminiscent of their original character only by their rhythms, while they are raised to the higher level of little tone pictures or character pieces.

Corelli followed the example of G. B. Vitali, Torelli and others, in extending the scope of the chamber sonata by the introduction of movements of free invention, which denoted an advance towards the modern sonata. Corelli was not destined to revolutionize the art of violin playing, but he consolidated the achievements of his predecessors, and, while keeping practically within the then usual compass of the three first positions, he treated the instrument more methodically, at the same time making use in his varied passage work of the possibilities of the violin strictly within the nature of the instrument.

The teaching of Corelli spread its influence on the development of the art of violin playing through his pupils throughout the whole of Europe. (1) G. B. Somis, who combined the art of Corelli with that of Vivaldi, founded the Turin school, from which emanated, among others, Giardini, Leclair, and Pugnani, the master of Viotti. (2) Geminiani, who acquainted the English with his master's art, became the teacher of Festing and of M. Dubourg, and laid down the principles of Corelli's teaching in "The Art of Playing on the Violin," the first serious and systematic violin tutor, published in London in 1740. (3) Locatelli, who settled at Amsterdam, developed the virtuoso side, and whose 24 capricci proved of great assistance to Paganini in his studies.

Vivaldi's influence as teacher of and composer for the violin was second only to that of Corelli. He surpassed the latter in the boldness and variety of his passage work, and he consolidated and extended the sonata form still further. His allegro movements are generally broader and more developed, while showing perfect symmetry and perfection in their construction. He is credited with the invention of the "Lombardian manner," which greatly fascinated the Roman people. It consisted in a short accented note, followed by a longer one, ♪♩. a well-known feature in Scottish and Irish music. An important achievement of his was the development and perfecting of the form of the "Italian Concerto," which J. S. Bach adopted after arranging several of his concertos.

Corelli and Vivaldi inaugurated a new epoch in the art of violin playing, which found its fullest expression in Tartini, who not only considerably advanced the technique of the violin, especially the art of bowing, but also developed the sonata still further, so that in both respects he served as model to future generations. He also improved the shape of the bow, as may be seen from the illustration of a bow which to all appearance belonged to him (*see* p. 22, vol. I). By his numerous pupils from all parts of Europe his art spread far and wide, and especially the Bohemians and Austrians benefited by his three years' sojourn with Count Kinsky in Prague and Vienna.

Another outstanding figure of this period was Francesco Maria Veracini, whom Tartini took for his model in style; his sonatas, rich in melodious invention, bold and new in their harmonic treatment, were not understood by his contemporaries, and only future generations appreciated them at their full value.

CARLO TOMASO PIANI, b. ca. 1685; d. Vienna, May 25, 1760. Violinist in the Bavarian Court chapel and from July 1, 1717, in the Imperial Court chapel, Vienna, with a salary of 30 thaler per month, which was raised to 75 florins in response to his complaint that his salary had been higher in Bavaria. When all salaries were reduced in 1741 he received only 800 florins per annum instead of 900 florins (Köchel, i and ii, 372).

SIGHICELLI. A family of eminent violinists: FILIPPO SIGHICELLI, b. San Cesario, Modena, 1686; d. Modena, Apr. 14, 1773; 1st violinist at the Court of Prince Hercules of Este. GIUSEPPE SIGHICELLI, his son; b. Modena, 1737; d. there, Nov. 8, 1826; capellmeister of Hercules of Este until the latter's expulsion by Napoleon. CARLO SIGHICELLI, son of Giuseppe, b. Modena, 1772; d. there, Apr. 7, 1806; violinist at above court. ANTONIO SIGHICELLI, son of Carlo, b. Modena, July 1, 1802; d. there, Oct. 20, 1883; esteemed violinist and conductor, first conductor at Cento then at Farrara, and 1835 –59 Ducal capellmeister at Modena. VINCENZO SIGHICELLI, son of Antonio, b. Cento, July 30, 1830; d. Paris, Feb. 15, 1905; violin pupil of Mayseder and Hellmesberger, composition pupil of Sechter in Vienna. During 1849–55 solo violinist and vice-capellmeister at Modena; from the latter year he lived in Paris. He wrote various compositions for the violin.

PIETRO CASTRUCCI, b. Rome, 1689 (Riemann: 1679); d. London, 1769 (Riemann: Dublin, Feb. 29, 1759). Pupil of Corelli. The Earl of Burlington took him into his service in 1715, and brought him to London, where he succeeded Corbett as leader at the Italian Opera, ca. 1718. Quantz heard him in 1727 when Handel was giving his operas there. Castrucci not only played the obbligato accompaniments in arias but also solos between the acts. He had invented an instrument which he called "Violetta Marina," and which he played also, alternately with the violin, at his concerts in York Buildings, and Hickford's room in Brewer Street, Golden Square. Handel employed two violette marine in his operas "Orlando" and "Sosarme," which were played by the brothers Castrucci, Pietro's brother Prospero having also settled in London. Pietro was very vain and irascible, and particularly jealous of Festing, who was not his equal as a virtuoso but of an amiable nature and gentlemanly deportment. It was a source of sport and amusement of many who knew him, when meeting him in the street to greet him with: "How do you do, Mr. Festing—ah—excuse me—Signor Castrucci?" and watch the result, which sometimes threatened to end in apoplexy. It was thought at one time that he was the prototype of Hogarth's "enraged musician," but it is more probable that this was Festing's brother, John Festin [*sic*], the oboist and flautist. Castrucci was undoubtedly a remarkable virtuoso of his time, but it is said (Riemann) that he was not free from mannerisms. He composed 12 solos, op. 1, a book of sonatas for violin with violone, (violoncello), or harpsichord, op. 2, dedicated to Princess Anne: not in any way remarkable. One sonata is repub. in Cartier's "L'Art du Violon." He also wrote 12 violin concertos (London, 1738).

PROSPERO CASTRUCCI, brother of Pietro, of whom only the following particulars are obtainable, was also in Handel's orchestra, where he played, besides the violin, the violetta marina with his brother. He succeeded Talbot Young as leader of the castle concerts in the City of London (*see* E. v. d. Str., "Romance of the Fiddle," p. 197). He composed 6 solos for violin and bass.

CARLO TESSARINI, b. Rimini, State of Rome, 1690; d. 17... He fixed the three-movement form of the sonata, and showed the beginning of the sonata form of the first movement (Schering, "Gesch. d. Instr. Konzerts"). Violinist at St. Mark's, Venice; Maestro di capella, hospital of St. Giovanni e Paolo, Venice, a position similar to that of Vivaldi; 1741, professore di violino in Urbino. On Sept. 6, 1752; gave a concert at Frankfort a/M. Finally concertmeister of Cardinal Wolfgang Hannibal (*see* Eitner). He published a tutor, "Grammatica di musica, etc.," ded. signed Roma li, Feb. 20, 1741, obl. fol.; French ed., Liège (R.C. of Mus.); French ed. pub. Amsterdam, 1760, with portrait. A musical grammar, etc., Edin.; an accurate method, etc., Welcker (B. Wagener). "Il maestro e discepolo da camera . . ." op. 2 (Urbino, Girol. Meinardi, 1734). Fétis says: "It is believed that he was a pupil of Corelli at Rome, as in his first compositions he closely copies the style of that master. He soon became prominent by his double talent of composer and executant, and in 1724 he had already become famous in Italy. Schering ("Geschichte des Instrumental Konzerts") points out his influence and the development of the symphonic form. Fétis disbelieves Gerbert and Burney's statement that he went to Amsterdam in 1762, when he would have been already 72 years of age. It is true, however, that he broke away from his early form of composition and developed a style which was entirely new. He wrote: "Sonate per due violini con un canone in fine" (Amsterdam, Roger; Paris, Le Clerc), sonate a due violini, lib. 1 and 2 (Ib.); 12 concertini grossi; 12 sonate a violino solo, e basso per organo (Paris, Venier); 6 divertimenti a due violini lib. 2; L'Arte di nuova modulazione, concerti grossi (Amsterdam and Paris, 1762); contrasto armonico, concerti grossi ibid, a nouvelle methode, etc. (Amsterdam; Italian, French and English eds.), a very primitive tutor, the Autogr. MS. dated "Roma 1741." (*See* Wki.)

GIUSEPPE TARTINI, b. Pirano, Istria, Apr. 8, 1692; d. Padua, Feb. 26, 1770. His father, Giovanni Antonio, was a member of a good Florentine family, who for his liberal donations to the church was raised to the rank of nobility. He destined Giuseppe for the church, and with that view sent him to the school of the Oratorio di San Filippo Neri, where, apart from his general education, he received also instruction in music and made such progress, that he was admitted into the Collegio dei Padri delle Scuole Pie at Capo d'Istria, where, apart from general studies in music, he also received lessons on the violin. The idea of joining the Order of the Minorite Friars had become distasteful to him, and he prevailed upon his father to permit him to enter, in 1710, the University of Padua as a law student. Fencing proved, however, a greater fascination than the latter, and his impulsiveness caused him not infrequently to be mixed up with duels and brawls.

5

Meanwhile he pursued with zeal his musical studies, and even began to give lessons therein. Among his pupils was a young girl, Elizabetta Premazone, a niece of Cardinal Cornaro, Bishop of Padua. Tartini fell desperately in love with this girl and they contracted a secret marriage, with the result that he was disowned by his parents, and threatened with imprisonment by the Cardinal. He fled from the town, intending to go to Rome, but when on the way he sought temporary refuge at the Monastery of S. Francis at Assisi, he found a relative in the person of the Father Guardian, who persuaded him to remain there in hiding for a time. He remained for two years, devoting himself to the study of the violin, and to theoretical studies under Father Boëmo (Bohuslav Czernohorsky, a distinguished composer). During this time he discovered what is generally known as the "third sound," which appears as the bass when two higher notes, thirds or sixths, are played on the violin, and henceforth he impressed the fact upon his pupils by telling them: "If you do not hear the bass your thirds or sixths are not true." The discipline of the monastery and his intercourse with the monks produced still more important results, as his irascible and quarrelsome nature had become calm and reflective, and his disposition had changed to one of gentleness and sweetness. He always played at divine service, when the musicians were hidden from the congregation by a curtain. On Aug. 1, 1715, the feast of S. Francis, when pilgrims from all parts of Italy came to pay homage at the tomb of the Saint, it happened that during the service the deacon accidentally moved the curtains, and Tartini was recognized by some Paduans, who spread the news in their town, where his wife languished for him. Soon after he learned that the Cardinal had forgiven him and that he as well as his parents had consented to his marriage, whereupon he returned to Padua. In 1716 he was invited to a contest with Veracini at the Palace of Mocenigo at Venice; but when he heard Veracini play just before that event, he recognized that the latter surpassed him, especially in the art of bowing, and he withdrew from the contest, to give himself up to another period of study to benefit from Veracini's example. He left his wife in the care of his brother and retired to Ancona, where he applied himself particularly to the technics of the bow until he had attained to the desired perfection. In 1721 he was invited to become solo violinist of the Church of S. Antonio at Padua, which had a chapel of 16 vocalists and 24 instrumentalists, under F. A. Valotti, considered to be one of the finest in Italy. On his appointment it was stipulated that he was exempt from giving any proof of his excellence, and he was moreover permitted leave of absence for playing elsewhere. The first opportunity for this came in 1723, when he was invited to play at the coronation of the Emperor Charles VI, at Prague, where he and his companion, the violoncellist Antonio Vandini, also a member of the chapel of S. Antonio, met with a most enthusiastic reception, and were induced by Count Kinsky, the Chancellor of Bohemia, to remain in his service. They accepted, but the climate disagreed with Tartini, whose health suffered therefrom, and family troubles being added to this (*see* Hortis, "Lettere di Gius. Tartini"), he returned with Vandini to Padua in 1726, visiting on the way his admirer M. Morosini di San Stefano at Venice, who interested himself in the misfortunes of his family (*see* E. H.-A.'s "Tartini" in Grove's Dictionary).

Tartini received many tempting offers to visit London and Paris, but after his return from Prague, no amount of money could induce him to leave his native country again. His answer to a proposal from Sir Edward Walpole to come to London was: "I have a wife, who is of the same mind as myself, and no children. We are contented with our condition, and if ever we have a wish, it is not one to possess more than we have." He was very charitable, and supported widows and orphans, paid for the education of children of poor people; to poor pupils he gave lessons at reduced fees, or even taught them gratuitously.

In 1728 he established at Padua a High School for violin playing which gained for itself the title of "School of the Nations," while he himself was called "Master of Nations," as his numerous pupils came from all parts of Europe, and included a large proportion of the leading violinists of the second half of the 18th century. Among the foremost may be mentioned Alberghi, Bini, Ferrari, J. G. Graun, Lahonssaye, Manfredi, Meneghini, Nardini, Pagin, also Pugnani, pupil of Somis, who finished his studies under Tartini, and Maddalena Lombardini-Sirmen, to whom Tartini addressed

7

in 1760 the still valuable letter on the "Art of Bowing," translated by Burney, and since reproduced in Geo. Hart's "The Violin," and many other books on the violin, as well as separately.

He was an indefatigable investigator of the scientific and theoretical part of his art, and tried to find a satisfactory explanation of the "third sound," and probably to clear his own ideas about this question, he wrote a "Trattato di musica" (Padua, 1754), but his scientific knowledge was not equal to the task, which did not find a satisfactory solution before the famous work of Helmholtz appeared. Tartini's "Trattato" was attacked by several scientists as well as by J. J. Rousseau, and a reply in Tartini's name appeared which is said to have for its real author his friend and pupil Count Thurn and Taxis, who is also believed to have written an answer, published at Venice in 1769, to Rousseau's attack. In 1767 Tartini published another book, "De' principij dell' armonia musicale," etc., in which he claimed the priority of the discovery of the third sound against Remieu, a Frenchman, who asserted that he had discovered the phenomenon in 1743.

In later years he wrote another compendious theoretical work, "Delle ragioni e delle proporzini," in 6 books, which he left to his friend Professor Colombo with the request that he should superintend its publication. Unfortunately Colombo died shortly after and the work appears to have been irretrievably lost except for portions of the material which served for the work and which are preserved in the Archives of Pirano. He occupied himself also with technical questions regarding the violin and the bow. For the instrument itself he used thicker strings than those that were chosen by his predecessors and contemporaries. To the bow, for which he chose a lighter wood, he gave a slight inward curve of the stick, which was somewhat longer than customary. He also diminished the size of the head and had the lower half of the stick fluted, which gave a surer grip. A bow, which most probably belonged to him, and is now in the possession of Mr. Howard-Head of London, is illustrated and described in the chapter on the bow.

Although the life of a virtuoso did not appeal to his nature, and he did not leave Italy again after his return from Prague, he toured occasionally in his own country. One such journey was undertaken shortly before 1740, at the request of Cardinal Olivieri, at whose palace at Rome he played before members of the aristocracy and the highest dignitaries of the Church, including Pope Clement XII, at whose request he wrote a Miserere which was performed in the Sistine Chapel on Ash Wednesday, 1768, but proved unworthy of the master's work and was never performed again. This, a Salve Regina for four voices, his last composition, and some canzone for two and three voices, both in the archives of S. Antonio, are the only vocal compositions known by him.

In 1768 his health began to fail him. He had an attack of convulsive paralysis from which he partly recovered, but soon after a cancerous growth formed in his foot which caused him intense suffering. His favourite pupil Nardini hurried to his bedside and tended him with loving care and devotion to the end. He was buried in the Church of S. Catherine, and a Requiem composed by his friend Vallotti was sung in the basilica of S. Antonio. The Abbé Fanzago delivered a eulogium, at the funeral service in the Servite Church, which was afterwards published with Tartini's portrait at Padua in 1770 and again in 1792.

Tartini's importance in the history of the violin is threefold: in the first place as executant, in the second place as teacher, and in the third place as composer. Of the player posterity can only form an idea by the accounts of his contemporaries, his art as a teacher was handed down to future generations through his pupils, but a number of his works are still, and will be, probably for centuries to come, the delight of music lovers. Although he had a remarkable technique, especially of the bow, he abhorred the display of mere virtuosity. His greatest strength lay apparently in the playing of the cantabile, in which he showed deep poetical feeling, yet with a noble reserve, which probably makes him akin to Spohr and Joachim. All seem to agree that he had a very beautiful singing tone, except Quantz, who for once, however, appears to have failed in his judgment, in which he alone runs contrary to all the rest. Lahoussay, who became his pupil, says: "Nothing could express my astonishment and admiration caused by the perfection and purity of his tone, the charm of expression, the magic of his bow, the all-round perfection of his performance.

9

Fayolle, in a note to Tartini's letter to Mme Sirmen, says that Tartini considered resin one-half of the art of violin playing, and that he prepared his own resin in the following manner: "Put resin and water in equal proportions into a glazed earthenware or silver vessel. Let it boil over a strong fire, and skim with a spoon all impurities that are thrown up in the boiling. When no more impurities appear on the surface, boil down the residue, and pour it into prepared boxes or into egg shells, which can be afterwards chipped off as the use will demand."

With Tartini the art of violin playing enters upon a new era. Up to then the figuration which we find already in the sonatas of Bassani and Torelli, has not undergone any fundamental change; although Corelli widened its scope, yet it became more or less stereotyped. Tartini's figuration is much bolder and far more varied, but important as his innovations are in this respect, they are still more so with regard to the sonata, and especially to the instrumental concerto. Their nature is discussed in detail, in A. Schering's "Geschichte des Instrumental Konzerts." The following are the salient points of his investigation. Tartini no longer belongs to the period of the concerto introduced by Torelli, he belongs to the quartet and symphony period, typified by his concertos in 4 parts pub. by Welcker, London. Vivaldi rounds off, synthesizes, and concludes the achievements of the old style masters; Tartini begins the new. Soli and Tutti show well-defined divisions, they show more artistic and thematic workmanship, and the form becomes more compact. Rondo types are used more and more for the final movements. His concerto form exercised a dominating influence and served as a model for his contemporaries, even including J. Christian Bach who wrote, before 1754, a harpsichord concerto "in Tartini's manner," which was found among the posthumous papers of Ph. E. Bach.

It is impossible to obtain a satisfactory view of Tartini's life work before a long promised, revised Italian ed. of his complete works has appeared. Only the smaller amount of these was published. Statements as to their number vary greatly, but it appears fairly safe to estimate the number of his sonatas at ca. 100, and of his concertos at over 127, apart from concerti grossi, and string quartets. Of that once favourite form of chamber music, the trio sonata, only one trio for 2 violins and bass has been published. According to Wasielewski a few more of this kind are preserved in the Basilica of S. Antonio at Padua, which cannot awaken any particular interest. A comprehensive list of his works appears in Eitner's "Quellen Lexikon." He left, according to most biographers, his autograph compositions to Count Thurn and Taxis, but Mr. Heron-Allen (Grove's Dictionary) says that the "Journal Encyclopédique de Venise" of 1775 contains a paragraph stating that Captain P. Tartini, his nephew, had deposited 42 sonatas, 6 sonatas and trios, 127 concertos, etc., with the violinist Antonio Zazzini, which were offered for sale by Carminer at Venice.

The best known of his sonatas is that known as "The Devil's Trill," composed during his exile at Assisi, and which owes its origin to a dream in which the Devil appears to him and plays a sonata, which however far surpassed that which he afterwards wrote down as far as he could remember. He told the story to Lalande, and it has since been recounted in numberless books. It is also known that he sought inspiration for his compositions in the poems of Petrarque, and that he would keep a certain line in his mind while at work, which he inscribed in cypher on the top of his MSS.; a number of these are still in existence, and have been deciphered by a certain Melchior Balbi, who possessed the key to the cypher. In beauty of melody, which always bears an elevated and dignified character, he is seldom approached, never surpassed, by any of his contemporaries, and only by the greatest of his successors.

PIETRO ANTONIO LOCATELLI, b. Bergamo, 1692 (Fétis and Wki.: 1693); d. Amsterdam, Apr. 1, 1764 (Fétis). Sent to Rome in early youth as a pupil of Corelli. According to Alexandri he was still at Rome on Mar. 17, 1714. On Mar. 15, 1725, he entered the service of the Landgrave of Hesse Darmstadt at Mantua (Alessandri, p. 90), during 1732–41 he appears to have lived at Amsterdam, where his compositions were pub. at that time, and, 1746, he conducted concerts there. On July 24, 1731, he received the privilege for the pub. of his works in Amsterdam, which was renewed May 12, 1746. In 1755 he produced a comic opera of his at Dresden. For critique of his playing, see *Allgemeine Music Zeitung Leipzig*, 1865 (?), No. 38. Compositions are in Eitner.

Although he was not the founder of a new school, he enlarged and enriched the technique of the violin by new passages and styles of bowing. The Count di San Rafaells praises him in most eulogistic terms in his "Lettere sul arte del suono." In spite of Burney's derogatory remarks, his sonatas and concertos, especially his concerti grossi, contain much that is excellent; and his share in the development of the sonata form is by no means inconsiderable. Paganini owed a great deal of his art to his close study of Locatelli's 24 caprices, which are really studies in transcendental technique, and as such have been often misjudged. He had a most astounding technique which called forth unqualified admiration wherever he appeared, and the charm of many of his compositions added no doubt to his success. A. Schering ("Gesch. des Justr. Konzerts," pp. 54–5) shows him as an innovator with regard to the concerto grosso, who like Tatrini belongs to a new epoch which broke with the old traditions. For his well-considered criticism we must refer students to his book, as it would lead us beyond the scope of this work. Some of his charming sonatas have been repub. by various editors, and his caprices have been edited by E. Nadaud as "L'Art du Violon" (Paris, Costallat & Co.).

FRANCESCO MARIA CATTANEO, b. Lodi, ca. 1697; d. Dresden, 1758. Was violinist in the Court chapel at Dresden from June 8, 1726, and succeeded Pisendel as concertmeister in 1756 with a salary of 1,200 thalers. He composed 3 violin concertos and some airs, which remained in MS., a MS. trio for 2 violins and bass, in Schwerin library, also a sonata for violin and cembalo, and sonata for violin and bass, signed Catango!

G. CATTANEO, Sonate a 3, op. 1, Modena, 1700 (Bol.).

LEONARDO BALZIANI. Italian violinist, living ca. 1700; composed some solos and trios for violin which were pub.

FILIPO CARLO (?) BELISI (BELLISI). An early 18th-century violin-composer of 12 sonate per camera a violino e violoncello, 1700. One of these sonatas is in a collective vol. pub. by Kirchhoff and Wig, 1887. Baletti e correnti for 2 violins, violoncello and B. C. (Bologna, 1691). Pougin calls him Filippo Carlo saying: "He was a violinist born at Bologna in the middle of the 17th century. In 1685 he was a member of the Academia Filarmonica."

BERNARDO DE ANGELIS, DETTO BERNARDUCCIO, b. Genoa, ca. 1700. Violinist in the town chapel at Lucca from July 24, 1736, to his death, July 16, 1757. Some psalms by De Angelis detto Rivotorto M.C., autograph, in S. Antonio Padua, are apparently not by the above.

GIOVANNO STEFFANO CARBONELLI, b. Rome, ca. 1700; d. London, 1772. A pupil of Corelli. After having already become known as an excellent violinist in Rome, the Duke of Rutland invited him to come to London in 1719 and live in his house. In recognition of his patron's kindness, he composed 12 solos for violin which he dedicated to the Duke. In 1720 he became leader at the newly founded Royal Academy of Music which performed Italian operas at the Haymarket Theatre and also played as soloist in public concerts with great success. He became so popular that Sir Richard Steele introduced him in one of his comedies (*see* E. v. d. Str., "The Romance of the Fiddle," p. 195.—For a programme of one of his concerts of 1722, Ib., p. 196). In 1725 he became the leader at Drury Lane, where he also played solos between the acts according to the custom of the time. For several years he played also at St. Paul's in the performances for the benefit of the sons of the clergy. He became leader of the orchestra in Handel's oratorio performances and relinquished his position at Drury Lane. Later on he began to import Italian wines, which occasioned the lines composed by Dr. Cooke for two voices:

> "Let Rubinelli charm the ear
> And sing, as erst, with voice divine,
> To Carbonelli I adhere;
> Instead of music give *me* wine."

(One more verse, see E. v. d. Str., "The Romance of the Fiddle," p. 197.)

His enterprise was highly successful, he became purveyor to the King, and the business was continued by his heirs, who altered the name to Carbonell. After having renounced the Roman Catholic faith and become a Protestant, he married the daughter of Mr. Warren, the Parish Clerk of St. James's,

Westminster. He composed "Sonate da Camera a violine e violone o cembalo," London, ca. 1722.

GIOVANNI PIETRO GUIGNON (GHIGNONE), b. Turin, Feb. 10, 1702; d. Versailles, Jan. 30, 1774. Last of the "Rois de violon et des Ménétriers." He was first a violoncellist, then he took up the violin, making such rapid progress that he became a redoubtable rival of Leclair. It is said that he was a pupil of Somis at Turin, and went in 1725 to Paris, where he played with great success at the Concert Spirituel. The *Mercure* notes his further successes for a number of years. Sometimes he appeared alone at the concerts, at other times in duets with Mondonville and afterwards with Gaviniés. For his solos he chose preferably the difficult concertos by Vivaldi. In 1730 he became a member of the Private Music of the Prince de Carignan, the potentate of the opera. In 1733 he entered also the King's chapel and became teacher of the Dauphin (afterwards Louis XV). The influence obtained thereby he used to have the once famous majesty of the Dumanoirs revived on his behalf, and to make this possible he applied for papers of naturalization, which were handed to him on May 6, 1741, and on June 15 he received the letters patent from the King appointing him King and Master of the Minstrels. In 1762 he retired with a pension from the Royal Chapel. The glory of his Minstrel Kingship brought him nothing but trouble with the French musicians, and after years of quarrels and lawsuits, he abdicated his sovereignty in Mar., 1773, and the 31st of that month the office was abolished by a Royal edict. Guignon did not long survive the loss of his illusory royalty; he succumbed after an apoplectic stroke. He had a brilliant technique, good, powerful tone and a graceful elegant style. On his op. 1 he calls himself 1st violin of the King of France and of Prince Carignan. He composed sonatas, duos and trios for violin (list in Eitner, "Quellen Lexikon"). Also a book of sonatas for 2 violincellos and pieces for horn. A MS. concerto signed Giov. Pietro Ghignone is in the Dresden Museum Library.

FRANCESCO CIAMPI, b. Massa di Carrara, 1704. Distinguished violin virtuoso and composer. He went to Venice, where a number of his operas were performed between 1728 and 1762.

Burney speaks highly of a mass and a miserere of his composition.

GIOVANNI BATTISTA TIBALDI, of Modena, where he was violinist in the Court chapel at the beginning of the 18th century. Composed sonate (12) a 3, 2 violini e violone o organo (Rome, Komarek), ded. signed Apr. 1, 1704; sonatas (12) in 3 parts for 2 violins and a thorough-bass, op. 1 (Walsh and Jos. Hare); 1 sonata for flute, violin and bass in Albinoni's 6 sonatas (Amsterdam, Roger) (in Medulla Musice). Fétis: "Composed 2 books of trios for 2 violins and bass," op. 1 and op. 2 (Amsterdam, Roger).

FRANCESCO BARBELLA. Early 18th-century violinist at Naples (Eitner). Composed violin sonatas, some of these have been repub. by Hofmeister (Leipzig).

EMMANUELE BARBELLA, b. Naples, 1704, where he died in 1773. Son and pupil of Francesco Barbella. At the death of the latter he received some advice from Zaga, and then became the pupil of Pasqualino Bini, a pupil of Tartini. His first master in counterpoint was Mich. Gabbalone, and after that Leonardo Leo, who said of him: "But for music, Barbella is an ass who knows nothing." He became however a clever violinist who trained some good pupils, the foremost being Raimondi. He composed, according to Fétis: 6 duos for 2 violins (London, n. d.); 6 sonatas for violin (London; not original, ?); 6 duos for violins, op. 3 (Paris); 6 duos for violoncello, op. 4 (Paris). Burney (iii, 561) gives a piece of his in double stopping, "Tinna nonna per prender sonno."

GIOVANNI ANTONIO PIANI (called DES PLANES), b. Naples, late 17th century. He went to France in 1704 and entered the service of A. de Bourbon, Count of Toulouse; he was apparently highly esteemed both as player and teacher. He returned to Italy, having amassed a considerable fortune and settled probably at Venice before 1738. In June of the latter year the *Mercure de France* brought out a sensational account of his having been convicted of forgery and having been condemned to have his hand cut off. Fétis relates the whole story, which was copied by all subsequent biographers, without seeing that the same paper in August, 1738, contradicts it and blames the reporter for his imprudence in relating it. Fétis also states that he was the teacher of Sénallié

(Sénaillé), which is likewise erroneous (*see* Sénallié). Piani composed sonatas for violin solo with 'cello and harpsichord, op. 1, ded. to the Count of Toulouse (Paris, 1712, and Amsterdam).

GIOVANNI PIANTANIDA, b. Florence, 1705; d. Bologna, ca. 1782. In 1734 he went to St. Petersburg with an Italian opera company and appeared with great success as soloist. During 1737–8 he gave successful concerts at Hamburg; thence he went to Holland, and in 1743 met also with success at the Concert Spirituel in Paris. Finally he returned to Italy and settled at Bologna, where Burney heard him in 1770 and declared him to be the best violinist in Italy at that time. He composed 6 violin concertos and 6 sonatas for 2 violins and bass or harpisichord, op. 1, pub. in Holland; the sonatas also in London, 1742. A sonata da camera (or more?) for violin and violoncello is in the library of the Friends of Music, Vienna. A Piantanida appears as violinist in the list of the members of the Dresden Court chapel in 1748. It is uncertain whether this is the above.

GIUS. BERGONZI (? relative of Carlo Bergonzi, who was active 1712–50). Composed Sinfonie da chiesa e concerti a 4, a due Violini concertati e due Ripieni con l'Alto Viola obligato col Basso per l'organo, op. 2 (Bologna); Sonate a 3, Bologna, 1705 (Bologna).

FILIPPO SALVIATI, b. ca. 1706; d. Vienna, Mar. 27, 1766. During 1718–27 Court scholar at the Imperial school, with a subvention of 20 thaler per month. He petitioned to go to Italy for study, but Fux reports, "although he has a fresh and fiery spirit he must not be left out of the sight (aus den Augen) of his master." He received, however, the permission and funds for travel and remained nearly nine years. On Nov. 25, 1727, he was appointed violin in the Court chapel with a salary of 460 florins and remained till his death. (Köchel, i, 2, 230, 384, 389, 414.)

GIOV. BAT. LAMPUGNANI, b. Milan, ca. 1706; d. there after or about 1789. Opera composer: 6 sonatas à 3, 2 violins and bass for harps. or violoncello, op. 1 (London, Walsh); 6 sonatas, do. do., op. 2.

CARLO FIORELLI. Violinist ca. 1706 at the Court of Bayreuth, where Birkenstock became his pupil for one year. He was

PIETRO ANTONIO LOCATELLI

GAETANO PUGNANI

1st violinist and chamber composer in the Dresden Court chapel ca. 1709 with an annual salary of 600 thaler (Fürstenau, 26, 50). Two instrumental MS. movements of his are in the library at Wolffenbüttel.

MICHELE MASCITI (MASCITTI) (called M^r. MICHEL in France), b. Naples in the last quarter of the 17th century; d. Paris, ca. 1750. Toured as violin virtuoso in Italy, Germany and the Netherlands and settled in Paris, where he entered the service of the Duke of Orleans. He wrote a large number of violin sonatas. The sonatas in the Vienna Musikfreunde library under Marcitti Michele "twice 12 sons. 1707" are no doubt by the above. Pub. at Amsterdam: 6 sonatas for violin and B.c. for the harpsichord; 15 sonatas do. do., op. 2; 12 sonatas do. do., op. 3; 12 sonatas for violin solo, op. 4; 12 sonatas for violin and violoncello, op. 5; 12 sonatas do. do., op. 6; concertos for violin solo, 2 ripieno violins and B.c., op. 7. The sonatas are dealt with in "Eighteenth Century Violin Sonatas" by E. v. d. Str., *The Strad*. Pougin states that between 1704 and 1731 up to 9 books of sonatas by him were pub. Although not of a high order they contain many charming, melodious movements.

GIOVANNE VENERANDO. Priest and violinist ca. 1708 in the Ducal chapel, Venice, with a salary of 15 ducats (Caffi, ii, 61).

PAOLO SALULINI, b. Siena, ca. 1709; d. there, Jan. 29, 1780. Studied under Padre Martini at the Liceo Musicale Bologna, became then 1st violin at Siena theatre, and on May 5, 1765, capellmeister at the cathedral. He composed violin concertos, sonatas for 2 violins and bass, symphonies, 3 Pastorale, a violino solo (Eitner) and a Requiem for the Emperor Franz I.

ANDREA FADINI. Early 18th-century Italian violinist-composer. 12 sonatas for 2 violins, violoncello and organ (Amsterdam, ca. 1710).

LODOVICA FERRONATI, Italian violinist and composer of the 17th–18th century. Composed 10 sonatas for violin and violoncello, op. 1, 1710, and Sonate, op. 1 (Venice, 1710) (Bol.); Sonate per camera a violino e cembalo (Venice, 1715) (Walther).

PIANI. Violinist in the Court chapel at Cassel, 1710–15 (Appel, who calls him Piana). This must be a different person from either Carlo Tomaso Piani or Giov. Antonio Piani.

FRANCESCO GUERINI, b. at Naples, ca. 1710; d. London, 1780. Was from 1740 to 1760 in the chapel of the Prince of Orange at the Hague. He went afterwards to London where he remained until he died. He wrote a considerable number of concertos, sonatas and duos for the violin, also 6 sonatas for violoncello, op. 9, and sonatas for the harpsichord, mostly pub. at Amsterdam. Some of his violin sonatas have been repub. (*see* Moffat).

LUIGI CANDIDO. Lived at Venice at the beginning of the 18th century. He was a violin virtuoso and composer, who wrote Sonate per camera, a violino solo e violoncello, op. 1 (Venice, 1712).

NICOLO ANGROPOLI. An early 18th-century violinist in the Imperial Chapel, Vienna, from July 1, 1713, till his death, June 22, 1732 (Köchel).

DOMENICO APUZZO. A violinist in the Imperial Chapel, Vienna, from July 1, 1713, to his death on Oct. 10, 1740.

ANGELO RAGAZZI. From July 1, 1713, to 1740, violinist in the Court chapel, Vienna; d. there Oct. 12, 1750. Pensioned in 1740 (Köchel, i). Composed Fant. a violoncello solo senza B. (MS., Dresden), Sinfonia in Sol a 2 violini e basso ed org. (MS., Milan Conser.), masses, etc., and instrumental music. A MS. "Concerto a violoncello concertato con 2 violini, viola, e basso," G minor, in Royal library, Dresden, is no doubt by the above, the spelling of the name on the MS., Angelo Regazzi, being an error of the copyist.

CARLO GIOVANNI TESTORI, b. Vercelli, Piedmont, 1714; d. there, 1782 (Fétis). Calls himself Maestro di musica e Professore di violino in Vercelli. He wrote some works on musical composition but apparently nothing for the violin. He was capellmeister at St. Eusebio, Vercelli. The titles on his books on musical theory, 1767–82, give no information as to his position. He was the only Italian, according to Fétis, who adopted the doctrine of Rameau.

DOMENICO GAVAZZI. Violinist in the chapel of St. Mark's, Venice, ca. 1714 (Caffi, ii, 62).

GIOVANNI CARLO VAITO. Mentioned by Hawkins (vol. v, 137–808) as an eminent violin virtuoso, among the most famous at Naples ca. 1715.

GIUSEPPE ANTONIO BRESCIANELLO. Violinist composer; in 1716 capellmeister to the Duke of Württemberg. Composed 12 concertos or symphonies for 2 violins, alto and bass (1733).

GIOVANNI MOSSI, b. Rome towards the end of the 17th century. A pupil of Corelli, appeared ca. 1720 as violinist and composer, 6 concertos for 6 instruments, op. 3 (Amsterdam 1730?) and 2 books of sonatas with bass respectively, violoncello, op. 1 and op. 5, all pub. Amsterdam (*see* Fétis and Eitner). *See* full analysis in E. v. d. Str., "Eighteenth-Century Sonatas." Fétis credits him with 20 concertos. He ranks among the best composers of his time. His concertos show affinity with Locatelli's style (*see* Schering, *ib.*).

FELICE DE GIARDINI, b. Turin, Apr. 12, 1716; d. Moscow, Dec. 17, 1796. Pupil of Paladini as choirboy at Milan cathedral; then violin pupil of Lorenzo Somis at Turin, but he failed to acquire the simplicity and grandeur of Corelli's school. In 1728 he went to Rome and soon after he was in the orchestra of the Sa. Carlo theatre, Naples. In 1748 he toured in Germany, appeared successfully in Paris, 1750, and made his debut in London, Apr. 27, 1751, where he gave 20 very successful subscription concerts with the oboist Thomas Vincent. In 1755 he became joint manager with Siga. Mingotti, and conductor of the Opera, where he was the first to introduce uniform bowing of the strings. In 1863 he became lessee, but having lost everything by 1765, he turned singing master. During 1770–76 he was leader of all provincial Festivals and 1782–83 again leader at the Italian Opera. On his violin solos op. 16 he calls himself Music Master of the Duke of Cumberland. Later he went to Italy, returned in 1789, but finding himself eclipsed by Wm. Cramer, he went, 1791, with a theatrical company to Moscow where he died in poverty. Fr. Benda and others praise the beauty and fulness of his tone, nobility of style and his rare gift of improvization. He left numerous compositions (*see* Eitner), which are, however, lacking in inspiration.

GIACOMO FACCO. Lived in 1720. Fétis says he wrote 12 concertos for 3 violins, viola, violoncello, and B.c., pub. at Amsterdam, 1720, probably the same as: Pensieri Adriarmonici Concerti, lib. I Nr. 1 to 6, lib. II Nr. 7 to 12, Amsterdam, E. Roger e Le Cene Nr. 469, Jeanne Roger Nr. 477 (Wagner library). In Mich. Corette's "L'Art de Violon" 1 piece signed only "Facco" (Eitner).

ANTONIO LUIGI BALDACINI. Italian violinist ca. 1720; wrote 2 sets of sonatas for 2 violins and bass. *See* Baldassini, i. 165.

PASQUALINO BINI, b. Pesaro, ca. 1720; d. Stuttgart, 1768 (Mendel). Cardinal Olivieri, who had taken the boy under his protection, sent him at the age of 15 to Tartini, with whom he studied for three years to such good purpose that when at a later time (according to Burney, iii, 562) a Mr. Wiseman, an Englishman, asked Tartini to give him lessons, the latter sent him to Bini saying: "I recommend you to a pupil of mine who plays better than myself, and I am proud of it as he is an angel in religion and morals." At the end of his studies Olivieri recalled him to Rome, where by the boldness of his style and the purity of intonation he astounded everybody, and Montanari, who was then considered the first, is said to have grieved so at Bini's superiority that he died broken-hearted. On learning that Tartini had changed his style and especially his bowing, Bini returned to him for another year and renewed his studies, at the end of which he was considered foremost in expression and technique. In Mar., 1754, he went to Stuttgart as capellmeister to the Duke of Württemberg, where he remained to his death. Of his compositions there exist: Sonata a solo MS. (violin and b.) (B.B.) and concerto in G for violin (Musikfreunde). One of his best pupils was Emmanuele Barbella.

CARLO ANTONIO CAMPION (Fétis: CAMPIONI), b. Livorno, ca. 1720; d. Florence, ca. 1793. A violinist and composer who became widely known by 7 sets of trios for 2 violins and bass, and 3 books of violin duets which were pub. in England, Germany and Holland. In 1764 he became capellmeister at the Court of Florence and henceforward devoted himself to church music. To Dr. Burney, who visited him in 1771 (?), he showed, among other of his works, a Te Deum which had been performed in 1767 by 200 performers. He also brought together an extensive and valuable collection of 16th- and 17th-century madrigals.

GIULIO MENEGHINI.   Early 18th-century pupil of Tartini and his successor as 1st violin at St. Antonio, Padua, from 1721 to ca. 1723.   Afterwards he does not appear to have filled any official position.   According to Lipinski (Wki., 150) he was also called "tromba," on account of his powerful tone, which led Gerber (i) into the error of speaking of "Giuletto Tromba" also as a successor of Tartini, but another person.

PIETRO NARDINI, b. Fibiana, Tuscany, 1722; d. Florence, May 7, 1793.   As a child he went with his parents to Leghorn, where he received his first lessons in music until he went to Tartini, whose pupil he was until the age of 24.   He then returned to Leghorn, where he played in the church and in concerts.   In 1753 he entered the service of the Duke Charles of Württemberg.   Leopold Mozart heard him there and praises his "Beauty, purity, and evenness of tone; in the cantabile style nobody surpasses him" (Sittard, iii, 55).   He left Stuttgart on the reconstruction of the chapel in 1767, went back to Leghorn, and two years later he went to Padua to his old master Tartini, whom he nursed like a son throughout his last illness.   In 177? he played before the Emperor Joseph II, who was so pleased that he presented him with a richly enamelled golden snuff-box.   Ca. 1770 he was appointed as 1st violinist and director of the Court chapel at Florence.   He died at the age of 71.   *See* Schubart's flowery panegyric in Wki., 146.   La Mara (i, 233) gives a letter of his of Jan. 30, 1790.   Notices by Burney (i, 184, 186, etc.).   Rangoni G. B., Elegio dell Abate Raimondo Leoni Piacenza.   Compositions in Eitner.   Many of his concertos remained in MS.   6 quartets were pub. at Florence as well as 6 violin duets.   Several of his sonatas have been repub. by David, Alard, Moffat, etc.   Nardini's sonatas are among the most remarkable of their time in respect of form, subject-matter and figuration, which show an uncommon freshness, virility and inventive genius.   Some of his slow movements are exceedingly beautiful melodies.

CHARLES CHABRAN (CHIABRANO), b. Turin, ca. 1723.   Nephew and pupil of Somis; member of the Royal Chapel at Turin in 1747.   He went to Paris in 1751, where he met with great success. In 1752 he was in London for some time. He composed 6 sonatas for violin and B.c., op. 1, pub. in Paris, also in London by Welcker. With other of Somis' pupils, he handed the latter and Corelli's art down to posterity. Some of his sonatas were repub. by Cartier, Alard, A. Moffat, etc. His brother, FRANCESCO CHABRAN, was a guitar player, and GAËTANO CHABRAN a 'cellist.

LUDOVICO (erroneously called GIOVANNI) MADONIS, b. Venice, about the end of the 17th century. In 1726 he went as conductor of an Italian opera company to Breslau, where Quantz heard him and praised his playing. In 1729 he went to Paris, where he played at the Concert Spirituel, and was appointed Royal chamber musician. In the same year he returned to Italy. In 1731 he went to St. Petersburg, accompanied by his uncle ANTONIO, a good violinist, though inferior to Ludovico. The latter remained there till 1767 at a salary of 3,000 roubles per annum. Ludovico composed sonatas for violin solo, op. 1; 3 violin concertos, and a "Recueil," pub. in Paris; also 12 symphonies for violin and B.c. dedicated to the Empress Anna.

GIUSEPPE MADONIS. Mentioned by Caffi (ii, 66) as violinist at St. Mark's, Venice, in 1786.

GIOVANNI VEROCAI. Apparently a violinist who came with an Italian opera company to Breslau in 1727, whence he went to Dresden, then to Moscow (Fétis) and to St. Petersburg, where he married the daughter of Reinhard Keiser. He then went to Hamburg, and ca. 1741 (?) to Brunswick, where he became Ducal concertmeister (Mizler, "Mus. Bibl.," ii, part iii, p. 174) and produced 2 operas, ca. 1734 (43?). He composed "Labyrint Musicale" for violino I and II, with explanations (Leipzig, J. G. Im. Breitkopf and another); "Labyrinthe Musicale" for 2 violins and bass, Vienna (Vienna Hofburg); a symphony, several operas, arias, etc.

DALL' OCHA. An early 18th-century pupil of A. Lolli; was the first teacher for the violin of Campagnoli at Bologna.

LORENZO GAETANO ZAVATERI. Early 18th-century "Bolognese Academico Filarmonico" Concerti da chiesa e da camera, op. 1 (in archive of St. Petronio); "divertimenti musicali per camera a violino e basso," op. 2, dedio alli signori dilettanti di V. (once in Borghese library).

MICHEL. A native of Naples who lived in Paris in the beginning of the 18th century and distinguished himself also as a composer (Pougin, Fétis).

FIORENZO À KEMPIS. An Italian musician of the beginning of the 18th century, who wrote 12 sonatas for violin, viol da gamba and bass (Hawkins, v, 82).

BARTOLOMEO MENESINI. Composer of 6 sonatas for 2 violins and bass (London, Hy. Fought) (B. Wagner, Musikfr., Vienna).

ALESSANDRO DE ROSSI, b. Rome, beginning of 18th century. A pupil of Franc. Gasparini, lived for some time at Vienna or Prague. Composed concerto E minor for 2 violins, 2 trombe da caccia, viola e basso (MS. in Musikfr.), and cantatas.

ANTONIO GUIDO GIOVANNI. An early 18th-century Italian violinist who apparently was for some time in the service of the Duke of Orleans in Paris, to whom he dedicated his "Premier livre de Sonates pour le violon" (Amsterdam, 1726).

GAETANO ORSINI. Apparently a violinist who composed 16 trios for 3 violins (Milan), Ricordi and 6 duos for 2 violins, and 'cello, op. 1, ca. 1730 (Brit. Mus.).

PIETRO ANTONIO AVANDONNO (AVONDANO), b. Naples, at the beginning of the 18th century; d. ca. 1786. A violoncellist. He wrote 12 sonatas for violin and bass, op. 1 (Amsterdam, 1732); also duets for violin and violoncello, pub. in Germany and in Paris, which were very popular. He also composed 2 operas and 2 oratorios. 3 sonatas for 2 violins and bass, MS., at Dresden, without Christian name, are no doubt by the above.

CARLO CECERE, b. in the Kingdom of Naples, early 18th century; violinist and composer; 2 comic operas of his were performed at the Teatro Nuovo, one in 1738.

MIROGLIO, L'AÎNÉ. Early 18th-century violinist and owner of the "Bureau d'abonnement musical," Paris. Composed sonatas a violon, et basse, op. 1, par M. (monsieur) Miroglio, Paris, chez l'auteur (Paris Nat.). Pougin found 6 violin sonatas by the elder Miroglio dedicated to Geminiani. His son and pupil, PIERRE JEAN MIROGLIO, who signed himself only Miroglio le cadet, b. Paris, ca. 1750, composed sonates pour le violon, op. 1; do. do., op. 2; sonates a 2 violons, op. 4 (all in Paris Nat.); 6 symphonies, op. 10 (Brit. Mus.); a sextet for strings and 2 horns (MS., Brussels Conser.). Fétis says Pierre Jean composed 5 books of violin sonatas with bass and several books of violin duets.

CLAUDIO, b. Lucca, early 18th century. Came to London and was for several years violinist at the Opera. Composed 6 solos for the violin (London, ca. 1740).

ANDREA ZANI, b. Casal Maggiore, Lombardy, beginning of 18th century. Lombardy belonging then to Austria, he was probably engaged at the Imperial Court in Vienna, where his op. 4 and 5 were pub., the latter in 1735. In his Concerti grossi he developed the principle of contrasting themes (Schering, ib., p. 100). His sonatas, which only rarely touch e, are rich in variety of figuration, contrapuntal and rhythmic devices, and in thematic and melodic invention. While some of his sonatas are Corellian in character, others approach the style of Haydn. The bass is often concerted and fairly difficult. In a note to his copy of the 14 sonatas op. 3, J. B. Cartier calls him a great composer and famous violin virtuoso. Besides these, Cartier had his 12 sonatas op. 5; 6 sonatas op. 6 (Paris, 1745); now in Brit. Mus. (E. v. d. Str., "Eighteenth Century Violin Sonatas," The *Strad*, Oct. Dec. 1920). Besides the sonatas he wrote: 12 Concerti à op. (only copy, Dresden Museum); 12 symphonies for 2 violins, gamba and organ (Amsterdam) and 6 concertos for violin in 7 parts (ib.).

# CHAPTER 34

# *Italy: to 1750*

FRANCESCO DAVOGLIO, b. Velletri, 1727.  He went to Paris, where he played at the Concert Spirituel in 1755.  Six works of solos, duos, and quartets of his composition were pub. in Paris between 1780 and 1784.

GIUSEPPE CASELLI, b. Bologna, 1727.  After gaining a great reputation as violinist in Italy, he was appointed solo violinist at the Russian Court at St. Petersburg in 1758.  He composed 6 solos for the violin.

ANTONIO LOLLI, b. Bergamo, between 1728 and 1733; d. Palermo, 1802.  According to all accounts he was almost entirely self-taught.  From 1755 he appears as 1st violinist in the documents of the Court chapel at Stuttgart, by the side of Nardini, whose superiority induced him to take a year's leave for further study.  He married an actress engaged at the Court.  In 1760 he appears to have toured in the Netherlands, when his first concertos were published at Amsterdam.  In 1765 he is called concertmeister in the Stuttgart chapel, of which a son of his appears already as a member in 1770.  On July 29, 1744, the Duke dismissed, for financial reasons, the greater part of his chapel, and probably also Lolli, who, together with his wife, received 4,000 thaler per annum.  He then went to St. Petersburg, where he gained the favour of Catherine II, who presented him with a bow with the inscription: "Archet fait par Catherine II pour l'incomparable Lolli."  In 1778 he left St. Petersburg on account of his health, and in 1779 he appeared in Paris at the Concert Spirituel, where previously he had played, in 1764.  He met with great success, although connoisseurs declared that he was playing too much for outward show.  From Paris he went to Madrid, where the Prince of Asturias presented him with a golden box filled with 350 ducats, while the director of the theatre paid him nightly 2,000 reales for playing 1 concerto and 2 solos. In 1785 he went to London, and Burney (Hist., iv, 680) tells us that "owing to the eccentricity of his style of composition and execution, he was regarded as a madman by most of the audience. In his freaks nothing can be imagined so wild, difficult, grotesque and even ridiculous as his compositions and performance." He adds, however, "I am convinced that in his lucid intervals he was in a serious style, a very great expressive and admirable performer." His musical knowledge was practically nil, he could not keep time, nor could he play at first sight, and when he was asked by the Prince of Wales to lead a Haydn quartet he almost broke down. In 1791 he was in Berlin with one of his sons, and thence went to Copenhagen; 1793 he was at Palermo, 1794 in Vienna, and 1796 at Naples, where Romberg heard him and found him but a shadow of his earlier form. Later he went to Palermo again, where he died after a prolonged illness and was buried in the church of the Capuchin friars near that town. Dittersdorf describes him from personal acquaintance as a handsome, perfect man of the world, of agreeable manners, modest and jovial. Others describe him as conceited, extravagant and dissolute. All are unanimous in their praise of his astounding virtuosity, his full and beautiful tone, wonderful technique of the bow as well as of the left hand. Schubart, in his customary extravagant eulogy, says: "Octaves and tenths he plays with perfect intonation, also double shakes in thirds and sixths. . . . His speed goes to the point of magic. . . . He goes into the most dizzy realms of sound and sometimes finishes a concerto with a note which appears the *non plus ultra* of all tones." These features of his playing are also mentioned by all the other musicians of note who heard him, and all regret that he used his extraordinary technique merely for senseless firework display. He composed 4 books of sonatas, op. 1, 3, 9, 10 (Amsterdam and Paris); 8 concertos, op. 2, 4, 5, 6 (Berlin and Paris); but of all these he only wrote the violin part, which had to be brought into form and provided with an accompaniment by others. He also pub. a method for violin, op. 8 (Berlin, Paris and Offenbach). Wasielewski Die Violine, p. 204, etc., quotes detailed descriptions from various contemporary writers.

GIORGIO ERBA, violinist of Milan, lived in Rome ca. 1730. He composed 10 sonate da camera a violino solo e basso, op. 1, Amsterdam, 1736. Mendel says he was probably the son of Dionisio Erba, who was in high esteem as a composer at Milan ca. 1690, and wrote the Magnificat which Handel used in "Israel in Egypt."

DOMENICO GALLO, b. Venice, ca. 1730. An eminent violin virtuoso who composed sei sonate a 2 violini e violoncello o cembalo Venzia Allesandri e Scattaglia (Milan Conser.). Other sonatas and 3 symphonies (trios for 2 violins and b. or string quartets) and church music remained in MS.

TOESCHI, real name Toesca della Castella Monte, a family of musicians:

ALESSANDRO TOESCHI, from Rome, 1731, concertmeister (violinist) in the Court chapel at Ludwigsburg (Stuttgart) with a salary of 750 florins (Sittard, ii, 123). During 1742–58 he was at Mannheim, concertmeister in the Court chapel and director of instrumental church music (Marpurg, ii, 567; Fr. Walter). Composed 1 violin concerto with string quartet in E flat major (MS. at Dresden); there is also a violin concerto with string quartet in A major under "Toesca" (MS. Cx. 1011) which may be by the above; 6 solos for flute with B. (Rostock). (*See* Lipowski.)

CARLO GIUSEPPE TOESCHI, b. in the Romagna (Papal State); d. Munich, Apr. 12, 1788. Real name Toësca della Castella Monte. (Rudhart, 167, says, however: b. 1722 at Padua.) In 1752 he was appointed in the Court chapel at Mannheim, where in 1759 he became concertmeister, afterwards also director of the chamber music (Riemann); (Fr. Walter from documents) (Wki. different again). In 1778 he went with the chapel to Munich, became director of Music 1780, and died there before Apr. 3, 1788; on Apr. 3 his death was communicated to the Elector and his salary divided among the younger members. He composed several ballets, symphonies, etc. (*see* Schubart—extract in Wki.). On his compositions he generally appears only as Carlo *or* Joseph (Giuseppe), seldom with both Christian names. Eitner mentions among his numerous compositions 1 duetto for cembalo and violin (Musikfr. B. M.), sonata for 2 violins and violoncello, sonatas

27

en trios, for clavecin, violin or flute and bass; trietti for 2 violins and bass, op. 7; 6 quartets for flute, violin, viola and bass, op. 3; 6 do. do. (MS. Karlsruhe), no violin concerto but 3 for flute and string quartet, etc., etc.; other chamber music (Riemann: 63 symphonies, and 1 repub. by H. Riemann, D.T.B., vol., vii, 2), ballets.

GIOVANNI BATTISTA TOESCHI, son of Carlo Gius. Toeschi, b. Mannheim (before 1745 as has hitherto been accepted, as he was already in the chapel in 1755); d. Munich, May 1, 1800. A pupil of Joh. Carl Stamitz, and of Cannabich for theory. (Fétis: succeeded Stamitz as solo violin and occasionally deputized as conductor for Cannabich.) In 1774 the lists mention him as concertmeister and director of the chapel with a salary of 700 florins, raised in the same year to 800 florins. In 1778 he went with the chapel to Munich, with the title of Court Director of Music (Hofmusikdirektor). In 1799 he received 1,200 florins. Wasielewski says that he was superior as composer to his father, and mentions 18 symphonies, 10 quartets, 6 trios. Eitner mentions 3 symphonies, quartet for flute, violin, viola d'amore and bass (Brit. Mus.), 6 duetti for 2 violins, 6 sonatas for 2 violins (London); 6 conversation sonatas for 2 violins and bass; 6 trio sonatas for 2 violins and bass (all in Brit. Mus.); sonata for viola d'amore and bass (Vienna, Hofburg); 24 symphonies MS. in Royal Hausbibliothek, Berlin, but some of these, according to the catalogue, may be by Carlo Guis. Fétis says his symphonies had great success in Paris before Haydn's symphonies were known.

CARLO TEODORO, GIOV. BATT. TOESCHI, b. Mannheim, Fétis says 1770, but this is too late, as Toeschi says in a petition of 1792 that he had been already 12 years in the Court chapel, where he must therefore have been appointed 1780, and consequently born before 1770. In 1785 and 1787 his salary was raised, although in 1788 he is mentioned as recently appointed violinist. He was still active in 1835, as the Brit. Mus. has a book of court ball waltzes of that year by Toesca di Castellamonte, which is evidently Carlo Teodore Toeschi.

GAETANO PUGNANI, b. Turin, Nov. 27, 1731; d. Turin, July 15, 1798. A pupil of Somis (he was trained in the traditions of Corelli) and afterwards Tartini; toured in Europe. In 1754 he had phenomenal success at the Concert Spirituel in Paris, and in 1768 in London (Pohl, ii, 370). Was appointed, 1752, 1st violinist at the Royal chapel, Turin, with a salary of 1,200 lire, and from 1775 with 1,500 lire. On Jan. 19, 1776, he became director-general of the Royal Chapel. His biography is based on documents in "Ricordi Musikztg.," 1891, p. 353, etc. A correct judgment of his very numerous compositions cannot be formed without greater knowledge than either Fétis or Wasielewski possessed. He composed a large number of sonatas, duos, trios, operas, oratorios, cantatas, etc. (list in Mendel-Reissmann Mus. Lexikon). Some works are by NICOLO PUGNANI, ed. by Ed. Lassen in Musikfr. Eitner doubts correctness of the Christian name. Wasielewski asserts that Pugnani combined the achievements of the schools of Corelli, Tartini and Vivaldi. At the age of 21 (Fétis says 25) he became conductor of the private music of the King of Sardinia. The *Mercure de France*, Feb. 2, 1754, states that he was greeted with enthusiasm by connoisseurs, who declare that they know of no greater talent. In London he was for some time leader of the Italian Opera. He toured till 1770, when he returned to Turin, became solo violin at the Court theatre and founded a school for violin playing, remaining active until he died. He was also an excellent conductor, and this art he transmitted successfully to his pupils Bruni, Polledro, etc. For personality, anecdotes, etc., *see also* Mason Clarke, Pougin, etc.

ALOISIO LODOVICO FRACASSINI, b. Orvieto, 1733; d. Bamberg, Oct. 9, 1798. Pupil of Tartini at Padua, and apparently also of Ferrandini, Munich, according to a receipt for 100 florins of Jan. 21, 1762. On Aug. 1, 1757, he was appointed (it is said at Tartini's recommendation) Court violinist in the chapel of the Bishop of Bamberg at a salary of 200 thalers with free board and residence. In 1764 he became 1st violinist and concertmeister and in 1782 received a rise of 80 florins fränk. Leopold Mozart writes about him: "And now I believe he is concertmeister or capellmeister, and that on account of his German wife, a singer from Würzburg." He had in 1762 married Anna Katharina Bayerin, soprano singer at the Wützburg Court chapel and an ardent defender of German music, who died June 21, 1793. The Bamberg Episcopal library contained many compositions by him as arias, serenades and 5 symphonies. (Marschalk, xvi, 58.)

IGNAZIO RAIMONDI, b. Naples, 1733 (1735?); d. London, at his house, 74, Great Portland Street, Jan. 14, 1813. He was the best pupil of Barbella, and went to Amsterdam in 1760, instituting concerts and pub. his first compositions. During 1762–80 he was director of the public concerts there, at which his symphony, "The Adventures of Telemachus," was performed on Jan. 13, 1777. After leaving Amsterdam he went to Paris, where in 1791 his opera "La Muette" was performed, evidently on a second visit (*see* Mendel, "Conversations Lexikon"), and settled in London early in 1880. Here his compositions became very popular, especially "The Favourite Musical Battle," produced at the Professional Concerts in 1785. On June 1, 1791, he appeared as violinist and composer at his benefit concert at the Hanover Square Rooms, assisted among others by Mme Mara and Lord Mornington. In the following year (others say in 1800) he gave 12 subscription concerts at Willis's Rooms, where he appeared as virtuoso and as leader of the orchestra. He composed for the violin 3 concertos (Berlin, Hummel); 4 string quartets, op. 10 (Ib.), and 2 sets of trios for 2 violins and violoncello (according to Grove); 3 trios for violin, violoncello (?) and bass, op. 11 (London); 6 sonatas for 2 violins, and for violin and viola (Amsterdam); 3 sonatas for violin and violoncello, op. 15, and 6 sonatas for do.

DOMENICO DALL' OGLIO, b. Padua, early 18th century; d. near Narva, Russia, 1764. An eminent violinist, who went to St. Petersburg in 1735 with his brother Giuseppe, the violoncellist. Both were attached to the Imperial Chapel. In 1764 they both left St. Petersburg to return to Italy, but Domenico died from an apoplectic stroke on the journey, near Varna. He composed symphonies, violin concertos and solos, and some solos for viola, of which, according to Fétis, copies were preserved in Germany.

MADDALENA SIRMEN *née* LOMBARDINI, b. Venice, about the middle of 1735. She received her first musical and general education at the "Ospidale dei Mendicanti" at Venice, one of the four "hospitals" (schools with music as chief subject) for young girls, mostly orphans. The Director there was the celebrated composer Bertoni, and under his guidance she became not only an excellent violinist but also a gifted singer

and harpsichord player; who her individual teachers were is
unknown.   Burney, in the diary of his journey to Italy, gives
an interesting account of the Ospidale dei Mendicanti.   After
leaving this school she went to Padua to perfect her violin-
playing under Tartini, who took great interest in her, and
under his loving care she developed into the great artist who
soon took the whole of Europe by storm.   When she began
to appear in public, ca. 1760, the Italians proclaimed her as
the rival of Nardini.   After her first successes she married
Lodovico de Sirmen, himself a distinguished violinist and
capellmeister of Santa Maria Maggiore at Bergamo, and
henceforth they toured together; but it was essentially
Maddalena who, by her brilliant technique, purity of intonation, beauty of style and tone, combined with her personal
beauty and charm, made the conquest of the public in every
town they visited.   Nor would it be right to attribute her
enormous success to the comparative novelty of a woman
violinist.   The care which Tartini bestowed upon her, and
which found expression in several letters, including the one of
Mar. 5, 1760 (*see* p. ii, 7-8) with important instructions on the
best way to study the violin, addressed to her at Venice, where
the autograph is preserved, and where she had returned at the
end of her sojourn at Padua, and likewise Burney's opinion,
who speaks from personal knowledge, are sufficient testimony
with regard to her talent.   At the beginning of 1768 she went
with her husband to Paris, where they were engaged to appear
at the Concert Spirituel on Aug. 18.   They were enjoined
by the management not to play anywhere in Paris before that
date, to heighten the curiosity of the public.   They played a
double concerto for 2 violins of Maddalena's composition, and
the *Mercure de France* records the fact in ecstatic terms.
They appeared again at these concerts on Sept. 8 and Dec. 9,
1768, and in Apr., 1769, with equal success, the greater share
of which fell to Maddalena, who eclipsed her husband.   In
1771 Signora Sirmen made her debut in London at the King's
Theatre, Haymarket, on Jan. 9, playing a concerto after the
duettino in the second act of J. C. Bach's oratorio "Gioas Rè
di Giuda" with unqualified success, which was repeated on
five other occasions in that month.   In Feb. she played at
Covent Garden, on the 15th between the first and second part
of "Judas Maccabæus" and on the 20th between the first and

second parts of the "Messiah," also at a number of other concerts. At her Benefit Concert at Almack's on Apr. 15, which was given under the direction of Bach and Abel, with the assistance of several celebrated artists, she played a concerto on the harpsichord. She repeated however her successes as a violinist at a number of concerts in May, the last of which for the season took place on May 28. In the following year she returned and played at most of the oratorio concerts of the season with ever-increasing popularity. On Apr. 1 she played a violin concerto by the violoncellist-composer Cirri, after the second part of the "Messiah," and on Apr. 10 she made her last appearance as a violinist in England at the newly founded Concert Spirituel at Covent Garden (*see* Grove, iv, pp. 773, etc.). In 1774 she visited London again, this time as a singer, appearing in Piccini's "La Buona Figliuola" at the King's Theatre; she also sang in other operas, but with only moderate success. Afterwards she sang at the Paris Opera; in 1782 she was engaged at the Dresden Court Opera. In 1785 she appeared once more as a violinist at the Paris Concert Spirituel, but without success, due to the old-fashioned and worn-out music which she played, as the *Mercure de France* tells us. Nothing appears to be known about her from that time onward, nor is it known when or where she died. Her published compositions consist of: 6 trios for 2 violins and 'cello obbligato, op. 1 (Welcker, Gerrard St., Soho); 6 string quartets (composed in conjunction with her husband), (Paris, Berault, and London, Longman & Broderip); 6 violin duets (ded. to Duke of Gloucester) (London, Wm. Napier); 6 violin concertos with small orchestra (Amsterdam, Hummel); 6 sonatas for 2 violins (Ib.); 6 concertos adapted for the harpsichord by Sigr. Giordani (London, Longman & Broderip, 1789). A concerto pub. in Venice is mentioned by J. A. Hiller. For the letter by Tartini, *see* G. Hart, "The Violin," p. 445.

GIUSEPPE CANAVASSO (JOSEPH CANAVAS). An Italian violinist from Piedmont who came to Paris in 1735, together with his elder brother Alessandro, an excellent 'cellist. Giuseppe, better known as Joseph Canavas, an eminent violinist, was in the first row of the 1st violins at the Concert Spirituel, where he appeared also as soloist until 1762, which, Pougin thinks, was the year of his death. He does not appear ever to have

FELICE DE GIARDINI

FEDERIGO FIORILLO

BARTOLOMEO CAMPAGNOLI

MILANOLLO SISTERS

been a member of the Opera orchestra and probably was chiefly engaged in teaching. He composed 6 sonatas for violin and bass, op. 1 (Paris, 1739), a second book of violin sonatas, and a cantatilla "Le Songe."

CONSTANTINO RUBERTI. A Neapolitan, and violinist in the Royal Chapel, Naples. His opera "Il Filippo" was performed there in 1735 at the Teatro Nuovo (Pougin).

MATTIA VENTO, b. Naples, ca. 1735; d. 1777. Opera composer; wrote 6 sonatas for 2 violins and bass (London) and 6 trios for 2 violins and bass, op. 1 (MS. Naples—perhaps the same ?), a large number of sonatas for cembalo con accompagnamento di violino (98), and trios for harpsichord, violin and violoncello, op. 2, 4, 5, 6, 7, 8, 9 and 12, 6 trios each.

FRANCESCO DREI, b. Siena, ca. 1737; d. there, Jan. 1, 1801. One of the most eminent pupils of Nardini. Fétis mentions sonatas, quartets and vocal pieces by him, pub. between 1760 and 1785. He excelled in the playing of an adagio.

ELEGIO CELESTINO, b. Rome, 1737 (Riemann: 1739); d. Ludwigslust, Mecklenburg-Schwerin, Jan. 24, 1812. He studied the violin at Rome, where Burney heard him in 1770 and considered him the best Roman violinist of his time. From 1775 to 1780 he toured in France and Germany (was, 1776, in Stuttgart Court orchestra) and in 1781 he became concertmeister in the Court chapel at Ludwigslust, which position he occupied to the time of his death. At the age of 60 he visited London, where he was considered one of the greatest artists of the time. In 1800 he returned to Ludwigslust. He composed, among others, 3 duos for violin and violoncello (Berlin, 1786) and 6 sonatas for violin and violoncello, op. 9 (London, Clementi, 1798). An excellent pupil of his was Christian Ludwig Dieter.

FILIPPO MANFREDI, b. Lucca, ca. 1738; d. Madrid, 1780. Pupil and friend of Boccherini, with whom he went on tour. They arrived together in Paris in 1768, where they met with an enthusiastic reception of their performances of Boccherini's works. As a soloist Manfredi apparently did not meet with the hoped-for success, according to a notice in *Mémoirs Secrets* of Apr. 2, 1768, which adds, moreover, "his music was found insipid, his execution broad and pithy, but his playing mad and disordered." One of the main features in his composition was the frequent use of octaves, which was new at the time. According to Fétis, whose dates, however, are incorrect, the two artists, on their way to France, visited several towns in Lombardy, remaining a long time at Turin and in the central provinces of France, arriving in Paris in 1768. According to C. F. Pohl they started at the end of that year or the beginning of 1769 for Spain. Other biographers state that they were still in Paris in 1772, when Manfredi's 6 solos, op. 1, were pub. there. Certain is that they both became chamber musicians of the Infante Don Luiz, brother of the King of Spain, in whose service Manfredi remained until his death. Apart from being the inseparable musical companion of Boccherini he was also his business manager; nor was he without merit as a composer, as may be seen from his sonata in Cartier's "L'Art du Violon" and sonata No. 6 in Alard's "Maîtres Classiques." Several concertos, trios, sonatas and solos were pub. in Paris, others remained in MS. at Madrid.

PIETRO GIANOTTI. A double-bass player at the Paris Opera, ca. 1738–58. Master in composition of Monsigny. Wrote: Sonate a violino o flauto solo col basso, op. 5; Nouveaux duos pour les deux violons ou pardessue de viole, op. 6; sonate a due violini senza basso, op. 7.

LA CHIARETTA. Is mentioned in a letter by Charles de Brosses, dated Venice, Aug. 29, 1739, in which he says: "La Chiaretta would undoubtedly be the first (foremost) violinist in Italy, if Anna Maria of the Hospitalettes did not even surpass her." Of neither have we more particulars.

TAGNANI. An Italian violinist of the 18th century who enjoyed a great reputation in his country. The president de Brosse, who heard him at Florence in 1739, describes him thus in his letters: "a little, affected violinist, whose playing is full of little, insipid tricks. He invented a key for the violin like those on the flute, which when pushed by the chin, descends upon the strings and acts as a mute. He has also added seven thin copper (brass?) strings which run under the bridge and a lot of other tricks, but in justice to him it must be said that he accompanies with perfection." This was evidently a violino d'amore, which, apart from the mute arrangement, continued to be used occasionally. A specimen was only recently (1932) sold by Messrs. Puttick & Simpson.

GAETANO BRUNETTI, b. Pisa, ca. 1740; d. Madrid, 1808. Received his first music lessons from his father, the capellmeister of Pisa Cathedral, who also caused him to receive instruction on the violin. Afterwards he studied under Nardini at Florence, whose style he imitated very successfully. When he had finished his studies he toured in Italy and Germany, and was for some time in the service of the Elector Palatine at Mannheim, where Mozart heard him in 1778 and admired his talent. Towards the end of 1779 he went to Paris, where his 6 trios for 2 violins and bass, op. 1, were pub., which, as well as some quartets, were unsuccessful. About this time Manfredi, the 1st violin in the private band of the King of Spain, died, and Boccherini, the director at the Court, chose Brunetti as his successor. He began now to study Boccherini's style of composition and assimilated it so well that his compositions so closely resembled the works of that master that those who were not connoisseurs placed them on the same level. He began now to intrigue against Boccherini, to whom he owed everything, and again succeeded so well that he forced him to resign, and secured his place, besides receiving an annuity from the Duke of Alba for composing chamber music which was to be performed nowhere but in the Duke's palace. When Napoleon entered Madrid in 1807 fear took hold of him to such an extent that he died from a stroke. He composed 3 books of violin duets pub. in Paris, and 18 sonatas with bass and airs variés for violin and violoncello, which remained in MS., as did most of his numerous orchestral and chamber works. Picquot, author of the biography of Boccherini, had in his collection 24 of his works; on one of these, dated 1766, he calls himself "Musician of the Prince of the Asturias," which makes it doubtful that he was a son of Antonio Brunetti II, who only married in 1752.

CLAUDIO ROMANO ROIERO (ROGERS ?). Instrumentalist in the first half of the 18th century. Composed 12 sonate a violino solo e basso (London, 1740) (B. Wagner, Eitner).

ANGELO MARIA SCACCIA. A distinguished violinist of Milan during the first half of the 18th century. Composed 6 concerti per violino con accompagnamento, op. 1 (Milano); concerti con violino obbligato, 2 violini, alto, e B.c. (Amsterdam, Roger), op. 1 (the same ?); in Berlin MS. concerto for violin in F major with 2 violins, viola, basso violone e cembalo; Dresden Mus., 2 concerti, C and E flat, for 2 violins, viola e basso, MS. Fétis mentions: 6 concertos for violin (Milan 1740). 2 concertos in MS. are in the private library of Mr. Newman Flower, viz. E minor and F major, with string orchestra (parts) and B.c.

GIACINTO SCHIATTI. A violinist-conductor, ca. 1740, at the Court, Baden-Durlach. He went to St. Petersburg in 1747 as member of the Imperial Court chapel, where he was greatly praised as an excellent violinist. Schubart says he was but a mediocre composer but a good conductor, and died ca. 1780 or 1785. Composed 6 sonatas for 2 violins and bass, op. 1 (Amsterdam, Hummel). Also other trios for 2 violins and bass, and flute sonatas, trios, etc.

GIUSEPPE DEMACHI, of Alessandria della Paglia in Piedmont; was, ca. 1740, violinist in the Court chapel at Turin. In 1771 he went to Geneva, and Pohl (ii, 370) mentions him as giving concerts in London in 1791. On the MS. of his symphony in E flat he describes himself as concertmeister of the Princess of Nassau Weilburg. Apart from symphonies and a kind of symphonic poem, "A Day in the Country," in 9 movements, he composed 6 sonatas for violin and bass, op. 1 (Paris, Le Menu); several violin concertos including 2 with orch., op. 16; trios for 2 violins and bass, and 1 duet in Vanhall's 3 duets, 1790 (Brit. Mus.).

FERDINANDO GALLIMBERTO (GALIMBERTI). A mid-18th-century violinist; b. at Milan, where he stood in high repute as violin virtuoso ca. 1740. Composed Sinfonia a 3: 2 violini e basso (Upsala); Trio a 2 violini e cembalo, and 2 sinfonie a 2 violini, viola e basso (MSS. in Darmstadt Lib.); also a number of sacred vocal works, some dating between 1744–58.

GIUSEPPE ANTONIO CAPUCCI, b. Brescia, 1740; d. Bergamo, Mar. 18, 1818. A pupil of Nazari and F. Bertoni (composition), studied the violin under Tartini, and was accounted one of his best pupils. In 1769 he visited London, where he met with great success and also had a ballet of his performed. On his return he was appointed master at the Musical Institute and conductor of the orchestra at the Church of Santa Maria Maggiore at Bergamo, which position he retained to the time of his death. According to Fétis he composed 2 violin concertos, quartets, quintets, and operatic music.

JOSEPHO ODOARDI, b. ca. 1740. A peasant from the neighbourhood of Asoli, county Ancona, who had a natural genius for violin-making, and though he never entered the workshop of a violin-maker, made some 200 excellent violins which are still sought after in Italy. He died at the early age of 28.

GIOVANNI ANDREA SABATINI, b. Naples, ca. 1740; d. there ca. 1808. An excellent violinist and composer. 6 sonatas for 2 violins and bass, op. 1 (London, 1770, Hy. Fougt; also later ed.). Special praise is bestowed on his funeral music for choruses on the death of Jomelli, 1774 (Fétis).

SALVADORE TINTI, b. Florence, ca. 1740; d. Venice, ca. 1800. According to an opera libretto he was 1st violin at the theatre at Florence in 1795. Composed 6 quartets, 3 for 2 violins, viola and violoncello, and 3 for flute, violin, viola, and violoncello (Brit. Mus.); also 3 quintets for 2 violins, 2 violas and violoncello (Traeg. Cat.).

FRANCESCO ZANNETTI (ZANETTI), b. Volterra, ca. 1740. A singer and opera composer whose works include: 6 sonatas each, for 2 violins and bass, op. 1, op. 3, op. 4, and several more sets, some pub. London; 6 sonatas for harpsichord with violin (London, Welcker). A favourite solo for violin, 6 quintetti for 3 violins, violoncello obbligato and B.c., op. 2.

GIOVANNINI. Italian violinist, pupil of Leclair, lived 1740–82 chiefly in Berlin; had a pasticcio performed in London in 1745 under the name of Count St. Germain; he was also known as song composer (Graefe's Collection of Odes, 1741 and 1743) and the song "Willst du Dein Herz mir schenken" which was attributed to Bach, but according to latest researches appears undoubtedly to be by Giovannini.

LUDOVICO (ALOYS) TOMASINI, b. Pesaro, 1741; d. Esterház, Apr. 25, 1808. He came from Italy with Prince Esterhazy, as his valet. After 1761 he became a concertmeister in the chapel, where he gained the friendship of Haydn, who used to say "Nobody plays my quartets so much to my satisfaction as you" (C. F. Pohl's Biog. of Haydn, i, 262). He never went on tour. Only once in 1775 he played at a concert of the Vienna Musical Artists' Society (Tonkünstler Societät). His salary rose gradually from 200 florins to 1,100 florins. In 1802 he became director of the chamber music. Prince Esterhazy held him in high esteem, and after his death provided liberally for his wife and those of his children who were still too young to look after themselves. Compositions are contained in the Archive of Eisenstadt (Pohl, iii, 263; iv, 17). Apart from these, Eitner traced: Concerto in A for violin; 2 sonatas and variations for violin and Bc. (Musikfr.); 10 string quartets; duos concert. for 2 violins; divertimenti a 4; 24 divertimenti. According to Riemann, he wrote 24 divertissements for Baryton, violin and 'cello, etc., for Prince Anton. Two of his daughters sang in the church and opera at Eisenstadt and two sons were good violinists.

LUIGI TOMASINI, b. Eisenstadt. Son of Ludovico, entered the Esterhazy chapel, 1796, as violinist; married without the Prince's permission the singer Sophie Groll (Croll), was dismissed and became concertmeister to the Duke of Mecklenburg Strelitz. The wife was engaged there as a singer. Both gave a concert in Berlin in 1812, when Tomasini played the violin concerto by Beethoven, which he played again in Vienna in 1814. From that time nothing is known about him, nor are any compositions of his known.

ANTONIO TOMASINI, b. Eisenstadt, Hungary, Feb. 17, 1775, as 2nd son of Ludovico Tomasini and godchild of Haydn; d. there, June 12, 1824. Entered the Esterhazy chapel at Eisenstadt, 1796. In 1811 he became leader of the 2nd violins and 1820 of the 1st. Pohl (iii, 263; iv, 382; v, 108) says that he was member of the Vienna Musicians' Society (Tonkünstler Societät). His career was ruined by his reckless life.

ALEXANDER MARIA ANTONIO FRIDZERI (FRITZERI, FRIXER, called de F.), b. Verona, Jan. 16, 1741; d. Antwerp, Oct. 16, 1825. Became blind in early youth and studied music, especially the violin, at Vicenza. He also had great talent for musical instrument-making, and when only 11 years old he made himself a mandolin on which he learned to play, and afterwards on several other instruments. On Mar. 25, 1768, he played at Frankfort a concerto by Gabignet, an otherwise unknown composer (perhaps meant for Gaviniés) (E. v. d. Str.) (Israel, ii). For three years he was organist at the chapel of the Madonna del Monte Berico at Vicenza, and at the age of 24 he toured as violinist and mandolinist through Italy and France to Paris, where he remained for two years, afterwards continuing his tours through Belgium and along the Rhine, meeting everywhere with great success. In Strassburg, where he remained over a year, he composed 2 operas. In 1771 the first 6 of his string quartets and 6 mandolin sonatas were pub. in Paris (Fétis says he had a music selling and publishing business there), and in 1773 an opera of his was performed there and well received. He then went on concert tours again in the South of France. In 1766 he had another opera performed in Paris with still greater success, and some time after that he lived for twelve years on the estate of the Count of Chateaugiron in Brittany, visiting Paris occasionally, once for the performance of another opera of his, and for the pub. of some of his violin concertos. His opera "Les Souliers Mordorés" was performed at Bonn in 1782. The Count fled on the outbreak of the Revolution and in 1790 Fridzeri settled at Nantes, where he founded a Philharmonic Academy. The war in the Vendée in 1794 drove him back to Paris, where he founded a similar academy and was elected a member of the Lycée des Arts. The bomb explosion in the rue Nicaise in Dec., 1801, which was opposite his house, destroyed all his belongings and compelled him to go on tour again with his talented daughters, one a violinist, the other a singer. They toured in the North of France and in Belgium, finally settling at Antwerp, where Fridzeri devoted himself to teaching and started a music and instrument business. Apart from the above-mentioned works he wrote violin duets, quartets, songs, etc. His compositions enjoyed great popularity in their time; they consisted of violin concertos, 4 violin duos, quartets, operas, a mass, a symphony, etc.

ANTONIO CONFORTI, b. Piemont, ca. 1743. Pupil of Pugnani. Burney met him in Vienna in 1772. Of his compositions only a few vocal pieces and harpsichord sonatas are known. Fétis mentions 2 books of violin sonatas by him. (He calls him Conforto—but his spelling of names is unreliable.,

Mendel mentions a Niccolo Conforto, whose opera "Antigone" was performed in London in 1757 twelve times running, and thinks he might be the same as above.

NICOLO PASQUALI.  Came, ca. 1743, to London where he appeared in public concerts in 1752; settled at Edinburgh, where he died in 1757.  (Burney, vii, 672; Pohl, ii, 370.) Burney (vii, 458) says that 2 arias by him were inserted in Hasse's opera "Semiramide."  Composed also 6 sonatas for violin and bass, op. 1 (London); 6 sonatas for 2 violins with a tenor and thorough bass, in 2 sets (London); an opera, an oratorio, 6 sonatas for 2 violoncellos (Paris, 1740) (these may be the same as 6 solos for 2 violoncellos comp. by Sigr. Pasqualino de Marzis, op. 2, London, J. Johnson); 12 English Songs (1750), harpsichord tutor, and a book on thoroughbass.

BERNARDINO POLAZZO.  According to Pougin, probably a pupil of Tartini, who wrote a book of 6 violin sonatas, pub. Paris, 1743.

DOMENICO BASCONI.  A native of Sicily.  During 1745–60 violinist in the Court orchestra at Mannheim, where he conducted the Intermezzi from 1753 to 1757, at a salary of 150 florins.  He also wrote pantomime music.

GIOVANNI MANE GIORNOVICHI (JARNOVICK), b. Palermo, 1745: d. St. Petersburg, Nov. 21, 1804; a pupil of Bolli; met with great success but his quarrelsome nature and free living drove him from town to town.  Reichardt and Dittersdorf praise his perfect purity of intonation, his clear and beautiful, though small, tone.  In 1770 he appeared at the Paris Concert Spirituel and became very popular, till discreditable affairs caused his departure in 1779.  In Sept., 1779, he gave concerts at Frankfort a/M. as "First violinist of France and concertmeister of Prince Rohan-Guimenée."  He then entered the service of the Prussian Crown Prince but left Berlin in 1783 after a quarrel with Duport, and toured all over Europe.  On May 4, 1791, he made his debut in London where, in contest with Viotti, he was defeated.  In 1796 at Hamburg he earned large sums by violin- and billiard-playing.  In 1802 he played at the Berlin Opera; later going to Petersburg where he was defeated in contest with Rode. He died suddenly while playing billiards. He left many compositions for violin (List in Eitner).

GIOVANNI GIUSEPPE CAMBINI, b. Leghorn, Feb. 13, 1746; d. Bicêtre, Dec. 29, 1825. Studied first under Polli, then under Manfredi and Nardini. In 1763 he went to Bologna, where for three years he studied composition under Padre Martini. At the end of that time he went to Naples, where he fell in love with a girl from his native town whom he married after exciting adventures. He went to Paris, where he was enabled to produce in 1770 some of his compositions at the Concert Spirituel, which made him the musical hero of the day. Encouraged by his success, he began to turn out compositions wholesale, which although of ever-decreasing musical value still testified to excellent craftsmanship. Fétis enumerates 60 symphonies, 29 concertante symphonies, 144 string quartets, more than 400 pieces for various instruments, 19 operas, ballets and vocal compositions. As a performer he stood in great repute and was even associated for some time with Boccherini in the latter's quartet performances. From 1788 to 1791 he was conductor at the theatre Beaujolais and from 1791 to 1794 at the theatre Louvois. He also engaged in literary work but after the Revolution he gradually fell into poverty and died in a workhouse. In his chamber music he made much of the viola, for which he wrote very effectively.

GASPARO GHIRETTI, b. Naples, ca. 1747; d. Parma, ca. 1797. A pupil of the Conservatoire della Pieta who became (1774) chamber musician (violin) at the Court of Ferdinand of Parma. He composed several books of sonatas and caprices and church music (Fétis).

NICOLO MESTRINO, b. Milan, 1748; d. Paris, Sept., 1790. He entered the chapel of Prince Esterhazy in Nov., 1780, and in 1785 went to Pressburg, being appointed to the chapel of Count Ladislaus Erdödy. In 1786 he was at Brussels and petitioned the Princess-Regent of Belgium on Aug. 18, 1786, unsuccessfully for the post of Court capellmeister. And Mestrino went to Paris, played at the Concert Spirituel and became in 1789 conductor at the newly founded theatre de Monsieur. He composed a number of concertos, duets, solos, sonatas, and studies. Fétis says: "Mestrino was a great musician." He trained some excellent pupils, among them Mlle de la Jonchère, who married the famous Ladurner. When Viotti established the Italian Opera in Paris in 1789 he chose Mestrino as conductor, but he died in the following year and was succeeded by Puppo.

TRANQUILINI. A violin virtuoso at Verona ca. 1748; teacher of Hupfeld (Gerber, i).

FERRARIS. A violinist mentioned in the Saxon State Archive of 1748.

GIUSEPPE PUPPO, b. Lucca, Feb. 14, 1749 (Riemann: June 12, 1749); d. Florence, Apr. 19, 1827. Studied the violin at the Conservatoire St. Onofrio, Naples; returned 1768 to Lucca, where he succeeded Manfredi as director of the orchestra, then he toured all over Europe. In 1777 he appeared as violinist in London (Pohl, ii, 371), and in 1784 settled in Paris, where he had earlier, 1775, acquired a footing. He now was appointed at the theatre de Monsieur with a salary of 2,400 francs, afterwards at theatre Feydeau and others. Under the Republic he became director of the orchestra (conductor ?), but in 1811 returned to Italy, where he lived at Naples, Florence, etc., then he sank into poverty until Ed. Taylor bought him a place in a Hospital, where he died. According to Fétis, in 1793–9 he was conductor at the "Théâtre Français de la République." In the latter year he lost that place through the amalgamation of the Théâtre Française de l'Odéon and that of the rue Richelieu. He composed 3 violin duos, 8 fantasias or studies for violin solo (both Paris, Beaucé), and 6 fantasies for pianoforte.

ANTONIO KOLICHI. An Italian violinist who wrote 6 violin sonatas, op. 1, Paris, ca. 1750 (Pougin).

MME TASCA (TOSCA), of Venice, "de la musique de l'empereur." Played a concerto, in the style of Vivaldi, of her own composition in Paris, Sept. 8, 1750 (M. Brenet, "Les Concerts en France," etc.).

ANTONIO TILE. A 1st violinist in the Court chapel, Turin, ca. 1750; received Dec. 29, 1750, 500 lire salary, raised Dec. 22, 1775, by 150 lire (Ricordi's "Gazetta," 1891, 456).

NICOLA FORENZA. A teacher of the violin at the Conservatoire Santo Onofrio, Naples, ca. 1750, and, as such, master of Ant. Sacchini, who at the beginning of his career played chiefly the violin, on which he was a good performer.

FRANZ ANTON BOURESI. Violinist in Munich. In 1750 at the Court chapel with a salary of 285 florins, which was raised to 475 florins when he became 1st violinist in 1765.

GIOVANNI CARMINATI. A Venetian, pupil of Tartini; lived as teacher of the violin at Lyons, ca. 1750–70. He appeared with success as soloist at the Concert Spirituel, Paris.

PIETRO FIDANZA, b. 1750. Composed 6 duos, dialogo per 2 violini, pub. Florence, 1780 (Gerber, ii). The Milan Conservatoire has: Sei Sonate per 2 violini (Firence, Stecchi e del Vivo) (Eitner).

GAETANO (CAJETANO) MATTIOLI, b. Venice, Aug. 7, 1750. A violin pupil of Angelo Moriggi. Conductor of opera at Bologna, Mantua and Parma; went to Germany and was appointed concertmeister at the Electoral Chapel, Bonn, May 26, 1774, with a salary of 1,000 florins. On Apr. 24, 1777, he became director of music there, but on May 18, 1784, he had to leave the country on account of debts (Thayer, i, 53 ff. and 80). Neefe says "he was full of fire, vivacity and fine feeling."

CIPRIANO-CORDIER (CORMIER in Eitner), b. Venice, ca. 1750; d. Warsaw, 1789. A pupil of Nazari at Venice, and excelled particularly in cantabile playing. He went to Poland as a youth, and became concertmeister, chamber virtuoso and teacher of Prince Sapicha in 1772. His violin compositions, concertos, etc., which were written to suit his particular style, were greatly admired and in strong demand. They helped to spread his fame and to gain for him a considerable fortune.

GIOVANNI BATTISTA GRAZIOLI, b. Venice, ca. 1750; d. Venice, ca. 1820. A composer; wrote 6 sonate per cembalo con violino, op. 3 (1799, Venezia, Ant Zatta e figlio) (Dresden MS.). A very beautiful Adagio from Sonata in G for violin and cembalo, arranged by Max Grünberg, is pub. by Carl Simon, Berlin. *See* Augener's Catalogue.

CARLO ZUCCARI of Milan (a MS. in the B.B. says "di casal Maggiore"); ca. 1750 violinist (leader?) at the Italian Opera, London; Wasielewski thinks he might be identical with the leader of the Milan orchestra whom Burney heard in 1770 and praised as an excellent player, and also with the Zuccarini, mentioned by Brenet ("Les Concerts en France") as having played at the Académie Royale, Paris, in 1737. He composed 3 trios for 2 violins and bass. Gerber states that he made himself known in 1761 through 6 violin concertos, which, like his following compositions, remained in MS.; 6 duets for violin and violoncello, one book of 7 and one of 3 sonatas for violin and bass. In the Brit. Mus. Lib. are sonatas for violin and bass, op. 1 (1730?), *see* E. v. d. Str., "Eighteenth-Century Sonatas," *The Strad*, Dec., 1919. He also composed: sonate a violino e basso o cembalo, ded. conte Jos. Ant. Arronati Visconti (Milano), op. 1 and 2 (12 sonatas pub. Milan without name of place or publisher); 6 sonatas for 2 violins with thorough bass for the harps (London, A. Hummel). In Dresden Mus. MS., 4 concerti a violino concertato with string quartet and one solo a violino e basso. One piece in Corette's "L'Art de Violon"; in Berlin 4 Adoramus in score MS.; in Brussels Conservatoire "Zuccarini Carlo, sonate per violino e basso," MS. Karlsruhe, "Carlo Zuccarini 1 sonata flute et basse G. major," score MS. (probably the same as above). Carlo Zuccari, "The True Method of Playing an Adagio" (London, R. Bremner, ca. 1770), containing 12 adagios with B.c., each in its simple form, and underneath with the customary embellishments, thus giving a useful key to the manner in which the adagios were executed by the Italian violinists of the time.

DOMENICO FERRARI, b. Piacenza, d. Paris, 1780, murdered (?) as embarking for England. Pupil of Tartini, then retired to Cremona ca. 1748 for further study. In 1749 he was greatly admired in Vienna. In 1754 he obtained a brilliant success at the Concert Spirituel, Paris, especially by his novel use of harmonics and octave passages. After touring Germany, appointed in the Stuttgart Court Chapel, together with Nardini, in 1758, but returned to Paris in 1770. Composed a Concerto and a solo for violin and 'cello (MSS. Musikfreunde); 3 sets of 6 sonatas each with bass; 6 trios for 2 violins and bass, etc. (*see* Eitner).

GIOVANNI BATTISTA NOFERI, b. in Italy in the first half of the 18th century. A distinguished violinist who appeared 1770 in London as violin virtuoso (Pohl, ii, 370). He wrote: 6 solos with bass, op. 2; 6 do. do., op. 8; 8 solos with bass for harpsichord or violoncello; a large number of duets for 2 violins with and without bass, also for violin and violoncello; trios for violin, viola and violoncello; dances for the theatre, etc. He left in MS. some concertos for the violin (Fétis).

MELCHIOR CHIESA. Capellmeister at Milan about the middle of the 18th century. Pougin enumerates him among the pupils of Tartini and states that he composed 6 trios for 2 violins and bass, op. 1 (Paris, engraved by Mme Leclair).

MICHAEL ANGELO FERACE. An 18th-century Neapolitan violinist. The Fitzwilliam Museum at Cambridge has "2 sonatas for 2 violins and violoncello, by Sigr . . ."

ANTONIO MARIA FILIPPI. Portrait of a violinist giving that name, but no date, in Liceo Mus., Bologna (Eitner).

PAGNI, is mentioned by Wasielewski as a pupil of Tartini. Probably Cesare Pagni, of whom the "Musikfreunde" in Vienna have 4 pianoforte quartets and 1 duet for violin and harpsichord.

GUILARDUCCI. Italian 18th-century violinist who, *vide* Fétis, wrote a concerto for violin which was pub. in Paris, no date.

ANOLGIO. Composed 6 sonatas a violon seul, 18th century (Paris Conserv.); 6 airs for violin which once were there also, have been lost.

DOMENICO ANTINORI DETTO MENEGUCCIO. Lived in the 18th century at Karlsruhe. Composed sonatas for violin and bass, in Karlsruhe library. No other particulars.

GIOVANNI DE SANTIS. An 18th-century Neapolitan violinist who lived at Naples about the middle of the century. His sonatas, etc., had been pirated by Wittvogel, Amsterdam. When this came to the knowledge of Santis, he started out to sue Wittvogel, but died on the journey. Known, are 6 sonate da camera a violino, violone e cimbalo, op. 1 (Amsterdam, Wittvogel); 12 sonate a flanto trav. o violino solo e B.c. o violoncello (Paris, Leclerc, Boivin), copy in Karlsruhe. Fétis says he composed 3 sets of sonatas and 6 concertos, surreptitiously published by Wittvogel.

# CHAPTER 35

## *Italy: to 1775*

THE Italian school of violin playing reached its zenith about the middle of the 18th century. Geminiani followed in the footsteps of his master, Corelli, whose technique he had developed to a much higher degree. He surpassed even his co-student, under the same master, G. B. Somis, who on the other hand had extended his art in other ways by amalgamating the teaching of Corelli with that of Vivaldi, and, proving a teacher of very great ability, founded the Piedmontese school at Turin, from which emerged, among other eminent violinists, G. B. Viotti, who may be looked upon as the father of modern violin playing.

Vivaldi had formed a style of his own, and developed and enlarged the form of the instrumental concerto to such an extent that Bach took him as his model therein. He also influenced the art of violin playing through his pupils, Regina Strinasachi and Pisendel, who was, moreover, a pupil of Torelli and of Montanari. F. M. Veracini again, excelled not only through his brilliant technique and by his entirely new style of great freedom and boldness, which Tartini took for his model, but also by the uncommon freedom in the melodic and harmonic treatment of his sonatas, which sometimes have such a modern physiognomy that they were not appreciated by his contemporaries. Tartini, on the other hand, pursued the work of his great predecessors, Corelli and Vivaldi, to far greater heights and depths as a composer as well as a player, and in both capacities he became the teacher of the whole of Europe. He made several improvements with regard to the fittings of the violin, and also the shape of the bow, as to the length and *cambre*, on which he advised the makers. A bow, said to have belonged to him, and to be the workmanship of the elder Tourte, is in the possession of

46

Mr. W. Howard Head, through whose courtesy we are able to give a reproduction (Ch. 3). The stick is fluted for about two-thirds of its upper length, and Tartini's name is engraved on the silver ferrule, the lettering appearing to belong unquestionably to the 18th century; there seems little doubt that it was one of Tartini's bows. Still further improvements in the construction of the bow were made by François Tourte in conjunction with Viotti. Viotti completed the great trinity in the firmament of Italian violin playing; although the field of his activity was outside his native country, and in spite of the fact that the period in which he devoted himself to teaching was but a short one, yet he must be looked upon as the father of modern violin playing and the founder of the French school, which from that time began to take a leading position in the art of violin playing. Viotti's compositions were an even greater advance upon Tartini's, as these had been on Corelli's, especially with regard to form and orchestration.

BARTOLOMEO CAMPAGNOLI, b. Cento, near Bologna, Sept. 10, 1751; d. Neustrelitz, Nov. 6, 1827. His first violin teacher was Dall'Ocha, a pupil of Lolli. In his twelfth year his father, a merchant, sent him to Modena to study under Paolo Guasta-robba, a pupil of Tartini. At the same time he studied composition, and in 1766 he became a violinist in the orchestra of Cento. In 1768 he was so fascinated by the young violinist Lamotta (about whom little is known, *see* Lamotta) that he accompanied him to Venice and Padua, where they remained together for several months. In 1770 he made a very successful debut at Rome and thence went to Faënza, where he remained for 6 months to benefit by his friendly intercourse with the violinist and capellmeister Paolo Alberghi. Then he went to Florence, where he continued his studies under Nardini, became leader of the 2nd violins at the Pergola theatre, and formed a close friendship with the young Cherubini. In 1775 he returned to Rome as leader of the 2nd violins at the Argentina theatre. After giving a number of concerts in various towns he became concertmeister of the Prince-Bishop of Freising from 1777 to 1779. Then he toured with the bassoon player Reinert in Poland. In 1780 he went to Dresden as director of the chapel of the Duke of Courland. In 1783 he toured in Northern Europe, remaining

47

for several months at Stockholm, where he was made a member of the Royal Academy. After his return to Dresden he visited, in 1784, his native country. In 1786 he returned again to Dresden, but paid another visit to Italy in 1788. In 1797 he became concertmeister at the "Gewandhaus" concerts at Leipzig and remained there, with the exception of a visit to Paris in 1809, until 1818, when he went as Court capellmeister to Neustrelitz and remained there for the rest of his life. Campagnoli is praised for his purity of intonation and perfect technique, but although he was trained by pupils of Tartini he lacked the power of tone and breadth of style of that school; on the other hand, he had not become acquainted with the important progress in violin playing brought about by the art of Viotti. Spohr, who praises his playing in many ways, describes his method as antiquated. His tutor, based on the teaching of Nardini, contains much valuable material, and the rules and principles which he expounds are incontestable, but the work lacks systematic progression. He composed concertos for violin and flute, sonatas for violin and bass, violin duets, duets for violin and flute, a number of solos, studies, etc., and the still famous caprices for viola. His two daughters were good operatic singers.

COLLIGNON, b. ca. 1751. A pupil of Lolli. Gave a concert at Frankfort a/M. on July 5, 1769, when he was 18 years old (Israel, 50).

GIUSEPPE MORIANI, b. Livorno, Aug. 16, 1752; still living there, according to an autograph letter, on Sept. 8, 1814. Studied the violin under Cambini and Nardini, and counterpoint under Luigi Boccherini. He excelled particularly in the rendering of Haydn's quartets and Boccherini's quintets. In 1812 he was conductor at the theatre at Livorno. He is said to have composed violin concertos and sonatas (Fétis), but none were known to Eitner.

PASSERINO. In London 1752 as violinist and viol d'amour player (Pohl, ii, 370).

ANGELO (ANGIOLO) MORIGI, b. Rimini, 1752; d. Parma, ca. 1788. A violin pupil of Tartini, as he states himself on his op. 2, and of Vallotti at Padua in counterpoint. He was appointed in 1785 as violinist at the Court of Parma and afterwards as director of music. He left a treatise on "fugal

Giov. Battista Viotti, from Mme. Viger-Lebrun's portrait from life. (Photograph by the author).

counterpoint" which was pub. after his death by his pupil Bonifacio Asioli. He composed 6 sonatas for violin and bass, op. 3 (London, J. Johnson); 2 sonatas do. with B.c. are in the Lib. of the Musikfr., and, in MS. copy in Brussels Conservatoire, 6 sonatas for 2 violins and thorough bass (London, Walsh). Fétis mentions also 6 sonatas for violin with bass, op. 1; 6 concerti grossi (Parma, 1758, and Amsterdam, 1762); 6 do. do., op. 4 (Parma, 1759).

FRANCESCO MONTALI. An 18th-century Neapolitan violinist and composer who went to Spain and became 1st violinist at Toledo Cathedral. Composed 6 sonatas for violin and B.c., 1752, and 6 do., 1759; sonatas for violin and violoncello, 1759; 12 trios for 2 violins and bass, 1751 (MS. in Duke of Alba's Lib., Madrid); a concerto for flute, harpsichord, 2 violins and bass; collaborated also in an opera "Endimione" (Madrid, 1752).

GIOVANNI BATTISTA VIOTTI, b. Fontanetto da Po, Piedmont, May 23, 1753; d. London, Mar. 3, 1824. There are so many detailed accounts of the varied fortunes of this great artist, that their recapitulation in this place appears unnecessary, especially as they would, for their adequate treatment, require more space than we could give them here. One of the best and most authoritative accounts is that by Mr. Edw. Heron-Allen in Grove's Dictionary, while all the best portraits of Viotti are reproduced in E. v. d. Str. "Viotti" in *Dio Musik*, June, 1902, and "Viottiana," in *The Connoisseur*, Nov., 1911. We shall therefore restrict our biography to the most essential facts. Viotti's father, a farrier and amateur horn player, taught him the elements of music, and he delighted in playing on a toy violin, purchased at a fair. At the age of 11 he was aided for about one year by a good all-round musician and lute player, Giovannini. In 1766 he played at a church festival at Strambino, where he attracted the attention of the Bishop, at whose recommendation the Marquis Voghera charged himself with his musical education. The characteristic story of how he astonished everybody by playing a difficult sonata by Ferrari at first sight has been told by all his biographers. The Marquis gave him Pugnani for his teacher, under whose care he made rapid progress. At the age of 14 he composed his first violin concerto in A minor, which was afterwards published as No. 3. In 1780 he went on tour for the first time with his master Pugnani, who held him in great affection. They first went to Geneva, where Viotti met with an enthusiastic reception, and thence to Dresden, and Berlin, where Frederic the Great honoured Viotti by frequently playing concerted music with him. From Berlin they went in the same year to Warsaw and thence to St. Petersburg where the Empress Catherine II overwhelmed Viotti with presents and tried to induce him to remain at her Court where Viotti met Giornovichi in an undecided contest (*see* Wasielewski, 159), which had its sequel ca. twelve years later in London to Giornovichi's discomfiture, but he left in 1781 with Pugnani, revisiting Berlin, and other northern cities, finally visiting London. How far Pugnani accompanied him appears uncertain; according to Wasielewski they probably parted at Berlin, and Pugnani did not go with Viotti to England as stated elsewhere. In London Viotti created a profound impression, eclipsing even the fame of Geminiani. Early in 1782 he went to Paris where, after a small private concert, he appeared at the Concert Spirituel on Mar. 15 with unparalleled success, which was repeated on frequent subsequent occasions. At one time he was leader of Prince Guéménée's band, and, later on, 1st violin in that of the Prince de Soubise. At his benefit concert on Apr. 29, 1783, Mme Mara was announced to sing, but jealous of Viotti's success at her own benefit concert, so it is said, refused at the last moment. On Sept. 8, 1783, he appeared for the last time at the Concert Spirituel, and at the height of his fame retired altogether from the public platform. Many reasons have been advanced for his doing so, one of these being his extreme sensibility, and disdain of the ignorant public. In 1784 Queen Marie Antoinette appointed him as her accompanist with a life pension of £150, and for the following years he devoted himself entirely to the service of the Court. In 1785 he was living with his friend Cherubini, where every Sunday musical academies were held, visited by all musicians and violinists of note, where Viotti's latest compositions were performed, and where he often played solos and concertos. In 1788 he joined Léonard (Léonard Antin), Queen Marie Antoinette's hairdresser, in the management of the theatre de Monsieur, where, with a brilliant company of singers of the first order, he started to produce Italian operas, under the patronage of the Comte de Provence, brother of Louis XVI. The venture promised to become a great success, but soon the rumblings of the Revolution made themselves heard, yet Viotti refused to give in. "A man should die at his post," he said; "for good sense always taught me that if honest men quitted their posts, the wicked gained an immense triumph" (E. Heron-Allen in Grove). He remained at his post, but donned for his protection the uniform of the National Guard. In 1790 the Court moved from Versailles to the Tuileries and Viotti was obliged to find another theatre. He removed his opera to the theatre de la foire Saint-Germain, which proved inadequate, and with the assistance of the intendant, Feydeau de Brou, and several wealthy nobles, he had the theatre Feydeau built, which was opened in 1791; but the conditions in Paris became more and more turbulent, and on the eve of the arrest of the King and Queen he left for London, where he arrived July 21 or 22, 1792, having lost practically all he possessed. As soon as Salomon had heard of Viotti's arrival he induced him to play at his concerts in Hanover Square, and in a short time he found a circle of influential friends and pupils. In July, 1793, he revisited his native country to arrange his own affairs as well as those of his brothers, who were still children, and after that he returned via Switzerland, Germany and Flanders to London, where he arrived in Dec. of that year.

About that time he made the acquaintance of Mr. and Mrs. Chinnery which ripened into closest friendship, so that he was eventually looked upon almost as a member of the family. This circle of friends was joined by Ad. Frederick, Duke of Cambridge, an amateur violinist, and pupil of Viotti, who wrote for him a book of violin duets. In 1794 and 1795 he played at nearly all Salomon's concerts, for which he composed the second series of his violin concertos, marked by letters only, which show him at the apex of his art; the first series, comprising the first 20 concertos, he composed in Paris, about 1782–3. In 1794 he began to take part in the direction of the Italian Opera at the King's Theatre, and on the retirement of Cramer, Viotti succeeded him as leader there. His life now ran a quiet course until Mar. 6, 1798, when, as he was spending the evening peacefully in the circle of his friends, he was arrested by the King's officers, and unceremoniously expelled from the country. Jacobites, enraged at his escape from France, had denounced him to the British Government for revolutionary intrigues and lèse majesté. Needless to say, it was an entirely baseless and spiteful slander, but feeling ran high, and Viotti, who was helpless, went to Schönefeld, a small place on the Dove-Elbe, near Hamburg, where his friend George Smith possessed a country seat which he put at his disposal, and where he occupied his enforced leisure hours by composition and correspondence with his friends, especially with Mrs. Chinnery and her children, who were his pupils, for whom he wrote little pieces. He also wrote some of his finest violin duets there, one book being dedicated to his friend Mr. Chinnery. The title page of this shows one of the best portrait engravings of Viotti. Part of his time was taken up in teaching the talented young Mannheim violinist, Friedrich Wilhelm Pixis, who had come to Hamburg with his father and brother Joh. Peter, the famous pianist, and who subsequently reflected great credit upon his great master. In 1801 he was allowed to return to his friends in London, where, finding his musical connexions more or less severed, he embarked in the wine trade with the financial and social support of Mrs. Chinnery; but like all his business undertakings this also was eventually to end in disaster. In 1802 he revisited Paris and produced his latest compositions in the circle of his artist friends who were loud in their praise, both of these and his playing, especially Baillot, who praises particularly his tone and his bowing.

At the end of the year Viotti was back in London, and from the Memoirs of Mme Viger-Lebrun, the famous French artist, we get a glance of the happy life he led at the time in the midst of the Chinnery family. Mme Lebrun, who spent a fortnight with them at Gilwell, their country house near Sewardstone (Epping Forest), relates how the beautiful and charming Mrs. Chinnery, a very good musician, Caroline, her 14-year-old daughter, a remarkably talented pianist, and Viotti gave them every night delightful concerts. It was about this time that Mme Lebrun painted the celebrated life-size portrait of Viotti which was believed to have been lost until Mr. Heron-Allen discovered it in the possession of a lineal descendant of Mrs. Chinnery, together with a miniature portrait of him by Trossarelli and miniatures of Mrs. Chinnery and her children, which through Mr. Heron-Allen's instrumentality were first reproduced from the writer's own photographs in his above-mentioned articles.[1]  Viotti's ever-increasing financial difficulties in connexion with his wine business drew him further and further away from his musical pursuits until 1813, when he took part in the formation of the Philharmonic Society, and even played in the orchestra at the opening concert on Mar. 8, 1813, under Salomon as leader.  Occasionally, however, he conducted the orchestra, and led one of his own quartets at one of the concerts of the first year.  In 1814 he paid a short visit to Paris.  When Baillot discovered his presence he hurriedly assembled his admirers and friends, who gave him a great ovation as the grand-master of his art, and when Cherubini embraced him before the assemblage their enthusiasm knew no bounds.  In 1818 his commercial ruin had apparently become complete and he returned again to Paris in an attempt to retrieve his fortunes. At a concert arranged in his honour he played his E minor concerto, when many in the audience were moved to tears. Through the influence of his old patron the Comte de Provence, who had mounted the throne as Louis XVIII, he was in 1819 appointed Director of the Opera and the Opera Italienne at a salary of 12,000 francs, but misfortune dogged his footsteps.  In the following year the Duc de Berry, the King's nephew, was assassinated on Feb. 13, as he came out of the Opera.  Viotti was in England at the time.  The Opera was removed to the rue Favart, but that theatre proving inadequate, it changed its quarters, after a two months' interval, in May, 1821, to the theatre Louvois.  After only four performances this proved also unsatisfactory, and after another interval the Opera was finally opened, at the rue Le Peletier, on Aug. 16, 1821.  All these changes had so seriously affected poor Viotti's financial position, that on Jan. 27, 1821, he wrote to the Baron de Ferté asking to send him some furniture, as after an absence of twenty-nine years he finds himself without household effects, and without the means to buy any.  Worn out by disenchantment, intrigues and mistrust—in some quarters he was blamed for the adversities of the Opera—he resigned his position at the Opera, but apparently continued

[1] Photo-reproduction in *Die Musik*, June, 1902.

for a short time the direction of the Théâtre Italienne. It may have been at least a small satisfaction to him when *Le Miroir* of Oct. 31, 1821, in speaking about his retirement, after praising his achievements as virtuoso and composer, says, "Never has the Théâtre Italienne appeared to us better managed" (then under Viotti). On March 13, 1822, he was still in Paris, as is evident from his will, made on that day, and now in the possession of Mr. E. Heron-Allen (*see* Grove, "Viotti"). It is a pathetic document which throws some light on the tragedy of his life and his lovable, sympathetic character. There is no doubt, however, that most of his misfortunes were of his own making by embarking on ventures which lay outside the domain of his art.

He returned to London soon after, broken in spirit and in health, and lived with the Chinnery family, falling into gradual decline, until he died at the house of Mrs. Chinnery, 5 Berkeley Street, Portman Square, at seven o'clock in the morning. The writer, in spite of laborious researches, has failed to discover his burial-place, which may be at Sewardstone, where several of Mrs. Chinnery's children were interred.

Viotti was the father of the modern school of classical violin playing. He inherited from his master Pugnani the combined art of Corelli, Vivaldi, and Tartini, and having evolved on the basis thereof a style of his own he handed it on to posterity through his numerous pupils, especially Rode, Pixis, Alday, Vacher, Cartier, Labarre, Libon, Mori, Pinto, and Robberechts. Viotti was the greatest virtuoso of his time, but he never debased his extraordinary technical powers by using them for any but the noblest and highest purposes of his art. He despised all mere technical display. His perfect command of the bow, brilliant technique of the left hand and perfect purity of intonation were accompanied by great beauty and fullness of tone and in the poetical expression of his cantabile playing he was without his equal. His technical heritage, transmitted through his pupils, is at least equalled, if not surpassed in its importance for the modern art of violin playing by his compositions. Viotti was the first who expanded the architectural forms of the violin concerto by adopting as far as possible Haydn's symphonic form, with well-contrasted subjects, and the use of the full symphony orchestra employed by the latter. His work is distinguished by nobility of thought and charm of thematic invention, especially his 9 concertos of the 2nd series.

Viotti was a cultured and refined man of courtly bearing, and dignified personality, yet simple and kind hearted. The unwholesome atmosphere of the decadent French Court had left him unspoiled. He possessed a personal magnetism which threw its spell over every audience as soon as he appeared on the platform. "There was something so grand, so inspiring, in his playing, that even the cleverest artist shrank in his presence, and became mediocre" (Heron-Allen quoting Miel). He left two violins, one very fine Stradivari, now in the possession of Messrs. W. E. Hill & Sons, and a Klotz (Sebastian?) which belonged to Mrs. Chinnery.

His compositions for the violin consist of 29 concertos with orchestra; 2 symphonies concertante for 2 violins, strings and wind; 12 sonatas for violin and piano; 3 divertissements for violin solo; 54 violin duets; 6 serenades for 2 violins; 3 popular airs for violin and piano; 36 trios for 2 violins and bass; 7 books of string quartets; 6 string quartets on popular airs. He composed also pianoforte sonatas and songs (*see* list in Grove V, 541, and Eitner). Messrs. W. E. Hill & Sons have also the autograph of a duet for one violin (in contrapuntal writing) which he composed for his friend Cherubini.

GIOVANNI BATTISTA MARELLA, a violin virtuoso who lived for some time in London, and gained a prize at the Catch Club in 1763. In 1753 a Marella appeared in London as violin virtuoso and one on the viol d'amour appeared in 1759 (Pohl, ii, 370, 374). They are in all probability one and the same. He signed himself with his full name on the following compositions: 6 sonatas for a violin and bass, ded. Aemilia Rob. Forster, op. 1 (Dublin, 1753); 6 soli a violino solo, ded. Conte Pembroke, op. 2 (London, 1757). In Walsh's Catch Club I, some songs, also in the modern Catch Club (J. Cox).

PIETRO ANTONIO AMADEO RASETTI (RAZETTTI). Of Turin, where his son (?) Amadeo was born 1754. He was appointed one of the Twenty-four Violins of the King in Paris, Dec. 18, 1760; sent to Naples in 1765 to engage new musicians (singers?) for the Royal chapel; pensioned 1776 with 1,000 lires. (Brenet, "Les Concerts en France.")

GIOVANNI FELICE MOSEL, b. Florence, ca. 1754; d. after 1812. A pupil of his father, who was a pupil of Tartini; afterwards he studied under Nardini. Appeared in public as virtuoso at the age of 15; appointed in the chapel of Grand Duke Leopold of Florence and succeeded in 1793 his master as 1st violinist and conductor of the chapel. In the *Magazine* of 1786 he is called célèbre professor di Fiorenze (*sic!*). In 1812 he was 1st violin at the theatre La Pergola (Fétis). Eitner only knows 6 duetti per 2 violini and sonata per violino e basso (Musikfr.). Fétis: 6 violin duets (Florence, 1783, and Paris, Pleyel); 6 duets, do. (Venice, 1791); also quartets; serenade for flute, 2 violas and violoncello; and in MS. sonatas for violin and bass, trios for 2 violins and violoncello, and symphonies.

ANGELO COLONNA. An 18th-century violinist of Venice; preceded Joh. Christ. Friedr. Bach as concertmeister of Count Wilhelm of Schaumburg-Lippe with a salary of 600 thaler per annum, but was dismissed Apr. 14, 1756. In 1786 he was violinist at S. Mark's, Venice, with a salary of 600 ducats. As composer he is chiefly known by the canzonetta "La Biondina in Gondola," which has become a popular air. In the Fitzwilliam Museum, Cambridge, is a MS. collection of 52 canzonettas for soprano and 8 minuets for violin and bass by him.

ANTONIO MESSIER. 1st violin in the Court chapel at Turin, May 28, 1756, with a salary of 200 lire, and from Jan. 11, 1785, with 450 lire in the same position (Ricordi, *Gazetta*, 1891, 456). Composed 6 concertos for violin, in Musikfreunde, Vienna; 2 concertos; 13 trios (mostly Ad$^o$. All$^o$. All$^o$.) for 2 violins and bass; and a symphony in MS. in Karlsruhe, signed G. A. Messier, are probably by the same.

ALESSANDRO ROLLA, b. Pavia, Apr. 22, 1757; d. Milan, Sept. 15, 1841. Studied under Fiorino at Milan, then under Renzi (who, ca. 1785, became 1st violin at the Court of Brazil) and Conti. In 1782 he was called to Parma and succeeded Georgi as 1st violin and director. In 1802 he returned to Milan as conductor at the Scala theatre, and in 1805 became 1st violin to Prince Eugene Beauharnais, viceroy of Italy, and professor at the Conservatoire. Paganini was among his pupils, but only for a few months. He made apparently a speciality of the viola, for which he wrote more concertos than for the violin. (For list of compositions, *see* Eitner.) One of his best pupils was Bern. Ferrara. He retained a youthful freshness of feeling in his playing to his ripe old age, and showed an ability as conductor which in Italy was rare in his time. He was a prolific composer of concertos, duets, etc., both for violin and for viola, also of chamber music. Only his duets survived until the latter part of the 19th century.

ANTONIO ROLLA, b. Parma, Apr. 18, 1798; d. Dresden, May 19, 1837. Son and pupil of Alessandro Rolla. In 1823–36 he was concertmeister in the Dresden Court orchestra. He composed one concerto and solo pieces for violin.

CARLO FALCO (Fétis calls him François; Mendel, Francesco). Appeared in London in 1759 (Pohl, ii, 370), where he published in 1763 "6 sonate per il violino solo col B.," also some harpsichord sonatas (*see* Eitner, who erroneously translates harpsicordo as "harp"). Fétis says: He went to France in 1773, where he became a member of the Royal chapel and published 6 solos for violin, op. 2, and a book of solfeggios, which were both re-pub. London in 1776.

ANTONIO BARTOLOMEO BRUNI, b. Coni, Piemont, Feb. 2, 1759; d. there, 1823. Pupil of Pugnani for the violin and Spezziani of Novara for composition. He was of a querulous nature, which accounts for the fact that he never remained long in any one position. In 1780 he made his debut at a Concert Spirituel, in 1781 he settled in Paris and became a violinist at the Comédie Italienne, and in 1789 he became conductor of the theatre de Monsieur, as successor of Mestrino, but was soon replaced by Lahoussaye. Afterwards he held that position at the Opéra-Comique with similar results. He was then appointed as director of the temporary Commission of Arts and in 1801 leader of the orchestra of the theatre des Bouffons, and proved himself a most able conductor. Never —says Fétis—were the voices better accompanied than under Bruni. He was succeeded in that position by Grasset, and retired to Passy whence after a long period of silence he emerged once more in 1816 with a little comic opera which was unsuccessful. Soon after that he returned to Coni. Among his numerous compositions are 8 books of sonatas for violin, some concertos, and 10 books of violin duets which have retained their popularity.

ANTONIO BARTOLOMEI (called MAURICE), b. Parma, 1760; still living in 1815. Commenced his studies at Turin in the school of Pugnani, finishing them under Morigi at Parma. His countrymen looked upon him as a violinist of great talent. He was 1st violin and director (conductor?) of the orchestra of the theatre at Parma. He wrote, according to Fétis, some solos for violin which remained in MS.

FRANCESCO GIULIANI, b. Florence, ca. 1760; was still fully active in Florence, 1812. Violinist, harpist, singing and harpsichord teacher at Florence; pupil of Nardini and Bartol. Felice (composition). For some time violinist at the Novo Teatro, Florence. According to a textbook (libretto) he was director and 1st violin at the Royal Theatre, Florence, in 1795. In the list of operas, Milan, 1785, he is mentioned as opera composer. He wrote duets for 2 violins, violin and violoncello; quartets, sonatas, concertos, etc., for harpsichord and other instruments.

LUCHINI. Of Milan, was appointed violinist at the Bologna theatre in 1761 (Dittersdorf, Autobiog., 108).

P. SPAGNOLETTI, b. Cremona, 1761; d. London, Sept. 23, 1834. He was appointed at the theatre, Bologna. Composed variations for violin and pianoforte, dances and songs (Brit. Mus.). He came to London in 1813, where he was for many years leader at the King's Theatre, and one of the original members of the Philharmonic Society.

GIOVANNI BATTISTA CIMADOR, b. Venice, 1761; d. London, ca. 1808. He was of a noble family and the Theatre Almanach de Gotha called him Count Cimador. He played the violin, the violoncello, and the pianoforte with equal perfection. In 1788 an interlude of his was performed at Venice with success, but Cimador was dissatisfied with it and renounced composing. Fétis says that the score, which was then in the Paris Conservatoire Library, proved it to be indeed very mediocre. Cimador settled in London, ca. 1791, as teacher of singing. As the orchestra of the Haymarket Theatre refused to perform the symphonies by Mozart on account of their difficulty, he felt very annoyed and arranged 6 of the finest for 2 violins,

2 violas, violoncello and double bass with a flute and libitum. This arrangement, which did credit to his musicianship, met with great success. He also composed 2 duos for 2 violins and 2 duos for violin and viola, as well as some songs; they were pub. in London.

LUIGI GRIMALDI MARCHESE DELLA PIETRA, b. Genoa, 1762; d. Turin, July 31, 1834. Of the family of the Princes of Monaco. In 1801 he was in Paris. A good violinist who wrote some pieces for violin (Masseangeli).

PROSPERO SILVA, b. Reggio, Dec. 5, 1762; d. there, Oct. 29, 1834. Violinist and director of music to the town, director of the School of Music, and violinist of the Duke Francesco IV. He trained many pupils, including Rosalind Grossi, whom he afterwards married (Valdrighi, xiv, 27).

A. OLIVIERI, b. Turin, 1763; lived at Paris, 1827; died probably soon after. He was for a long time in the Court chapel at Turin. Fétis says he was a pupil of Pugnani, and for a long time at the Court of the King of Sardinia and the theatre at Turin. He was often engaged by a member of the Court circle, who paid him liberally. One evening he kept his patron's company waiting so long that they became impatient. When he arrived, his patron reprimanded him severely. Olivieri listened without uttering a word, which irritated the former, who became more and more abusive until Olivieri lost his patience and knocked him on the head with his violin, breaking it to pieces; then he ran out of the house and fled to Naples. When the French Revolutionary army appeared there he proclaimed openly his sympathy with their principles, which would have made it unsafe for him to remain there when they left. Consequently he went to Paris in their wake and there he had pub. variations on a Neapolitan air with quartet accomp. and airs with variations with violoncello. He went to Lisbon a few years later, but returned to Paris in 1814. Fétis knew him there in 1827, when he had abandoned playing on account of excessive stoutness. He played with brilliance and delicacy, but lack of feeling, rather cold.

REGINA STRINASACCHI, b. Ostiglia, near Mantua, 1764; d. Dresden, 1839. She received her musical and general education at the Ospidale della Pietà at Venice, and soon distinguished herself both as a violinist and as a guitar player, but

she chose the violin as her principal instrument.   At the end of
her studies she went to Paris, where she benefited still further
by the presence there of a number of famous violinists, and
played, according to Fétis (Pougin denies his statement), with
great success at the Concert Spirituel.   In 1777 she toured with
her brother in Germany and they appeared on Nov. 21 with great
success at Frankfort a/M.   In 1780–3 she toured in Italy and
was greatly admired as an eminent virtuoso, as well as for her
beauty and personal charm.   In 1784 she visited Vienna, where
she met Mozart, who wrote to his father on Apr. 24: . . . "The
famous Strinasacchi from Mantua is here, a very good violinist;
she plays with much taste and expression.   I am doing just
now a sonata for her which we have to play together next
Thursday."   The sonata in B flat (Köchel, 454) was performed that day in the presence of the Imperial Court, without
a previous rehearsal.   Strinasacchi only received the copy of
her part that very morning, and as Mozart had no time to write
out the piano part, he played the whole of it from sheets of
music paper which had only barlines and a few hurried notes.
The result was a great success, but the Emperor Joseph had
noticed from his box the blank look of the piano part and asked
for Mozart to come and show it, when the truth was revealed—
to his astonishment.   The final MS. of this sonata, now in the
possession of F. G. Kurtz of Liverpool (Grove), still allows one
to judge of its original condition.   In Dec., 1785, Strinasacchi
went to Salzburg, and on Dec. 7 Leopold Mozart, in a letter
to his daughter, confirms his son's opinion of her: "She plays
not a note without feeling; even in the symphonies she plays
everything with expression, and nobody can play her Adagio
with more feeling and more touchingly; her whole heart
and soul is in the melody she plays and just as beautiful, and
powerful is her tone.   Altogether I find that a really talented
woman plays with more expression than a man."   In 1785
she married the violoncello virtuoso J. C. Schlick, chamber
musician at the Court of Gotha, with whom she toured far and
wide, the two frequently playing double concertos by Schlick
which were well received by the public.   A violoncello
concerto which appears in Traeg's catalogue of 1799 as by
Strinasacchi, is, according to Joh. Klingenberg, also by
Schlick ("History of Violoncello," i, 211).   With their
daughter, an excellent pianist, they toured as a trio, and as such

appeared at Leipzig, 1799–1800. After the death of her husband in 1825, Strinasacchi went to Dresden, where she resided till she died.

LORENZO FRANCESCHI. From Sept. 5, 1764, to Mar. 28, 1791, when he died, violinist in the municipal band of Lucca, with a salary of 2 scudi per month (Nerici, 211).

FRANCESCO SOZZI, b. Florence, ca. 1765. Pupil of Nardini. Belonged, ca. 1790, to the chapel of the Duke of Tuscany. On the invasion of the French he went to Germany and lived as 1st violinist at the theatre at Augsburg in 1801; went to Vienna, thence toured in Hungary, Poland and Russia, and returned to Augsburg in 1811, and 1817 to Foligno, after which no further particulars are available. He composed 40 caprices or studies op. posth., Milan, Ricordi (copy in Milan Conservatoire); they bear the inscription "composti in Foligno 1817"; also variations, trios and quartets for strings; 3 violin duos, op. 6 (Augsburg, Gombart); Italian airs with variations (Ib.).

GIOVANNI CONRADO ROVANTINI. A violinist at the Electoral Court of Treves. Went 1765 to Bonn as member of the Electoral Chapel, and died at the end of 1766. His son Franz, a teacher of music (violin?), died Sept. 9, 1781, aged 24.

GIORGIO CHELOTTI. In Jan., 1767, he became violinist in the Grand Ducal chapel, Florence, and in the autumn of 1779 1st violinist (leader) of the opera at the Teatro degli Intrepidi there.

JOSEPH TRANI. A violinist in the Vienna Court chapel, 1767–88; d. 1797, aged 90 (Köchel, i). A violinist, Trani, in the service of the Prince of Hildburghausen, was the teacher of Dittersdorf in 1750. As he was already advanced in years he was absolved from service, and only was employed as a teacher (Ditter's Autobiog.). This was probably the father of the above.

P. DA VELLA, b. Malta. A violinist who lived in Paris about the middle of the 18th century. Fétis says he composed 6 sonatas a 3, 2 violins and bass, op. 1, Paris, 1768 (Brit. Mus.), also 6 quatuors.

LUIGI DE SIRMEN. Violinist and capellmeister at Sta Maria Maddalena, Bergamo; married Maddalena Lombardini (q.v.). He composed 3 trios for 2 violins and bass (Paris, 1769).

GIUSEPPE? FARINELLI, b. Este (Padra), May 7, 1769; d. Trieste, Dec. 12, 1836. Probably the composer of Tre sonate per il pianoforte col acc. di violino, ded. Eugenio Napoleone di Francia. Venezia, proprieta del autore. Giacinto Maina, incise in Venezia, 2 Stb., obl. fol. (Musikfreunde).

S<sup>GRA</sup> PARRAVICINI, *nee* GANDINI (her mother was a noted singer), b. Turin, 1769; d. 183. According to Fétis a pupil of Viotti (Pougin contradicts this), who enjoyed a great reputation as virtuoso. During 1797–1802 she appeared in Paris, first at the theatre Louvois and 1798 at the Société Olympique. Afterwards she went to Germany and was still playing in public in 1827. Mason Clarke says: 1797 in Paris, 1799 at Leipzig, 1800 at Dresden; 1801 in Paris again, where she was received with enthusiasm at the Fridzeri concerts. In 1802 she appeared again in Berlin with unabated success. About this time she was divorced, became the mistress of Count Albergati, and passed henceforth as his wife. In 1805 she was presented as the Countess Albergati at the Court of Ludwigslust. About this time she seems to have withdrawn from the concert platform but, according to Fétis, she reappeared in Germany in 1820 and in 1827 she gave concerts at Munich, where, despite her 58 years, the vigour of her bow was greatly admired. The German musical papers of ca. 1802 praise her fullness of tone, purity of intonation, facile mastery of technical difficulties, elegant bowing, and sympathetic, graceful style with avoidance of too many unnecessary embellishments. Spohr, who heard her in later life, says that she played cantabile passages with a passable tone on a beautiful Stradivari violin, but with bad taste, and condemns her use of meaningless embellishments, impure intonation, unclean techique and bad bowing.

LUIGIA GERBINI, b. ca. 1770 (Baptie). A pupil of Pugnani and afterwards of Viotti. According to a notice in the *Allgemeine Musikalische Zeitung*, Vienna, 1807 (No. 25), she possessed a power of tone and brilliant technique almost incredible for a woman; another notice in the same paper (1811, p. 737), reporting a concert of hers in Paris, speaks in similar terms, and ranks her with the first virtuosi of the time, praising moreover her power of expression and artistic rendering of a concerto by Spohr, the difficulties of which she mastered with a graceful ease.   She was also a good singer, and appeared in both capacities in an Italian pasticcio, "Il Dilettante," at the theatre de Monsieur, Paris, on Nov. 13, 1790.   The *Journal de Paris*, in noticing the performance, praises both her singing and her playing in glowing terms.   Pougin, who records the fact, adds, however, that apparently the success of the piece was not a lasting one, as it was only given twice.   Mlle Gerbini then went to Lisbon, where she played violin concertos between the acts at the Italian theatre, with great success.   Her singing pleased likewise and she was engaged at the theatre as a singer and remained until Feb., 1801, when she went to Madrid. From that time all particulars are wanting.

FABIO.   A late 18th-century Italian violinist; according to Pougin, conductor at the San Carlo theatre at Naples in 1770.

GIOVANNI ZANNI.   Italian violinist of the second half of the 18th century who composed some sonatas for violin and B.c. Two of these were pub. in a collective volume by C. and S. Thompson, London, ca. 1770.   They are in the conventional style of the time.

FERDINANDO MAZZANTI, b. Rome, 17. .; where Burney visited him in 1770.   He was a distinguished violinist, singer and composer who had collected a large quantity of books and manuscripts, including most of the works of Palestrina.   His own compositions comprised quintets, quartets, and trios for strings as well as operas.   The Abbate Santini at Rome had some canzonettas with pianoforte accompaniment under his name.   He showed to Burney the MS. of a treatise on music, which he was writing at that time.

STEFANO N. detto SPADINA, GENTILUOMO DALMATINO.   Evidently a good amateur violinist, who composed: Sei Sonate a due violini, op. 6, Amsterdam, Hummel, ca. 1770 (Brit. Mus.). They are very interesting (*see* E. v. d. Str., "Eighteenth-Century Violin Sonatas," *The Strad*, Sept., 1923).   6 sonate a violino e basso in fine un capriccio, op. 3, Paris, Bayard (Leo Liepm.).   Twelve Italian Menuets for 2 violins and bass, London, Thorowgood and Horne (score in Milan Cons.); some pieces in J. B. Cartier's "L'Art du Violon."

GIOACHINO TRAVERSA, of Piedmont. Pupil of Pugnani. Entered the service of Prince Carignan as 1st violinist and appeared as soloist at the Concert Spirituel in 1770. He was an excellent virtuoso who in tone and temperament surpassed all his contemporaries. He is praised for the beauty of his tone and lightness and elegance of bowing. Fétis mentions 4 works of his composition. Eitner only traced: 6 sonates à violon seul avec la Basse, oe 2 (Paris, aux adresses ordinaires de musique; B. Wagner); 6 quatuors concert. pour 2 violons, A et B (Paris, Sieber); 6 quatuors dialogués pour 2 violons, A et B (Paris); also a violin concerto with orchestra, op. 5 (Paris, Bailleux).

PAOLO ALBERGHI. Violinist and capellmeister at Faënza, ca. 1770 (*see* Campagnoli), of whom nothing else is known. Mendel mentions a highly esteemed church composer, IGNAZIO ALBERGHI, about whose life likewise nothing is known. Mendel suggests that he might be identical with Tartini's pupil of that name; if it were not for the different Christian names one might conclude that he was identical also with Paolo. With regard to the Christian names, however, some mistake or confusion seems not impossible.

ALBERGHI. A pupil of Tartini, possibly identical with Ignazio Alberghi (*see* above), an 18th-century church composer, whose offertories and vespers were very popular.

ARAGONI. Composed sonatas for 2 violins and bass, ca. 1770, Thompson; pub. one of these in a book with 5 by other composers (Brit. Mus.).

COUNT BENEVENTO DI SAN RAFFAELE. An 18th-century amateur violinist and Royal director of studies at Turin. Composed: 6 duets (sonatas?) for violin, pub. London, 1770, and afterwards also in Paris. He also wrote two letters on the art of music ("sopra l'arte del suono") in "La Raccolta degli opusculi di Milano," tomi 28 and 29, Vicenza, 1778.

ANDREA ROBERTI DEGLI ALMERI. A violinist, ca. 1770; pupil of Tartini (Tebaldini, 79).

MODELE. A violinist who lived, ca. 1770, at Florence. Mentioned with praise in Burney's travels (diary), who heard him play a concerto for 2 violins with his son.

ANTONIO NAZARI (NAZARRI). A pupil of Tartini and in 1770 a violinist at S. Mark's, Venice (Burney, i, 116, 129). In 1786, soloist (concertist) there with a salary of 100 ducats; in 1792 still there (Caffi, ii, 58, 64). A pupil of his was Gius. Ant. Capuzzi.

MICHELE NARCI. A violinist and, ca. 1770, conductor at the theatre Fiorentino, Naples (Burney i, 262). Composed concerto di violino e basso and sonata for 2 violins, viola and bass (Musikfr.); 6 sonatas, harpsich. and violin, London, ca. 1775; also a sacred song in Autogr. (Brit. Mus.).

GIUSEPPE SIGNORETTI. Settled in Paris, ca. 1770, where he had some string quartets pub.; in Liepmannssohn Cat: P. Signorelli, "Méthode contenant les principes de la Musique et du violon," La Haye, 1777, Williams, 3 parts in 1 vol., 4°. Eitner says: according to all indications he is the same as above, the different spelling being an error. He was a pupil of Tartini. Fétis refers to 12 books of 6 string quartets, each published in Paris, where he was living in 1786.

GIUSEPPE MARIA FESTA, b. Trani (Naples), ca. 1771; d. Naples, Apr. 7, 1839. He received his first instruction from his father, afterwards studying under Francesco Mercieri (Fétis) and Giardini, and finally under Lolli. Ca. 1798, when he had already gained a considerable reputation in Southern Italy, he accompanied Lord Hamilton, the Ambassador, to Constantinople, but after a few months he went to Milan. In 1816 he became concertmeister at the S. Carlo Theatre, Naples, later on holding the same position also in the private band of the King of the two Sicilies. He is said to have been a conductor of unusual merit and Gerber (ii) says that he was one of the few (*sic!*) great violinists that Italy produced. Rossini said that he was an excellent quartet player, and that he confessed that all the best he knew he owed to Ludwig Spohr, with whom he stood in friendly intercourse while at Naples (Ferd. Hiller, "Tonleben unserer Zeit," Leipzig, 1868). He composed, among others, 3 string quartets, op. 9, and some church music. According to Fétis, he was in 1802 conductor of the Opera at Lodi, became violinist at the theatre S. Carlo, Naples, in 1805, and afterwards conductor which he was still in 1836 (and probably till he died, E. v. d. Str.). His sister Francesca was a famous singer who died in St. Petersburg, 1836.

GIUSEPPE SCARAMELLI, b. Venice, 1771 (Mendel: 1761). He was 1st violin-conductor at the theatre at Trieste in 1811, afterwards he was for some time at Vienna (Köchel?) and finally settled at Florence. He composed, according to Fétis, some 30 works, of which however the latter knew only: Rondo variato for violin and horn "principale" with orchestra (Florence, Cipriani); 2 string quartets, Nos. 1 and 2 (Ib.); variations for 2 violins, op. 8 (Vienna, Cappi); 3 sonatas for violin and bass, op. 1 (Vienna, Mollo). He also wrote an Essay on the duties of a 1st violinist-conductor of an orchestra (Saggie sopra i doveri di un primo violino direttore d'orchestra), Trieste, Weiss, 1811, 8vo, 51 pp.

LUIGI (LUDOVICO) CAMPANELLI, b. Florence, 1771. One of the best pupils of Nardini; was violinist and capellmeister at the Court of Toscana. In 1802 he became 1st violinist to Ferdinand I, King of Etruria. He composed for the violin sonatas, duets, trios, as well as quartets, etc. Fétis says that many of his MSS. are to be met with in various parts of Italy.

ANGELO FRANCESCO CUCCO, violinist in the Court chapel at Turin, July 7, 1771 to 1782, receiving a salary of 300 lire per annum (Ricordi, 1891, p. 457).

CARLO CANOBIO. An Italian violinist who, after touring in his native country, ca. 1780, was appointed in the orchestra of the Opera at St. Petersburg in 1790. He is said to have returned to Italy in 1796 and to have died soon after. He composed 6 duos for flute and violin (Paris, 1780). Riemann says: During 1779–1800, chamber musician in St. Petersburg; wrote, 1773–5, 3 ballets for Venice; in St. Petersburg 2 ballets, a historical play (with Sarti and Paschkewitz); 2 symphonies; 6 sonatas for guitar and violin, op. 2; arias and duets.

JOSEPH (GIUSEPPE) AGUS. A pupil of Nardini; violinist in London, 1773 (Pohl, ii, 370).

J. F. AGUS. Wrote glees and airs for violin and violoncello (Reeves Cat., 1882).

FRANCESCO BIOTO. Violinist in Dresden Court chapel, ca. 1773, with a salary of 200 thaler.

FRANCESCO VACCARI, b. Modena, ca. 1773; d. in Portugal after 1847. He commenced to study the violin at the age of 5 and progressed so rapidly that two years later he could play at sight any kind of music. Pugnani, who heard him about that period, was astonished at the boldness of his playing. Towards his tenth year he became a pupil of Nardini at Florence. At 13 he went to Mantua to give concerts. There he met Wenzel Pichl, who placed before him a concerto, which he played in public at sight. Parma, Piacenza, Verona, Padua, and Venice were visited next, and everywhere he met with great success. After having lived at Milan for some years, the King of Spain engaged him for his chapel in 1804. This position, which was as agreeable as it was advantageous, he lost through the war in 1808. Obliged to tour again, he arrived in Paris in 1809, but after a short stay there, went on tour in Germany. In 1815, after visiting England, he went to Lisbon, and thence returned to Madrid, where he entered the service of King Ferdinand; but the events of 1823 made him once more lose that position. He went again to Paris, and paid a second visit to London in that year. There he played at one of the Philharmonic Concerts where he had played also with great success on his first visit eight years before (1815). A contemporary critic speaks of his playing in most enthusiastic terms, praising his perfect intonation, beauty of tone, gracefulness and taste and a style free from all trickery. He returned to Portugal where, according to Fétis, he still was about 1843. His compositions for violin, pub. in Paris, consist of duets op. 1 and 2; variations on "God save the King"; potpourri varié on the Fandango and "Robin Adair"; l'Ecossaise nocturne.

GIOVANNI GIORGI. Appeared 1774 in London as violinist (Pohl, ii, 370); probably the pupil of Tartini of that name (Pougin, 104).

LUIGI BORGHI. A pupil of Pugnani, esteemed both as virtuoso and composer, who settled in London in 1774, and appeared in 1777 also as a viola player. At the Handel commemoration festival in Westminster Abbey, 1784, he was leader of the 2nd violins, and he was also 2nd violinist in Cramer's quartet at the Professional Concerts. Apparently he was still in London in 1787, as some symphonies of his were pub. there in that year; but in 1788 he appears to have been in Berlin, as a violoncello concerto, dated Oct. 24, 1788, is in the Royal house-library there. 3 concertos for violin, op. 2; 6 duos for 2 violins, op. 4; 6 duets for violin and viola, op. 6, were all pub. in Berlin. He composed also: 6 sonatas for violin and bass, op. 1 (Paris); 6 concertos, op. 2 (various eds.); 6 solos for do. do., op. 3 (Amsterdam); 6 divertimentos for 2 violins, op. 3a (various eds., including Longman & Broderip, ed., 1785); 6 solos, op. 4 (for the author—with title page engraved by Bartolozzi, 1783); 6 duets for violin and viola or 'cello, op. 5 (London, ca. 1785); 64 cadences or solos for the violin, op. 11 (London, ca. 1790). Alard republished op. 5, No. 1; Jensen edited 2 sonatas (Augener) and A. Moffat, 1 sonata. He composed also a book of Italian canzonettas, and with others the opera "Dames" for the King's Theatre in 1783; he was manager of the Italian Opera at the Panthéon in 1790, and married the prima donna Cassentini.

COSTANZI. Mentioned by Pougin as a pupil of Tartini. No other particulars are given. May have been a relative of Giov. Batt. Costanzi, a Roman violoncellist, 1704–78.

VITTORIA D'ALL' OCCA, b. Bologna. Violin virtuoso, ca. middle or after the middle of the 18th century. She toured a great deal and appeared at Milan in 1788. Another violinist bearing that name, but whose Christian name is unknown, was a pupil of Lolli, and the first teacher of Campagnoli (*q.v.*), ca. 1760, but nothing else is known about him.

GIOV. ANT. GIAIJ. Composer. In Dresden Mus., Concerto a violin conc. with string quartet; several symphonies (no date given).

GUGLIETTO TROMBA. Gerber (i) writes, after Burney (i, 92), that he was a pupil of Tartini, after whose death he became his successor. Gerber says the same of Giulio Meneghini.

ANDREA BAGHETTI. A solo col violino e basso, MS. by him in Dresden Mus. (no date, 18th century).

# CHAPTER 36

## Italy: to 1800

BOURO. Appeared in 1776 at Turin as violin virtuoso with great success. Nothing else is known.

FELICE (ALESSANDRO) DE RADICATI, b. Turin, 1778; d. Vienna, Apr. 14, 1823. A member of an impoverished noble family; pupil of Pugnani; went on tour; played in London 1806–7. His wife, Teresia Bertinotti, was a singer who appeared in Vienna from 1805 to 1807. Radicati was in 1815 appointed as violinist at San Petronio and as teacher at the Liceo Musicale at Bologna, also as 1st violinist and conductor at the theatre, where his opera, "Ricciardo cuor de lione," was performed. In 1816 he toured in Lombardy; in 1818 he went to Vienna, where in 1823 he met with a carriage accident which eventually proved fatal. He was held in high esteem as composer not only for his instrument but also in the field of opera and chamber music, especially the string quartet, although the claims of his biographer Regli are exaggerated. Composed: Gran sonate p. violino acc. di alto, op. 10 (Musikfr.), duets for 2 violins, op. 3, 9, 19, 20; trios, op. 7, 13, 20(?); quartets, quintets for strings; Aria, "In questo tomba" (Mollo, Vienna); operas, etc.

ANDREA RESTORI, b. ca. 1778, Pontremoli, Toscana. Studied under Fanini and Ramaggi at Lucca. Afterwards with Rolla at Parma for violin and composition; became then 1st violin and conductor at the theatre of his native town. He composed, according to Fétis, 4 violin concertos, 6 books of violin duets and 10 symphonies.

GIUSEFFO PERRUCONE (detto PASQUALINO). In 1779 conductor of the orchestra for the ballet at La Scala theatre, Milan, 1789; 1st violinist at that theatre for the ballet (Cambiasi, 115). In the textbook of Paër's "La Rossana" (B.B.)

of 1795, he is called 1st violinist at the above theatre. The office of 1st violinist, i.e. leader, and conductor were generally combined at that time.

ANGELO MARIA BENINCORI, b. Brescia, Mar. 28, 1779; d. at Belleville, near Paris, Dec. 30, 1821. At the age of 3 he went to Parma with his father, who had become secretary to the reigning Duke. At 5 he became a pupil of Rolla for the violin and of Ghiretti for composition. Before he was 8 years old he played a violin concerto before the Duke, who rewarded him with a repeater watch. At the death of his father the Prince placed him in a college for the study of languages, but his enthusiasm for music made him steal some hours of the night for the study of his beloved violin. When the Duke heard of it he ordered him to be placed again under Rolla, and afterwards he studied composition under several masters, including Cimarosa, and composed a mass at the age of 14 which met with success. In 1797 he went to Spain with his elder brother, where they were forced, through adverse circumstances, to earn their living by giving concerts. Soon afterwards the brother died, and Angelo Maria returned to Italy, where an opera, "Nitetti," of his met with success which was repeated when he had it performed at Vienna. There he became acquainted with Haydn, and his admiration for the latter's quartets caused him to write a number of quartets, of which Fétis speaks in terms of high praise as works showing distinct individuality. The first book of these is dedicated to Haydn. The first 2 books, followed afterwards by several more sets, were pub. in Germany and re-pub. in Paris. He settled in the latter city in 1803, devoting himself to the composition of operas which met with little success, so that he was obliged to resort to teaching. In 1818 he was charged with composing the final acts of Isouard's opera, "La Lampe Merveilleuse" (The Magic Lamp). He finished the work in 1821, but died a few weeks before its first performance, which proved a brilliant success.

PROSPERO CAUCIELLO. A violinist (?) in the Royal Chapel of Naples in 1780. He composed 2 books of 6 duos each for 2 violins; 5 quintets for violin or flute; 3 symphonies, all pub. about the above date at Lyons; also trios for 2 violins and violoncello, op. 4. (Gerber and Magazin.)

G. FESTONI. Played a violin concerto of his own composition
in London ca. 1780, which remained in MS., and Gerber (ii)
speaks of 2 trios for 2 violins and bass pub. in London, Preston,
1797.

BERNARDO ANGELINI. Of the school of Tartini. The Royal
Lib., Berlin, has an autograph of a "Sonata a Violino solo
e Basso," Ad⁰., All⁰., Ad⁰., All⁰., Melodic composition, the
middle Adagio full of feeling. "A favourite solo for the
Violin and Harps.", fol., ca. 1780 (Brit. Mus.), by
Angelini . . .; is probably by Bernardo Angelini.

BORRA. Violin virtuoso; pupil of Pugnani, lived at Turin;
composed 2 violin concertos (Lyons, 1780).

ANGELO PUCCINI, b. Leghorn, 1781. He received his first
violin training from Vanacci; afterwards he went to Florence,
where he studied the violin under S. Tinti and composition
under Zingarelli, continuing the latter study under Cecchi
after his return to Leghorn. He composed violin sonatas,
concertos and duets.

GIOVANNI BATTISTA POLLEDRO, b. Casalmonferrato alla Piova,
near Turin, June 10, 1781; d. there, Aug. 15, 1853. His
first teacher for violin was Mauro Calderara, then Gaetano
Vai, 1st violin at the cathedral, both of Asti. After a
thorough grounding in the works of Corelli and other old
masters he became the pupil of Somis at Turin. In his
fifteenth year he toured in Lombardy and on his return he gave
some concerts at Turin, when he attracted the attention of
Pugnani, who offered to give him further instruction, of which
Polledro eagerly availed himself; but about six months later
Pugnani's failing health compelled him to abandon all teaching. On his recommendation, however, Polledro was appointed violinist at the Royal Theatre, Turin. In 1801 he
went to Milan, where he gave some concerts and was engaged
in the Royal Chapel, but in 1804 he became 1st violinist at
the church of Sta Maria Maggiore, Bergamo. The troubles
of the Napoleonic war obliged him to quit this town and he
started on a prolonged concert tour, which led him to Moscow,
where he remained for five years in the service of Prince
Tatischev; after that time he visited St. Petersburg, Warsaw,
Berlin, and Dresden, where he was engaged as concertmeister
from 1814 to 1824. In the latter year the King of Sardinia

induced him to return to Turin for the reorganization of the Royal chapel and made him director-general of the instrumental music. A nervous stroke in 1844 caused him to retire to his native town, where he died after nine years of suffering. He composed 8 concertos, airs variés, trios for 2 violins and bass, duets, studies, etc., all for violin, but most of these proved of no lasting value; Schradieck re-edited his studies; he also wrote a sinfonia pastorale, a mass and a miserere.

ANTONIO FUMAGALI (FUMAGALLI?). An eminent Italian violinist of the second half of the 18th century, who toured in Germany ca. 1782.

FRANCESCO GALEAZZI, b. Turin, 1783 (Riemann: 1785); d. Rome, 1819. Settled as violinist and composer in Rome, where he was for many years 1st violinist at the Teatro del Valle. He pub. a work in 2 volumes: "Elementi Teoretico practici con un saggio sopra l'arte di suonare il violino analizzato (with examples) . . .," Roma, 1791 and 1796. A second ed. appeared in 1817 (Ascoli, Franc. Cardi), corrected and augmented by the author, with new tables. This work became favourably known in Germany through Fränzl. As there is a letter by him dated Ascoli, Oct. 17, 1816, it seems evident that he lived there for at least two years. He also composed 6 trios for 2 violins and viola, Milan Cons.).

LANZONI. Played in 1784 as violin virtuoso in London (Pohl, ii, 370).

FRANCESCO ANSALDI, b. Vercelli, Piedmont, 1785. A violin pupil of his uncle, the noted Pietro Sessi. He became an eminent violinist, Portuguese court-capellmeister and followed, afterwards, Dom Pedro to Rio de Janeiro. He composed violin concertos which were considered works of eminent importance, but they were never pub.

POLIDORI. An Italian violinist who lived in Paris ca. 1785. He composed 6 trios for 2 violins and bass, op. 1 (Paris, Louis).

D. FRANCESCO NEGRI. 1st violin at S. Mark's, Venice, in 1786, with a salary of 60 ducats (Caffi, ii, 69), sonata a violoncello e bass, MS. (B.B.) probably by him. MS. 3 trios 2 violins and bass in Brit. Mus. named only "Negri," doubtful if by him.

FERDINANDO GASSE, b. Naples, Mar. 1, 1788. Went to Paris in early youth and became a pupil of the Conservatoire in the year VI of the Republic (1798–99), where he studied the violin under Kreutzer, while Catel and Gossec taught him harmony and composition. In 1805 he gained the Grand Prix of the Academy and was sent thereby to Rome, where he produced some more important compositions which were praised by Mehul. In 1812 he returned to Paris and re-entered the orchestra of the Grand Opera, in which he had been a violinist before he went to Rome. He remained in that position until 1835, when he was pensioned. He composed several operas which were produced in Paris. For the violin he wrote some easy sonatas with bass and several sets of duets.

LODOVICO MOLINO, b. Fossano. Succeeded his master, G. Pugnani (according to Wasielewski, Regli does not mention him amongst the pupils), as 1st violin at Turin theatre in 1788, where he was afterwards musical director. He was also a harp virtuoso, and played both instruments in Paris, 1809. In 1803 he brought out airs variés pour guitar avec acc. de violon, Paris, Pellet (Gerber, ii). Trio in La per violino, viola e chitarra; duo concert. pour 2 violons, op. 13, No. 2 in Milan Cons. Fétis says he composed 1 concerto in D for violin (Paris, Pleyel); 3 duos concert., op. 8, 11, 13 (Paris, Cousineau); pieces for pianoforte and songs.

GIACOMO CONTI (not to be confounded with the castrato of the same name but surnamed Giziello), b. Vienna, 1804. In 1790 he was 1st violin in the Russian Imperial Chapel, as well as in that of Prince Potemkin, and in 1793 he was conductor at the Italian Opera in Vienna. He composed 5 violin concertos, 2 books of sonatas, 3 books of duets, op. 6, 9 and 10, and 1 book of solos, op. 8.

PIETRO CONTI. Another violinist. Pub. a concerto for violin (Amsterdam, 1760).

GIOVANNI FRANCESCHINI. An 18th-century violinist from Naples. Gerber (i) mentions 6 duos for violin, pub. Amsterdam as by him. The Society of the Friends of Music, Vienna, has 2 concertos with accompaniment, and the Brit. Mus. 6 sonates a 2 violins, oe. 2, Amsterdam and Berlin, Hummel, ca. 1790 (probably the above?); also 6 trios for 2 violins and bass, op. 1 (Eitner).

MADAME GARBINI, b. Italy, . . . Appeared 1791 at the theatre de Monsieur in Paris as a singer, and played between the acts violin concertos by Viotti, etc., with the greatest success. Afterwards she appeared with equal success at other Parisian theatres. She had a brilliant technique, a good tone and played with great expression. As a singer she ranked among the best of her time. Further particulars are wanting. Apparently identical with Luigia Gerbini (*q.v.*). The name being misspelt by some writers.

PIETRO ROVELLI, b. Bergamo, Feb. 6, 1793; d. there, Sept. 8, 1838. A pupil of R. Kreutzer in Paris. Returning to Bergamo, he became capellmeister at the church of Sta Maria Maggiore and at the theatre. He married Micheline, the daughter of Förster of Vienna, teacher of composition, who was an eminent pianist. During 1817–18 he was concertmeister in the Royal chapel, Munich. He composed some excellent studies, which have been re-ed. by E. Singer.

LORENZO MOSER. A late 18th-century "professore di violino e supranumerario della Real capella (Naples)." He wrote the music for two ballets by Domenico Lefevre, performed at Naples 1793 and 1794 (Eitner, "Zusätze.")

GIULIO MARIA LUCCHESI, b. Pisa, 17... A pupil of Moriani and Nardini for violin and of Cecchi for composition; lived for a time in Vienna and afterwards entered the service of the Archbishop of Salzburg. He returned to Italy in 1799, and appears to have died soon after. Composed 3 duets for 2 violins, op. 1 (Vienna, 1794; repub. Basle, 1795), and 3 duets op. 2 (Augsburg, Gombart, 1796); 6 sonatas for pianoforte and violin, op. 3 (Ib., 1796), also symphonies and vocal compositions (Fétis). Eitner knows only 3 sonatinas, op. 3.

GAETANO VAI. An 18th-century Italian violinist, chiefly known as master of Giambattista Polledro. He was for a considerable period first in Paris, then in Geneva. A post in the Royal chapel in Turin, which was offered him, he declined, preferring to be independent. Regli praises his purity of intonation, rhythmical precision and an uncommon talent for improvisation. Ca. 1795 or earlier he settled at Asti as 1st violinist at the cathedral and in the town orchestra.

P. VIGNETTI. Composed: Caprices pour le violon, op. 2 (Paris, 1798; notice in *Leipzig Zeitung*, i, 15); 6 études pour violon avec le doigté indiqué pour en faciliter l'exécution, oe 2 (Paris, Sieber) (Milan Cons.).

ABBATE GIULIO VISCONTI. Of the late 18th century. Composed concerto in A for violin with oboi, corni and archileuto MS. (Milan Cons.); a viola concerto in C with orchestra, MS. (Dresden Mus.); 9 intonazioni per violino MS. (Milan Cons.); Ib. vocal compositions, MS. and print.

MAURO ALAY. A composer of the 18th century. The Newman Flower collection has 6 violin concertos by him.

LUIGI TONELLI. Apparently a violinist of the late 18th century. Traeg's Catalogue enumerates 1 concerto for violin and sonatas for violin (without Christian name); 3 duetti concertanti per violino e violoncello, op. posthumous in Musikfr. Lib., Vienna, which seems to point to his final residence in that town; a Metodo completo per il violino (Milan, Ricordi) is in the Milan Cons. Lib.

GIUSEPPE DE VICENTI. Was living in St. Petersburg at the end of the 18th century. Composed 6 duos for 2 violins, op. 1, liv. 1, 2. Gerber (ii) thinks he is probably identical with Vincenti, the ballet composer and viola virtuoso in the Imperial Chapel.

GIACOMO ZUCCHI. An 18th–19th-century violinist. In Musikfr., Vienna: has 3 serenate per violino, 2 viole e basso, op. 3; 2 divertimenti for violin and quartet; the second with orchestra; Adagio e Tema con var. per violino et orchestra. Duetto per 2 violini œuv. posth.; quintet for flute, violin, 2 violas and duetto per flanto e clavicembalo.

ANTONIO STULICHI. A Neapolitan violinist of the latter half of the 18th century; is mentioned by Pougin as the author of a book of violin sonatas pub. in France.

POLLANI. A late 18th-century violinist of Rome; is mentioned by Wasielewski as a pupil of Nardini without further particulars; Pougin enumerates him among the pupils of Tartini as "Polani," giving only the surname.

ANTONIO BONAZZI, b. Cremona, ?; d. Mantua, 1802. Described by Fétis as one of the best violinists in Italy. He left a collection of about 1,000 concertos, quintets, quartets, etc., for violin or flute, among them a great number of his own composition. He also possessed 42 violins by Stradivari, Guarnieri, Amati, and other famous masters, valued at 6,500 ducats (ca. £3,000).

FERDINANDO PONTELIBRO, surnamed AJUTANTINI (Fétis: PONTE-LIBERO). A pupil of Rolla who lived in Milan, where he died ca. 1820. He composed string trios and quartets, a symphony and other instrumental and vocal music. Fétis says he composed 3 trios for 2 violins and bass, op. 3; 3 duos for 2 violins, op. 2; 3 string quartets, op. 4, all pub. Paris, Carli; ballets, etc.

ANGELO CASIROLA, b. Tortona, ?. Created a sensation at Milan in 1824 by playing with a fixed bow (?—Mendel: mit fest-stehendem Bogen) the most difficult pieces on the G string. (It reads as if he had moved the violin against a fixed bow. Evidently a charlatan.)

# CHAPTER 37

# *Netherlands*

GERMAIN FRANÇOIS LEMIRE, b. Antwerp, ca. 1726; d. there, July 21, 1813. About 1782 he was violinist at the cathedral, and from 1772 to (ca.) 1812 1st violinist and conductor at the Antwerp theatre (Gregoir, "Panth.," iii, 58; vi, 31; in vi, p. 26, he mentions an "A. Lemire" as violinist at the theatre in 1772).

ANTONIO LORENZITI, b. The Hague, ca. 1740. Son of a musician in the chapel of the Prince of Orange; pupil of Locatelli. About 1767 he was given the post of capellmeister at the cathedral at Nancy. His compositions included "sei Trietti per camera per 2 violini e basso, op. 2 (Paris, Landini); La Camme pour violon avec acc. d'alto e basse; symphonies, an opera, quartets, etc. Fétis adds: 6 duos for violin and viola, op. 3 (Paris, Heina); 6 duos concertants for 2 violins op. 8 (Paris, Heina, 1775).

LORENZITI. A violin virtuoso who played at Sg.ª Molza's concert at Frankfort a/M. (Israel, 35) on Sept. 6, 1748, as mentioned by Eitner. This almost suggests a misreading of Lorenziti, or perhaps he was the father of Antonio.

FRIEDRICH SCHWINDL (SCHWINDEL), b. Amsterdam, ca. 1740; d. Aug. 11, 1786, at Karlsruhe. A virtuoso on the violin, flute and pianoforte; of a roaming disposition, but of eminent talent. On his op. 1 he calls himself concert-director of Count von Wiedt Runquell (Runkel?); and on op. 10, Maître de concert de S.A.S. Mj. le Margrave de Bade Durlach. Reichard speaks of him as founder and director of an amateur concert at Mühlhausen, in Switzerland, who composed Sing-spiele and French operettas. Burney speaks of him (ii, 102, and iii, 248). Schubart (p. 231) says: "A popular violin composer, famous throughout Germany. His compositions are not difficult and therefore the more attractive for amateurs. His style of playing (Vortrag) is fluent and his mind inclines to a sweet melancholy, and for this reason he became a favourite with the sentimentally inclined" (Empfindsamen) (Gerber, i and ii). Composed violin sonatas, operas and operettas. According to Fétis, it was want of financial success that drove him from place to place.

PIETER HELLENDAAL, b. Rotterdam, went to Italy in 1740 and was a pupil of Tartini. In 1744 he lived at Amsterdam according to his pub. compositions, went thence to Leyden, where he appears in the matriculation book of the University on Jan. 8, 1749, as Musicus; settled afterwards in London, where he appeared as virtuoso in 1752 and gained a prize of the Catch Club. He was a fertile composer of concertos, sonatas and solos for violin, also glees, psalms, etc.; 6 sonatas for violin and bass, op. 1—fairly difficult; 6 sonatas for violin solo.

A. C. STEGEWY, b. Zwolle, Overyssel, first half of the 18th century. Violinist and organist. He composed 6 sonatas for violin, 3 sonatas for flute, violin, and bass; 3 idem for 2 flutes and bass (Amsterdam, 1760).

JEAN BAPTISTE MOULINGHEM, b. Haarlem, 1751. In Paris he was in the orchestra of the Comédie Italienne ca. 1774 to 1809, when he was pensioned. He wrote an opera-vaudeville, a symphonie périodique (Paris, 1784), and other instrumental compositions.

LOUIS CHARLES MOULINGHEM, his brother, b. Haarlem, 1753. Studied the violin at Amsterdam, was violinist in the chapel of Prince Charles of Lorraine, and afterwards became conductor in touring companies. In 1785 he went to Paris as teacher. He composed operettas (Fétis mentions 7) for various smaller theatres.

JOSEPH FODOR, L'AÎNÉ, b. Venloo, ca. 1752; d. St. Petersburg, Oct. 3, 1828. Son of an Hungarian officer. Studied from ca. 1766 under Franz Benda in Berlin. He toured for several years as a virtuoso in the Netherlands, Germany, and France, with eminent success. In 1780 he went to Paris, where he appeared successfully at the Concert Spirituel on Dec. 8, 1781 (Gregoir, "Panth." iii), and settled in that city in 1787.

In his "2, livre de Duos" he calls himself 1st violinist of the Duke of Montmorency. About 1794 he went to Russia, where he settled at St. Petersburg. He wrote 13 violin concertos, 13 sonatas, solos, duets, also quartets (42) and songs (*see* Eitner). The celebrated singer, Josephine Fodor Mainville, was his daughter. His brothers were pianists in Paris and Amsterdam. Spohr, who heard him in 1802, found him lacking in taste and feeling, and disapproves of his manner of bowing, but acknowledges his great technical skill.

ERNST SCHICK, b. The Hague, Oct., 1756; d. Berlin, Dec. 10, 1815 (Becker, iii, 139, says 1814). The son of a dancing-master who destined him for that art, but he preferred the violin, which he studied already in tender years and showed such talent that concertmeister Georg Anton Kreusser asked to have him as a pupil. At Amsterdam in 1770 he heard Esser and Lolli and took especially the latter as his model. In 1774 he was appointed violin in the Mayence Court chapel, where he afterwards also became conductor of the Opera (Reichardt, 1791, 221). He went on tour in 1779 and on Nov. 5 played at Frankfort; he conducted and played in a concert of Mme Steffani on April 9. In 1783 he went on tour with Tricklir, the violoncellist, and instituted quartet soirées in Berlin with Benda and Hoffmann, where he cultivated especially Haydn's music (Sittard, i, 130). In 1793 he became chamber musician in the Royal Chapel there, and advanced to the post of concertmeister in 1813. In 1804 he instituted subscription concerts with Bohrer. His wife, *née* Hamel, was a famous concert-singer. He composed: 6 (?) violin concertos (Fétis, 6 concertos) with orchestra (Berlin, 1785) and songs including some Freemason songs. (Cramer, i, 749, 764; Gerber, i, 2; Ledebur; Israel, 69, 72.) According to Cramer he was one of the most successful imitators of Lolli's style, of which, so Gerber says, he freed himself in later years.

PIERRE JOSEPH GUISLAIN, b. Bergen op Zoom, ca. 1757 (1756); d. Antwerp, Mar. 2, 1811. Violinist at the Antwerp opera and a soloist in high repute as exponent of the concerts of Viotti, Kreutzer and Rode. Also conductor of several amateur and orchestral societies; tried to popularize Haydn and Mozart. He composed a violin concerto, and 6 sonatas for 2 violins, op. 1 (Antwerp, J. L. Wauters) (Gregoir, "Panth.," vi, 49).

PETER DAHMEN, b. ca. 1757; brother of Hermann Dahmen. A solo violinist first at Leeuwarden, then at Utrecht; composed trios and quartets.

HEINRICH CHRISTIAN KLEINE (called HEIN K.), b. the Hague, July 28, 1765; d. Amsterdam (?), Aug. 23, 1839. Belonged to a family of distinguished Dutch musicians. His grandfather, JOH. WILH. KLEINE, was a good violinist at The Hague who eventually went to Paris, where he died. His father was a clarinet player in the Royal chapel at The Hague; his three brothers joined the band of Napoleon's Guards, went with them to Russia in 1812 and perished from cold near Vilna. "Hein" received his first lessons from his father, then from various masters, including Spohr, and progressed so rapidly that he was able to appear successfully in public as a soloist at an early age. At Amsterdam, where he then lived, he soon became a public favourite and his co-operation at concerts was eagerly sought after. He also conducted on many occasions and was for twenty-five years an honorary member of the Society Felix Meritis. In his latter years he was attacked by a nervous trembling and had to restrict his activity to the teaching of advanced pupils.

JACOB JOSES BALTHAZAR MARTINN (real name, MARTIN), b. Antwerp, May 1, 1775; d. Paris, Oct. 10, 1836. Son of the bandmaster in an Austrian regiment. As a choirboy at St. Jacques, Antwerp, he began to compose for the church in his tenth year. In 1793 he became a violinist at the Vaudeville theatre and afterwards at the Grand Opera, Paris. On the foundation of the Imperial Lyceums he became professor of violin at the Lycée de Charlemagne, which position he occupied until his death. He composed for the violin 20 books of duets, also one for flute and violin; string quartets, trios for the flute, violin, 'cello; viola sonatas; tutors for violin and viola; symphonies for wind instruments, etc.

VAN HECKE (VANECK), b. ca. 1780. A teacher of singing and guitar; he wrote "Méthode de Violon" (Paris, Frère). Cramer (i, 105) calls him Vanhecke, as does Gerber (i), and attributes to him duos for 2 violins pub. in Paris, 1783.

He invented a plucked instrument with 12 strings called Bissex (Fétis).

JOSEPH SCHMITT, b. Amsterdam, 178?; d. Frankfort a/M., 1810. Son of Joseph Schmitt. A violinist and conductor; pupil of Baillot and Rode at the Paris Conservatoire, who early acquired the reputation of a brilliant virtuoso. He was appointed concertmeister at the Frankfort theatre, where he died quite young.

LA HAY, b. Amsterdam, 17..; d. Ofvansjö (Gestrikland). Violinist and concertmeister of Louisa Ulrika of Sweden, capellmeister and pioneer of Swedish concert life; founder of the Gotenburg Academy of Music in 1782. He was largely responsible for advancing the musical life of Sweden.

F. J. WITTENBERG. In the second half of 18th century he was 1st violinist in the chapel of the Stathouder of the Netherlands. Composed 6 duos for 2 violins, op. 1 (1786); 6 trios for 2 violins and bass, op. 2; 3 concertos for violin and orchestra, op. 3; The Hague.

WILHELM HEINRICH DAHMEN, b. Amsterdam, Mar. 27, 1797; d. Nymwegen, Dec. 15, 1847. A member of a numerous family of musicians, and pupil of his father. In his seventeenth year he was already solo violinist at the Amsterdam theatre, and in the following year conductor at Nymwegen, where he remained till his death. He was solo violinist to King William I of the Netherlands, and an excellent quartet player.

JOSEPH RUDERSDORF, b. Amsterdam, 1799 (Riemann, 1788?); d. Königsberg, 1866. At the age of 8 he played a concerto by Pleyel in public. In 1822 he was engaged by Prince Bariatinsky at Ivanovskoi, Russia, and in 1825 he became concertmeister at Hamburg. Thence he went to Dublin where he remained for over twenty years. In 1851 he went to Berlin where he remained for six years, and conducted successively the orchestras at Sommers-Salon, Kemperhof and at Kroll's. During that time he played at 1,300 concerts, having a repertoire of over 600 solos. About 1857 he settled at Königsberg. His daughter was the famous singer Hermine Küchenmeister-Rudersdorf. He composed numerous violin solos, 22 easy violin duets, an overture, songs, etc., which are of no interest.

# CHAPTER 38

# *Poland*

BASILIUS VON BOHDANOWICZ, b. in Poland, 1754; d. Vienna, 1819. A violinist, and the father of eight children, to all of whom he gave a musical training. He settled in Vienna, where he gave concerts with his children which reached the height of charlatanism. The first number, entitled "Les premices du monde," was a violin solo sonata for 3 players with 3 bows and 12 fingers on one instrument, after which the four sisters Bohdanowicz played an andantino with variations for eight hands on one pianoforte; some were regular variety-trick turns. He composed 3 duos for 2 violins, violin solos, pianoforte pieces, etc., pub. in and after 1798.

JOHANN KLECZINSKY (KLETZINSKY KLETSCHINSKY), b. in Poland, ca. 1756; d. Vienna, Aug. 6, 1828. He was a member of the Court chapel there from Jan. 6, 1803, to the time of his death. Gyrowetz mentions him on several occasions in his autobiography. In 1781 he was engaged by the Countess Breuner. When Gyrowetz was in Rome he refers to him as concertmeister. He composed some duets, variations and a pianoforte trio pub. in Vienna, and concerto, op. 1, Lemberg. Fétis says he was in Vienna, 1797.

FELIX YANIEWICZ, b. Vilna, Poland, ca. 1750, but Baptie says ca. 1762; d. Edinburgh, 1848. He was engaged for some time at the court of King Stanislaus at Nancy and went to Paris ca. 1770, where his first violin concertos were pub. After that he travelled in Italy, and in 1776 he went to London (Fétis says he gave a concert at Milan in 1786 and then went to London) as leader-conductor at the Italian Opera. In 1787 he played at the Concert Spirituel and lost (according to Pohl) all his possessions at the outbreak of the Revolution. He married an Englishwoman and had a son and two daughters, of whom the elder became an excellent pianist. He is said to have possessed a solid technique, brilliant in octave playing and an expressive cantabile, and was also an excellent conductor. He composed 5 violin concertos and 6 trios for 2 violins and bass, all pub. in Paris.

AUGUSTE FRÉDÉRIC DURAND (real name DURANOWSKI), b. Warsaw, ca. 1770, and was still living in 1834. His father, who was in the Polish Court chapel, was his first teacher. In 1787 he went to Paris and was a pupil of Viotti, who found him to possess exceptional talent, artistic nature and a remarkable facility to master the greatest technical difficulties. Afterwards he toured. In 1790 he was 1st violin at the Brussels Opera, but mostly toured until he settled at Strassburg (Lowinski, Fétis). He composed concertos, airs with variations, fantasias, and solos with and without orchestra, also German songs, pub. at Dresden (*Leipzig Zeitung*, iii, 703). In 1794 and 1795 he toured in Germany and Italy, where his prodigious facility was greatly admired. Suddenly he forsook his art and became adjutant to a general in the French army. He became mixed up in some rather serious affair at Milan. Through the influence of the general he was set free, but had to resign his position in the army and went to Germany where, from 1810 to 1814, he led a roving life, going from one place to another all over the country, from Prague to Warsaw, Leipzig, Frankfort, Mayence, etc. In 1810 he played with great success at the Court of Cassel, and in the following year before the Grand Duke of Darmstadt at Aschaffenburg. At last, feeling the want of a quieter life, he accepted in 1814 the place of 1st violin at the theatre and concert orchestra of Strassburg, where he was still at the end of 1834, according to Fétis, having only undertaken a few short tours in France and Germany during that period. Paganini, who knew Durand during his early youth, told Fétis that he owed his whole art to Durand, and it appears moreover that the tale of Paganini's imprisonment may have had its origin in Durand's escapade at Milan, at least his famous letter to the *Revue Musicale* in Paris, 1833, seems to point to this. Fétis says that Durand invented many tricks of bowing which none but himself were able to execute. He also maintains that Durand was never fully appreciated according to his merit.

AUGUST GERKE, b. in Poland, ca. 1790. Violinist and composer, of whom Fétis says that his work was wanting neither in charm nor originality. His works for the violin consist of Sicilienne variée and potpourri with orchestra, op. 5 and 6 (Leipzig, Breitkopf and Härtel). Potpourri with quartet, op. 3 and 20 (?), (Ib.); trio for 2 violins and violoncello, op. 2 and 8 (Ib.): duos for 2 violins, op. 1, 7 and 16 (Ib.); also overtures, one with violin principal, op. 10; piano pieces, etc.

# CHAPTER 39

# *Russia*

IVAN BÖHM, b. Moscow, 1723; d. Berlin, 1764. Studied first under Piantanida at Moscow, and was afterwards sent to Berlin to continue his studies under Johann Gottlieb Graun, becoming one of his best pupils. In 1740 he became a Court musician in the chapel of Frederic II in Berlin, which position he retained till he died. He composed violin solos and trios, which remained in MS.

YVAN CHANDOSCHKIN, b. 1765 (?); d. Petersburg, 1804. A pupil of Tito Porto, an Italian violinist. He became chamber musician in the Court chapel of Catherine II, and enjoyed great popularity as virtuoso and composer. He wrote numerous violin pieces, mostly folk songs and popular romances with variations; 3 sonatas for violin solo have been repub. by Jürgenson. Chandoschkin is one of the earliest Russian violinists mentioned in "Mus. Lexicons." He was also a guitar player.

SPRINGER. In 1760 a solo violinist and concertmeister at the Court of St. Petersburg. Reichardt, in his letters, places him in a line with Pisendel.

IGNAZ DOBRZYNSKI, b. in Volhynia, 1777; d. there in 1841. He was violinist in the chapel of Count Ilinski at Ramanov, and author of several operas and ballets. Afterwards he went to Winniça, then to Krzemieniec, in 1827 to Warsaw, and later retired to his native place. His son, IGNAZ FELIX, was capellmeister at the theatre, Warsaw.

FRANZ XAVER BLYMA, d. Kiev, May, 1822. A good violinist, and conductor at the Moscow theatre in 1796. He appears to have relinquished that post in 1801 and entered the service of Count von Comburleys. Composed solos and potpourris for violin and orchestra; 3 airs with variations for violin with

85

a 2nd violin and bass (Leipzig, Breitkopf and Härtel); the Traeg Catalogue of 1799 Vienna, enumerates a violin concerto with orchestra in MS. by him; he also composed 2 symphonies, the first pub. at Moscow, the second by Simrock at Bonn.

# CHAPTER 40

# Scandinavia

JOHAN HELMICH ROMAN, b. Stockholm, Oct. 26, 1694; d. at his country seat of Haraldsmala, near Kalmar, Oct. 19, 1758. The son of the Royal concertmeister Johan Roman. He is called the father of Swedish music. At the age of 7 he was already playing the violin in the Court orchestra, of which, in 1710, he became a regular member. At the expense of the Princess Ulrika Eleonora he went to London, where for several years he studied composition under Ariosti and Dr. Pepusch. He was looked upon as a distinguished violinist and as such was for some time in the service of the Duke of Newcastle. In 1720 he returned to Stockholm, where in 1729 he became Court capellmeister. From 1737 to 1739 he visited Italy, France and England on account of his health. Roman was in correspondence with the greatest musicians of his time, many of whom were his personal friends. In 1740 he became a member of the Swedish Academy of Science and retired in 1745 to his country seat, where he died from cancer in the tongue. Many of his numerous compositions, all in MS. except 12 flute sonatas (1727) and "Assagio" (essay) a violino solo (1740), perished in a fire at Åbö in 1827, yet a thematic catalogue by Patrik Vretblad in his Monograph of Roman "Swenska Musikus Fader" (Stockholm, 1914, 2 vols.) enumerates a very large number of works, including for violin: 5 concertos, ca. 20 sonatas with B.c., 17 trio sonatas for 2 violins and B.c., violin duets and studies. His other works comprise symphonies, overtures, suites, concerti grossi, many vocal works of various kinds, musical treatises, etc.

JOHANN ERNST HARTMANN, b. in Silesia, 1726. At first concertmeister at Plön, and from 1768 concertmeister in the Royal Court chapel, Copenhagen, where he died 1791. He was the ancestor of an illustrious family of Danish musicians,

including the composers Joh. E. Hartmann, father-in-law of
N. Gade, and Emil Hartmann. Composed symphonies,
operas, etc., and contributed Danish and Norwegian songs
for La Borde's essays. The Danish National anthem is an
air from his opera "Die Fischer." (Gerber, i, 2; Cramer, i,
949; Reichardt, 1781, 83, 84; Forkel, i, 135; *Leipzig Zeitung*,
38, 527.)

FREITOFT. About 1746 celebrated as violin virtuoso; was
secretary and chamber musician to King Frederic V of
Denmark. On his travels, especially in Italy, he had acquired
artistic skill as well as scientific knowledge.

PETER LEM, b. Copenhagen, ca. 1753; d. there, 1826. A
violin pupil of Hartmann, who, after several years of tuition,
caused him to travel, to perfect himself technically and
musically. On his return he was appointed 1st violinist at
the Court with a salary of 1,000 thaler which, after the death
of his master in 1791, was increased to 1,200 thaler, and he
became professor at the Conservatoire and solo violin at the
Court. He trained many excellent pupils. A violin concerto of his was published in Vienna in 1785 and a harpsichord
rondo appears in Traeg's Catalogue.

CLAUS SCHALL, b. Copenhagen, Apr. 28, 1757; d. at his
country seat, Kongens Syngby, Aug. 10, 1835. Son of a
dancing-master and dancing-pupil at the Royal theatre,
he became violinist in the orchestra; in 1776 "Repetitor," in 1792 concertmeister, and in 1817 capellmeister;
pensioned in 1834. Highly esteemed as ballet-composer.
He was acquainted with Cherubini and Viotti. In Denmark and Germany he was looked upon as a distinguished
violinist and composer of merit. He appeared with success at Hamburg, Berlin, Dresden, Frankfort a/M., Paris,
and in Italy. On his return to Copenhagen he became
concertmeister and chevalier of the Daneborg order. He
trained many good pupils, several of whom became violinists
in the Royal chapel. Composed 5 concertos for violin
(Copenhagen and Paris); 6 solos with B.c. (London, Bland);
Grand solo pour le violo avec accp. d'un 2^nd violon, op. 1, par C.
Schall, Maître de music du théâtre de S.M. le roi de Danne-
mark et Norwège, op. 1; duos for 2 violins, op. 1, 2 (Paris,

Pleyel, Sieber); études de l'archet et du doigter (Hamburg, Boehme); some dances for orchestra, ballets, 1 opera.

OLAF WILLMANN, b. Nefvitshöz (Skåne), Feb. 13, 1780; d. Stockholm, Apr. 5, 1844. He first studied law and philosophy, then devoted himself entirely to the violin and musical theory, etc. Travelled abroad to perfect himself in violin playing, with excellent results. In 1813 he was a viola player and from 1814 violinist in the Stockholm Court chapel. He instituted a school of music, at which he taught, and was looked upon as an eminent Swedish violinist.

JOHANN DAVID ZANDER, d. Stockholm, Feb. 21, 1796. The son of a member of the Royal chapel, Stockholm, and became an eminent violinist and viola player in the Royal chapel, in which he rose to the position of second capellmeister, holding that office till his death. He composed incidental music to many plays, also an overture (1787) in the older French style for Stenborg's Folk theatre.

JOHANN FRIEDRICH BERWALD, b. Stockholm, Dec. 4, 1787; d. there Aug. 26, 1861. Son of the bassoon and violin player G. J. Berwald. Toured in his younger years as violin virtuoso; became concertmeister in 1815 and in 1823 Court capellmeister at Stockholm. Composed violin concertos and sonatas, string quartets, one string quintet, orchestral works, cantatas, etc.

PETER FUNCK, b. 1789; d. 1859. An excellent Danish violinist who became concertmeister in the Royal chapel, Copenhagen.

WALDEMAR THRANE, b. Christiania, 1790; d. there, 1828. A pupil of Claus Schall and of Baillot, Habenek and Reicha, Paris Conservatoire. In 1817 conductor of the Oslo Musical Society and Musical Lyceum, and formed a string quartet. He made his debut at Stockholm in 1819. In 1828 he became capellmeister at Christiania but died of consumption in the same year. During his illness he was supported in the performance of his duties by Ole Bull, then a young student. He composed the first Norwegian opera, "Fjeldeventyret," overtures, cantatas and orchestral dances.

MADS GREGERS DAM, b. Svenborg, Denmark, Apr. 2, 1791; d. Berlin, 1859. Born of poor parents, and showing early talent for the violin, he was in 1796 placed under the Svensborg town musician, where he became the most-sought-after violinist at dances in the country all around. At the age of 12 he went to Copenhagen to study under the chamber musician, Gregers Simonson, who procured him engagements for concerts, where he appeared with great success, and gained the means for his subsistence. In 1806 he was a member of the Royal chapel at Copenhagen; some time after he resolved to perfect himself in Germany. He appeared there in several towns with continued success. In 1811 and 1812 he was in Berlin, where he was appointed as violinist in the Royal chapel, and in 1827 became also conductor of the Symphony concerts, and occupied this position, greatly honoured and respected, to the time of his death. His compositions included an Adagio and Polonaise, 3 violin duos and a string quartet.

## CHAPTER 41

## *Spain*

JOSÉ HERRANDO. In 1750 a violinist in the Royal chapel of the Incarnation at Madrid. He wrote a tutor: "Arte y puntual expliciación del modo de tocar el violon" (Paris dedication dated 1756); also chamber music works MSS. in Bologna Lic. Mus. and Madrid; 18 new Spanish Minuets (London, 1760).

CARLO D' ORDOÑEZ (ORDONNETZ, ORDINEZ). A born Spaniard who went to Vienna, where, ca. 1760, he was registrar at the Court of Justice and a good violinist and composer. In the academies (concerts) of the Tonkünstler Society, Vienna, his cantatas and symphonies were often performed. Hanslick (113) says that he was even a member of the Court chapel; Mendel, who gives the date as 1766, corroborates this, but in Köchel he does not appear as such. A "Singspiel" of his was performed in Vienna in 1779. He composed 2 sonatas for violin and bass; 6 trios for 2 violins and bass; 12 minuets for do. do.; 4 divertimenti a 3; 8 divertimenti for string quartet; 12 quartets, op. 1 and 2; symphonies, the above Singspiel, and, according to Fétis, 6 string quartets, op. 1 (Lyons, 1780).

OLIVER. Spanish Court-virtuoso. Gave a concert at Frankfort a/M., Apr. 18, 1765 (Israel, 47), and appeared in London in 1767 (Pohl, ii, 370).

NICOLAS XIMENES. Appeared in London as violinist, 1772 (Pohl, ii, 370). Composed 6 solos for a violin, dedicated to the Earl of Sandwich (London, Welcker). Pohl, ii, 371, also mentions a violoncellist XIMENES who appeared in London at the same time.

ANTONIO XIMENES. A late 18th-century 1st violinist at the Cathedral at Alicante. Composed 3 sonatas for violin and bass, op. 2 (Paris, Vidal, ca. 1780).

LUC GUENÉE, b. Cadiz, Aug. 19, 1787. Became Gavinié's pupil at the Paris Conservatoire in 1797. Afterwards he studied under Rode, and gained the first prize for violin playing in 1797. He then became violinist at the theatre in the rue de Louvois after renewed studies under Mazas. He studied theory under various masters and finally under Reicha. In 1809 he joined the orchestra of the opera and was pensioned after twenty-five years' service, when he became conductor at the theatre of the Palais Royal. In spite of all his careful training he was apparently never more than a good orchestral player. He composed for violin: A concerto with orchestra; 3 duets for 2 violins each, op. 1 and 2; trios for 2 violins and bass, op. 5; 6 caprices with bass, op. 6; 3 string quartets, op. 4, all pub. in Paris; also some operas and various music for the theatre.

CARLO FRANCESCO ALMEYDA. In 1798 a violinist at the Court of Spain; 6 string quartets, op. 2 (Paris, Pleyel, pub. 1798). He is said to have been born at Burgos. (Quartets reviewed in *Leipzig Zeitung*, 1, 555.)

DON PAOLO GUASTAROBBA. An 18th-century Spanish violinist who figures among the pupils of Tartini.

JOSÉ MAURICIO NUNES GARCIA. In Dresden Mus., there are, by him, 5 concerti a violino concert. with string quartet (MS. ?).

VIDIGAL. An 18th-century Portuguese guitarist and violinist. Vasconcelles refers to him at some length.

## CHAPTER 42

## *Switzerland*

KASPAR (GASPARO) FRITZ (FRIZ), b. Geneva, Feb. 18, 1716; d. there, Mar. 23, 1783. A pupil of Somis at Turin. Burney, who heard him at Geneva in 1770, praises his technique, his tone and excellent style of bowing. Composed 6 solos for a violin with a bass for the violoncello and harpsichord, op. 2 (London, Walsh, 1742); 6 sonate à violino solo e basso, op. 3; 6 sonatas for 2 violins (Walsh); 6 sonate à 2 violini e basso, op. 4 (Paris); also symphonies and 6 sonate à 4 strom. à 2 violini, alto viola, cembalo e violoncello, op. 1 (London, Walsh, 1742); 1 harpsichord concerto; one allegro movement, in Cartier's collection.

JEAN BAPTISTE EDOUARD DUPUY, b. Corcelles, near Neuchâtel, ca. 1770; d. Stockholm, Apr. 3, 1822. A pupil of Chabrand for violin, and Dussek for pianoforte, in Paris. He succeeded J. Q. P. Schulz as capellmeister at the Court of Prince Heinrich at Rheinsberg. In 1793 he toured as violinist and was engaged as second concertmeister at the Court of Stockholm, appearing also as singer, but was expelled for singing revolutionary songs. He went thence to Copenhagen in the same capacities and in 1806 had his opera, "Youth and Foolishness," performed there, which has retained its popularity. In 1809, however, he was expelled from Copenhagen also. In 1812, after a short sojourn in Paris, he was recalled to Stockholm as capellmeister and remained there to the time of his death. He composed solos for violin, a flute concerto, choral songs, etc.

DOMINIK ABEGG. A native of Schwyz, late 18th century. Lived for a long period in Italy, where he studied the violin (Schubiger, ii, 53), returned to Schwyz, 1798 (Eitner; Schubiger, ii, 53).

# PART III

# HISTORY OF THE VIOLIN FROM 1800 TO THE PRESENT DAY

## CHAPTER 43

# History of the Violin from 1800 to the Present Day

THE art of violin-playing, which had been carefully nursed and tended on Italian soil from its birth until the tender plant had brought forth a profusion of beautiful flowers, began, like all arts, to show a rapid decline in that country during the latter part of the 18th century. The works and precepts of the great masters fell into disuse and were forgotten. Religious, political and social conditions drove the Italian people to seek their pleasures in the shallow sensuous enjoyment of cloying melodies, and even the genius of Rossini only served to lull them into that mental somnolence of *dolce far niente*. No young artists arose to take the place of Tartini, Veracini, etc. The last heir to the achievements of Corelli and his successors, Viotti, had taken up his abode in Paris and London. His very antithesis, Paganini, that brilliant meteor in the musical firmament, did not arise from any school, nor did he found one, but his influence on the art of violin-playing is immeasurable. Viotti, on the other hand, transmitted the art of Corelli to his pupils and became the founder of the great French school, which throughout the 19th century stood foremost for elegance and grace in bowing, and style of rendering, as well as for brilliance of left-hand technique. It was brought to a high state of perfection by Rode, Kreutzer, Baillot, and Habeneck, the master of Alard, who was the teacher of Sarasate, the greatest virtuoso which the French school has produced so far. Its tendency was to cultivate essentially the virtuoso element, and in this it was closely allied to the Belgian school, which had, however, certain characteristics of its own, particularly in the style of its compositions which, mostly of an ephemeral nature, were decidedly elegant and melodious. The foremost representatives of this school were De Beriot, Vieuxtemps, Léonard, Thomson and Ysaye, whose educational influence extended over the whole of Europe. With the deaths of Franz Benda, and the Mannheim masters, the importance of Berlin and Munich for the art of violin-playing suffered a temporary obscuration, until there arose in Cassel a star of the first magnitude in the person of Spohr. His was the antithesis of the French art of violin-playing. His great technique of the bow followed an entirely opposite direction to that of the French masters. Nothing was done to excite applause; staccato, springbow, spiccato, etc., he condemned as trivial effects, and played all quick running passages with detached bows. His style was noble and dignified, his tone broad and powerful, and his cantabile full of expression without sentimentality. His tradition was carried on by his numerous pupils, foremost among whom were Ries, Pott, Kômpel, Hartmann, Bott and the brothers Bargheer. His pupil Ferd. David, however, deviated from his master's teaching. It was Joachim who followed in many respects the tradition of Spohr; he had the same noble and commanding personality, the same breadth and grandeur of style combined with an even greater technique, without that rigidity and heaviness from which Spohr's playing was not free. Joachim had, moreover, a far wider artistic outlook. When he became director of the Berlin High School for Music, that city became once more the centre of German violin-playing.

In Vienna Joachim's master Böhm, and Hellmesberger, father and son, carried on the best traditions of the German school until the arrival of Ševčik, who completely revolutionized the technical side of playing and especially of teaching. In England the art of violin-playing had received a fresh impetus with the opening of the Royal Academy of Music, in the early part of the century, where Mori and Sainton trained a number of excellent pupils, and their work is carried on by a number of eminent teachers. The same is the case with the Royal College of Music, where Henry Holmes, and R. Gompertz, who represented the Joachim School, were the first distinguished professors of violin, and the Guildhall School of Music which at one time counted the great Wilhelmj among its professors, and Trinity College of Music have also produced many excellent violinists. The activity of all these various schools has raised the general standard of violin-playing beyond recognition and enabled composers to write orchestral passages for the violin which the players of fifty years ago would have been quite unable to execute.

# VIOLINISTS OF THE PERIOD

VIOLINISTS OF THE PERIOD

# CHAPTER 44

## *Australia*

MAUD McCARTHY, b. Australia.   Showed remarkable musical
talent from early childhood; pupil of Ferd. Arbos from her
eighth to her fifteenth year.   In the first years of this century
she made her debut as a soloist in London, achieving great
success with the Beethoven and Brahms concertos, and at the
age of 12 she had already played in public concertos by Bach,
Mendelssohn, Bruch, Wieniawski, Saint-Saëns, Lalo, etc.;
at 15 she was a finished artist, with a repertory of an almost
incredible number of all the principal violin concertos and solo
pieces.   About that time she devoted her talent largely to the
performance of chamber music, and gave sonata recitals with
Fanny Davies, L. Borwick, Dohnany and others.   She made
her debut in Boston, Mass., ca. 1903, where she played the
Brahms concerto with great success, afterwards touring in the
United States, which she visited again the following year,
when she received an offer for 30 concerts for the winter of
1904–5.   This she declined as she wished to study for another
year or two in Europe.   Eventually she became an ardent
theosophist, and was taken by Mrs. Besant to Adyar, but
returned after a few years and married Mr. Fouldes, the
composer, in the performance of whose works she takes part
as well as in the performance of Indian music, but she has not
since been heard as a violinist in any important public concert,
although she gave some broadcast performances of Indian
music in 1929–30.

LEILA DOUBLEDAY, b. in Australia, 1894 (?).   In early childhood she studied the pianoforte, gaining several prizes at
Festivals, and at the age of 10 she gained a scholarship at the
Melbourne Conservatoire, where she took up violin-playing
as a second study, but soon felt that it attracted her more than
the pianoforte.   At the age of 12 she gave successful concerts

as a pianist, and then her mother took her to Vienna for further studies. There she decided to devote herself to the study of the violin under A. Rosé, who took great interest in her, and while giving her two weekly lessons instead of one, for three years, gave her a fourth year of free tuition. After that she made her debut in Vienna with Bruno Walther's orchestra, and then she gave, at Rosé's recommendation, an orchestral concert, which the latter, departing from his rule, conducted, with very favourable results for his pupil. She toured successfully for some years and in ca. 1926 formed a trio with Max Pirani (whom she married afterwards), pianoforte, and Chs. Hambourg, violoncello; which has become favourably known in London and the Provinces as the Pirani Trio.

ALMA MOODIE, b. Brisbane, Australia, Sept. 12, 1900. During 1907–10 a pupil of Ces. Thomson at the Brussels Conservatoire. She played in concerts with Max Reger in 1913; renewed her studies under C. Flesch in 1919. She is one of the foremost modern violinists, distinguished by breadth and power of style and tone, and was the first to bring out Pfitzner's violin concerto. She resides at Zürich.

ERNEST TOY, b. in Australia. Went to the United States of America, ca. 1920, where he held several important appointments as teacher of the violin. About 1922 he gave up teaching and toured all over the States as a soloist. Early in 1923 he went with his wife for a 5 months' trip to Australia, and although this was intended for a holiday he made several appearances on the concert platform during that time. He made his permanent quarters at Chicago.

# CHAPTER 45

## *Austria: to 1850*

JOSEPH MAYSEDER, b. Vienna, Oct. 26, 1789; d. there, Nov. 21, 1863. Son of a decorative (scene ?) painter, whose talent attracted the attention and patronage of the Court Councillor Sonnenfels (von Sonnleithner ?), who enabled him to become a pupil of Suche and Wranitzky and afterwards of Schuppanzigh. He gave his first concert in 1800. On Oct. 16, 1814, the young violinist, who had already acquired a widespread reputation, was leader of the violins on the memorable occasion of the first performance of Schubert's first Mass in F at the church of Lichtenthal, Vienna. His style was distinguished more by grace and elegance than by breadth and power, but it was to the taste of the Viennese, with whom the brilliant pleasing piquancy of his playing made him a great and lasting favourite. He was noted for the charm of his rendering of Haydn's quartets. In his younger years he was 2nd violinist in the famous Schuppanzigh quartet. He never went on tour except for a visit to Paris in 1820. From 1816 he was an Imperial chamber virtuoso at St. Stephen's Cathedral and at the Opera, and 1835 he became concertmeister in the Imperial Chapel. His compositions are distinguished by grace and elegance, good musicianship and very effective treatment of the violin. Hence his concertos and solo pieces remained in favour for a long time, but his numerous chamber music works are wanting in inspiration and depth of thought.

JOSEPH STRAUSS, b. Brünn, 1793; d. Karlsruhe, Dec. 2, 1866. Son of a violinist who was concertmeister at one of the minor Italian Courts and did not wish Joseph to become a musician, but gave him teachers for the violin and the pianoforte. After the father's death he was taken to Vienna, where he commenced more serious studies under C. Blumenthal, Urbani and Schuppanzigh; Jos. Teyber and Albrechtsberger taught him harmony and counterpoint. At the age of 12 he played a violin solo at the theatre on the Wien, between the acts of a play. Riemann says he became violinist at the Court Opera. After some years of success in Vienna both as a soloist and orchestral player, he went to Pesth as solo violinist at the theatre, and there he brought out some of his more important and orchestral compositions. In 1813 he became conductor at Temesvar and in 1814 he went to Hermannstadt, where he produced two operas, as well as a mass, two cantatas and some violin solos. In 1817 he went to Brünn, where he brought out important sacred works as well as a concerto and solos for violin. Thence he went to Prague, where he gained the friendship of D. Weber and Wittaczek; later he went on a concert tour through Germany and Switzerland, and in 1822 was called to Strassburg to organize and conduct the German opera. In 1823 he went to Mannheim where he produced Spontini's "Fernando Cortez" with such success that the Grand Duke of Baden charged him with the direction of the Court concerts at Karlsruhe, and after Danzi's death nominated him his successor as Court capellmeister, a position which he held until he retired in 1863. He wrote several successful operas for Karlsruhe, including the "Werwolf," which was performed also in Vienna over fifty times. In 1840 he conducted the German opera in London as well as his prize symphony at the Philharmonic Society. Among his pub. compositions are a number of airs with variations, a string quartet and songs.

KARL DITTERS VON DITTERSDORF, b. Vienna, Nov. 2, 1739; d. at the castle Rothlhotta, near Neuhaus (Neuhof), Bohemia, Oct. 31 (Riemann: 24), 1799. His first teacher for the violin was König, but after about three years he studied under Karl (Wasielewski says "Joseph") Zügler, on whose advice he played in the orchestra of the Benedictine church. There he had one day to play a solo at first sight in place of the violinist Karl Huber. He acquitted himself so well of that task that General Prince Joseph Friedrich of Hildburghausen took him as a page and violinist in his private band, where in his twelfth year he had to play a solo almost every Friday at the Academies which the Prince gave to members of the nobility. He also was placed for further tuition under Trani, who made him study the sonatas by Locatelli. Ditters says: "As old-fashioned as these sonatas may sound now, I can strongly recommend them to every pupil of the violin, not to play as solos but for practice. He will thereby make great progress in fingering, various bowings, arpeggios, double stops, etc." He played also works by Zuccari, Tartini, and Ferrari. When the latter was in Vienna, Trani became his intimate friend, and he accompanied Ferrari's solos wherever the latter played. Thereby he was able to make a close study of Ferrari's technique in every detail, which he adopted henceforth, and though he appeared no longer as a soloist, he was a gifted teacher, and able to transmit it to his pupils. Thus Ditters succeeded in acquiring that style and technique to such an extent that he could play Ferrari's pieces in the composer's own manner. On account of this, many Viennese called him jocularly "Ferrari's little ape." At the same time he studied composition under Capellmeister Bono, and besides he had to learn Latin, French, Italian, as well as fencing, dancing and riding. All this had a happy influence upon his mental development; unfortunately it came to an end when in 1760 the Prince left Vienna, but not before he had procured him a place in the Imperial Court orchestra. In 1762 he went with Gluck, then Court-capellmeister, to Bologna for the performance of Gluck's opera "Clelia." On that occasion he made friends with the famous Padre Martini, and Farinelli. On his return he resumed his former duties, and in 1764 he went with other picked members to Frankfort a/M. for the festivities in connexion with the coronation of Joseph II as German Emperor. Differences with the new intendant, Count Spork, arising after his return, he left the Imperial Chapel and succeeded Mich. Haydn as capellmeister of the Bishop of Grosswardein, Hungary, where he developed a great activity as composer. Apart from symphonies, string quartets, violin concertos, masses and motets he wrote 4 oratorios to librettos of his friend Metastasio, and also his first operas for the new theatre of the Bishop. The latter disbanded his chapel in 1769, and Ditters went on tour in Germany. At Breslau the Prince-Bishop von Schafgotsch, residing at Johannesberg, attracted him to his Court, procured him from the Pope the title of Knight of the Golden Spur as a New Year's gift, 1770, and made him forestmaster of the Principality of Neisse (a sinecure). He was given the formation of a little theatre, for which he engaged Viennese artists, including Mlle Nicolini, who afterwards became his wife. In 1770 he wrote his famous oratorio "Esther" for the Musicians' Widows' Society. The MS. is preserved in the National Library. In 1773 the Bishop made him Governor of Freienwaldau and procured for him the Imperial diploma of nobility. In 1768 he was again in Vienna to conduct performances of 12 symphonies after the Metamorphoses by Ovid, an oratorio and several of his operas, including his "Doctor and Apotheker," which on account of its melodiousness and charming spontaneous music held the stage for over a century. In 1789 he earned fresh laurels in Berlin with his works and was greatly honoured by the King. His happy and successful career received a rude shock when the Bishop died in 1795, and he was dismissed from all his positions. He was then afflicted with gout and podagra, and only after much trouble he was in 1797 awarded a pension of only 500 florins. The great artist and composer of still popular works was threatened with want and misery when Baron Ignaz von Stillfried took him and his family to live at his castle Rothlhotta, near Neuhaus (Bohemia). There he dictated his autobiography to his son. It was finished only two days before his death and pub. at Leipzig, 1801, for the benefit of his family. Dittersdorf was a remarkable violinist in his time. When on their visit to Bologna, Gluck and Dittersdorf attended vespers at St. Paolo, where Spagnoletti played a concerto by Tartini with great success. Ditters was to play there on the following evening, and Gluck remarked: "Now you may count for certain upon the applause of your audience to-morrow as both your composition and your style of playing are more modern." Gluck's prediction proved true. As a composer, Dittersdorf is at the present time chiefly remembered for his string quartets, which for their spontaneous humour and melodious charm, approach Haydn in eternal youthfulness.

JOSEPH BENES (BENESH), b. Batelov, Moravia, Jan. 11, 1793. Violinist in the orchestra at Baden, near Vienna, and Pressburg. Started on tour in Italy in 1819, and became concertmeister at Laibach in 1823. In 1832 he became a member of the Imperial Chapel in Vienna. Composed violin pieces and songs which were pub.

FRANZ PECHATSCHEK, II, b. Vienna, July 4, 1793; d. Karlsruhe, Sept. 15, 1840. A pupil of his father. As early as 1801 and 1802 he played before the Viennese Court and in 1803 he gave, with his father, two concerts at Prague, where he played a concerto by Fodor, an adagio by Rode and variations of his own composition. Foerster was his teacher of harmony and composition. In 1805 he made a successful debut at the Vienna Prater concerts, and after renewed studies, including that of the guitar, he became a second concertmeister at the theatre on the Wien. In 1818 he was called to Hanover as 1st violinist in the Court orchestra. In 1824–5 he toured with great success in South Germany and in 1827 the Grand Duke of Baden appointed him as concertmeister at his Court in Karlsruhe. In 1832 he visited Paris but, according to Fétis, he was there looked upon as a feeble imitation of Paganini. There is no doubt that he developed chiefly the virtuoso side of his art, to which his now antiquated compositions testify, but his great and continued success all over Germany and Austria is ascribed to his bold and infallible technique and purity of intonation. In 1837 he went to Baden-Baden in the hope of restoring his failing health. He composed a concertino, a concertante duo for 2 violins, a number of violin solos and a string quartet.

JOSEPH PANNY, b. Kohlmitzberg, Austria, Oct. 23, 1794; d. Mainz, Sept. 7, 1838. A pupil of his father and, in theory, of his grandfather; violinist and composer of merit, also good organist. In Vienna, where he took his final studies in composition under Eybler, he attracted in 1828 the notice of Paganini, whom he joined on his concert tours, but they separated. Panny continued touring, giving concerts in all the principal towns of Germany and Austria. He composed a scena for violin and orchestra (for Paganini), a sonata for the G string, solo pieces for violin, easy string quartets, op. 15; trios, a clarinet sonata, masses, a requiem, songs, etc. Paganini played his dramatic scena with orchestra at his farewell concert in Vienna in 1828. Panny sojourned successively at Hamburg, Bergen in Norway, Altona, as conductor at Wesserling in the Alsace, and finally settled at Mayence in 1836. There he founded a School of Music, where Peter Cornelius was for a time his pupil, and married, but died only two years later.

ANTON SCHINDLER, b. Meedl, near Neustadt, Moravia, June 13, 1795; d. Bockenheim, near Frankfort a/M., Jan. 16, 1864. Studied law at Vienna and at the same time the violin, pianoforte, composition and æsthetics. In 1822 he became leader-conductor at the Josephstadt theatre, and 1825 at the Kärntnertor theatre. During the winter of 1823–4 he had all Beethoven's symphonies performed under the master's supervision. His lifelong friendship with Beethoven is told in his biography of the great master, whom he served with unfaltering devotion. In 1831 Schindler became capellmeister at Münster, Westphalia, and 1835–40 at Aix-la-Chapelle; afterwards he travelled a great deal, visiting also Paris, whence he gives some interesting glimpses of the state of violin-playing there, at that time, in his Beethoven biography (copious extracts in Wki., "Die Violine," under Schindler). In 1848 he settled finally at Bockenheim.

JOSEF STADLER, b. Vienna, Oct. 13, 1796. Studied the violin under a relative and at the age of 16 became 1st violinist at the Leopoldstadt theatre, where he rose to the post of capellmeister in 1819. From 1831 he was the only solo violinist at the cathedral of St. Stephen. He composed the music for three pantomimes, also solos (variations, rondos, etc.), as well as 30 studies for violin.

FERDINAND SIMON GASSNER, b. Vienna, Jan. 6, 1798; d. Karlsruhe, Feb. 25, 1851. He showed marked talent for the violin and music generally in childhood. In early years he went to Karlsruhe, where his father became scene painter for the Court theatre. There he visited the Latin college (Gymnasium) and received regular lessons on the violin. He was destined for a scientific career, but instead of entering the University he became an accessory violinist in the Court orchestra, where his talent as a violinist, as well as composer of an operetta, attracted the attention of the Court musicians Danzi, Fesca and Brandl, who henceforth took his further musical education in hand. In 1816 he became 1st violinist at the New National theatre at Mayence, and soon afterwards, deputy chorusmaster and conductor. Gottfried Weber became his friend there and assisted him in his theoretical studies. In 1818 he gave a concert at Giessen which was so successful that he was appointed as director of music at the University of that town and there he resumed also his scientific studies and became Doctor of Philosophy in 1819. From that time he developed a widespread activity as conductor, organizer of music festivals, composer writer on music, and originator of the musical periodical *Cäcilia*, etc. In 1826 he returned to Karlsruhe as member of the Court chapel, became teacher of singing at the Court theatre and in 1830 chorusmaster and musical director there; whenever he did not conduct he played in the orchestra as leader of the violins. In his latter years he wrote also a theoretical work, ed. a musical periodical and an abbreviated edition of Schilling's Musical Dictionary.

GEORG HELLMESBERGER, SEN., b. Vienna, Apr. 24, 1800; d. Neuwaldegg, near Vienna, Aug. 16, 1873. He started his musical career as a soprano choirboy in the Imperial Chapel as successor to F. Schubert, received his first violin lessons from his father and continued under Böhm at the Conservatoire of the Friends of Music, where Emmanuel Förster was his master for composition. In 1821 he became assistant teacher for violin, in 1825 titular professor and in 1833 actual professor at the Conservatoire. In 1829 he succeeded Schuppanzigh as conductor at the Court opera and in 1830 was appointed as a member of the Court chapel. As virtuoso he toured successfully in Austria, Hungary, and Bohemia. He was pensioned in 1867. As a teacher he stood in the foremost rank of his contemporaries, counting among his pupils E. Ernst, M. Hauser, J. Joachim, L. Auer, and his sons Georg and Josef. His pub. compositions are: 2 concertos, several sets of variations, solo pieces, and a string quartet.

ALBERT RAIMUND, EDLER VON KAAN, b. Vienna, 1802. He belonged to a Hungarian noble family; studied the violin under Mayseder, joined an Austrian cavalry regiment in which he advanced to the rank of captain, whereon he resigned and toured in Italy as a violin virtuoso with great success, which followed him also to Vienna, where he appeared again in 1840, and then appears to have retired into private life.

STRAUSS FAMILY. The family of the Waltz-classics deserve a place here as they are not only unequalled in the charm of their dance compositions but also by the manner by which they played them, which absolutely electrified their audiences, so that it was a saying in Vienna: "Leute hebt's Füsserl auf—heut geigt der Strauss." (People lift your feet—to-day Strauss is playing.)

JOHANN STRAUSS (the father), b. Vienna, Mar. 14, 1804; d. there, Sept. 25, 1849. The son of an innkeeper, had some lessons on the violin from an obscure musician, but by his natural talent and indefatigable study he soon became an excellent player, who, at his father's house with his friends, studied the string quartets of some of the best masters. In 1819 he joined Launer's quartet, which played dance music at various inns, as a viola player, and when that blossomed out into a full orchestra he became its deputy conductor. In 1825 he started his own orchestra, which eventually acquired European fame. For a detailed history of this orchestra and the various members of the family see the dictionaries of Grove, Riemann, etc., as well as the special biographies. We can here only enumerate them.

JOHANN STRAUSS, b. Vienna, Oct. 25, 1825; d. there, June 3, 1899; eldest son of the above. He surpassed his father both as composer and as violinist-conductor. His "Blue Danube" is a favourite all the world over, as well as many of his other waltzes and charming operettas. He formed an orchestra of his own in 1844, but after his father's death took over the conductorship of the latter's orchestra and toured all over Europe and even visited America. After his marriage in 1863 he devoted himself chiefly to composition and handed over the orchestra to his brothers, but conducted the Imperial Court balls till 1870.

JOSEPH STRAUSS, brother of the preceding, b. Vienna, Apr. 25, 1827; d. Warsaw, July 22, 1870. He was also a fertile and talented composer of dance music, but did not attain the fame of his brother.

EDUARD STRAUSS, b. Vienna, Feb. 14, 1835; d. there, Dec. 28, 1916. The third brother, who succeeded Johann as conductor of the orchestra and the Court balls. He also was an excellent violinist and a composer of dance music.

MORITZ SCHÖN, b. Krönau, Moravia, 1808; d. Breslau, Apr. 8, 1885. He originally intended to become a schoolmaster, but showed such talent for the violin that at the age of $14\frac{1}{2}$ he

JOSEPH MAYSEDER

GEORG HELLMESBERGER (the elder)
By kindness of Prof. O. E. Deutsch.

JACOB DONT
By kindness of Prof. O. E. Deutsch.

ANDREAS ROMBERG
By kindness of Prof. O. E. Deutsch.

became chamber musician to the Princess Lynar at Drehnau, where he continued his violin studies under the musical director Löbmann. In 1827 he was engaged by Count Brühl as supernumerary in the Royal chapel, Berlin, where he took still further lessons from Moser and Hub. Ries; then he went to Brunswick to benefit by the advice of the brothers Müller, of quartet fame, and finally finished his violinistic education under Spohr at Cassel, who gave him an excellent testimonial. Armed with this, he went on tour and eventually settled at Breslau, where he was capellmeister at the theatre from 1835 to 1841. After that he founded a school for violin-playing there, and was co-founder of the Philharmonic Society. He composed violin duets which, on account of their pleasing melodious character, are still largely used, as well as some of his numerous, excellent studies. His other violin compositions have become more or less obsolete.

HEINRICH PROCH, b. Vienna, July 22, 1809; d. there, Dec. 18, 1878. Studied law at the University and at the same time he cultivated the violin to such good purpose that in 1833 and 1834 he played in many concerts as soloist with such success that he decided to follow music as a profession. In 1837 he became capellmeister at the Josephstädter theatre and in 1840 at the Court Opera, which position he held until 1870. When the New Comic Opera was opened he filled once more the place of conductor, but the enterprise came to an early end. Proch became more widely known by his songs, which were of the popular ballad type, and in great favour in most countries. His vocal variations with flute obbligato were a favourite item in the repertoire of Mme Peschka-Leutner. He was also a most successful singing-master who, as well as Mme Peschka-Leutner, counted among his pupils Mmes Dustmann, Rokitansky, and Titjens.

HEINRICH WILHELM ERNST, b. Brünn, Moravia, May 6, 1814; d. Nice, Oct. 8, 1865. In early childhood he showed a remarkable talent for music. He studied at the Vienna Conservatoire, violin under Böhm and Mayseder, and composition under Seyfried; at the age of 16 he went on tour, a fully fledged virtuoso, appearing at Munich, Stuttgart, Frankfort, etc. On the way, he went to Paris, where he renewed his studies under de Beriot, and remained for some years. Paganini appeared there in 1832 and Ernst never missed an opportunity to hear him and to study his style, which he did to such good purpose that he acquired many features of his technique, and it was also about that time that he wrote his famous variations on the "Carneval de Venice," one of the most brilliant firework pieces for the violin, which, however, is based largely on reminiscences of Paganini's variations on the same subject, and, like most of his works, remained unpub. He approached so near Paganini, both in the style of the composition and in its execution, that the latter once jokingly remarked: "Il faut se méfier de vous." Ernst was certainly the nearest approach to Paganini, but he possessed higher artistic qualities which show themselves also in his compositions as well as in interesting and important novel technical features. In 1834 he began again to tour all over Europe and in 1843 he paid his first visit to London, for which he conceived a great affection, revisiting it again and again until 1858, sometimes for lengthened sojourns, while in the intervals he continued his triumphal tours on the Continent. In 1859 a spinal complaint began to show itself which culminated in paralysis in the spring of 1862. His large-hearted and princely munificence during the hey-day of his career, had left him to face sickness in its most depressing form, in reduced circumstances. His admirable personal qualities, however, had made him many friends, who failed him not to the last. *The Times* of June 23, 1862, announces that the Monday Popular concert of that evening would be "exclusively for the benefit of Herr Ernst; that the performers—M. M. Joachim and Laub (violins), Molique (viola), Piatti and Davidoff (violoncello), Charles Halle (pianoforte), Mr. Santley and Mme Sainton-Dolby (vocalists) and Mr. Benedict (conductor)—have one and all tendered their services; and that a MS. quartet from Herr Ernst's own pen would be played. He lingered still for three years, unable to use his beloved violin. *The Times*, in announcing his death, said, "This is one of the cases in which departure can only be welcomed as relief." The *Athenæum* in its obituary said, "A more amiable man never breathed than Ernst; nor one of a better heart, a finer intelligence and a more generous and unenvying nature. A certain languor of temperament, approaching to indolence, and of late years aggravated by illness, prevented him from doing full justice to his powers, either as a creative musician or a member of society; but his friends will recollect him not merely by his nobility of nature, incapable of intrigue, jealousy and suspicion, but also by his quick and delicate sense of humour. As an artist he cannot be overrated among the violinists. One of the greatest violinists of the 19th century, he was nevertheless subject to moods which sometimes adversely affected his technique as well as intonation. Although he is praised by his contemporaries for his soulful and temperamental playing of classical chamber music, yet he was not above the virtuoso habit of introducing his own embellishment into the works of the great masters."

His compositions show a deeper poetical feeling than those of his contemporary virtuoso composers but most of them show the wear of time; even the once so popular "Elegy" is not often heard now, and the elegant and charming "Pensées Fugitives" which he wrote in conjunction with Heller, are almost forgotten. His concerto in F sharp minor, however, is a genuinely inspired work, and like the fine "Othello Fantasia" contains so many features of technical violinistic interest and offer such opportunity for the display of the highest virtuosity that they will always be welcome to the few who can effectively master their enormous difficulties. His many other fantasies, nocturnes, etc., as well as his chamber music compositions, have disappeared in the stream of time.

JACOB DONT, b. Vienna, Mar. 2, 1815; d. there, Nov. 17, 1888. The son of the violoncellist, Jos. Val. Dont. Pupil of Böhm and Hellmesberger at the Vienna Conservatoire. In 1831 he became a violinist at the Burg-theatre, and in 1834 teacher at the Conservatoire and member of the Imperial Chapel. He distinguished himself as a soloist as well as chamber music player and teacher, his most eminent pupil being L. von Auer. As a composer he earned the praises of Spohr. He wrote violin concertos, solos, studies, quartets, etc. His studies, which possess musical value, are standard works for the study of the violin, especially in its advanced stages.

MATHIAS DURST, b. Vienna, Aug. 18, 1815. A pupil of Hellmesberger and Böhm, who became a violinist at the Burg theatre, and in 1841 a member of the Imperial Chapel. Later he was a professor of the Church Music Society. He was held in great esteem as a soloist and still more as a quartet player. He composed solos for violins, duets, quartets, also overtures; only part of these were pub.

KARL HAFNER, b. Vienna, Nov. 23, 1815; d. Hamburg, Jan., 1861. A pupil of Jansa; he became concertmeister at Hamburg, where, among his many good pupils, was O. von Königslöw.

WENZEL FEIGERL, b. Vienna, 1815. Studied the violin at the Vienna Conservatoire, and became at first violinist at the Josephstadt theatre, but soon was appointed at the Court Opera. In 1834 he went to Hungary, and afterwards to Moscow, where he was esteemed as an excellent violinist and an artist of distinction.

LOUIS ELLER, b. Graz, June 9, 1820; d. Pau, France, July 12, 1862. A pupil of Hysel at Graz, he played in public at the age of 9. In 1836 he became more widely known by his successful debut in Vienna. In 1842 he became concert-meister at Salzburg. He toured with continued success in Austria, Hungary, Switzerland, Southern Europe. In 1844 he visited Paris, and went with Gottschalk to Spain and Portugal. A pulmonary complaint, to which he eventually succumbed, hindered the free exercise of his art. He composed a number of violin solos and studies. He settled at Pau, from where he paid several visits to Paris and the principal towns of Germany where his brilliant technique and refined style was greatly appreciated.

KARL HEISSLER, b. Vienna, Jan. 18, 1823. Pupil of Jos. Böhm, Matth. Durst, Geo. Hellmesberger; from 1843 violinist in the Imperial Chapel, and professor of violin at the Conservatoire and conductor of the orchestra of the Friends of Music. Mendel, who ranks him with the best violinists of his time, says that he excelled both as soloist and as chamber music player.

LUDWIG MINCUS, b. Vienna, 1827. During 1853–5 conductor of Prince Jussupov's orchestra in St. Petersburg; 1861–72 solo violinist and music inspector of the Imperial theatre, and for a time professor at the Moscow Conservatoire.

In 1872 he became ballet composer for the Imperial theatre, St. Petersburg. Afterwards he settled in Vienna, where one of his ballets, composed for Paris in 1866 in collaboration with Delibes, had been performed.

JOSEPH HELLMESBERGER, SEN., b. Vienna, Nov. 3, 1828; d. there, Oct. 24, 1893. Son and pupil of Georg. Hellmesberger, who toured with him and his brother Georg through Germany and England in 1847, where they appeared at one of Ella's Musical Union concerts, London. In 1849 he formed a permanent quartet with Heissler, Durst and Schlesinger which gave the first concert on Nov. 4, that year, becoming famous throughout the musical world and reviving many important but for some reason or other neglected chamber works. On Dec. 26, 1861, he gave a performance of Schubert's great octet which had not been heard since Schuppanzigh produced it for the first and only previous time at Schubert's last subscription concert on Apr. 16, 1827 (O. E. Deutsch "Franz Schubert," i, 393), and on Feb. 23, 1862, he gave the first public performance of Schubert's quartet in B flat major, op. 168. In 1851 he became director and conductor of the Society of the Friends of Music and teacher at the Conservatoire, and in 1859, when these positions were separated, Herbeck became conductor of the concerts, while Hellmesberger remained director of the society. In 1860 he was appointed as concertmeister at the Imperial opera, and in 1863 he succeeded Mayseder as solo violinist in the Imperial Chapel (Institute for church music), the first time that seniority was set aside in favour of greater talent. In 1877 he became Court Capellmeister, retiring in 1893. In 1855 he was president of the jury for musical instruments at the Paris Exhibition and received the Knight's Cross of the Legion of Honour and a special medal. As a virtuoso Hellmesberger is described as a combination of Joachim and Sarasate, possessing the classical breadth and dignity of the former and the brilliancy and limpid tone of the latter. He proved himself an excellent conductor who raised the orchestra of the Friends of Music to a high standard of perfection and at their concerts gave a first public hearing to many young violinists, who afterwards became eminent artists. He recalled Mozart's feat of writing down Allegri's "Miserere" from memory after hearing it performed, by writing out a whole new concerto by de Beriot after hearing it in 1840 at two rehearsals where it was played by Teresa Milanollo, who possessed the MS. and wished to reserve it exclusively for her own use. Robin Legge, quoting from obituary notices in Viennese papers, relates that he raised himself on his death-bed and, beating time with his hands, said: "One, two, three! now the organ comes in." He received the freedom of the city of Vienna and many orders from the Austrian Emperor and other kings and princes.

GEORG HELLMESBERGER, JUN., b. Vienna, Jan. 27, 1830; d. Hanover, Nov. 12, 1852. Son and pupil of his father. He toured successfully in Germany and England in 1847 with his father and his brother, and became concertmeister at the Court of Hanover in 1850. Two operas of his were performed at Hanover and he left a number of compositions, including symphonies in MS. His daughter Rosa became a singer at the Vienna Opera.

E. RAPPOLDI, b. Vienna, Feb. 21, 1831; d. Dresden, May 16, 1903. At first he intended to become a pianist, but exchanged that instrument for the violin, which he studied successively under Jansa and Böhm and composition under Sechter. During 1854–61 he was violinist at the Vienna Opera and toured occasionally in Germany, Holland and Belgium. From 1861 to 1866 he was concertmeister at Rotterdam, and from that time till 1870 opera conductor successively at Lübeck, Stettin and Prague. During 1871–7 he was teacher at the Berlin High School for music, and for some longer period viola player in the Joachim quartet. In 1876 he received the title of Royal Professor. On Oct. 1, 1877, he was appointed Court concertmeister until 1898 at Dresden, and professor at the Conservatoire until his death. He belonged to the serious type of virtuosos and excelled equally as soloist and chamber-music player, having also a high reputation as teacher. His wife was an excellent pianist and pupil of Liszt. Rappoldi composed quartets, sonatas, songs, also some orchestral works.

MORITZ KÄSSMAYER, b. Vienna, 1831; d. there, Nov. 9, 1884. A pupil of Preyer and Sechter at the Conservatoire; violinist at the Imperial Court Opera. Composed 5 string quartets; suite for string orchestra; an opera, church music, songs, etc. He was a musical humourist of the highest order.

HEINRICH KARL HERMANN DE AHNA, b. Vienna, June 22, 1833; d. Berlin, Nov. 1, 1892. Pupil of Mayseder, finished his studies at the Prague Conservatoire under Mildner. In 1849 he became chamber virtuoso of the Duke of Coburg-Gotha and in the same year went to England, where his classical style combined with great virtuosity was greatly admired, and he remained there some time, but suddenly resolved to enter the military career. In 1850 he returned to Vienna, entered the army Oct. 1, 1851 (Riemann), as sub-lieutenant, served in the Italian campaign, and was promoted to the rank of 1st lieutenant. After peace had been declared, his love for music gained once more the upper hand, and he toured successfully in Germany and Holland. As Ferdinand Laub had left Berlin, a violinist of the first rank was wanting there, and de Ahna was offered the post as Royal Chamber Musician in 1862, which he accepted the more readily as his mother and sister had already settled there. In 1868 he received the title and position of Royal Concertmeister. He excelled as soloist as well as chamber-music player in his regular soirées. He was a well-educated, amiable, and most unselfish man, who ungrudgingly gave his services to many young or less fortunate musicians who for their concerts could not afford to engage a first-class artist. His many excellent qualities decided the Minister of Education, on the opening of the Royal Academy of Arts in 1869, to appoint him as first teacher for the violin and the viola, under Joachim. He joined the latter's famous quartet as 2nd violin. With Barth and Hausmann he instituted trio soirées which stood in high repute. His rendering of the works of the classical masters is described as unsurpassable. He was the fortunate owner of a Strad, of which Ehrlich said that it had the finest and most powerful tone of any he ever heard. It was, moreover, remarkable by a knot in the wood of the table, a rare occurrence in a Strad (Robin Legge).

KARL HOFMANN, b. Vienna, Apr. 3, 1835; d. there, Dec. 12, 1909. Violinist in the Vienna Court chapel and professor at the Conservatoire. Composed a violin concerto; waltzes for string quartet and pianoforte; an opera and instructive works.

WILMA MARIA FRANZISKA NERUDA, b. Brünn, Austria, Mar. 21, 1839; d. Berlin, Apr. 15, 1911. Of a distinguished family of violinists and musicians, dating back to the 17th century. She began to play the violin in her early childhood under the tuition of her father, Joseph Neruda, an esteemed organist, who after some time placed her under Jansa. In 1846 she made her debut in Vienna, together with her sister Amalie, a pianist, when she astounded even that severe critic Ed. Hanslick by her perfect technique, fullness of tone, purity of intonation, and her soulful cantilena, and these qualities she developed still further, so that afterwards it was truthfully said of her that she combined female grace with manly power and intellect. She was the female counterpart of Joachim; she also had that quiet, noble dignity, abhorring all outward show and affectation, and like him she strove for the highest ideals in art, eschewing everything trivial or indifferent. Joined by their brother Franz, the violoncellist, the sisters toured with unabated success all over Germany and the Netherlands. Wilma made her London debut on Apr. 30, 1849, and this was followed by many other concerts. On June 11 she played a de Beriot concerto at a Philharmonic concert. For several years the family continued touring, chiefly in Russia. In 1862 Wilma received the title of Chamber Virtuoso. In 1864 she was in Paris, where she played with immense success at the Pasdeloup, Conservatoire, and other concerts, and at that time she married the Swedish capellmeister and composer Ludwig Norman, with whom she went to Stockholm as soloist, and teacher at the Royal Academy of Music. In 1869 she separated from her husband, and went to London, where, on May 17, she played at the Philharmonic Society, and was persuaded by Vieuxtemps to remain till the winter, when she enhanced her reputation by her unrivalled leadership at a series of Monday Popular Concerts before Christmas. From that time until 1898 she was in London for every spring and winter season and played at many of the principal concerts, including the Popular Concerts in London and also in the provinces. Norman having died in 1885, she married Sir Charles Hallé on July 26, 1888, and they frequently appeared on the concert platform together until Hallé's death in 1895. In 1896 a committee headed by the Prince of Wales, the Kings of Denmark and Sweden, and many influential admirers, acquired a palace at Asolo, near Venice, which they presented to her as a mark of universal esteem. After the death of her eldest son in 1898 she went to reside in Berlin, whence she continued to tour on the Continent and to pay her annual visits to London. In 1901 Queen Alexandra conferred upon her the title of Violinist to the Queen. Her magnificent Stradivari violin, dated 1709, was presented to her in 1876 by H.R.H. the Duke of Edinburgh, and the Earls of Dudley and of Hardwicke.

GEORG FRANK, b. Vienna, 1845; d. Odessa, Apr. 13, 1871. A pupil of Jos. Hellmesberger. He combined beauty of tone with a brilliant technique, and the pursuit of high artistic ideals which won him universal sympathy. He toured successfully in Austria, Hungary, Bulgaria, etc., as far as Odessa. Princess Woronzoff, in admiration of his playing, presented him with a fine Guarnerius violin. He was for a short time violinist at the Vienna Court opera, but on account of his health he accepted the position of director of the Russian Society of the Friends of Music at Odessa in the hope that he might find recovery in the milder climate, but tuberculosis brought a promising career to an untimely end.

# CHAPTER 46

# *Austria: to Present Day*

JOHANN SCHRAMMEL, b. Vienna, May 22, 1850; d. there, June 17, 1893. A member of an old family of Viennese musicians, pupil of G. and J. Hellmesberger, K. Heissler and L. Weiss; at first military bandsman, founded with his brother JOSEPH SCHRAMMEL (violinist, b. 1852; d. 1895), Dänzer (clarinet), Strohmayer (guitar), the quartet known as "D'Schrammeln" in 1877, which roused the Viennese to the height of enthusiasm and extended its fame to even wider circles. In 1891 the clarinet was replaced by a chromatic harmonica. Johann composed 150 pieces for this quartet in the Viennese waltz-and-folk-tune style, some of which became widely popular. He also published "Old Austrian Folk-tunes to 1860" and a Schrammel-operetta, "Wiener Kinder," which, in O. Skalla's arrangement, was performed at the Strauss theatre in 1917. Quartets of this and similar combinations are the descendants of those of the Styrian fiddlers who, down to the beginning of the 19th century, used to come down the Danube from Linz on rafts and boats and played in the beer- and wine-houses in Vienna. They have now in some cases reached a high artistic standard. The writer heard such a quartet of 2 violins, harmonica and bass guitar at the house of Mr. van Hoboken, founder of the photogram archive of the National Library, Vienna, at the end of the International Schubert research Congress in 1928, which by the exquisite delicacy, artistic rendering and beauty of tone proved a revelation to a company of eminent musicians from all parts of Europe.

JOSEPH HELLMESBERGER, JUN., b. Vienna, Apr. 9, 1855; d. there, Apr. 25, 1907. A pupil of his father, Joseph Hellmesberger, in whose quartet he became 2nd violinist in 1870. From 1878 he was solo violinist in the Court chapel and professor of violin at the Conservatoire. He held the post of conductor at various theatres, and from 1884 that of concertmeister at the Court opera and conductor of the ballet. In 1886 he became capellmeister at the Court opera. He composed 10 operettas which were performed in Vienna, Munich and Hamburg between 1880 and 1890, also 6 ballets and other pieces for the theatre. In 1899 he was appointed vice-capellmeister and 1900–2 he was first Court capellmeister. In the winter 1904–5 he was Court capellmeister at Stuttgart.

RICHARD SAHLA, b. Graz, Sept. 17, 1855. Studied the violin for four years at the school of the Styrian Musical Union at Graz under Concertmeister Ferd. Casper, a pupil of Mildner, also pianoforte under Kuno Hess and Hoppe and composition under Dr. Meyer (Remy); he made his debut in public as a violinist at the age of 7, and appeared with great success on many subsequent occasions at Graz, where on four occasions he gained a prize at the music school. During 1868–72 he continued his studies at the Leipzig Conservatoire under Ferd. David and Röntgen, but benefited chiefly by observing the style of great violinists who played at the Gewandhaus concerts, where, after gaining the violin prize at the Conservatoire, he made his first appearance early in 1873. During 1876–7 he was concertmeister at Gothenburg, and 1878–80 at the Court opera, Vienna, where he gave a farewell concert for the benefit of the orchestral fund, playing the Paganini concerto with unqualified success. After that he toured for ca. two years, and then, during 1882–8, he was concertmeister at Hanover, where he introduced himself with the Paganini concerto with his own cadenza, achieving, according to the notice in the *Signale*, a veritable triumph, and in the andante from the 4th concerto by Mozart, and a capriccio by Fiorillo, which followed, he proved that he possessed "not only a phenomenal technique, but also a big tone and noble warmth of feeling." During 1888–1919 he was capellmeister at Bückeburg, where he re-organized the chapel, founded a school for orchestral players, which developed into the Conservatoire and an Oratorio society. He has received the title of professor, and lives since 1919 at Stadthagen, having appeared since then at many towns, as far as Odessa, both as virtuoso and as conductor. He composed for violin concert-pieces, a reverie, fantasia on Carinthian folk tunes, Roumanian rhapsody, and ballade with pianoforte; also a number of songs.

HANS WESSELY, b. Vienna, 1862; d. Innsbruck, Sept., 1926. He began to study the violin at the age of 9, continuing at the Vienna Conservatoire from 1873 to 1878 under Heissler and Hellmesberger and after that for three years as a private pupil of Grün, which created some ill-feeling on the part of Hellmesberger, but was an incentive to Wessely to do his best in justification of the change. In 1883 he made his debut as a soloist with great success and was praised even by the severe Hanslick. About this time he played the Brahms concerto to the composer, who was a customer of his father, a glover, and who with a twinkle in his eye remarked: "Can't you play me something more interesting than that?" The next three years he spent in Berlin, where he played at most of the important concerts, and after that he toured in Sweden with Benno Schönberger. In 1890 he came to London, where he made his debut at the Saturday Crystal Palace concerts under Manns, and a gentleman who had heard him play brought him to the notice of the Prince of Wales (afterwards King Edward), who a few months later commanded him, through Sir Arthur Sullivan, to play at Marlborough House. In the same year he succeeded Sainton—pending the arrival of Sauret—as teacher at the Royal Academy of Music, and remained at that Academy until, in 1900, he formed a permanent quartet with Spencer Dyke, E. Tomlinson and Patterson Parker, which became very popular and gave regular concerts in London. Both as soloist and a teacher Wessely stood in high esteem. At the age of 21 he gave two orchestral concerts in Vienna where, in consequence of his success, he was engaged to play the 7th concerto by Spohr at the Philharmonic Society under Richter, and afterwards he toured in Europe. With a brilliant technique and powerful tone he combined the qualities of a serious and thoughtful artist. He was the fortunate possessor of a Stradivari violin of the best period.

MARIE SOLDAT-ROEGER, b. Graz, Mar. 25, 1864. At an early age she received pianoforte and organ lessons from her father, an organist, and in her eighth year became a violin pupil of Edward Pleiner. She had already occasionally taken her father's place at the organ, when at the age of 10 she played "Vieuxtemps Phantasie-Caprice" at a concert of the Steier Musical Union, and at 13 she played Bruch's G minor Concerto, when she was touring in Austria. Soon afterwards, her father died, and the poor circumstances of the family compelled her to earn her daily bread. In 1878 Pleiner also died and her violin was neglected for a time. In that year she heard Joachim at Graz, and his playing aroused in her such enthusiasm that she sought his advice as to her career and in consequence she placed herself under Spohr's pupil, A. Pott, at Graz. In 1879 she went on tour again in Austria, and in Pörtschach she made the acquaintance of Brahms, who accompanied at her concert Mme Dustmann in some of his own songs, and was so much impressed by Marie's playing that, learning of her desire to become a pupil of Joachim, he recommended her personally to that master. After hearing her play the Mendelssohn Concerto, Joachim accepted her as a pupil and she studied under him from 1879 till 1882 at the Berlin High School of Music, which she left after gaining the Mendelssohn Prize, but after that she still took private lessons from Joachim. From that time onwards she toured extensively in most European countries. In 1885, at a concert conducted by Hans Richter, she played the Brahms Concerto, the rendering of which, as well as that of the Beethoven Concerto, places her among the foremost women violinists. Brahms gave her somewhat of a shock on the above-mentioned occasion, when he insisted on making some alterations in the Cadenza of his concerto on the day before the concert. She acquitted herself, however, so well of her task that she obtained a brilliant success and Brahms presented her with a fan and an edition de luxe of his Concerto. She often used to play his latest compositions with him at his house. She was also a great favourite of Mme Schumann, whose guest she was whenever she visited Frankfort. She was an excellent chamber-music player and appeared frequently at the London Popular Concerts at the old St. James's Hall, where she always found an enthusiastic audience. While she was studying in Berlin she formed a quartet with Agnes Tschetchulin, Gabrielle Roy, and Lucie Campbell, which acquired a high reputation and which was chosen to appear at the Beethoven Festival at Bonn, by the side of the Joachim quartet. An interesting account of her career is given by Mrs. B. Henson in *The Strad*, vol. xx, p. 444 (1910). In 1889 she married the Viennese lawyer Roeger, since when she appears under the double name of Soldat-Roeger. Without in any way neglecting the technical part of her art she stresses the musical side. Her playing is distinguished by great virility.

MARIANNE EISSLER, b. Brünn, Moravia, Nov. 18, 1865. A pupil of Hessler and a violinist of merit who often played with great success, in the latter decades of the 19th century, in London, together with her sister Clara, an excellent harpist. The two sisters were favourites at the English Court.

GABRIELE WIETROWETZ, b. Laibach, Austria, Jan. 13, 1866. Entered the violin school of the Graz Musical Union, where she was at first a pupil of A. Geyer and in the higher class of Concertmeister F. Casper. At the end of her studies she gained the 1st prize and Count Aichelburg, one of the directors of the Musical Union, presented her with a valuable violin, while the board of directors granted her a scholarship which enabled her, in the autumn of 1882, to go to Berlin, where she entered the High School of Music and studied under Em. Wirth and Joachim. At the end of the first year she gained the Mendelssohn Prize for violin playing, which, at the end of the third year, she also carried off for the second time. Her first important public appearance was at the St. Cecilia's festival at Münster, Westphalia, where she played the Brahms Concerto with great success. She then toured in Switzerland, Sweden and Norway. In 1892 she made her debut in London at the Crystal Palace and was afterwards often heard at the Popular and Philharmonic concerts where her broad, masterly style and excellent technique were admired. During 1902–11 she was a teacher at the Berlin High school and went to live at Charlottenburg, where she was still living in 1920.

RUDOLF FITZNER, b. Ernstbrunn, Lower Austria, May 4, 1868. Studied the violin under Grün at the Vienna Conservatoire, 1882–7. After that he was a violinist in various orchestras, eventually as concertmeister; but in 1894 he formed a permanent quartet which was highly successful and has since been touring all over Europe as well as in Russia and Egypt. Since 1911 he has been chamber virtuoso of the King of Roumania. His permanent home is in Vienna.

LOUIS (LUIGI) VON KUNITS, b. Vienna, 1870. Violin pupil of J. Kral; J. M. Grün and O. Ševčik; composition of Bruckner; musical history of Hanslick; he also studied law and philosophy. During 1893–6 at Chicago; 1897 concertmeister in the symphony orchestra and teacher at the Conservatoire at Pittsburg. Afterwards he toured for two years as soloist in Europe, and became teacher at the Canadian Music Academy of Toronto in 1912. Contributed instructive articles to the *Canadian Journal of Music* and became conductor of the Symphony orchestra and leader of a string quartet. In 1926 Toronto University bestowed upon him the honorary degree of Mus. Doc. He has composed some works for chamber music.

FRITZ KREISLER, b. Vienna, Feb. 2, 1875. Being the son of a very musical doctor, he heard good chamber music from earliest childhood. At the age of 4 he began to study the violin under Concertmeister Jacques Auber of the Ring Theatre, and at 7 he became the pupil of Hellmesberger at the Conservatoire, which he left after gaining the 1st prize in 1885. He then studied for two more years under Massart at the Paris Conservatoire, where he again carried off the 1st prize among 42 competitors. He then went on tour in America with the pianist Moritz Rosenthal. After that he returned to Vienna to complete his general education, then he served his year in the army, at the end of which he passed his officer's examination and became an officer in the Reserve. At times he wavered in the choice of his career between that of a medical man, an officer or a musician, which however was soon decided in favour of the last. He made his home in Berlin and thence he toured with ever-increasing success in Europe and America. During the Great War he served as an officer in the Austrian army and was wounded. Fortunately his arms and hands were not affected and soon after the war, when he had quite recovered, he began touring again, and it was recognized that his technique was, if anything, greater than before, while his understanding of the works of the great masters became even greater and more matured. His tone is full and round and of exquisite quality, and the technique of both bow and the left hand place him in the front rank of virtuosos, but as an artist very few come near him. In the noble breadth and deep understanding of the works of the masters he occupies the place that once was filled by Joachim, although he has so far not occupied himself to any particular extent with chamber music, for which his solo playing hardly leaves him time. He has written a considerable number of solo pieces, some of which have become universal favourites. He has also made arrangements of and ed. a large number of mostly 18th-century compositions, which in many cases had become quite unknown. During 1915–19 he toured America. In the latter year he returned to Europe and has since divided his time between Europe and America. Apart from his pieces and arrangements for violin he wrote a string quartet in A minor, an operetta "Apple Blossom" (New York, 1919), and "Four Weeks in the Trenches: The War Book of a Violinist" (1918).

ADOLF REBNER, b. Vienna, Nov. 21, 1876. A pupil of Grün at the Vienna Conservatoire, where he gained the 1st prizes in 1891; then studied under Marsick at the Paris Conservatoire. Since 1896 he has lived at Frankfort a/M., where he was for several years first concertmeister at the Opera, and leader of the Museum's Quartet. He also belonged for ten years to a trio with Prof. Friedberg and Joh. Hegar. In 1906 he succeeded Heermann as violin teacher at the Hoch Conservatoire. In 1915 he formed a quartet with Davisson, Natterer and Hegar which has toured with eminent success in Germany, England, France and Spain. He has also made himself known as an excellent soloist all over Europe.

JOSEPH GUSTAV MRACZEK, b. Brünn, Mar. 12, 1878. Son and pupil of Franz M., cellist and music teacher, was a choirboy at Brünn churches, passed through the school of the Brünn Music Union and was, 1894–6, a pupil of Jos. Hellmesberger, Stocker, Grädener and Löwe at the Vienna Conservatoire. After touring for one year as violin virtuoso, he was concertmeister at the Brünn theatre, 1897–1902, and violin teacher at the school of the Brünn Music Union, 1898–1918. Since 1919 he has been at the head of a master class for composition at the Dresden Conservatoire, and 1919 to 1924 also conductor of the Dresden Philharmonic orchestra.

*Elliott & Fry, Ltd.*

*Wilma Norman Neruda*

LADY HALLE
(Mme. Norman Neruda)

In 1916 he was awarded the title of Professor by the Austrian Government. He has composed some pieces for violin and pianoforte, also a pianoforte quintet and a string quartet, but his more important work lies in his operas and orchestral compositions.

ROBERT POLLAK, b. Vienna, Jan. 18, 1880. A pupil of Hans Sitt at the Leipzig Conservatoire. Studied for some time under Carl Flesch and went afterwards to Geneva, where he finished his studies 1903–5 under Marteau and Carl Flesch. From 1906 to 1914 he was teacher of violin concurrently at the Conservatoires of Geneva and, 1912–14, of Lausanne and fulfilled many concert engagements in many towns on the European continent as well as in America. Just before the outbreak of the War in 1914 he had gone to Russia where, as a prisoner of war, he was sent first to Astrakhan, then to Saratov. After the outbreak of the Revolution he was allowed to go to Moscow, where he gave a concert which caused such enthusiasm that he was engaged as professor for the violin at the Moscow Conservatoire, a position he held until 1919, when he felt the political and social conditions becoming so intolerable that he returned to Vienna, and there, in the autumn of that year, he gave a concert with such success that he was appointed Ondricek's successor at the Neue Wiener Conservatorium. In 1924 he became leader of the Vienna Buxbaum quartet; in Oct., 1926, he became professor of the master class of the San Francisco Conservatoire and leader of the Californian string quartet. He composed a one-act opera.

ERICA MORINI, b. Trieste, Austria, 1905. Her mother is Austrian, her father also, though of Italian extraction. She received her first violin lessons from her father and afterwards she studied successively under Rosa Hochmann, Jacob Grün, and finally for several years under Ševčik at Prague, passing through his master class at the age of 9. As she received her education at Vienna she prefers to be called Viennese. At the age of 11 she appeared with uncommon success at the Gewandhaus, Leipzig, under Nikisch, and on more than one occasion she played at the Beethoven Festival in Vienna, an unusual honour for one so young. The unsettled conditions in Europe after the War caused her to visit America where, during four years, she gave recitals and played with most of the leading symphony orchestras. In Jan., 1924, she made her debut at a Sunday concert at the Albert Hall, London, where she made a very favourable impression which was fully confirmed when she appeared again at that Hall in 1925. She has since toured with unabated success practically all over Europe. Fräulein Morini is the fortunate owner of a fine Stradivari of 1727.

WÖLFI (WÖLFI SCHNEIDERHAHN), b. in Austria, 1915. A pupil of Ševčik and Professor Winkler of Vienna. After finishing his studies he toured with great success all over Europe and made his debut in London at a private concert under the auspices of the Austrian Minister. Soon afterwards he gave a concert at the Albert Hall with Maria Jeritza and met with a most enthusiastic reception, which was repeated on his subsequent appearances. He forms another addition to the lengthening list of wonderful virtuosos proceeding from the school of the Bohemian Wizard. He is however not mere virtuoso, but his interpretative powers are also praised. He is also said to be a keen student of the liberal arts, especially mathematics, and hopes to matriculate at the age of 18.

JULIUS GRUNEWALD. A pupil of M. Mildner, Prague.

MARGARETE KOLBE. A pupil of Ševčik and member of the Vienna ladies' quartet.

FRITZ SEDLAK. An excellent contemporary violinist, living in Vienna, where he has formed a permanent quartet with V. Borri, G. Gruber, and W. Winkler, which has won for itself golden opinions. In the autumn of 1927 they gave a series of eight concerts devoted to the chamber-music works by Schubert, in conjunction with other distinguished artists. The performances were marked by great delicacy and intelligence of phrasing and a beautiful quality and balance of tone.

# CHAPTER 47

## *Belgium*

BELGIUM did not produce any violinists of outstanding merit until de Bériot, who may be looked upon as the founder of the Belgian school of violin-playing, and who was epoch-making in his treatment of the instrument. His compositions, without having any claim to profundity or lasting value, show a natural flow of pleasing melody, and elegance of form. His studies are among the best that have been written for the instrument, and as a teacher, especially in the art of bowing, he made Brussels, together with Paris, the centre for the art of violin-playing, especially with regard to the lighter kinds of bowing, a position which it held throughout the greater part of the 19th century. In 1813 the Civic School of Music was established, which in 1824 became the Royal Conservatoire, at which de Bériot trained a large number of eminent pupils, foremost among whom stood Vieuxtemps who followed his master at the Conservatoire, at which later on C. Thomson and E. Ysaÿe shone as particular stars among teachers. Through Thomson the Liège Conservatoire, founded in 1827 and reorganized in 1832, had also become an important school for violin-playing, and its reputation was still further consolidated by his successor, Ovide Musin.

JEAN BAPTISTE TOLBEQUE, b. Hanzinne, Belgium, Apr. 17, 1797; d. Paris, Oct. 23, 1869. A pupil of Kreutzer for violin and Reicha for composition. During 1820 to 1825 he was violinist at the Italian Opera and after that he became a successful conductor of and composer for dance music orchestras and also played the viola at the Conservatoire concerts.

AUGUSTE JOSEPH TOLBEQUE, b. Hanzinne, Feb. 28, 1801; d. Paris, May 27, 1869. As his brother Jean Baptiste, a pupil

131

of Kreutzer. He was a good solo violinist and also a member of the Grand Opera orchestra, and that of the Conservatoire concerts, and afterwards of the Royal Opera, London.

CHARLES JOSEPH TOLBEQUE, b. Paris, May 27, 1806; d. there, Dec. 29, 1835. The youngest of the three brothers, and also a pupil of Kreutzer. He became conductor at the Théâtre des Variétés and, as his brothers, played also at the Conservatoire concerts. He wrote also some successful music for the above theatre.

ANDRÉ ROBBERECHTS, b. Brussels, Dec. 13, 1797; d. Paris, May 23, 1860. He commenced the study of the violin under van der Planken, an excellent teacher of Brussels. At the beginning of 1814 he entered the Paris Conservatoire and on Dec. 29 of that year gained the accessist for violin. But on the entry of the Allied armies a few months later, the Conservatoire was closed, and he obtained private lessons from Baillot, afterwards returning to Brussels. There he was allowed to play to Viotti, then on a visit to that town, who was so pleased with the young artist's playing that he accepted him as a pupil. For several years Robberechts studied under that great master and acquired that perfect technique and sound musicianship which distinguished his playing and enabled him to become one of the best teachers of his time, and de Beriot, his most distinguished pupil, always gratefully acknowledged the debt he owed him in that respect. In 1820 Robberechts returned to Brussels, where he became 1st solo violinist to King Guillaume with 1,500 florins per annum. The events of 1830 deprived him of that position and he went to Paris, where he remained to the end, with the exception of some concert tours in the French provinces. His numerous compositions for the violin are of no particular value.

LAMBERT JOSEPH MEERTS, b. Brussels, Jan. 6, 1800; d. there, May 12, 1863. Intended for a commercial career, he studied the violin at first as amateur, but later on altered circumstances compelled him to turn it to profitable account, and consequently he became at the age of 14 repetitor and 1st violinist at the Antwerp theatre, studying at the same time the violin under Fritzeri; afterwards he went to Paris and became a pupil of van der Planken, Lafont, Habeneck and Baillot. In 1828 he became violinist in the Brussels Town Orchestra, where he was appointed solo violinist in 1832; in 1833 he studied composition and in 1835 he became professor for the violin at the Brussels Conservatoire. As a teacher he ranked almost on a footing of equality with de Bériot. He wrote a method for the violin and of his numerous studies many are still in use, several books of them have been repub. by Augener, Ltd., London.

FRANÇOIS JEAN BAPTISTE SEGHERS, b. Brussels, Jan. 17, 1801; d. Margency, near Paris, Feb. 2, 1881. A pupil of Concert-meister Gensse at Brussels and afterwards of Baillot at the Paris Conservatoire. He was a co-founder of the Conservatoire concerts, and founder of the society Ste Cécile, where he arranged and conducted excellent performances of orchestral and choral works from 1848 to 1854, after which he retired into private life, and the society soon ceased to exist.

JOSEPH GHYS, b. Gand, 1801; d. St. Petersburg, Aug. 22, 1848. A pupil of Lafont. At the age of 20 he made some successful tours as violin virtuoso, afterwards settling as teacher at Amiens, and later on at Nantes. In 1832 he resumed his concert tours, first in France, 1835 in Belgium together with Servais, afterwards in England, and 1837 in Germany and Austria. In 1844 he went to Russia and in 1848 he succumbed to an attack of the cholera at St. Petersburg. He composed a concerto, studies and drawing-room pieces for the violin; more valuable are his carefully bowed and fingered editions of the works of great masters. He is now best known by his arrangement of the so-called "Air de Louis XIII" which in reality is an air from Baltazarini's Ballet Comic of 1581 (*see* i, p. 45). His son, HENRI GHYS, lived in Paris as violinist and composer.

CHARLES AUGUST DE BÉRIOT, b. Louvain, Feb. 20, 1802; d. Brussels, Apr. 8, 1870. Born of an old Belgian noble family, he showed early talent for music. He was attracted by the methods adopted in teaching French and literature of Jacotot, a French humanist, of Louvain, whose procedure was to make the pupil independent from the teacher by constant suggestion, and by implanting self-control raise him to intellectual emancipation and self-reliance. These became Bériot's guiding principles throughout his life. His first musical tuition he received from Tiby, a local musician who was his guardian, and his progress was so rapid that in his ninth year he played a concerto by Viotti in public (Baker). In 1821 he went to Paris and played to Viotti, who told him: "You have a good style, try to perfect it, listen to all men of talent and imitate none." He entered the Conservatoire to study under Baillot, but left it again after a few months as he was afraid that the influence of his master would destroy the individuality of his style. For some time, however, he studied under Robberechts, a pupil of Viotti, after which he continued his studies in retirement and then went to England, where he met with great success. He played at a Philharmonic concert in 1826, also at a Norwich and several other provincial festivals. Returning to Brussels, King William nominated him chamber virtuoso with a pension of 2,000 guilders, both of which he lost through the Revolution of 1830. He went on tour in Germany, Italy, France and England, this time with Marie Malibran-Garcia, whose beautiful singing he took for a model, and to that he owed to a great extent the beauty of his style. He married her in or about 1832, but she died in 1836 through a riding accident. De Bériot, who was deeply devoted to her, was thrown in a state of apathy, from which he succeeded in rousing himself by a supreme effort of his will power, after a considerable time. In 1840 he started on his last concert tour through Germany to Vienna. He succeeded Baillot as professor at the Paris Conservatoire in 1842, but in 1843 he exchanged that position for one of first professor of violin at the Brussels Conservatoire. Nerve trouble compelled him to resign from the latter in 1852, and in 1858 he had the misfortune to become not only blind but also paralysed in his left arm. He bore his misfortune with great fortitude, and devoted himself to composition, producing, in collaboration with G. A. Osborne, Thalberg, Benedikt and others, a considerable number of violin pieces of various kinds, which though lacking in deeper thought are refined in character. They show a natural flow of melody and his inventive genius in the great variety of his passage work, which is most effectively written for the violin and hence very grateful for the player, apart from its pedagogic value. De Bériot was the father of the Belgian school and exercised also a considerable influence upon the French school. Not representing any one particular school, he synthesized the achievements of all, and carried the result still further on modern lines. His tone was not powerful but of great beauty and sweetness, his technique both of the left hand and the bow had few rivals, his intonation was faultless, and his playing distinguished by grace and elegance. He composed 10 violin concertos, many solos, airs-variés, 6 books of studies, 49 duos brilliants for pianoforte and violin, 4 pianoforte trios, and a tutor in 3 parts. His most distinguished pupils were Vieuxtemps and Prume. His son and only child, also CHARLES AUGUST, was a good pianist and violinist who composed some salon pieces.

CHARLES WAROT, b. Dunkirk, Nov. 14, 1804; d. Brussels, July 29, 1836. A brother of the violoncellist CONST. N. A. WAROT. Charles was a pupil of his father and the blind violinist Fridzeri. He appeared for some time successfully in various towns as a soloist, but soon devoted himself entirely to composition, his first opera being performed at Antwerp in 1829 and well received. Several more followed; he also wrote a number of works for the church.

JOSEPH TERBY, b. Louvain, July 4, 1808; d. there, May 19, 1879. Son of Jos. Terby. He was a pupil of Robberechts in Paris and on his return to Belgium he received the title of violinist to the King of the Netherlands. He succeeded his father as capellmeister at Louvain and left an important collection of instruments and valuable music MS.

ANTOINE BESSEMUS, b. Antwerp, Apr. 6, 1809; d. there, Oct. 19, 1868. During 1826–9 he studied under Baillot at the Paris Conservatoire; then he was for some time violinist at the Opéra Italienne, after which he toured successfully in the Netherlands, Italy, England and Germany, eventually returning to Paris, where he gave successful chamber-music concerts. From 1847 to 1852 he was director of the Société Royale d'Harmonie at Antwerp. He composed fantasias and other pieces, 12 grandes études, 12 grandes duos de concert for violin, string quartets, orchestral works, church music, etc.

LAMBERT JOSEPH MASSART, b. Liège, July 19, 1811; d. Paris, Feb. 13, 1892. Received his first violin lessons from an amateur at Liège, a Mr. Delaven, who procured for him a scholarship from King William I of the Netherlands, which, with an additional subsidy from the town of Liège, enabled him to study as a private pupil under R. Kreutzer in Paris, as Cherubini (so it is said) would not admit foreigners to the Conservatoire. Massart became an eminent virtuoso and appeared as such with great success, but a certain degree of nervousness prevented his following the career of a soloist and he devoted himself to teaching, in which he rose to great heights, and in 1843 he was appointed as teacher at the Paris Conservatoire, which had refused him as a pupil. He counts among his numerous pupils many who rose to prominence, foremost among them being Lotto, Wieniawsky, Sarasate, Teresina Tua, Marsick, Fritz Kreisler and others. He was an admirable quartet player and together with his wife, an excellent pianist, he gave delightful chamber-music concerts. He also composed some solo pieces for the violin. He retired in 1890.

JEAN BAPTISTE SINGELÉE, b. Brussels, Sept. 25, 1812; d. Ostend, Sept. 29, 1875. A pupil of Wéry at the Brussels Conservatoire from 1828. He toured in France with his daughter LOUISE SINGELÉE, a pupil of his, and he was for some time solo violinist and conductor in Paris and at Marseille. His daughter became celebrated as an operatic singer. In 1839 he succeeded Meerts as solo violinist in the Brussels orchestra, and in 1852 he became conductor of the orchestra at Gand. He composed 144 works for violin, including 2 concertos, numerous operatic fantasias, which were very popular among amateurs during the latter half of the 19th century. His brother, CHARLES SINGELÉE, b. 1809, d. Brussels, Aug., 1867, was also a violinist of distinction.

FRANÇOIS TERBY, b. Louvain, 1813; still living there ca. 1883. Son of the elder Joseph Terby; he became teacher of the violin at the Music Academy of Louvain, and wrote compositions for violin (Brussels, Schott).

ALEXANDRE JOSEPH MONTAGNEY D' ARTÔT, b. Brussels, Jan. 25, 1815; d. Ville d'Avray, near Paris, July 20, 1845. Pupil of his father, who, although himself a horn player, taught him the violin, and he progressed so rapidly that before long he played successfully a concerto by Viotti at the theatre. Then he became a pupil of Snel, who after some time advised him

*Petit, Paris.*

EDOUARD LALO

HUBERT LÉONARD

CÉSAR THOMSON

LOUIS VAN WAEFELGHEM, seated, and
GEORGE SAINT-GEORGE
From a photograph taken by the latter.

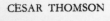

*t & Fry, Ltd.*

HENRI VIEUXTEMPS
From an engraving in the possession of Messrs. W. E. Hill & Sons.

EUGÈNE YSAŸE

to go to Paris. In 1824 he entered the Paris Conservatoire as a pupil of Rodolphe and August Kreutzer, and before he finished his studies at the age of 12 he was twice awarded the prize at the concours. After a passing visit to Brussels he went to London, where he created quite a sensation. Then he returned to Paris, where he played for some time as a soloist and in some orchestras, and from there went on tour in the South of France, Belgium, England, Holland, Germany, Russia and Italy. In 1843 he visited America, but on his return he developed a pulmonary disease which ended fatally about two years later. According to Fétis his tone was not big, but he had a brilliant technique and graceful style, which is reflected in his compositions, which are of the drawing-room type.

FRANÇOIS HUBERT PRUME, b. Stavelot, near Liège, June 3, 1816; d. there, July 14, 1849. Showed early talent for the violin, which he studied first at the Liège Conservatoire (1827) and afterwards under Habeneck at the Paris Conservatoire. In 1833 he was appointed teacher at the Liège Conservatoire. In 1839 he toured successfully in Germany, where the Duke of Gotha bestowed upon him the title of concertmeister. On his return to Liège he resumed his duties at the Conservatoire, but not long after he developed eye trouble, which led to complete blindness. He had to relinquish his position and retired to Stavelot, where he gradually fell a prey to melancholy, which destroyed his vitality and led to his early death. His playing was smooth and elegant but inclined to weakly sentimentality, which is also expressed in his once very popular "Mélancolie" for violin and orchestra, op. 1. He also composed a book of studies, op. 2, and 2 concert pieces. One of his foremost pupils was his nephew, F. H. Jehin-Prume, who surpassed him in virtuosity. He formed a famous trio with de Konski and Monsigny, and toured with Patti, Jenny Lind, Rubinstein, etc. (*See also* ii, 142.)

HUBERT LÉONARD, b. Bellaire, Belgium, Apr. 7, 1819; d. Paris, May 6, 1890. He began to study the violin at the age of 9 under Rouma, a violinist at Liège, who took a fatherly interest in him. At the age of 16 he found a patron in the wife of a rich merchant at Brussels who enabled him to study in Paris, where in 1836 he entered the Conservatoire as a

pupil of Habeneck. At the same time he became a violinist
at the Théâtre des Variétés; afterwards he went to the Opéra-
Comique and then to the Grand Opera. In 1839 he left
the Conservatoire, but remained in Paris until 1844, when
he went on a concert tour which brought him first to Liège
and then to Leipzig, where Mendelssohn took a kindly interest
in him and gave him some good advice with regard to composition. Meanwhile he had, on Apr. 4, played at the
Leipzig theatre, where his variations on a theme by Haydn
were much applauded and his perfect technique, sympathetic
tone and elegant phrasing and brilliant staccato were greatly
admired. In 1845 he played with renewed success at the
great Beethoven festival at Bonn, and in 1846 at Dresden,
Berlin and the Rhenish Music festival at Aix-la-Chapelle,
where among other works he played a concerto of his own
composition. In 1847 he visited Sweden and returned via
Hamburg, where he gave two successful concerts. A visit
to Vienna in 1848 was cut short by the outbreak of the
Revolution. In the year 1852 he succeeded de Beriot, who
had retired on account of ill-health, as professor for violin
at the Brussels Conservatoire, where he worthily upheld the
traditions of that famous school. In 1851 he married Antonia
Sitcher de Mendi, a niece of Manuel Garcia and herself an
eminent singer. In the following winter they gave concerts
together at Paris which made them popular favourites. Afterwards they toured with unabated success in France, Holland,
Denmark, Sweden, Norway and Russia. In 1866 he relinquished his position at the Conservatoire on account of
ill-health and in the following year he settled in Paris, where
he still continued now and again to teach and to play in concerts. The list of his compositions is a very long one, but
most proved children of their time, including his studies and
his tutor. Still interesting are his editions of old violin compositions. He followed, on the whole, more serious lines
than the majority of the Franco-Belgian school. He was
also an ardent champion of the important modern composers and did much to introduce Brahms, César Franck and
others in Paris. Among his numerous pupils he counts many
now eminent artists, including Besekirski, Taborowski, Dan-
gremont, Marteau, Marsick, Musin, Nachéz, and César
Thomson.

JEAN NICHOLAS CÉLESTIN TINGRI, b. Verviers, Sept. 7, 1819. Studied the violin at the Paris Conservatoire from 1832 to 1837. After that he appeared as a soloist at many concerts and in 1844 to 1845 toured in the South of France and in Germany. After his return to Paris he gave matinées at which he produced quartets and quintets of his own composition, and eventually settled at Cambrai as teacher. In 1857 he appeared once more in Paris, where he played some of his own compositions in various concerts.

HENRI VIEUXTEMPS, b. Verviers, Feb. 20, 1820; d. Mustapha, Algiers, June 6, 1881. He was the son of a retired soldier who played some instruments and had taken up instrument-making. As an infant he showed delight in hearing his father play the violin, and at the age of 2 he spent hours in scraping on a toy fiddle. At $4\frac{1}{2}$ years he could read music and an enthusiastic amateur placed him under Lecloux, a good violinist. At the age of 6 he played with great success Rode's 5th concerto and variations by Fontaine with orchestra at a public concert. In 1827 he went on a tour through Belgium and Holland in the company of his father and his master. At Brussels he met with de Bériot, who was so fascinated by his playing that he taught him gratuitously for some time, and made him acquainted with the works of the great masters of the violin. In 1828 he accompanied de Bériot to Paris, where he played in concerts of his master who procured for him also an annuity from King William, which he lost however at the outbreak of the Revolution. In 1833 he went on his first, very successful, concert tour, visiting the principal German towns, and going on to Vienna, where for some time he studied composition under Simon Sechter, and afterwards he met with Molique at Stuttgart, who was not without influence on his style and technique. In December, 1834, he went to Paris without finding a chance to appear in public, and he therefore went on to London, but without meeting with the desired success. In the summer of 1835 he went to Paris to study composition under Reicha, whose methods were less profound than expeditious; but Vieuxtemps did not consider the strict counterpoint of much use for his purpose. Soon afterwards he wrote his first compositions, which he played on a tour in Holland in 1836, whence he paid a second visit to Vienna, where he had them pub. In 1838 he appeared

with great success at the theatre and at the Philanthropic
Society's concert at the church of St. Augustine's in fantasias
and parts of concertos which contained some happy ideas but
were lacking in form.   Immediately after these concerts he
went to Russia, giving concerts at Leipzig, Dresden, Prague
and Berlin on the way.   Attacked by illness, he was delayed
for two months at a small Russian town.   In St. Petersburg
he met with great success and wrote a new concerto which
so far surpassed his previous compositions that evil tongues
in Paris and Brussels suggested it was not his own work,
but these ill-natured remarks were completely confounded by
his subsequent creations.   Back in Brussels, he played his
new concerto and a fantasia on July 7, 1840, at a concert
for the members of the theatre orchestra conducted by Fétis,
and met with an enthusiastic reception, which was surpassed
even by the outbursts that greeted him in the following
August at Antwerp when he played at the unveiling of the
Rubens statue, on which occasion the Minister decorated him
with the Order of Leopold.   In the winter of that year he met
also with the most emphatic approval of the critical Paris audience, and then revisited Holland, Germany, paid a third visit to
Vienna, gave a number of concerts in Poland and returned to
Brussels in June, 1843.   At the end of that year he went to
America, where he remained for about two years, after which
he went to Russia, where in 1846 the Tsar appointed him his
solo violinist, and professor at the St. Petersburg Conservatoire in the hope that he would train talented pupils; but in
1852 Vieuxtemps left that position, forsaking his pension,
and started touring again.   In 1856 (Riemann: 1857) he
went to America with Thalberg.   It was said that the artistic
side of his playing suffered from the then prevailing artisan-
like conditions in American musical life, but when he
returned to Europe he continued to hold his position in the
front rank of violinists.   In 1870 he visited America for the
third time, in company with Christine Nilsson and Marie
Krebs.   The periods of rest between his tours, which extended
also to Turkey, he spent either in Paris or at his villa in
Drei-Eichenhain, Frankfort a/M.   From 1871 he carried on
the traditions of de Bériot as first professor of violin at the
Brussels Conservatoire.   In 1873 a stroke paralysed his left
side, which prevented him from playing.   Although he slowly

recovered, his career as a virtuoso was ended, yet he continued for a time to teach at the Conservatoire, hoping against hope for a final recovery, and in this hope he visited Algiers in 1881, where he died. A monument was erected in his memory at Verviers in 1898.

His wife, Josephine Eder, was a distinguished pianist, who accompanied him on all his tours until she died in 1868.

Of his numerous compositions, his "Fantaise Caprice" is perhaps the most valuable for modern concert use. (For list, *see* Riemann and Wasielewski.) Vieuxtemps was also an excellent viola player and possessed a fine instrument. He wrote for it a sonata and an elegy both with alternate violoncello part.

JOSEPH DUPONT, b. Liège, Aug. 21, 1821; d. there, Feb. 13, 1861. A pupil successively of Wanson and Prume at the Liège Conservatoire, where he progressed so rapidly that he was appointed there as teacher of the violin when he had barely reached the age of 17. He wrote also a few compositions for the violin, and 2 operas.

ALOYS KETTENUS, b. Verviers, Feb. 22, 1823; d. London, Oct. 3, 1896. Studied the violin and composition at the Liège Conservatoire, which he had to leave before his studies were finished. He returned to Verviers, where he continued to study without a master. In 1841 he became violinist at the Aix-la-Chapelle theatre and then toured as soloist in middle and south Germany. In 1845 he was appointed a concertmeister at Mannheim, where he made further studies in composition under Vincenz Lachner. In 1855 he settled in London. In Mannheim he was the teacher of Jean Becker, who always spoke of him with affection, and said that the best part of his technique he owed to that excellent master. An opera, "Stella," by Kettenus was performed at Brussels in 1862 without much success. He also composed concert pieces for violin and other instruments, and songs.

JACQUES DUPUIS, b. Liège, Oct. 21, 1830; d. there, June 20, 1870. A pupil of Prume for violin and Daussoigne-Méhul for composition; became violin teacher at the Liège Conservatoire in 1850. He toured successfully as virtuoso in Belgium, France, England and Germany. He composed violin concertos of merit, sonatas, etc.; only a few were pub.

JOSEPH MERTENS, b. Antwerp, Feb. 17, 1834. Belgian violinist and composer; was 1st violinist at the theatre and teacher at the Antwerp Conservatoire. He composed 8 operas in the Flemish language which were well received, an oratorio, romances for pianoforte and songs.

FRANTZ HENRY JÉHIN (Jéhin-Prume), b. Spaa, Apr.18, 1839; d. Montreal, Canada, May 29, 1899. Nephew and pupil of Prume, Bériot, Léonard, Vieuxtemps, Wieniawsky; after successful tours succeeded de Bériot as violinist to the King, 1862. After touring Europe and America he went to Montreal; then succeeded Vieuxtemps at Bruxelles Conservatoire, where Ysaÿe was among his pupils; returned to Montreal ca. 1893. Composed 2 concertos, and solos for violin, also vocal music.

LOUIS VAN WAEFELGHEM, b. Bruges, Jan. 13, 1840; d. Paris, June 19, 1908. A pupil of Meerts (violin) and Fétis (composition) at the Brussels Conservatoire, which he left in 1860 and appeared with success as soloist at Weimar and Dresden. There he met Lipinski, who became his friend and protector, and placed him as solo violinist at the Budapest Opera. In 1863 he went on tour again, but remained in Paris, where he devoted himself to the study of the viola and filled engagements in the orchestras of Pasdeloup and of the opera, acting also on various occasions as examiner and prize adjudicator for that instrument at the Paris Conservatoire. After the Franco-Prussian War he was induced to come to London for the opera season at Her Majesty's Theatre and the concerts of the Musical Union, where he played quartets with Joachim, Auer, Vieuxtemps, Sivori and Sarasate and henceforth returned regularly every season. He had meanwhile also made a close study of the viole d'amour and formed an ensemble with L. Diémer, harpsichord; L. Grillet, vielle; and J. Delsart, viol da gamba; the Société des Instruments Anciens; and on May 2, 1895, they made their debut at the Salle Pleyel, Paris. During the season of 1897 they gave several most successful concerts at the Salle Erard, London. Van Waefelghem was perhaps unequalled, certainly unsurpassed as viole d'amour player, for which instrument he wrote some effective solos and transcriptions of older pieces (Paris, Durand). He was a Chevalier of the Legion of Honour, of the Portuguese Order of Christ and the Belgian "Ordre de Leopold." The viole d'amour on which he usually played was one by Eberle, but he also had a particularly handsome one by Paolo Aletzie, dated 1720, which he acquired from Messrs. Hill & Sons. (For a more detailed account see *The Strad*, Nov., 1908.)

MARTIN PIERRE JOSEPH MARSICK, b. Jupille, near Liège, Mar. 9, 1848; d. Paris, Oct. 21, 1924. His father began to teach him music when he was 7 years old, and a year later he sent him to the Liège Conservatoire, where at the age of 10 he gained the first prize. Then he began to study the violin under Desiré Hynberg, and in 1864 he was awarded the large gold medal, a rare distinction. He was also an excellent pianist and organist. From 1865 to 1867 he studied at the Brussels Conservatoire under Léonard, at the expense of the Princess of Chimay. During 1868–9 he was a pupil of Massart at the Paris Conservatoire, and finally he studied, 1870–1, under Joachim at the Berlin High School, having received a scholarship from the Belgian Government. In 1873 he made his debut at the Concerts Populaires in Paris with the 4th concerto by Vieuxtemps who, being present, complimented him highly on his performance. After this he toured with great success in most European countries and established his fame as one of the foremost virtuosos. In 1892 he became professor of violin at the Paris Conservatoire. He composed 3 violin concertos and a number of effective solo pieces. With Rémy, van Waefelghem and Delsart he formed a quartet which acquired European fame.

OVIDE MUSIN, b. Nandrin, near Liège, Sept. 22, 1854; d. New York (?), at the beginning of 1930. Entered the Liège Conservatoire, where he studied under Hynberg, and after two years gained the 1st prize for violin-playing. In 1870 he became a pupil of Hubert Léonard, whom he followed to the Paris Conservatoire, where he gained the gold medal for solo and quartet playing, and in the following year he made his debut by taking the place of Léonard at a concert. In 1873 he began to tour, and in 1874 he formed the Quartet for Modern Music, more particularly with a view to popularize Brahms in Paris. During the following years he continued touring, until Mapleson induced him to come to London, in 1877, where he remained for five years. He visited London for the last time in 1888, when on May 6 he played a Concertstück by Leop. Damrosch, the orchestra being conducted by Walter Damrosch. He toured again round the world, returning to Liège in 1897, succeeding César Thomson as violin professor at the Conservatoire. In 1908 he went again to New York, where he established a school for violin-playing. He was a prolific composer of solos, etc., for the violin, and wrote also "The Belgian School of the Violin" (4 vols., 1916) and "My Memories" (1920).

CÉSAR THOMSON, b. Liège, Mar. 17, 1857. Received his first violin lessons from his father, a Scandinavian musician; at the age of 7 he became a pupil first of Jacques Dupuis, then of Léonard at the Liège Conservatoire, which he left in 1869, after gaining the gold medal. In 1873 he became chamber musician in Baron von Dervies's orchestra at Lugano, where he married in 1877. After touring for some years in Italy he became concertmeister in Bilse's orchestra, Berlin. In 1883 he became third teacher of the violin at the Liège Conservatoire, where finally he was first teacher till 1897, touring a great deal in between. In 1898 he settled at Brussels, where he formed a string quartet with T. Lamoureux, Vanhout and E. Jacobs, and became Ysaÿe's successor at the Conservatoire. In 1924 he went to Ithaca (U.S.A.) as teacher at the Conservatoire. He is one of the most brilliant representatives of the Belgian school of violin-playing, who combines with an extraordinary technique excellent musical taste and musicianship. He wrote a number of compositions for violin of a virtuoso character, studies, arrangements, and editions of old Italian violin music.

EUGÈNE YSAŸE, b. Liège, July 16, 1858; d. Brussels, May 13, 1931. He received his first violin lessons at the age of 5 from his father, a violinist and capellmeister. A little later he became a pupil of Rodolphe Massart for violin and of M. Dupuis for harmony, at the Liège Conservatoire, where he gained a 2nd prize with Ovide Musin in 1867. In 1873 he studied with Wieniawsky, and, 1876, Vieuxtemps, after hearing him play one of his concertos at Antwerp, obtained for him a subsidy from the Government for three years' further study. During that time he received many private lessons from Vieuxtemps, who not only held him in high esteem but also conceived a personal friendship for him, and when he was nearing his end at Algiers he sent a message to Ysaÿe to come

MORITZ MILDNER
From an Engraving presented by him to
his late pupil, George Saint-George.

ANTON BENNEWITZ
By kindness of Prof. O. E. Deutsch.

and play him some of his compositions, but alas! it was too late. In 1879 Ysaÿe played at Pauline Lucca's concerts at Aix-la-Chapelle and Cologne, where he made the acquaintance of Ferd. Hiller, who introduced him to Joachim. The latter, after hearing him play a Vieuxtemps concerto, is reported to have said: "I never heard the violin played before like that." Whichever way one takes this ambiguous remark, it shows that he was impressed with his originality. Through Hiller's influence he played the Mendelssohn concerto at a Gürzenich concert in Cologne in Oct., 1879, and afterwards he went to Frankfort, where he met J. Raff, and played with Mme Schumann. During 1880–1 he was conductor of the Bilse orchestra in Berlin, and after that he toured in Norway with Ole Bull's son as impresario. In 1883 he played at a Paris Conservatoire Concert under Colonne, in 1886–98 he was violin professor at the Brussels Conservatoire, and during that time he founded the Ysaÿe orchestral concerts, which he conducted as well as managed successfully from a business point of view. After that he toured again. In 1889 he made his London debut with the Beethoven concerto at a Philharmonic Concert, and in the autumn of that year he made his first appearance at the Popular Concerts. In 1894 he visited America for the first time, and toured there with great success, also on several subsequent occasions, but he refused the offer to succeed Seidl as conductor of the New York Philharmonic Society in 1898. In 1896 he gave three concerts (one with orchestra) in London, and one in 1899. In Mar., 1899, he played Bach's E major concerto at a Philharmonic Concert under Nikisch in Berlin, where an audience steeped in classical traditions was roused to enthusiasm by the poetry and dignity of his rendering. Soon after he played with equal success at Dresden. In Feb., 1900, he led quartets at the Popular Concerts in London and later on he played trios with Busoni and Hugo Becker in the Queen's Hall. In 1901 he brought his own quartet over from Brussels and introduced several modern chamber works, new to London audiences. In 1904 he gave two orchestral concerts, which his friend and pupil R. Ortmans conducted, and in Oct., 1909, he gave a strongly individual performance of the Brahms concerto. He also gave sonata recitals with the pianist, Raoul Pugno, for several years running. The War caused him to seek refuge in London for some years, but in 1918 he went to America as conductor of the Cincinnati orchestra. In 1922 he returned to Belgium in failing health, and in 1929 he had his right leg amputated, but made so wonderful a recovery, that he was able to take up the direction of his concerts in Brussels again. In Mar., 1931, his opera "Peter the Coalminer" was produced at Liège, but he was then too ill to be present. Ysaÿe is one of the outstanding figures in the history of the violin. He combined a marvellous technique with a rich and powerful tone, and the masterly handling of his bow served as a model for all young violinists. He overcame the greatest difficulties with that playful ease which marks the perfect virtuoso, and all was combined with an immense individuality and true artistic feeling. His taste was truly catholic, and while he was a remarkable interpretor of Bach, he brought out the sonata by Cés. Franck, which was written for him, the sonata by his countryman Guilleaume Lekeu, and many other works by modern composers. He had several valuable instruments, including a beautiful Stradivari of the latter period which was stolen while he was playing at the Opera House at St. Petersburg in 1908, and never recovered; but his favourite was a very perfect Guarnerius del Jesu, the gift of a pupil, a talented Dutch lady who afterwards became his sister-in-law.

ARMAND PARENT, b. Liège, Feb. 5, 1863. Studied the violin at the Liège Conservatoire, and during 1882–3 was concert-meister in Bilse's orchestra, Berlin. From 1883 to 1889 he was solo violinist in the Colonne orchestra in Paris; in 1890 he gave quartet soirées with P. Loiseau, Vieux and Fournier, where he brought forward chiefly the chamber-music works by Brahms and the young French school. He was also first professor of the higher violin class of the Schola Cantorum. He composed a violin sonata, pieces for violin, 2 quartets, a quintet and songs, and wrote several works for teaching purposes, including a "Méthode complète" for the violin, in 5 parts.

HENRI VERBRUGGHEN, b. Brussels, 18... Intended for the medical career, he studied nevertheless the violin from early boyhood with such success that he played with his first master at the "Cercle Artistique" at the age of 9. Not long after that, he appeared with great success in Paris, when Jos. Wieniawsky, the brother of Henri, persuaded his mother to let him study under Hubay at the Brussels Conservatoire, which he entered in 1886, but he still had to pursue his other studies. When Ysaÿe succeeded Hubay at the Conservatoire, Verbrugghen became a pupil of the latter, in whose house he lived also until 1889 when he carried off the 1st prize for violin and was declared by *La Gazette* to have been the most interesting among the 35 competitors. He remained two more years with Ysaÿe, whom he accompanied on his first visit to London where he remained for some months, afterwards touring in Belgium, France and Holland. In 1899 he played at a Berlin Philharmonic Concert, conducted on that occasion by Mr. (now Sir) Henry Wood. Afterwards he was, for one year, principal professor for violin at the Irish Academy of Music, Dublin; then leader and deputy conductor of the Scottish Orchestra, Glasgow, and 1904 leader of the Promenade Concerts, Queen's Hall, London. Some years ago he settled in the United States of America, where he is highly esteemed as soloist, leader and conductor.

JULIETTE FOLVILLE, b. Liège, Jan. 5, 1870. Received her first music lessons from her father, a barrister and music amateur; then studied the violin successively under Malherbe, O. Musin, and Cés. Thomson, and composition under Radoux at Liège, also pianoforte under Delaborde in Paris, and showed remarkable talent in all. From 1879 she appeared in public as violin virtuoso. During 1898–1914 she was teacher at the Liège Conservatoire. At the beginning of the War she settled at Bournemouth and appears still as soloist in England. She composed a violin concerto and pieces for violin, concertos and pieces for violoncello and for pianoforte; an opera, vocal compositions with orchestra; orchestral suites, symphonic poems, organ pieces, motets, etc.

MATHIEU CRICKBOOM, b. Hodimont, Liège, Mar. 2, 1871. During 1888–94 a member of the Ysaÿe quartet; 1894–6 leader of the quartet of the Société Nationale, Paris (director, Vinc. d'Indy). From 1896 to 1905, concertmeister of the Music Academy and the Philharmonic Society, Barcelona; 1910 teacher at Liège Conservatoire and 1919 do. at the Brussels Conservatoire. He has an excellent technique as well as poetical feeling. He has written several didactic works and composed for violin: a sonata, solo pieces, studies,

editions of works by older masters; chant élégiaque for violoncello and pianoforte; songs.

ALBERT JACQUES ZIMMER, b. Liège, Jan. 5, 1874. Studied the
violin first at the Conservatoire there, then at that of Brussels
under Ysaÿe. In 1896 he formed with Ghigo, Barsen (now
Piel) and Gaillard (now Doehard) a permanent quartet which
ranks with the best of its kind. In 1905 he founded a Bach
society, which, before the War, gave concerts at Brussels.
He was teacher at the Geneva Conservatoire until he succeeded
Cés. Thomson at the Brussels Conservatoire in 1924.

IRMA SETHE, b. Brussels, Apr. 28, 1876. Began to study the
violin at the age of 5 under Jokisch, and after three months she
was already able to play a Mozart sonata. Five years later she
made her public debut at Marchiennes, Belgium, with a de
Bériot concerto and Saint-Saëns' Rondo Capriccioso, and in the
following year she played at the Instrumentalverein, Aix-la-
Chapelle. Her success on both occasions was so great that
she received numerous offers of engagements, which her
mother wisely declined as a danger to the child's health.
While on summer holidays in Germany she met Wilhelmj,
who for two months gave her daily lessons which occupied the
whole of the mornings and which proved very fruitful. At the
end of the holidays Wilhelmj presented her with a violin.
She continued, however, her regular studies under Jokisch
until she was 14. On the advice of Ysaÿe she then entered
the Brussels Conservatoire, where after eight months she
gained the 1st prize in 1891, and continuing her studies for
three more years she gained not only other prizes, but also
frequently took over Ysaÿe's classes during his absence, as his
deputy. In 1894 she played together with Ysaÿe at a number
of concerts at Brussels, and afterwards toured with great
success in Germany. In 1895 she made her debut at the old
St. James's Hall, London, playing the Mendelssohn concerto,
and several movements from the Bach solo sonatas, and was
greeted with unbounded enthusiasm. Her unfailing technique, full and broad tone, and artistic intelligence placed her
at once among the foremost violinists of the time.

ÉMILE CHAUMONT, b. Liège, Mar. 29, 1878. Studied the
violin at first at the Liège Conservatoire, which he left in 1896

with a prize.    During 1896–8 he studied at the Berlin High School under Halir and Bruch (composition).    On his return he became concertmeister at the Ysaÿe concerts at Brussels and, since 1919, he is professor of the master class at the Conservatoire.    He has composed some solos; 36 progressive studies; an elementary tutor, editions of works of old masters, songs, etc.

EDOUARD DERU, b. Verviers, 187?; d. San Francisco, Mar. 27, 1928.    Entered the Verviers Conservatoire at a very early age and carried off several prizes.    In 1886, after the appointment of Ysaÿe as teacher at the Brussels Conservatoire, Deru became his first pupil and his close friend.    He gained the 1st prize with distinction after becoming solo violin at Ysaÿe's concerts.    Soon afterwards he was appointed solo violinist at the theatre de la Monnaie, where people often went, especially to hear him play a solo part, especially the Meditation from "Thais," which he always had to repeat.    About this time he also became solo violinist at the Kursaal at Ostend.    When King Albert ascended the throne, Deru became the violin teacher of Queen Elizabeth, on Ysaÿe's recommendation, and soon after he was appointed violinist to the Court, the first upon whom that honour was bestowed.    In 1906 he was the soloist at the Saint-Saëns' festival at Ostend, at the composer's own choice, who conducted in person.    He toured in Belgium, Holland and Germany.    In 1912 he gave concerts in Berlin and Cologne, and when the Germans entered Brussels, a German officer, who had heard and admired him and recognized him when he was vainly endeavouring to obtain a passport, helped him successfully to achieve his purpose.    He then went to London, where he remained for some years.    In Mar., 1915, he joined Ysaÿe in a memorable performance of Bach's double concerto at the Queen's Hall, London.    He had already visited America on the advice of Ysaÿe, soon after his marriage in 1902, and met with great success, especially in San Francisco and Los Angeles, but homesickness drove him back.    On his return he was appointed teacher at the Liège Conservatoire, where he remained for three or four years.    In later years he visited America again, and was about to return from San Francisco to celebrate his silver wedding in Belgium, when he had a fatal seizure.    After his death, the town of Verviers carried out in his memory his long-cherished plan to found a prize for violin-playing at the Verviers Conservatoire; it was competed for for the first time in Nov., 1928.

HENRIETTE SCHMIDT, b. Brussels, 18... The pupil of her father, then of Hubay and Ysaÿe at the Brussels Conservatoire. At the end of her studies she toured successfully on the Continent and ca. 1903 she made her debut in London with such gratifying results that she decided to make England her headquarters, while continuing her tours in various countries. In Nov., 1908, she gave a recital at the Bechstein Hall, when she played a sonata by Fauré and Poème by Chausson. She is particularly praised for breadth of style, almost masculine power, and thoughtful rendering of the works of early 18th-century masters.

GODEFROID DEVREESE, b. Courtrai, Jan. 22, 1893. Studied the violin under Thomson and Ysaÿe and composition under Gilson and Rasse at the Brussels Conservatoire. During 1919–24 he was conductor at the French Opera at Antwerp and Waux-Hall at Brussels. Since 1925 he has been violinist in the Concert-gebouw-orchestra at Amsterdam. He wrote sonatas for violin and pianoforte, and for violoncello and pianoforte; cantatas, orchestral works, ballets, and pianoforte pieces.

DESIRÉ DEFAUW. A contemporary Belgian violinist who gave a very successful concert with orchestra in London ca. 1907, and since the War has settled in London, where he has gained the reputation of an excellent chamber-music player.

## CHAPTER 48

## *Bohemia*

FROM the beginning of the 18th century Bohemia had already produced eminent violinists, as Benda, Stamitz, etc., but the field of their activity lay in Germany, although the great Bohemian nobles did much to encourage the cultivation of music in their country by maintaining private orchestras or at least a chamber-music ensemble. In the 19th century they took an important step further, by founding the Prague Conservatoire, which was opened on Mar. 30, 1811. Fr. Wm. Pixis brought to this the traditions of the Mannheim school and transmitted them, although in somewhat modified form, to his pupils. One of these, Mildner, succeeded him at the Conservatoire and distinguished himself as a teacher who gave to the Conservatoire another eminent teacher in the person of Bennewitz, who succeeded him in 1866, while a number of Mildner's other pupils acquired fame in foreign countries. Among his numerous pupils who came into prominence like Haliř, Ondřiček, three of the founders of the Bohemian quartet, etc., is O. Ševčik, who has revolutionized violin teaching and reached the pinnacle of that art, while in some respects carrying on, in uninterrupted line, the traditions of the Prague school which is the embodiment of musical art in Bohemia.

LEOPOLD JANSA, b. Wildenschwerdt, Bohemia, Mar. 23, 1795; d. Vienna, Jan. 24, 1875. His first master for singing, violin and pianoforte playing and organ was the local schoolmaster, Jahada; under his cousin Zizius he became a good organist, while during his time at the grammar school he perfected himself on the violin, and afterwards, when in 1817 he was sent to Vienna to study law, he appeared repeatedly as a solo violinist in public with great success. Encouraged by his countryman, the Court organist, Worzischek, he decided to devote himself entirely to music and studied composition under Em. Förster. He succeeded in establishing a reputation as virtuoso in spite of the difficulties which comparison with Böhm and Mayseder placed in his way.   In 1823 he became a chamber musician in the chapel of Count von Brunswick in Hungary; in 1824 he was appointed as Imperial chamber virtuoso in the Vienna Court chapel, and in 1834 as director of music and professor of violin at the University.   Before the death of Schuppanzigh he had already taken the latter's place in the famous quartet which he kept alive with various associates until 1849, when he was joined by Heissler, Durst and Schlesinger, and these quartet concerts formed the backbone of serious music in light-hearted, frivolous Vienna.   In 1849 Jansa went to London, where he was induced to play at a concert for the benefit of the Hungarian refugees which had been driven from their country by the Revolution.   This act of kindness not only cost him his dismissal from his posts, but he was also exiled and obliged to establish himself as virtuoso and teacher in London.   In 1867 he was pardoned, and in 1868 he returned to Vienna, where he met with a jubilant reception from the artists and the public, and was accorded a pension.   He retired to Salzburg, but after a short time returned again to Vienna and appeared once more in public in 1872.   He wrote violin concertos and concertinos, fantasias, rondos, variations, and solos, which on account of their excellent violinistic writing and pleasing melodiousness remained favourites for a long time, especially for teaching purposes.   He also composed string quartets, trios, and duets, as well as church music. His style was neat and sympathetic, his intonation pure, but his playing was more suave than grand.   He held his right arm rather high, which prevented complete freedom in the conduct of the bow.   Among his many pupils was Wilma Neruda, afterwards Lady Hallé.

JOHANN WENCESLAUS KALLIWODA, b. Prague, Mar. 21, 1800; d. Karlsruhe, Dec. 3 (Wki., Dec. 4), 1866.   He studied under Pixis for the violin and Dionys Weber for composition, at the Prague Conservatoire from 1810 to 1816, when he became a violinist in the Prague Municipal orchestra.   In 1822 he went on a successful concert tour, and in 1823 met at Munich with the Prince Fürstenberg, who engaged him as capell-meister of his chapel at Donaueschingen, which position he resigned in 1866 to retire into private life to Karlsruhe. His numerous concertos, solos, etc., for the violin, very popular during the 19th century, as well as symphonies, operas, chamber music, etc., are too much children of his time to be of lasting value. His style was graceful and pleasing, but lacking in power and grandeur.

KARL MARIA VON BOCKLET, b. Prague, 1801; d. Vienna, July 15, 1881. Studied the violin under Pixis, pianoforte under Zawora, and composition under Dionys Weber. In 1820 he was violinist at the Theater an der Wien, but afterwards devoted himself entirely to pianoforte playing, and was the pianist at various first performances of Schubert's works (*see* N. Flower, "Schubert"). Beethoven was also interested in him.

JOSEPH LABITZKI, b. Schönfeld, near Eger, Bohemia, July 4, 1802; d. Karlsbad, Aug. 19, 1881. His first teacher was Karl Veit, school- and choirmaster at Petschau, where his parents had removed, and from him he learned to play various instruments as well as singing and harmony. From his 12th year, when he lost his father, he had to earn his own living, studying by himself at the same time and composing little pieces. In the summer of 1820 he became 1st violin in the Marienbad orchestra and in 1821 in that of Karlsbad. Soon after he formed an orchestra of his own and with this he visited, in 1822/23, Ratisbon, Nuremberg, Augsburg and Munich with such success that it encouraged him to extend his tours until 1835 also to other parts of Germany. Munich he visited repeatedly and was for a time also engaged by the Russian Ambassador there, Count Woronzov Daschkov, and on these occasions he studied composition under P. von Winter. His first dances were pub. there in 1827. He also paid repeated visits to Vienna, Prague, Stuttgart and on the outbreak of the Polish Revolution also Warsaw. In 1835 he became conductor of the Karlsbad orchestra. From that time onward he toured only occasionally with his orchestra; his visits to St. Petersburg in 1839 and to London in 1850 obtained most brilliant results, the latter being also the last. From that time he remained as a most popular dance composer and conductor entirely in Karlsbad, where in 1872 he celebrated his jubilee as conductor, and in 1874 that of his golden wedding. Apart from his very popular dances he has composed also string quartets, concertos, divertissements, variations, etc., for the violin and other instruments. Tony Labitzki, a daughter of Joseph, became an operatic singer and was for many years at the Frankfort opera, retiring in 1872.

AUGUST LABITZKI, b. Petschau, Oct. 22, 1832. Son of Joseph Labitzki. Studied first at the Prague Conservatoire and afterwards under Ferd. David (violin) and M. Hauptmann (composition) at the Leipzig Conservatoire. He toured successfully as violinist, became concertmeister in the Karlsbad orchestra in 1853 and afterwards succeeded his father as conductor there. He also composed dance music and solos for violin.

WILHELM LABITZKI, another son of Joseph, studied, like his brother, first at Prague then at Leipzig, and went as violinist to Toronto, Canada.

FRIEDRICH WENZEL BEZDĚK, b. Prague, Sept. 24, 1804. A pupil of Pixis at the Prague Conservatoire. In 1837 he founded the Philharmonic Society and conducted the Italian Opera at Trient; then he was professor at the Prague Conservatoire and conductor at the theatre there. From 1846 he was violinist at the Court Opera, Vienna. He composed string quartets, songs, and pianoforte pieces.

JOSEPH SLAWJK, b. Jinetz (Jince), near Pribram, Bohemia, Mar. 1, 1806 (Riemann: Mar. 26); d. Budapest, May 30, 1833. The son of a schoolmaster who taught him from his seventh year the violin, pianoforte, organ and the elements of music. Count Wrbna, whose attention had been drawn to the boy, granted him the means to visit the Prague Conservatoire as a pupil of Pixis. While still a pupil there he composed a violin concerto, variations, and a string quartet. In 1823 he became a member of the Prague theatre orchestra, and in Feb., 1825, he went to Vienna, where he made his debut with Schubert's Introduction and Polonaise at his concert. In 1828 he heard Paganini in Vienna, who made so great an impression on him that he decided to take him for his model, and the great master, who took an interest in him, gave him some instruction. After Paganini's departure he went to Paris to study under Baillot; but soon after, in 1829, he received his nomination as titular member of the Imperial

Chapel, which compelled him to return to Vienna, where in
1829 he was also appointed at the Imperial opera and for
several years he studied Paganini's style of playing. On
Apr. 28, 1833, he gave his last concert in Vienna intending
to go on a prolonged tour, but at Pesth he was seized with
typhus fever which terminated fatally on May 30. He composed a Grand Potpourri with quartet accompaniment, op. 1,
and a Fantasia (both Vienna, Diabelli), and 2 concertos, 1
double concerto for 2 violins, 4 airs with variations, a rondeau
and a string quartet which remained in MS. Slawjk was not
only a virtuoso of a high order, he possessed also a poetical
temperament which caused Schubert to compose for him his
Fantasia in C, op. 159, which he played at his concert at the
"Landhaussaal" on Jan. 20, 1828, with the pianist von
Bocklet, also a friend of Schubert. The Press was not favourably inclined either towards him or the piece (*see* O. E. Deutsch,
"F. Schubert," i, 450). While he was in Paris, Chopin
took a friendly interest in him and called him the second
Paganini.

JAN URBANEEK, b. Slanik, Bohemia, Jan. 31, 1809. An
eminent Bohemian violinist, who studied at the Prague
Conservatoire under Pixis. He was concertmeister at the
Königstadt theatre in Berlin.

SIEGMUND KOLLESCHOWSKI, b. Prague, ca. 1809. Violinist
and church composer; lived at Prague as choirmaster of St.
Stephen's.

MORITZ MILDNER, b. Türmitz, Bohemia, Nov. 7, 1812; d.
Prague, Dec. 4, 1865. A pupil at the Prague Conservatoire
of Pixis, whom he succeeded in 1842 as teacher at that
institute. He was also concertmeister at the theatre. He
was one of the most eminent teachers of the time who counted
among his pupils Laub, J. Grunewald, Em. Wirth, Hrimaly,
Bennewitz, Rebicek, Skalitzky, Zajic. He never embarked
upon the virtuoso career and the true merit of this great artist
and teacher has never been rightly appreciated, except by
his pupils, on account of his unassuming personality and
retiring disposition.

JOSEPH SOKOL, b. Březno, near Jungbunzlau, Bohemia, Jan.
27, 1821; d. St. Petersburg, Aug. 9, 1858. The son of a
surgeon, who instructed him in violin-, pianoforte- and organ-

playing as well as in singing. On Count Kaunitz' recommendation he sent him to the Prague Conservatoire in 1831. While still a student he played at one of the Conservatoire concerts an Adagio and a Polonaise in the style of Mayseder, of his own composition with great success. In 1835 he composed an overture which he conducted himself and which was performed at the coronation of the Emperor Ferdinand, for which the Emperor presented him with a diamond ring. In 1837 his second overture was performed and this was followed by a rondo for the violin, a symphony, and an opera. In 1839 he was called to Vilna, where unfortunately he began to develop habits of intemperance which gradually became worse after he was, in 1841, engaged in St. Petersburg, first in the orchestra of Herrmann and then in that of Strauss. His failing prevented him from becoming an important instrumental composer, and cut short a promising career.

RAYMUND DREYSCHOCK, b. Zack, Bohemia (Riemann), Aug. 30, 1824; d. Stötteritz, near Leipzig, Feb. 6, 1869. He received his higher training under Pixis at Prague. He toured with his brother Alexander, the famous pianist, until 1850, when he became second concertmeister in the orchestra and teacher of the violin at the Conservatoire, Leipzig. A disease of the brain, for which he went to a sanatorium at Stötteritz, developed shortly before his death. His wife transferred her highly successful vocal academy to Berlin in 1870.

THEODOR PIXIS, b. Prague, Apr. 15, 1831; d. Cologne, Aug. 1, 1856. Son of Friedr. Wm. Pixis, who was his first teacher for the violin. In 1846 he went to Paris to continue his studies under Baillot. In 1850 he became concertmeister by the side of Hartmann in the Cologne orchestra, and professor at the Conservatoire. The writer remembers many musicians and amateurs in that town who spoke of his brilliant technique and elegant style, but consumption ended prematurely a promising career.

FERDINAND LAUB, b. Prague, Jan. 19, 1832; d. Gries, near Bozen, Mar. 17, 1875. Son of the musician Erasmus Laub, who was his first teacher. Before the age of 6 he was already able to play the popular Variations by de Bériot; in his ninth year he had toured already with great success in Bohemia, and in these tours he found a patron and protector in Count Protstatzi-Liechtenstein. After a concert which he gave in 1834 M. Mildner offered him free tuition, which offer young Laub turned to the best advantage under that eminent master at the Prague Conservatoire. About this time both Ernst and Berlioz heard him play and gave him every encouragement. The Grand Duke Stephan, who also heard him at that period, was so pleased with his playing that he presented him with a fine Amati violin and a letter of recommendation to Vienna. In 1847 he paid his first visit to that city where he gave a series of concerts which proved a great success both artistically and financially. After that he toured in South Germany and thence he went to Paris, where he found a friend in Berlioz. Next he returned to Vienna; in 1851 he went to London and in 1853 he succeeded Joachim as concertmeister and chamber musician at Weimar, but only two years later he accepted the post as teacher at the Stern Conservatoire in Berlin. In 1856 he became a chamber virtuoso and concertmeister in the Royal chapel there, and gave a series of chamber-music concerts every winter, where, from 1856 to 1862, the chamber works of the great masters of the past and present were performed in the greatest perfection, and especially the later quartets by Beethoven, which as yet were but little known. In 1864 he left Berlin to go on a prolonged tour through Belgium, Holland and South Germany with Carlotta Patti, Alfr. Jaëll and Kellermann (violoncellist). At the end of the tour he went to Vienna for a few months, and then he started on another tour to Russia, where in 1866 he was engaged as concertmeister of the Russian Music Society and 1st professor of violin at the Conservatoire in Moscow with frequent vacations which he employed by touring abroad. The Russian climate and mode of living, however, affected his health. He suffered from liver and kidney trouble, in 1874 he had to resign his position, and in Nov. he arrived in Karlsbad in a very low state of health, dropsy having developed through his other ailments. He hoped for a cure by the use of the waters and there was some improvement when on the advice of the doctors he went to seek a milder climate at Gries, near Bozen. There the improvement continued and he was already planning tours to Italy and to Paris when a relapse set in to which he succumbed. Laub had an extraordinary brilliant technique of fingers and bow. His tone was powerful and of great beauty, and above all his playing was soulful with a noble reserve and artistic appreciation of the works he performed. Like most great artists, however, he was subject to moods which sometimes adversely influenced his playing. Of a number of compositions only his Polonaise is still a favourite.

ANTON BENNEWITZ, b. Privrat, near Leitomischl, Bohemia, Mar. 26, 1833; d. Hirschberg, beginning of June, 1926. Studied the violin under Mildner and composition under J. H. Kittl at the Prague Conservatoire. After completing his studies he was for some time as 1st violinist at the Prague theatre, and toured in Austria, Germany, France and Belgium; then he became concertmeister at the Mozarteum at Salzburg, and later on he was in the same capacity at Stuttgart. In 1866 he succeeded Mildner as professor for violin at the Prague Conservatoire, of which he became the principal in 1882 and was pensioned in 1901, retiring into privacy first to Teplitz-Schönau, then to Hirschberg, near Leipa. He was famed as a teacher and counted among his pupils such names as Halir, Ondřiček, Zajic, Kopeski, as well as K. Hofmann, J. Suck and O. Nedbal, three members of the Bohemian quartet, etc., etc. Bennewitz had a beautiful and soulful tone, his playing was elegant and full of temperament. His wife was an excellent singer at the National theatre, Prague.

EMANUEL WIRTH, b. Luditz, Bohemia, Oct. 18, 1842; d. Berlin, Jan. 5, 1923. During 1854–61 pupil of Kittl and M. Mildner at the Prague Conservatoire; 1861–3 concertmeister in the Kur-orchestra at Baden-Baden; from 1864 concertmeister at the German opera, and the society concerts, teacher at the Conservatoire, and leader of permanent quartet at Rotterdam. In 1877 he took, at Joachim's request, Rappoldi's place in the former's quartet, which he occupied to the end, except in the winter of 1906/7, when, on account of eye-trouble, Klingler had to deputize for him; but at the last performance of the quartet on Apr. 6, 1907, Wirth was in his place again. He also gave regular trio soirées in Berlin with H. Barth and Hausmann. He was teacher of violin at the Berlin High School of Music until his retirement in 1910. He appeared as a soloist in many of the principal towns of Germany and Holland as well as in Vienna and in London.

ADALBERT HŘIMALY, b. Pilsen, 1842. The eldest of four sons of the cathedral organist; like his brothers, he received his musical training at the Prague Conservatoire and for some time formed with them the once famous Hřimaly quartet. Afterwards he became concertmeister at Gotenburg and then returned to Prague in a similar capacity. Next he was capellmeister at the German Landestheatre there, and after that, director of the Musical Union at Czernovitz. He composed an opera, a string quartet and vocal music.

KARL ŠEBOR, b. Brandeis, Bohemia, July 18, 1843. Studied the violin at the Prague Conservatoire, also composition under Kittl, and toured with success as a violin virtuoso in Russia and Poland, where he was also active as a teacher; then he became capellmeister at the Erfurt theatre, and during 1864–7 was in the same capacity at the Bohemian theatre, Prague; in 1871 he became military bandmaster in Vienna. He composed a quartet and a quintet for strings, pianoforte pieces, songs, choral songs, various operas and a prize cantata for the laying of the foundation-stone of the Bohemian theatre, Prague.

JOHANN HŘIMALY, b. Pilsen, Apr. 13, 1844; d. Moscow, 1915. After some preliminary lessons on the violin from his father and the local choirmaster he was from 1855 to 1861 pupil of Mildner at the Prague Conservatoire. His progress was so rapid that as a student he achieved great success in three of the public concerts of the Conservatoire. For some time he was a member of the Hřimaly quartet (*see* Adalbert Hřimaly). During 1862–8 he was concertmeister at Amsterdam, occasionally touring as a soloist. In order to be near Ferd. Laub, whom he had taken for his model, he went to Moscow in 1869 as teacher at the Conservatoire, and when Laub died in 1875 he succeeded him as 1st professor of violin, as well as concertmeister of the symphony concerts and leader of the quartet of the Imperial Russian Music Society. He spread still further the traditions of the Prague school of violin playing, already previously introduced by Laub, and did a great deal for the advancement of musical art in Russia, which began with the foundation of the Conservatoires of St. Petersburg in 1862 and Moscow in 1866. In his latter years Hřimaly devoted himself chiefly to teaching, in which capacity he was highly successful, having among his pupils, Barcewicz, Petschnikov, Luboschütz, Mogilewski, Zirelstein, etc. A festival was given by the Imperial Music Society in Mar., 1910, to celebrate the 40th year of Hřimaly's professorship. His scale and double stop studies were widely used; he also made a new ed. of Mazas's tutor.

OTTOKAR KOPECKÝ, b. Chŏtebŏr, Apr. 29, 1850. After studying at the Grammar School at Pilsen, he went under Bennewitz at the Prague Conservatoire from 1867 to 1870. After finishing his studies he became capellmeister at the theatre and teacher of the violin at Brünn. In 1873 he was engaged at the Mozarteum at Salzburg and afterwards in the Court chapel at Sondershausen. In 1878 he settled at Hamburg, where he became concertmeister in Laub's orchestra, touring with that through Russia and Germany. Returning to Hamburg he became teacher at the von Bernuth Conservatoire and 1890–6 1st concertmeister at the Philharmonic Society there. He also formed a string quartet with Vermehrer, Nissch and Kruse, which was very successful. In 1896 he retired from his position as concertmeister, devoting himself entirely to solo playing and teaching at the Conservatoire, and he counts among his numerous pupils the German Crown Prince and Prince Adalbert. He received the title of a Royal Prussian professor and chamber virtuoso of Schwarzburg-Sondershausen.

HANS SITT, b. Prague, Sept. 21, 1850; d. Leipzig, Mar. 10, 1922. His father was a well-known violin-maker. He began to play the violin in his childhood, and was acclaimed a remarkable prodigy when in early boyhood he played a concerto by Pixis at a Prague theatre. His father wisely refrained from exploiting his early talent and sent him to the Prague Conservatoire, where he studied the violin successively under Mildner and Bennewitz, and composition under Kittl and Krejči. At the end of his studies he toured successfully in Germany, and in 1867 he was appointed concertmeister at Breslau, where he also succeeded Schuch in 1870 as conductor at the Lobe theatre, and afterwards held a similar position first at Prague and 1873–80 at Chemnitz. Thence he went

GIOV. PIETRO GUIGNON

EMANUEL WIRTH

FRANZ ONDŘIČZEK

OSKAR NEDBAL

to Nice as conductor of the private chapel of Baron Dervies until that famous chapel, which had so many eminent musicians as members, was disbanded, after the death of the Baron. Sitt then went to Leipzig, where he started the highly successful Crystal Palace Popular Concerts and also frequently appeared as soloist. In 1883 he was appointed teacher of the violin at Leipzig Conservatoire after he had previously joined the famous Brodsky quartet as viola player. At the Conservatoire he conducted also the examination concerts and in 1885 he succeeded Herzogenberg as conductor of the Leipzig Bach society. He also conducted the "Sängerbund," the teachers' vocal society. He retired in 1921. He composed 3 violin concertos, 4 concertinos, 3 pupils' concertinos, and a large number of solo pieces, violin duets, albums of pieces for students, studies, etc., as well as numerous orchestral and choral works. He also edited many classical works. He stood in high esteem as a teacher.

HANS GERSTNER, b. Luditz, Bohemia, Aug. 17, 1851. Studied violin under Bennewitz at the Prague Conservatoire; became violinist at the Landestheater and member of the Bennewitz-Hegenbarth quartet at Prague. In 1871 he became teacher at the (then) State-Conservatoire and the theatre at Laibach, where he became also concertmeister of the Philharmonic Society, and in 1822 founded the Chamber Music Union of the Philharmonic Society. In 1914 he became "Director of Music" and lives there, still as esteemed teacher (1928).

OTTAKAR ŠEVČIK, b. Horaždowitz, Bohemia, Mar. 22, 1852, as the son of a schoolmaster, who taught him singing and pianoforte playing from early childhood, and from his eighth year also violin-playing; after two years he was able to play variations by Kalliwoda. His father, who did not wish him to become a musician, sent him to the Grammar School (Gymnasium) at Prague, where he became also a choirboy at one church and an alto-solo boy at another, which entailed the neglect of the pianoforte and the violin. A well-to-do Leipzig citizen (Mr. Flammiger), sojourning at Prague, who heard him sing and discovered his general musical talent, offered to provide for his musical education, and consequently he entered the Prague Conservatoire as a pupil of Bennewitz. He progressed so quickly, that on the conclusion of his studies in 1870 he was appointed concertmeister at the Mozarteum at Salzburg, where he remained for three years, appearing occasionally as soloist at Prague and in Vienna. In 1873 he became concertmeister at the newly founded Opéra-Comique in Vienna, but when in the following year that was changed into the Ring Theater, he went to Russia, where he was appointed concertmeister at Charkov, and in 1875 professor at the Imperial Music Society's School at Kiev, which he completely reorganized, and for this was decorated, in 1886, with the Order of Stanislaus. It was there that he evolved that system of teaching which eventually made him the "Master of Masters" in our time as Corelli was called in his time. At Kiev he was attacked by an eye trouble which necessitated an operation and resulted in the loss of the left eye. In 1892, Bennewitz, who had become director of the Prague Conservatoire, induced him to become principal professor at that institute, and from that time he devoted himself chiefly to teaching, only occasionally appearing as a soloist, his last public appearance being in 1898. One of his first pupils in 1892 was Jan Kubelik, then 12 years old and possessed of exceptional facility for the technique of the violin. Trained on Ševčik's new method he left the Conservatoire in 1898 to start on his triumphal tour throughout the world as a violinist magician of his time. Soon after, Kocian followed, and when in 1902 Mary Hall celebrated her triumphs in London, pupils from all parts of the world flocked to Prague to study under the master whose system had produced such wonderful results. This induced Ševčik to establish a summer school at the picturesque little Bohemian town of Prachatice. In 1906 a number of his pupils (their number is variously given as 75 and 100) gave a concert in his honour which was so successful that it had to be repeated on several subsequent days, and for the first time made the people of Prague aware of the activities and the importance of the master who dwelt in their midst. Soon afterwards he relinquished his position at the Conservatoire, to undergo an operation for his breathing organs, which was successfully performed. The following years he lived without any fixed appointment, teaching privately. In 1909 he accepted the position of principal of the violin department of the Vienna Academy of Music. On Dec. 12 he gave a concert at the

Queen's Hall, London, when he conducted the Queen's Hall orchestra for his pupils, Daisy Kennedy, Rosa Ehrlich, Nora Duesberg, David Hochstein, Vladimir Resnikoff, and Frank Williams, from the Vienna Academy, who all played concertos or parts of concertos, and did the greatest credit to their master, who received an enthusiastic ovation at the end of the concert. In 1919 Ševčik returned to the Prague Conservatoire, which had meanwhile become a national institution. His summer school has since then been moved to Pisek. In 1933 (May), at the age of 81, he came to London to found the first English "Masters' School" for virtuosi at the Guildhall School of Music. His principles are laid down in a "Method," op. 1, consisting of 4 books, followed by several other books dealing with various parts of violin technique, pub. by Bosworth & Co., Vienna and London. He also wrote a series of Bohemian dances for violin solo. The number of his pupils amounts to 600 or more; they comprise the sons of Wilhelmj and Hugo Heermann and the daughter of Wieniawski. The most prominent of his pupils will be found under their respective countries. Three of his pupils, Bohuslav Lhotsky, Karl Prochatska, Karl Moravec, with the violoncellist B. Vasca (now A. Fingeland) founded the Ševčik quartet at Warsaw in 1903. They reside now at Prague, make frequent tours in Europe, and visited England, 1913 and 1923.

JAN SLUNIČKO, b. Humpoletz, Bohemia, Mar. 23, 1852; d. Augsburg, May 5, 1923. A violin pupil of J. T. Höger's School of Music, and in 1864–70 of Mildner and Bennewitz at the Conservatoire, Prague; concertmeister at the Oratorio Union, afterwards teacher at and, from 1905, director of the School of Music at Augsburg. Composed 6 violin sonatas, a number of books of studies which were widely used, also violin and pianoforte pieces.

FLORIAN ZAJIC, b. Unhóst, Bohemia, May 4, 1853; d. Berlin, end of May, 1926. Born of poor parents and showing early signs of exceptional talent, he found a patron in a Freemason, who sent him to the Prague Conservatoire where he studied for eight years under Mildner and Bennewitz. He then was for a short time concertmeister at the Augsburg theatre, but soon was called to Mannheim by Vinc. Lachner as leader at the Court theatre; at the same time he was privately occupied, and played as solo violinist at the Subscription concerts. Among his pupils there was the daughter of the former minister and Privy Councillor President Lamey; they fell in love with each other and Zajic was thereby spurred on by dint of hard study to gain a position which would help to overcome the obvious obstacles. He achieved his object when in 1881 he played at Strassburg Conservatoire as successor of Lotto. During the vacations he toured as virtuoso in Germany with marked success. In 1885 he became the fortunate possessor of Ferd. David's Joseph Guarnerius, one of the finest specimens in existence, for the sum of £800. After having established his reputation in Germany as a violinist of the first order, he went to Paris to play at Pasdeloup's Concerts Populaires. Pasdeloup had worked his hardest to overcome the hatred of the French against German artists, and when Zajic appeared at the Cirque d'Hiver there were among a more or less well-disposed audience a number of ill-natured individuals who received him with hisses and cat-calls. He calmly stood his ground until the unmannerly disturbers had been forcibly removed; then he played a Vieuxtemps concerto with such poetry, beauty of tone and brilliancy that he was acclaimed with thunderous applause, and when at Pasdeloup's request he appeared again a fortnight later he was hailed as the hero of the day. Even at the captious Leipzig, his rendering of Bach's Chaconne and Bruch's G minor concerto, as well as his quartet playing received unstinted praise. From 1889 to 1891 he was at Hamburg, and in the latter year he succeeded Sauret as professor of violin at the Stern Conservatoire.

JOSEF HIEBSCH, b. Tyasa, Bohemia, Oct. 7, 1854; d. Karlsbad, Apr. 10, 1897. Choirboy in the Royal chapel, Dresden; in 1869 at the Seminary at Leitmeritz; violin pupil of Dont in Vienna and music master at the teacher's seminary there. Wrote "Guide for Elementary Violin Teaching" (1880: enlarged 1884); Collection of Violin Duets (12 books); "Method of Violin Teaching" (comparative method, similar to Riemann's work for the pianoforte), and other theoretical works (*see* Riemann).

EUGEN GRÜNBERG, b. Lemberg, Galicia, Oct. 30, 1854.

Studied the violin under Heissler (?), composition under Bruckner and Dessoff, and chamber music under Hellmesberger. During 1881–91 violinist, Leipzig Gewandhaus orchestra and afterwards successor of Eichberg as violin teacher at the Boston, Mass. Conservatoire. From 1899 teacher of violin, viola and ensemble playing at the New English Conservatoire. Composed a "Suite im antiken Stil" for violin and pianoforte; cadenza to Brahms' violin concerto, studies for violin, a symphony, ballets, Viennese dances, etc.; also wrote: "The Violinist's Manual" (N.Y., 1897); "Theory of Violin Playing"; contributions to various journals (Theo Baker, 1900).

MIROSLAV (really JOSEPH) WEBER, b. Prague, Nov. 9, 1854; d. Munich, Jan. 1, 1906. From his sixth year a pupil of his father, conductor at the National theatre (Landestheater), Prague. Two years later he played before the Emperor Ferdinand at Castle Reichstadt, and during the winter 1863–4 he toured with great success in the Austrian Empire. During 1864–8 he studied first privately under A. Hora (pianoforte), V. Vinăr and Prucha (composition), then at the Prague School of Organists, where he obtained also instruction in composition. From 1870 to 1873 he was under Krejči and Bennewitz at the upper classes of the Conservatoire. In 1873 he was appointed solo violinist in the Court chapel at Sondershausen. There he was stimulated, through Concertmeister Uhlrich, to acquaint himself with the treasures of chamber music. During the summer of 1874 he filled the post of conductor at the Royal Bohemian theatre at Prague, returning again to Sondershausen until Sept., 1875, when he became first concertmeister at the Darmstadt Court theatre, where from 1880 he filled also the post of second conductor and formed a permanent quartet. On June 1, 1883, he succeeded Rebiček as first concertmeister in the orchestra and second conductor at the opera, Wiesbaden, where in 1889 he received the title of Royal Director of Music. In 1893 he resigned his position and went to Munich as second concertmeister, and from 1901 first concertmeister in B. Walter's place, which post he occupied to the time of his death. At Munich he formed a string quartet with W. Leitner, Bihrle and Ebner. He composed a violin concerto, 2 string quartets, 1 string quintet, 1 septet for wind and strings, 2 suites for orchestra, 2 operas, 1 ballet, and incidental music to two plays. His chamber works, which all received prizes, deserve to be more widely known.

KARL HALIŘ, b. Hohenelbe, Bohemia, Feb. 1, 1859; d. Berlin, Dec. 21, 1909. He received his first lessons from his father, and studied from 1867 to 1873 under Bennewitz at the Prague Conservatoire, and after receiving the 1st prize there, he studied for two years, 1874–6, under Joachim. From 1876 to 1879 he was solo violinist in Bilse's orchestra in Berlin, and afterwards concertmeister at Königsberg. In 1881 he toured in Italy and the South of France and on his return he became concertmeister at Mannheim, where he remained from 1882 to 1884, when he was called to Weimar in the same capacity. There, in 1888, he married Theresa Zerbst, the distinguished concert singer. At the Bach Festival at Eisenach in 1884 he played the famous double concerto with Joachim, which turned into a perfect triumph for the two masters. In 1886 he played Gernsheim's violin concerto in Berlin at a Philharmonic Concert, and afterwards he toured in Russia and France and introduced Lalo's concerto in Paris, always with undiminished success. In 1888 he was leader at the Wagner Festival at Bayreuth. In 1889 he was offered the post of leader at the Dresden Opera, but refused on account of the greater freedom he enjoyed at Weimar. In 1890 he toured in Switzerland, Belgium, Germany and Austria, and played at the Tonkünstlerverein festivals at Wiesbaden and Eisenach. In 1893 he went to Berlin as professor of violin and as de Ahna's successor in the Joachim quartet, with which he was associated until Joachim's death. A quartet which he had formed in Berlin with Markees, Müller and Dechert, with himself as leader, was dissolved in 1898. In 1896 he toured as soloist in America. Haliř was not only in possession of a brilliant and faultless technique of both left hand and bow, but also of those higher musical qualities which stamped him as one of the great artists of his time. His style resembled in many respects that of his master Joachim. He excelled both as virtuoso and chamber-music player.

ANDREAS KADLETZ, b. Dobris, Bohemia, Feb. 18, 1859. A violin pupil of Bennewitz at the Prague Conservatoire and of L. v. Auer in St. Petersburg; composition under A. Bernhardt. He became concertmeister at the Imperial Russian Opera, and singing-master at 2 grammar schools. Wrote studies and other didactic works for violin, one opera and several ballets.

FRANZ ONDŘIČEK, b. in the Hradschin palace at Prague, Apr. 29, 1859; d. Milan, Apr., 1922. His father, a violinist at the Landestheater and leader of a dance band, gave him his first lessons in music and violin-playing, and so apt a pupil proved the boy that he was soon able to play in his father's band. At the age of 14 he became for three years a pupil of Bennewitz at the Prague Conservatoire. A wealthy Prague merchant then provided him with the means for further study under Massart at the Paris Conservatoire, which he left after two years, with the 1st prize, and after making his debut at the Pasdeloup concerts with great success, he went to London, Brussels and other Continental towns. In 1882–3 he met with enthusiastic receptions in Berlin and in Vienna. There he settled permanently and founded, 1911, the New Vienna Conservatoire, of which he was the director and teacher of the violin. Among his notable pupils there was his future wife, Ella Stiller-Ondřiček, and J. Orel. With the Court musicians Silbinger and Junek, he formed, in 1908, a string quartet which became favourably known as the Ondřiček quartet. In the autumn of 1919 he was appointed as professor of the master-class at the State Conservatoire at Prague. He has written a concerto and other compositions for violin, including 15 artists' studies, also a Method for the Violin, and a Rhapsody "Bohème" for orchestra.

KARL ONDŘIČEK, a younger brother of Franz Ondřiček, was, in the eighties and nineties of last century, first concertmeister at the National Bohemian theatre at Prague. He then went in a similar capacity to Boston, Mass.

EMANUEL ONDŘIČEK, a pupil of Ševčik, was living in New York ca. 1918.

HEINRICH BANDLER, b. Rumburg, Bohemia, Nov. 19, 1870. During 1882–8 a pupil of A. Bennewitz at the Prague Conservatoire, and of Joachim, in Berlin, from 1893–5; solo viola player at the Breslau Orchestra Union; from 1896 concertmeister of the Hamburg Philharmonic Society. He is also the leader of a permanent quartet bearing his name.

KAREL HOFFMANN, b. Prague, Dec. 12, 1872; pupil of Benne-witz at the Prague Conservatoire. He formed with Suk Nedbal and Berger, afterwards Wihan, the world-famed Bohemian quartet in which later on G. Herold and L. Zelenka replaced Nedbal and Wihan, respectively. Since 1922 Hoff-mann has conducted the Meisterklasse (master-class) at the State Conservatoire, Prague.

ANTON WITEK, b. Saaz, Bohemia, Jan. 7, 1873. During 1884–8 a pupil of A. Bennewitz at the Prague Conservatoire. In 1894 concertmeister in the Berlin Philharmonic orchestra; 1910–19 concertmeister in the Boston, Mass., Symphony orchestra, and at the same time teacher at von Ende's Academy of Music in New York; and 1900 to 1918 leader of the Witek-Malkin trio. From 1920, concertmeister in the Frankfort a/M. Symphony orchestra and from 1924 likewise in the Bayreuth Festival orchestra. From 1891 he gave regular sonata recitals with the Danish pianist Vita Gerhard, whom he married in 1910; she died July 25, 1925, at Bayreuth. In 1926 he married the American violinist, Alma Rosengren, who was a member of the permanent quartet which he had formed in 1925. He wrote a few works for teaching purposes, partly still in MS.

JOSEF SUK, b. Křečowitz, Jan. 4, 1874. A pupil of his father, a school-teacher, and of A. Bennewitz (music theory, K. Knittl, K. Stoker); composition, Dvořak. In 1892 he joined the Bohemian quartet as 2nd violin, and since 1922 has been teacher of composition at the Prague Conservatoire. He is one of the foremost Czeskian composers, who wrote a fantasia for violin and orchestra, a number of chamber-music works as well as important choral and orchestral works (list in Riemann). In 1898 he married Dvořak's daughter, Ottilia, who died July 5, 1905.

OSKAR NEDBAL, b. Tabor, Bohemia, Mar. 26, 1874, d. Prague, Dec. 24, 1930. Studied first the trumpet, which however he soon exchanged for the violin, becoming a violin pupil of Bennewitz, composition of Dvořak, at the Prague Conserva-toire, where he studied from 1885 to 1892. With his co-students K. Hoffmann, Jos. Suk and O. Berger, he formed the famous Bohemian quartet in which he was the viola player until 1906, when he went to Vienna as conductor of

MIROSLAV WEBER
By kindness of Prof. O. E. Deutsch.

EDMUND SINGER
By kindness of the Stuttgart Conservatoire Authorities.

JENO HUBAY

FLORIAN ZAJIC

E.N.A.

JOSEPH SLAWJK
From one of his Concert Programmes
kindly supplied by Prof. O. E. Deutsch.

PROSPER P. C. SAINTON
From a portrait in the possession of
Messrs. W. E. Hill & Sons.

the Vienna Tonal Artists' orchestra (until 1919), for some time being also capellmeister at the Volksoper. He composed a sonata for violin and pianoforte, op. 9, a number of ballets, 1 operetta, 1 opera, some orchestral works, and pianoforte pieces. His compositions show a distinctly national colouring.

JOSEF KONBA, b. Prague, Mar. 21, 1880. A pupil of Bennewitz and Ševčik at the Prague Conservatoire; composition under F. Morak. Is concertmeister at the German theatre at Prague. Composed a sonata and pieces for violin, also sonatinas and pieces for pianoforte.

JAN KUBELIK, b. Michle, near Prague, July 5, 1880. The son of a musical gardener who gave him his first lessons on the violin, after which he became a pupil of Ondřiček and progressed so rapidly that he was soon able to appear in public and arouse interest in himself. From 1892 to 1898 he was Ševčik's pupil at the Prague Conservatoire, after which he appeared in Vienna and Budapesth in a number of concerts with phenomenal success. Then he began to tour all over Europe and America, twice extending his tours right round the world with ever-increasing success, both artistically and financially, which enabled him to acquire an estate in Bohemia which he afterwards exchanged for one near Sillein in Slovakia. He married a Hungarian Countess and for a time he devoted himself to the cultivation of his estate in Sillein as well as to composition and the compiling of a new violin method, living at times at Abbazia; but within the last few years he has resumed touring again, compelled through serious losses owing to the Great War, and was for a longer period in America, returning via England in Jan.–Feb. 1930. He is the fortunate owner of the famous Emperor Strad. He composed 6 violin concertos.

LEO FUNTEK, b. Laibach, Aug. 21, 1885. Studied the violin at the Leipzig Conservatoire; became concertmeister in the Helsingfors Philharmonic orchestra in 1906. During 1909–10 conductor at Wiburg (Wiepuri); 1911–14 violin teacher at the Helsingfors Conservatoire; 1914–19 concertmeister in the Royal chapel, Stockholm, returning in 1919 to Helsingfors as teacher at the Conservatoire. Since 1925 he has been capellmeister at the Helsingfors opera; also music critic and excellent accompanist. Wrote arrangements for violin and pianoforte, also arrangements and transcriptions for orchestra.

BEDRICH VOLDAN, b. Hlinsko, near Chrudim, Bohemia, Dec. 14, 1892. The son of an organist. During 1907–13 pupil of St. Suchý at the Prague Conservatoire; 1913–14 concertmeister in Sweden; during the War music teacher and organist to Count Otto Czernin at Hlušice, near N. Bydžov. At the end of the War, he toured with his wife in Bohemia and Moravia. Since 1920 he has been teacher at the National Conservatoire at Prague. He composed for violin (with pianoforte) Pierrot, and Scherzo, op. 6; Wedding suite, op. 8; concerto piccolo, op. 18; a new violin tutor (called Violin-Taylorism); a melodrama, piano pieces. Songs, etc., are still in MS.

JOSEPH BLAHA, b. Bohemia, latter half of the 19th century. Studied the violin at the Prague Conservatoire under Bennewitz. Appeared as solo violinist in various towns and was teacher of the violin at the Royal Academy of Music in London, ca. 1915.

WENZEL HUML, pupil of Ševčik; was, ca. 1910, teacher of violin at the Agram Conservatoire.

HUGO KORTSCHAK. A pupil of Ševčik, who went to Frankfort a/M. at the invitation of Heermann, with whom he afterwards went to Chicago.

VASA PRIHODA. A young Czeko-Slovakian violinist who made his debut in London in Feb., 1926. He is reported to have a wonderful technique, but has yet to prove his musicianship (*Strad*, Feb., 1926).

# CHAPTER 49
## *Canada*

NORA CLENCH, b. Canada 18... Commenced the study of the violin at a very early age, and gave a successful concert at Rochester, N.Y., on Apr. 18, 1891, and in October of that year she went to Brussels for further study under Ysaÿe. In Sept., 1892, she appeared several times with great success at Ostend and since then she has been touring on the Continent and in England. She studied for some time under Brodsky and finally under Joachim. In 1896 she played the Mendelssohn concerto with great success at the Hovingham Musical Festival, in 1897 at the Ballad concerts, Queen's Hall, etc., and in Dec., 1905, she appeared at a concert of the North London Orchestral Society. About that time she formed a quartet with Lucy Stone, Cecilia Gates and May Mukle which gave six concerts in the spring of 1905, at which, apart from classical works, she produced quartets by Tanejev, Debussy, Hugo Wolf, and a quintet with horn by Holbrooke.

KATHLEEN PARLOW, b. Calgary, 1890. She began as a little child to play on a toy fiddle and when, after the death of her father, the mother removed to San Francisco, Mr. Conrad, a cousin, who was a well-known teacher, instructed her for four years, after which she became a pupil of Henry Holmes. At that time she had already met with enthusiastic receptions as a prodigy in various Canadian towns. At the age of 14 she gave two very successful concerts in London and also played before Queen Alexandra. It was intended that she should continue her studies under Holmes, but the death of the latter frustrated that plan, and she was enabled by the generous assistance of Lord Strathcona to study under von Auer at the St. Petersburg Conservatoire, receiving also additional private lessons from him. She has the distinction of having been the first foreign as well as the only female pupil in von Auer's class. At the end of the year von Auer arranged a "Press Matinée" to bring her to the notice of the leading musical circles in St. Petersburg. The enthusiastic notices in the papers encouraged her to give nine concerts, the proceeds of which enabled her to study there for another six months, results which were partly due to the patronage of the Grand Duke Michael and of the English Ambassador, Sir A. Nicholson. At the end of that time she gave six very successful concerts and then went to Ostend, where she played Glazounoff's concerto at a Russian Festival, conducted by the composer. Next she went to Berlin, where she gave six concerts, at the last two of which the house was sold out. A tour through Scandinavia followed, and after a concert under Safonoff at Copenhagen she was presented by an admirer with the magnificent Joseph Guarnerius violin of 1735 which formerly belonged to Viotti. She played before King Haakon and Queen Maud of Norway, who presented her with a valuable brooch. Her tours extended through Germany, Holland and Belgium. Her debut in London did not meet with the same success she had on the Continent, but subsequent appearances raised her in the favour of the public. In 1909 she played the Tschaikowsky concerto at the Queen's Hall symphony concerts and at a command performance at Marlborough House.

## CHAPTER 50

## *France: to 1825*

THE French school of violin-playing, properly speaking, took its inception from the appearance of Viotti at the Concert Spirituel, Paris, in 1782. In an account of this in the *Allgemeine Music Zeitung, Leipzig* (vol. xiv, p. 435), it says: ". . . He played a concerto of his own composition, and one found in this, as in all subsequent ones, an originality which appeared to have reached the highest of its class to the present time, a fertile inventive power, a happy boldness, the full fire of youth, but controlled by pure and noble taste, which never allows it to overstep the limits of the beautiful. And now as for the execution! Power and grace, how closely united! How perfect his Adagio! His Allegro, how brilliant! His playing created an extraordinary amount of enthusiasm when he was heard for the first time."

He remained for ten years in Paris, and during that period he gave to French violin-playing that impetus which soon after raised it to its dominant position. This was chiefly brought about by his example and his compositions, which presented to the players new and grateful problems. Direct pupils he had but few, the most important being P. Rode, while Kreutzer and Baillot, by taking every opportunity to hear and see Viotti play, took him for their model and studied his style. These three became the shining lights in the French violinistic firmament, handing down the art of Viotti, although Rode's influence, like that of his master, made itself felt more by his playing and his compositions than by direct teaching, although a few, like J. Böhm and E. Rietz, benefited for a time by his personal instructions. Kreutzer and Baillot, on the other hand, consolidated the principles and characteristics of the French school; they excelled less as soloists then as teachers. In the latter capacity they displayed a long and beneficent activity on the lines of the classical school of Viotti.

With the next generation there came, however, a change, which emphasized the elegant, graceful, brilliant, in fact the virtuoso side of the art of violin-playing. This showed itself in Kreutzer's famous pupil C. P. Lafont, in whose playing as well as in his numerous, now antiquated, compositions the virtuoso element predominated. Habeneck, the contemporary of Kreutzer, Rode, and pupil of Baillot, although he shone pre-eminently as conductor, was most influential in the evolution of the French school for violin-playing, as the master of Léonard, Prume, Maurin, Sainton, who spread his art in England, and especially of Alard, that brilliant professor of the Conservatoire who counted among his pupils the great Sarasate and Garcin, and edited the valuable collection of 18th-century violin compositions, "Les Maîtres Classiques," while his tutor and studies became standard works. Although essentially a virtuoso, he partook also of the serious side of his art, and this was even more the case with Sarasate. Léonard, on the other hand, developed, as well as his pupils, Cés Thomson, O. Musin, Tiv. Nachez, etc., essentially the virtuoso element; this was also, if to a minor degree, the case with Baillot's pupil Chas. Dancla, whose excellent studies, duets and little pieces were all through the 19th century largely used by amateur violin students throughout Europe.

Massart, the pupil of Kreutzer, and Maurin, pupil of Baillot and Habeneck, both excelled as teachers at the Paris Conservatoire, where they carried on the more serious traditions of their respective masters almost to the very end of the century.

Maurin did much for the advancement of string quartet-playing and was the first to perform in his chamber-music concerts, with Chevillard as violoncellist, the last quartets by Beethoven. His foremost pupil, Lucien Capet (see p. 191), who was also an excellent soloist, followed his master in cultivating the art of quartet-playing. We possess no further particulars about Henri Berthelier, a solo violinist at the Paris Opera and the Conservatoire Concerts, who succeeded Maurin as professor of the Paris Conservatoire in 1894.

The advance in the technique of violin-playing, especially in the art of bowing, was a very marked one from the middle of the 19th century, and in this the French and Belgian schools held a leading position.

JEAN JOSEPH VIDAL, b. Sorèze, ca. 1789; d. Paris, June 14, 1867. Entered the Paris Conservatoire in 1805, where he studied the violin under Kreutzer. In 1810–11 he played in concerts as soloist with great success, and afterwards he was for nearly twenty years 2nd violinist in Baillot's famous quartet. He was highly esteemed as a teacher of the violin.

JEAN MARIE BECQUIÉ DE PEYREVILLE, b. Toulouse, 1797; d. Paris, Jan., 1876. Entered the Paris Conservatoire as a pupil of Rod. Kreutzer on Oct. 20, 1820; studied afterwards under Jean N. A. Kreutzer. He played successively in several opera orchestras in Paris, and composed various pieces for violin.

NARCISSE GIRARD, b. Nantes, Jan. 27, 1797; d. Paris, Jan. 16, 1860. During 1817–20 a pupil of Baillot and Cherubini in composition at the Paris Conservatoire. Was capellmeister at the Italian Opera from 1830 to 1852, combining with it, in 1837, the same position at the Opéra-Comique and 1846 at the Grand Opera, as successor to Habeneck. Became violin professor at the Paris Conservatoire and conductor of the Conservatoire concerts in 1847, and in 1856 director-general of music of the Grand Opera. He died from a stroke while conducting "Les Huguenots." Of his compositions one knows only a little opera which had great success at the Opéra-Comique in 1841.

PANTALÉON BATTU, b. Paris, 1799; d. there, Jan. 17, 1870. A pupil of R. Kreutzer at the Conservatoire, where he gained the 1st prize in 1822, rousing the audience to a pitch of enthusiasms which made it impossible for the jury to restrain their acclamation. Then followed his success as a soloist at the Concert Spirituel, the Opera and the concerts of the Conservatoire, of which he was a co-founder. He became a member of the Royal chapel until 1830, and in 1846 second conductor at the Opera. He was also chosen by the Academy of Arts to conduct the performances of cantatas which had gained the "prix de Rome." In 1859 he retired into private life, honoured and respected as an excellent and modest artist. As a composer he kept himself free from the influence of Kreutzer, his master. He composed 2 violin concertos, op. 1 and 3; 3 violin duets, op. 2; thème varié with orchestra and some romances with pianoforte.

PIERRE JULIEN NARGEOT, b. Paris, Mar. 15, 1799. He entered the Paris Conservatoire Oct. 1, 1813, and became a pupil of Kreutzer. At the end of his studies he was for some years in the orchestra of the Opéra-Comique, then at the Opéra Italienne, and after that at the Grand Opera, where he was in 1840, according to Fétis. He composed an air-varié with pianoforte, op. 1.

THEODORE ALEXANDRE TILMANT, b. Valenciennes, July 8, 1799; d. Asnières, near Paris, May 7, 1878. A pupil of Kreutzer at the Paris Conservatoire, where he obtained the 1st prize; he then became 1st violinist at the Théâtre Italienne, and 1825 at the Grand Opera; 1834 he became 2nd and 1838 1st conductor at the Théâtre Italienne. In the latter year he instituted chamber-music soirées in conjunction with his brother ALEXANDRE, a good violoncellist, for the performance of works by Haydn, Mozart and Beethoven. In 1849 he succeeded Labarrés as conductor at the Opéra-Comique, and he also conducted the Concerts du Gymnase Musical, and in 1868 retired to Asnières.

VICTOR GRIVEL, b. at the beginning of the 19th century. For many years 1st violinist at the theatre at Grenoble. He pub. a pamphlet, "Vernis des anciens luthiers d'Italie, perdu depuis le milieu du XVIII siècle, retrouvé par V. Grivel" (Grenoble, Allier, 1867, 8a, 21 pp.); a favourable report about it was given by the Statistical Society of Science and Art: "Rapport sur le vernis inventé par Mr. Victor Grivel" (Ib., 1867).

LE CARPENTIER, d. Paris, 1827 or 1828. A teacher of the violin, who wrote a "Méthode de Violon" (Paris, Frey).

ALEXANDRE PARISOT, b. Orleans, 1800 (Mendel); living there ca. 1840 as violinist, teacher of music and composer. Wrote 2 violin concertos, 1 book of 3 duos concertants for 2 violins, and one book of 6 do. do. not difficult; 40 easy and progressive studies for violin; a symphony for full orchestra, and a book on the Elements of Music ("Principes de Musique," all pub. Orleans, Demar).

JOSEPH CLAVEL, b. Nantes, 1800. Entered the Paris Conservatoire in 1813 as violin pupil of Kreutzer and obtained the 1st prize for violin playing in 1818, after which he became an auxiliary teacher at the Conservatoire and 1st violinist at the Opéra Italienne. In 1830 he went over to the Grand Opera. In the Conservatoire orchestra he was leader of the 2nd violins until he was pensioned. He composed violin sonatas, duets, variations, romances and string quartets.

VICTOR MAGNIEN, b. Epinal, Department des Voges, Nov. 19, 1804; d. Lille, June, 1885. Began to play the violin at the age of 10; in 1817 he became a pupil of R. Kreutzer in Paris, and of Carulli for the guitar, and two years later he appeared in public with great success as a virtuoso on both instruments. In 1820 he went to Colmar, where his parents had settled, and he became a favourite in the best families there on account of his talent. It was then only that he resolved to make music his profession, he soon had a large number of pupils, and from Colmar he went for three months in every year to Paris for further studies under Baillot, Lafont and Fétis. After the Revolution in 1830 he went to Beauvais as conductor of the Philharmonic Union and director of the School for Singing. In 1846 he became director of the Conservatoire at Lille. He composed concertos, fantasias, variations studies, etc., for violin, duos for violin and guitar pieces and other instruments; also church music and a book of musical theory.

JOSEPH LOMAGNE, b. Perpignan, 1804; d. there, 1868. A pupil of Coste there, then of Kreutzer at the Paris Conservatoire; solo violinist at theatres of Nîmes and Bordeaux. In 1842 he founded a Conservatoire of which he was director and teacher of violin till he died. Composed studies for violin, church music and an opera.

NAPOLÉON ANTOINE EUGÈNE LÉON DE SAINT-LUBIN, b. Turin, July 5, 1805, d. Berlin, Feb. 13, 1850. He was the son of a French officer emigrant and teacher of French who went from Turin to Hamburg. Léon commenced his musical studies by playing the harp, which he soon exchanged for the violin. At the age of 9 he played a violin concerto in public. In 1817 he played in Berlin, and then in Dresden, where he received lessons from Polledro. In 1818 he went to Frankfort-on-the-Main, where he studied under Spohr for one year, after which he toured in Germany and in 1820 settled in Vienna for a time to study composition; in 1823 he became violinist at the Josephstadt theatre there, and in 1827 2nd conductor. About that time he wrote a melodrama, "Belisar," several violin concertos and a symphony. After hearing Paganini, he retired to Hungary to devote himself to renewed study of the violin. One year of that time he spent at the house of Count Ladislav Festetics. On his return to Vienna he gave some concerts with brilliant success. He composed several ballets, a fairy opera, string quartets and pianoforte trios. In 1830 he was called to Berlin as conductor of the Koenigstadt theatre, which position he occupied until 1847. He composed in all 5 violin concertos, an octet, quartets, trios, several operas, ballets, etc. At his house he had frequent musical reunions and quartet parties, in which the greatest artists, such as Mendelssohn, Spohr, Liszt, etc., used to take part. The past few years of his life he was constantly ailing. Jenö Hubay re-edited 6 caprices for violin by Saint-Lubin.

CHARLES FRANÇOIS JUPIN, b. Chambery, Nov. 30, 1805; d. Paris, June 12, 1839. In 1807 the family moved to Turin, where, at the age of 8, Charles received his first violin lessons from Monticelli, an old musician, and afterwards from Georgis, 1st violin of the theatre of Prince de Carignan. At the age of barely 11 he played at the Turin theatre a concerto by Rode with such success that his father decided to take him to Paris, but his slender means compelled him to give concerts to pay for the expense of the journey. At Chaumont-sur-Marne he was received by M. de Boucheporn, a high Government official and music enthusiast, who gave him a letter of recommendation to Baillot, who placed him in the Conservatoire under his own care. In 1823 he shared the 1st violin prize with Philippe, another of Baillot's pupils who died soon afterwards. In 1824 he played a symphony concertante by Baillot with the latter at the Opera. When the Odéon theatre was organized he became solo violinist, and 18 months later he left Paris to go on tour. Arrived at Turin, where he rejoined his family, he received a letter from the Mayor of Strassburg, who on Baillot's recommendation offered him the position of professor of violin and conductor of the town orchestra; this he accepted, entered upon his duties at the beginning of 1826 and from thence took an active and successful part in the organization of music festivals in the Alsace. At the closing of the Strassburg theatre in 1835 he settled in Paris as 2nd conductor at the Opéra-Comique. His playing was solid yet at the same time very brilliant. He composed a violin concerto, a fantasia for violin and pianoforte variations, etc., a pianoforte trio and a string trio.

AUGUSTE SEURIOT. Entered the Paris Conservatoire in 1808 as pupil of the elder Jean Kreutzer; afterwards he was for a short time at the Opéra-Comique. Fétis thinks that he settled after that in a provincial town. He composed for violin, 3 duos concertans, op. 1 and 6, duos faciles et progressifs on popular tunes, both pub. in Paris.

JEAN BAPTISTE PHILEMON DE CUVILLON, b. Dunkerk (?), May 13, 1809. A descendant of an old noble family. Entered the Paris Conservatoire in 1824; studied the violin under Habeneck and composition under Reicha. In 1825 he gained the 2nd, and in 1826 the 1st prize for violin-playing. In 1829 he also studied law at the University, became Licentiate and distinguished himself by brilliant disputations. Soon afterwards he devoted himself exclusively to music. During 1843-8 he was assistant professor in Habeneck's class. He became 1st violinist at the Opera, at the Conservatoire concerts, and in the Imperial Chapel. He occupied his position at the Opera till after 1880. Some violin compositions of Cuvillon were pub. in Paris.

EUGÈNE SAUZAY, b. Paris, July 14, 1809; d. Paris, Jan. 24, 1901. His first teacher for the violin was Vidal, and from 1824, when he entered the Conservatoire, Guerin and afterwards Baillot, while Reicha was his master in composition. He gained prizes in various subjects, but chiefly distinguished himself as violinist, and succeeded his former master Vidal in the famous Baillot quartet as 2nd violin and afterwards Urhan, as viola, till 1840. He married the daughter of Baillot and instituted musical soirées at his house in which, apart from his wife and his elder son as pianists, the violoncellist Norblin, the pianist Boely and afterwards Franchomme and others took an active part. At a later period they were given in public and sometimes with orchestra at the Salle Pleyel. In 1840 he was appointed solo violinist to Louis Philippe, later on leader of the 2nd violins to Napoleon III, and in 1860 he succeeded Girard as professor at the Conservatoire, and eventually was decorated with the Order of the Legion of Honour. He composed a number of pieces for the violin as well as for other instruments, a string trio, Études harmoniques (op. 13), and studies on the quartets of Haydn, Mozart and Beethoven with a thematic catalogue thereof (1861).

PROSPER PHILIPPE CATHERINE SAINTON, b. Toulouse, June 5, 1813; d. London, Oct. 17, 1890. Entered the Paris Conservatoire Dec. 20, 1831, and became a pupil of Habeneck. At the end of his studies he played for some time in the orchestra of the Grand Opera, and then toured in South Germany, Upper Italy, Russia, Sweden and Denmark. In 1840 he became teacher of the violin at the Toulouse music school. In 1844 he came to London, where his elegance of style and beauty of tone was so much admired that he was, in 1845, appointed violin professor at the Royal Academy of Music, leader of the Queen's band, and at Her Majesty's Theatre, as well as chamber musician to the Queen, which post he filled until 1856. In 1860 he married the eminent singer Charlotte Dolby, who as Mme Sainton-Dolby was for many years a great popular favourite. During the latter years of his life Sainton lived in retirement. He wrote a number of compositions for the violin. Robin Legge, in "Celebrated Violinists," says that "at the last Birmingham Festival before his death, every violinist in the orchestra had been either a direct pupil of Sainton's or a pupil of a pupil."

DELPHIN JEAN ALARD, b. Bayonne, Mar. 8, 1815; d. Paris, Feb. 22, 1888. He studied the violin from childhood, and appeared successfully in public at the age of 10. In 1827 he entered the Paris Conservatoire and was admitted to F. A. Habeneck's class, but only as a hearer, studying musical theory under Fétis. After gaining numerous prizes, he left the Conservatoire, but remained a member of the concert society of that institute, and was 1840 appointed solo violinist in the Royal Band of Louis Philippe. In 1843 he succeeded Baillot as professor of violin at the Conservatoire and instituted, in conjunction with the violoncellist A. Franchomme, chamber-music soirées which enjoyed great popularity. In 1850 he was made a Chevalier of the Legion of Honour, and in 1858 he became 1st solo violinist of the Imperial Chapel, which was dissolved after the fall of Napoleon III. In 1875 Alard retired into private life and surrendered his place at the Conservatoire to Maurin. Alard had a brilliant technique combined with great purity of intonation, beauty of tone, and musical intelligence. His numerous compositions are practically forgotten; his excellent tutor, however, was used in all European countries (as well as his valuable collected ed. of old sonatas, "Les Maîtres Classiques") and is still valuable to violin students. He trained many excellent pupils, foremost standing Sarasate and Garcin. Through the famous Luthier Vuillaume, his father-in-law, he acquired one of the most beautiful Strads in existence, which was afterwards sold to a Scotsman.

LOUIS MICHEL ADOLPHE DELOFFRE, b. Paris, July, 1817; d. there, Jan. 8, 1876. A pupil first of his father, then of Bellon, Lafont, and Baillot; solo violinist in the orchestra of Musard père. He settled at London, where he was engaged at Her Majesty's Theatre, the Philharmonic and Sacred Harmonic Societies, and the Musical Union. He visited Paris annually to give trio soirées with his wife, a good pianist, and the violoncellist Pilet. In 1851 he returned there permanently as conductor of the Théâtre Lyrique, where he produced among others the operas of Gluck, Mozart, and Weber. He composed 2 symphonies and chamber music; each of his 2 string quartets were awarded a prize.

AMEDÉE DUBOIS, b. Tournay, July 17, 1818; d. there, Oct. 1, 1865. His first teacher was a local violinist Moreau, and from 1836 Wéry at the Brussels Conservatoire, which he left in 1839 after gaining several prizes. He then gave some successful concerts in Paris, where he became concertmeister at the Casino Paganini, and later on he toured in France and the Netherlands. In 1851 he was appointed director of the Communal School of Music at Tournay. Some violin compositions of his were pub. in Paris, but they are not considered to be of outstanding value.

JEAN BAPTISTE CHARLES DANCLA, b. Bagnères de Bigorre, Dec. 19, 1818; d. Tunis, Nov. 9, 1907.   At the age of 10 he played the 7th concerto by Rode to the composer, who was so impressed by the boy's talent that he caused his immediate entry into the Paris Conservatoire, where he was at first a pupil of Guérin and afterwards of Baillot for the violin and of Halévy and Barton for composition.   After gaining many prizes (including one for a cantata) he was, in 1837, appointed 2nd solo-violinist at the Opéra-Comique, and after brilliant successes as a virtuoso in numerous concerts he became, early in 1857, an assistant teacher of the violin at the Conservatoire, and a professor in 1860.   With his brothers LEOPOLD (violin) and ARNAUD (violoncello) he gave chamber-music soirées which enjoyed great popularity.   He was a very prolific composer for his instrument, who possessed an excellent style and graceful melodious invention, but of a superficial order.   His works are, however, most effective for the instrument, and his method, as well as his studies and duets, are of lasting value for teaching, while his concertos, solos, fantasias as well as his symphonies, quartets and other chamber works are antiquated.

JULES MERCIER, b. Dijon, Apr. 23, 1819; d. there Mar. 5, 1868.   A pupil of his father and of Lejeune.   He went to Paris to study at the Conservatoire but fell seriously ill and had to return to Dijon.   After a time, however, he toured in France, Alsace Lorraine and played also at Karlsruhe, Würzburg and Stuttgart, everywhere meeting with great success. In Frankfort a/M., however, he fell ill again and had to return. At Dijon he founded and conducted the Philharmonic Society and exercised a beneficial influence upon the musical life of the town.   He was very popular everywhere, and how much his early death was mourned even in wider circles was shown by the fact that over thirty musical societies were represented at his funeral.   His compositions for the violin were pub. by Brandus, Paris.

EUGÈNE CHAINE, b. Charleville, Ardennes, Dec. 1, 1819.   A pupil of the Paris Conservatoire under Clavel and Habeneck. He was an excellent violinist who settled permanently at Paris as virtuoso and teacher.   He composed some violin concertos and numerous pieces.

JULES ARMINGAUD, b. Bayonne, May 3, 1820; d. Paris, Feb. 27, 1900.   After studying the violin in his native town he went in 1839 to Paris to perfect himself at the Conservatoire, but was not accepted, as he was already too far advanced. From that time he became a violinist at the Paris Opera, and formed a quartet with Leon Jacquard, E. Salo, and Mas, which became famous for its perfect ensemble, and the cultivation of Beethoven's then little-known quartets, especially the later works.   After the addition of some wood-wind players they adopted the name of Société Classique.   In 1855 the quartet only toured in Germany as far as Berlin and evoked the greatest admiration, especially for their rendering of the, rarely perfectly heard, later Beethoven quartets.   Armingaud composed a number of violin pieces in a florid, showy style which were pub. in Paris.

MLLE BRESSON, ca. 1820 noted in Paris as excellent violinist, pianist and composer of minor pieces for pianoforte and violin and pianoforte and harp which became favourably known also in Germany.   From 1827 she disappeared from public view.

CHARLES VICTOR ARTHUR SAINT-LEON, b. Paris, Apr. 17, 1821; d. there, Dec. 2, 1870.   A famous ballet dancer, who wrote the libretti of many of his ballets, in which he appeared with his wife, Fanni Ceritto.   He was also celebrated as a violin virtuoso and composed some violin concertos.   Mendel says of him: Son of the ballet master at the Court of Stuttgart, he learned both dancing and violin playing; in his fourteenth year he appeared as solo violinist at concerts; 1838 he toured all over Europe with great success as violin virtuoso and dancer. After his marriage with Fanny Cerrito he appeared, together with the latter, in ballets, mostly written and composed by himself as dancer and violinist.   He wrote and produced in this way also 2 ballets for the Paris Grand Opera; in the latter, part of the music was by Eug. Gautier; in later years he appeared no longer as dancer but produced a number of very popular ballets in Paris, partly in collaboration with others. As a violinist he combined a brilliant technique with pleasing grace of delivery.   His ballet Tartini, finally called "Le

Violon du Diable," in which he played the title rôle, met with great success both in Italy and at the Paris Opera.

JEAN PIERRE MAURIN, b. Avignon, Feb. 14, 1822; d. Paris, Mar. 16, 1894. In June, 1838, he joined the preparatory class of Guérin at the Paris Conservatoire where afterwards he was a pupil successively of Baillot and of Habeneck. After gaining several prizes he appeared in public as a soloist and proved himself an excellent virtuoso. Together with the violoncellist Chevillard, he founded a string quartet called the "Société des Derniers Quatuors de Beethoven" which acquired European fame. In 1875 he succeeded Alard as professor of violin at the Paris Conservatoire where he trained many excellent pupils, the foremost being Lucien Capet.

LEOPOLD DANCLA, b. Bagnères de Bigorre, July 1, 1823; d. Paris, Mar. 29, 1895. A pupil of Baillot at the Paris Conservatoire, where he gained the 2nd prize in 1840, and the 1st prize in 1842. He became afterwards a violinist at the Grand Opera, and professor at the Conservatoire. He composed some pieces for violin, studies, and 3 string quartets.

EDOUARD VICTOIRE ANTOINE LALO, b. Lille, Jan. 27 (17?), 1823; d. Paris, Apr. 22, 1892. After finishing his studies at the Lille Conservatoire where he studied under Habeneck, Schulhoff and Crevecoeur, he went to Paris in 1858 to join J. Arminghaud's string quartet as viola, with Mas as 2nd violin and L. Jacquard as violoncello. From 1860 onward he devoted himself chiefly to composition. Apart from operas, ballets, concertos for various instruments, chamber and vocal music he wrote 4 violin concertos, op. 20, N⁰· 1 ded. to Sarasate; N⁰· 2 is the Symphonie Espagnole; Fantaisie Norvegienne; Concerto Russe; a sonata, a duo concertante; and characteristic pieces for violin. Although the first concerto was dedicated to him, Sarasate played more often the Symphonie Espagnole, which has kept its place in the repertoire of violinists, as it is not only brilliant and effective from the violinistic point of view, but also from the purely musical aspect.

ALEXANDRE MALIBRAN, b. Paris, Nov. 10, 1823; d. there, May 13 (Riemann: 12), 1867. A pupil of Sauzay in Paris. In 1845 he married an excellent pianist with whom he toured in Germany and settled in the same year at Cassel, where he made further studies under Spohr. A few years later he returned to Paris where he started in 1860 a musical periodical, *Union Instrumentale*, which was but short-lived; and at Brussels in 1864, *Le Monde Musical*. In 1860 he went to Frankfort a/M. as musical editor of the French paper *Le Chroniqueur*. His attempts to start concerts at the Gaité Theatre, Paris, concerts similar to the Pasdeloup concerts, were abortive. He composed a number of violin pieces, orchestral works, chamber music, and a mass for male chorus for the Legion of Honour. He also wrote a biography of Spohr with a list of the latter's pupils from 1805 to 1856 in German (Frankfort a/M., 1860).

JEAN JACQUES DEBILLEMONT, b. Dijon, Dec. 12, 1824; d. Paris, Feb. 14, 1879. Began to study the violin at the age of 9; entered the Paris Conservatoire in 1839 as a violin pupil of Alard, studying theory and composition under Leborne and Carafa. He was for some time violinist at the Opéra-Comique. He returned to Dijon to get some of his early operas performed, but settled permanently in Paris in 1859, where he brought out a number of operettas, operas, etc. He was for some years conductor of the concerts of the Société des Beaux-arts, and afterwards at the theatre Porte Saint-Martin.

# CHAPTER 51

# France: to Present Day

ISIDOR CAHEN, b. Paris, Mar. 25, 1826. Studied at the Paris Conservatoire and became a distinguished violinist and composer for his instrument (Mendel).

LÉON ALBERT L'HÔTE, b. Paris, May 21, 1828 (Baptie: 31). Studied at the Paris Conservatoire, where he gained several prizes including the 1st. Became solo violinist at the Théâtre Italienne. Composed a romance for violin, orchestral, chamber music, and choral works.

JULES AUGUSTE GARCIN (SALOMON), b. Bourges, July 11, 1830; d. Paris, Oct. 10, 1896; his real name was Salomon. In his ninth year he entered the preparatory class of the Paris Conservatoire. In 1843 he became a violin pupil of Clavel and in 1846 of Alard, while Bazin and Adam were his teachers for theory and composition. After gaining several prizes at the Conservatoire he joined the orchestra of the Grand Opera in 1856, where he became solo violinist and 3rd conductor in 1871. In 1875 he was also appointed as teacher of the violin at the Conservatoire. In 1881 he became 2nd and 1885–92 1st conductor of the Conservatoire concerts in succession of Deldevez. He composed a violin concerto and other pieces for violin.

CHARLES LAMOUREUX, b. Bordeaux, Sept. 28, 1834; d. Paris, Dec. 21, 1899. A pupil of Girard at the Paris Conservatoire, where he gained the 1st prize for violin-playing in 1854. After that he played for a time in the orchestras of the Gymnase and the Grand Opera, then after some further studies under Tolbecque, Leborne and Chauvet, he formed a chamber-music society with Colblain, Adam and Rignault. In 1873 he founded the Société de Musique Sacrée, for the performance of Bach's cantatas and Handel's oratorios. After occupying various positions as conductor, in 1878 he succeeded Deldevez in that capacity at the Grand Opera, and in 1881 he founded the *Nouveaux Concerts*, which became generally known as the *Concerts Lamoureux*, which were eventually taken over by his son-in-law Camille Chevillard.

EDOUARD (real name JUDAS) COLONNE, b. Bordeaux, July 23, 1838. Pupil of Girard and Sauzay (violin), Elwart and Ambr. Thomas (composition) at the Paris Conservatoire; 1st violinist at the Opera until 1871, when he became conductor of the Concert Nationale. In 1874 he founded the Concert du Châtelet, where he brought out all the great works of Berlioz, and many of modern German composers. In 1878 he conducted the concerts of the Great Paris Exhibition, and 1892 he became conductor of the Paris Opera.

PAUL JULIEN, b. Brest, Feb. 12, 1841; d. Paris, Mar. 7, 1860. A pupil of the Paris Conservatoire. He was greatly admired as a soloist in his public appearances. During 1853–7 he toured very successfully in America and returned to France, where he resumed his concert playing, although with already impaired health, which soon was to end a promising career.

CAMILLA URSO, b. Nantes, June 13, 1842; d. New York, Jan. 20, 1902. A pupil of Massart at the Paris Conservatoire. Toured from 1852, first with Sonntag and Alboni, afterwards alone. In 1860 she married a Mr. F. Luère, but toured again from 1863. She did a great deal to advance the cultivation of the violin in America.

ÉMILE SAURET, b. Dun-le-Roi (Cher), May 22, 1852; d. London, Feb. 12, 1920. Began his study of the violin at the Paris Conservatoire, afterwards studied under de Beriot at the Brussels Conservatoire. In 1866 he began to tour in England, France and Italy, 1870–4 in America and 1877 in Germany. He lived for some years in Berlin, where in 1880–91 he was violin teacher at the Stern Conservatoire, and in the latter year succeeded Sainton at the Royal Academy of Music in London. In 1903 he went to Chicago as teacher at the Ziegfeld Conservatoire, but returned in 1906, going first to Geneva, then to Berlin, and 1908 to London again, where he remained. He was twice married; his first wife was Teresa Careño, but they separated after a few years and he married afterwards a lady from Düsseldorf. His compositions for violin consist of 2 violin concertos, a rhapsody with orchestra, op. 59; 2 pieces with orchestra, op. 60; a number of pieces with pianoforte; he also wrote some pieces for string orchestra. He counted among his pupils a large number of eminent violinists of this and the previous generation; foremost among the latter was Tor Aulin.

PAUL VIARDOT, b. Château Courtavent, near Paris, July 20, 1857. Son of the famous singer Pauline Viardot-Garcia and pupil of his cousin Léonard. He made his debut at the concert Pasdeloup with great success. He was afterwards concertmeister in various orchestras, including those of the Grand Opera, Paris, the Concerts Populaires, Lille, the Concerts Classiques at Marseilles, etc. He has toured as a virtuoso in Europe, America, South Africa, etc., sometimes in company of Rubinstein, Saint-Saëns, Raoul Pugno, and others. He is professor of violin and examiner at the Paris Conservatoire and composed violin pieces, chamber music, symphonic poems and suites for orchestra. He also wrote a History of Music in Scandinavia, and other works on music.

CHARLES MARTIN TORNOV LOEFFLER, b. Mülhausen, Alsace, Jan. 30, 1861. Violin pupil of Léonard and Massart at the Paris Conservatoire and of Joachim at the Berlin High School of Music, and in composition of Guiraud and Fr. Kiel. He was for some time a member of the Pasdeloup orchestra in Paris and then of that of Baron von Dervies at Nice and Lugano. In 1881 he settled at Boston, Mass., where for many years he was a member of the Symphony orchestra, but since 1903 devoted himself exclusively to teaching and composition. He composed a suite for violin and orchestra, "Les Veillées de l'Ukraine" (1891); Divertimento for violin and orchestra, a minor (1897); a string quartet; 4 poems for violin, viola and pianoforte, op. 5; music for four string players (1923); a string sextet; an octet for strings, harp, and two pianofortes; 2 rhapsodies for oboe, viola, and pianoforte (1901); 2 operas, a number of important orchestral and choral works, songs, etc.

EDOUARD NADAUD, b. Paris, Apr. 14, 1862. Received his first violin lessons from his father and played successfully in public at the age of 6. In 1873 he entered the Conservatoire, where he studied under Chas. Dancla until 1880, when he left with the 1st prize. After that he appeared as soloist at the Pasdeloup, Lamoureux and the Conservatoire concerts. At the latter he was for a time 2nd concertmeister. He is not only a brilliant soloist but also an excellent chamber music player and as such has been associated with Rubinstein, Diemer, Pugno and others. He is an excellent teacher and has published several works of studies, including an edition of Locatelli's caprices. He succeeded his master Chas. Dancla as professor at the Conservatoire and is honorary member and secretary of the society of the Conservatoire concerts, apart from holding other honorary offices.

EUGÈNE MAURICE HAYOT, b. Provins, May 8, 1862. A pupil of Massart at the Paris Conservatoire, where he gained the 1st prize in 1883; he played with great success at the Pasdeloup, Colonne, Lamoureux, Conservatoire, and many other concerts in Paris, the provinces and abroad. About 1895 he formed a permanent quartet with Touché, succeeded by André, Denayer, and Salmon, which was connected with the concerts of "La Trompette," the Cercle Volney and the Union Artistique, and also gave independent concerts. They also visited the principal towns of Europe, where they appeared with signal success. Hayot, who has a great reputation as a teacher, was professor of the Paris Conservatoire from 1894 to 1896.

SERGE ACHILLE RIVARDE, b. on board ship between Havre and New York, Oct. 31, 1865. His father, Paolo Rivarde, a Spanish violinist, gave him the first lessons on that instrument. His mother was American and they settled in New York, where he received further lessons successively from Felix Simon, Henri Wieniawski and Joseph White, a man of colour. At the age of 11 he entered the Paris Conservatoire, where he studied under Dancla, and in July, 1879, shared the 1st prize for violin playing with Ondříček. During 1881–5 he was in America and gave up playing for a time, but in 1885–91 he was a member of the Lamoureux orchestra, and in July, 1894, he made his London debut at a Nikisch concert at the Queen's Hall where he gave a superb rendering of the Beethoven concerto with immense success. Wilhelmj, Sauret, Ysaÿe and Nachez, who were all present on the occasion, were unanimous in their praise of the young virtuoso. Although of Franco-Spanish descent, he shows a decided leaning to the German school, reminding one in the breadth and power of his style of the Joachim school. This is particularly marked in his rendering of the Bach sonatas, which combines depth of thought and feeling with noble dignity and grandeur. At a Crystal Palace concert in the same year he proved by his playing of Lalo's "Symphonie Espagnole" that he also commands the lighter graces of his art to their fullest extent. In 1899 he was appointed teacher of the violin at the Royal College of Music, London, continuing to appear as a soloist in England and abroad, but chiefly devoting himself to teaching. In 1924 he founded a school of his own for violin playing, but without relinquishing his position at the R.C.M., where he is highly esteemed as teacher of solo and ensemble playing. His manual "Violin-playing" was published in 1922. Rivarde is a great admirer of the violins made by Szepessy Béla, on one of whose instruments he played even at public concerts, although he possesses some fine Italian violins.

RENÉ ORTMANS, b. Fontainebleau, 1866. Son of a noted landscape painter and amateur violoncellist (pupil of F. Servais); René Ortmans was a violin pupil of Sighicelli, then of Lefont, and from 1880 to 1884 of I. Maurin at the Paris Conservatoire. In the latter year he was also a 1st violinist in the Pasdeloup orchestra, a post which he held until the orchestra was disbanded in 1884, and when the famous conductor died in 1887, Ortmans conducted the orchestra at the funeral ceremony. At the age of 12 he had already made his public debut, and a few years later he gave concerts on his own account for which he engaged artists from Paris and acted as his own impresario. In 1884 he came, armed with letters of introduction from Gounod, to Sir Julius Benedict and Aug. Manns, who engaged him for the Crystal Palace, where he appeared in 1885, after a serious illness, and was so successful that many other engagements followed in London and in the provinces. When the writer organized regular chamber concerts at the North-East London Institute, newly founded by Prof. E. Prout, Ortmans became their leader for two years and acted in the same capacity at the Musical Artists' Society. In 1890 he was appointed teacher at Augen's college, Harley St., and soon after also at the

London Academy, and on the death of Pollitzer in 1900 he succeeded the latter as chief teacher of violin and conductor of the orchestra which he brought to a high degree of efficiency. In 1904 his friend Ysaÿe engaged him to conduct his two orchestral concerts at St. James's Hall, which drew the attention of the public to his decided talent in that direction. His chief interest centred however in chamber music and he was forming a quartet with the intention of bringing out works by modern composers when he strained his arm through over-work and had to abandon solo playing for a long time. He was also teacher and conductor of the orchestra at the Hampstead Conservatoire and highly esteemed in both capacities. Ortmans has composed some effective solo pieces for violin, and a Prelude and Bourrée of his so pleased Ysaÿe that he played them at the Monday Popular concerts in 1901. He also has an interesting collection of violins, including one of the rare Stradivaris with beechwood back, dated 1729, and a fine collection of bows by famous makers. About 1909 he conducted the Audrey Chapman orchestra which, apart from concerts in the Queen's Hall, provided free concerts in poor districts of London.

LUCIEN CAPET, b. Paris, 1873. A violin pupil of the Paris Conservatoire. After finishing his studies he became solo violinist in the Lamoureux orchestra, and 1899–1903 teacher at the Bordeaux Conservatoire. In 1903 he formed a quartet, bearing his name, with which he toured with great success throughout Europe and in 1907 he became professor of ensemble playing at the Paris Conservatoire, resuming his activities with his quartet (C. Delobelle, 2nd violin; H. Benoit, viola; M. Henri, violoncello) in 1919. He has acquired a high reputation as a successful teacher, and Gusikov is mentioned (ca. 1910) as standing in the front rank of his numerous successful pupils.

HENRI MARTEAU, b. Reims, Mar. 31, 1874. His father, a former burgomaster of Reims, was an amateur violinist, his German mother was a daughter of the pianist Schwendy. Many notable artists visited the house; the pianist Planté was his godfather, and Sivori evoked such enthusiasm in the then 5-year-old boy that he decided to become a violinist, and he commenced his studies under Bünzli, a Swiss violinist. Afterwards he studied for nine years under Léonard, received some thirty lessons from Sivori, and in 1892 he was for ten months a pupil of Garcin at the Paris Conservatoire, which he left with the 1st prize for violin. His opinion of Sivori as a teacher was not very favourable. He studied under him Paganini's concertos and caprices as well as studies and operatic concert fantasias by Sivori, who insisted on his imitating exactly Paganini's manner as that master had handed it down to him; that the then 11-year-old boy was able to do this speaks well for his exceptional talent and technical facility. He had already appeared in public at the age of 10, when he took the place of Léonard, who was indisposed. At the end of Mar., 1885, he played the Andante and last movement of the Mendelssohn concerto at Dresden, and in Dec., 1887, the G minor concerto by Bruch in Vienna at Hans Richter's concert. In 1891 he returned to Paris after a prolonged sojourn in Berlin, bringing with him the Brahms violin concerto which he was the first to play in the French capital. Both he and the work were received with great enthusiasm and shortly after this he gave chamber-music soirées with Raoul Pugno at Reims; then he resumed his studies under Garcin as stated above. After receiving the 1st prize in 1892 he went on tour in the United States of America, to which he paid a second visit in 1893. In the two following years he toured repeatedly in Scandinavia, and after serving his year in the army in 1895 he toured in France, Switzerland, the Balkan States, Russia, etc. In 1896 he conducted a performance of his "La Voix de Jeanne d'Arc" for soprano, chorus and orchestra at Götenburg. In 1899 he appeared with great success in Berlin, and in 1900 he became teacher at the Geneva Conservatoire, where he founded a quartet with E. Reymond, W. Pahnke and Ad. Rehberg, and gave sonata recitals with Ed. Risler. During this time he had among many talented pupils Florizel von Reuter, Pecsi, L. V. Laar, Lindelöf, Sommer, Weinmann, Pollak, Junna, Breuning, and H. Blume. In 1908 he became Joachim's successor at the Berlin Hochschule, to which the grand master himself, whose tutor he had translated into French, had recommended him. He continued his occasional concert tours, but devoted himself chiefly to teaching until the War brought his activity in Berlin to a sad end in 1915. Until

ERRE MARIE FRANCOIS BAILLOT DE SALES

CORENTIN HABENECK

J. B. CHARLES DANCLA

J. DELPHIN ALARD

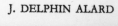
*re Petit, Paris.*

1920 he was then 2nd capellmeister at Göteborg, 1921–4 1st teacher, then rector at the Prague German Academy for music and dramatic art; 1926–7 teacher at the Leipzig Conservatoire and 1928 that of Dresden. He has made his home at Lichtenberg, Upper Franconia. He has composed for the violin: 2 concertos, the first in A major, op. 15, in the form of a suite, the second, op. 18, in C major; fantasia for organ and violin, op. 27; sonata fantastica for violin solo, op. 35; pieces for violin and pianoforte, op. 2; studies for violin, op. 14, 19, 25 (6 books); many arrangements of pieces; also a symphony and other orchestral as well as choral works, chamber music, songs, etc. (*see* list in Riemann).

JACQUES THIBAUD, b. Bordeaux, Sept. 27, 1880. Appeared in public as a violinist at Angers at the age of 13. He then became a pupil of Marsick at the Paris Conservatoire and at the end of his studies became a member of the Colonne orchestra, in which he soon rose to the position of solo violinist. He then toured extensively in Europe and America and ranks among the foremost living violinists as well on account of his perfect technique as of his great power of poetical expression.

WILLIAM CANTRELLE, b. Paris, Nov. 20, 1888. A pupil of Rémy at the Paris Conservatoire, which he left in 1905 after gaining the 1st prize. He was solo violinist, 1908–12, at the Concerts Rouge; 1913–21 at the Concerts Touche, as well as 1917 and 1918 in the combined Colonne and Lamoureux orchestra, and 1922 at the Concerts Colonne.

RÉNÉE CHEMET-DECREUX, b. Boulogne-sur-Seine, 1888?. Entered the Paris Conservatoire as a pupil of Mme Roy Got, and afterwards of M. Berthelier. She toured successfully on the Continent, and appeared in 1904 at the Promenade and the Symphony concerts at the Queen's Hall under Sir Henry Wood. Since then she has frequently appeared in London, and late in 1930 she gave a sonata recital at the B.B.C.

MARIUS ROBERT MAX CASADESUS, b. Paris, Oct. 24, 1892. Gained the 1st prize for violin at the Paris Conservatoire in 1914, and composed some quartets, solo pieces, etc. He is a member of a distinguished family of musicians, of whom the best known is HENRI GUSTAVE CASADESUS, viola and viole d'amour virtuoso, the founder and head of the Société des Instruments Anciens.

L. GANNE, b. Paris.   A pupil of Ševčik, has become known as a composer and arranger of music of a popular nature.

# CHAPTER 52

## *Germany: to 1825*

AT the end of the 18th century both the Berlin (Benda) and the Mannheim-Munich (Stamitz, Cannabich, etc.) schools began to decline, but four new centres formed to carry on, not only their traditions, but likewise those of Viotti; they were at Cassel, Leipzig, Vienna and Prague.

The dominating figure in the violinistic world of Germany at the beginning of the 19th century was Ludwig Spohr. The Cassel school began with his arrival there, and finished with his death, although his teaching, and especially his system of bowing, was spread throughout Europe and even America by his numerous pupils. He laid great importance on the art of bowing; but the fancy bowings, spiccato, spring bow, etc., he abhorred. He cultivated long strokes of the bow, producing a tone of great breadth and power, yet always beautiful; a perfect cantabile was his ideal, and the singing quality of the instrument was to him the most important. His style was dignified, of great nobility, and he always strove to impart the poetical, inner meaning of a composition. His concertos and violin duets rank among the best of their kind, and some of the former, which were included in the repertoire of every serious virtuoso until recent times, as well as the great duets, unequalled to the present day, added greatly to his influence as teacher, in the advancement of violin-playing.

The Leipzig school, which commenced with the foundation of the world-famous Conservatoire in 1843, followed Spohr's traditions through his pupil Ferd. David, only in a much modified form. If the latter had many and serious faults, it cannot be denied that he was an eminent teacher, and that those of his pupils who steered free from his mannerisms, like Wilhelmj, Heckmann, A. Hilf and others, owed much of their success to his excellent teaching. Leipzig became through him the German centre for the art of violin-playing.

The father of the Vienna school, which rivalled that of Leipzig in importance, was Schuppanzigh, the leader of Prince Rasoumowsky's famous private quartet. He was trained in the traditions of the classical school, to which he remained a staunch adherent, while his pupil Mayseder inclined more to the virtuoso element. Mayseder's influence upon the art of violin-playing lay chiefly in his compositions, which were effective, and largely used as material for study, while as executant he handed down his art to many pupils, the most prominent of whom were Adelburg, De Ahna, Hafner, Hauser, Panofka and Wolf. More important for the Viennese school was Jos. Böhm who was appointed as teacher for the violin at the School of Music of the Society of Friends of Music on its foundation in 1819. He devoted himself chiefly to teaching, and trained many eminent violinists, among whom Joachim, Hellmesberger, Singer, Rappoldi and Grün became famous teachers in their turn. They were worthily succeeded by Rosé, and from 1909 to 1919 Ševčik, the greatest of modern teachers, who completely revolutionized the system of violin study, stood at the head of that department at the Vienna Conservatoire. Although he was the master of most of the great virtuosos of modern times he did not neglect the more serious and important side of his art, and on the whole it cannot be said that, in spite of the fact that the technique of violinists has increased to an astounding extent since the middle of the 19th century, virtuosity as an aim by itself has been followed so much as in former times.

The musical life of Vienna and Prague have always been closely bound up, as the Imperial Court as well as the great nobles of Austria and Bohemia, mostly keen patrons of music, resided alternately in the two capitals. Although their national folk-music differed widely, being essentially German in character in Vienna, and as distinctly Slavonic in Prague, yet German music and culture dominated throughout the greater part of the 19th century, until the national Czeskian character found expression in the works of Smetana and Dvořak. The German schools of Mannheim and Berlin owed their inception to Bohemian violinists, while Mannheim, in the person of Friedrich Pixis, gave to the Prague Conservatoire, which was opened in 1811, its first professor for the violin, and his pupil, M. Mildner, spread the fame of that institute throughout Europe by the eminence of many of his numerous pupils, of whom Laub and Hřimaly became professors at the Moscow Conservatoire, Zajic at that of Strassburg, E. Wirth at the Berlin Hochschule; Skalitzky settled as teacher, soloist and chamber-music player at Bremen, and Bennewitz followed his master at the Prague Conservatoire, where during thirty-five years as director and professor, he trained a large number of eminent violinists, of whom Halíř became famous as member—afterwards leader of the Joachim quartet, and professor at the Berlin Hochschule. The greatest star among his pupils, as a teacher, is unquestionably O. Ševčik, who followed his master at the Conservatoire and became famous throughout the whole of the world.

LOUIS SPOHR, b. Brunswick, Apr. 5, 1784; d. Cassel, Oct. 22, 1859. He was born in the house of his maternal grandfather, a clergyman, and in 1786, his father, a physician, settled at Seesen. Both parents were musical: the father played the flute and the mother played the pianoforte and sang. The boy's innate gift for music was thus fostered from earliest childhood and at the age of 4 he sang duets with his mother at their musical evening practices. At his urgent request his father bought him a little fiddle at a fair, on which he began to play all day long. The rector Riemenschneider then took him in hand and taught him the elements of violin-playing, and very soon he took part with his parents in a trio for piano, flute and violin by Kalkbrenner. About 1790–1 Dufour, a French language teacher and good amateur violinist and violoncellist, became his violin teacher, and recognizing the boy's exceptional talent, as he had already, without instruction, made several attempts at composition, he persuaded the father to let him follow his natural bent for a musical career and send him to Brunswick for systematic tuition. There he studied theory and composition under Hartung, a surly old organist, whose method did not stimulate his thirst for knowledge, and before long failing health prevented the poor old man from instructing him any longer. Spohr never had any other lessons in these subjects, which henceforth he studied by close examination of the scores of the great masters. His teacher for the violin was the chamber musician Kunisch, under whom he progressed so well that at the beginning of 1799 he played a concerto of his own with so much success that he was asked to repeat it at a Court concert, accompanied by the Ducal band. Kunisch recommended that he should henceforward receive the tuition of Concertmeister Maucourt. After one year's work under that master he went on tour, first visiting Hamburg with a few letters of introduction, but the 14-year-old boy failed to obtain a hearing, and having exhausted his resources, he sent on his luggage to Brunswick, himself returning on foot. On his return he wrote a petition to the Duke, himself an amateur violinist, who, after having heard him play again, appointed him as violinist in the Court orchestra and promised to defray the expenses of his further tuition under one of the great masters of the time. Viotti was approached but he was absorbed in his wine business. Ferdinand Eck, who was considered the most famous violinist after Viotti, was then asked; but he recommended his brother Franz. The Duke invited the latter to Brunswick, and having satisfied himself about his ability, decided that Spohr should become his pupil for one year. As Eck was just starting on a journey to Russia, Spohr was allowed to accompany him. They started at the beginning of 1802 but stayed for a prolonged period at Hamburg and Strelitz, which gave Eck a favourable opportunity to devote much time to his pupil. After visiting all the principal towns on the Baltic they arrived at St. Petersburg on Dec. 23 of that year, and remained till June, 1803. During the whole of that period Spohr, who had the figure and strength of a young giant, practised for ten hours every day. He also composed among other things his violin concerto, op. 1, which is quite in the style of Rode, and the violin duets, op. 3, during that time. Through Eck he had absorbed the principles of the Mannheim school which he amplified by the intuition of his genius. He felt, however, that he still lacked many essential details, especially with regard to the art of bowing. On his return to Brunswick in July he found Rode there, whom he forthwith took for his model, and succeeded in copying him very closely, until he developed a style of his own. After having given

198

a very successful concert at Brunswick, he was appointed 1st violin in the Court chapel. Honourable as this was it could not satisfy the ambition of a genius like Spohr, and in 1804 he went on a tour which was eventually to lead him to Paris; but at Göttingen he had the misfortune that just before entering the town his portmanteau with his precious Guarnerius violin, the gift of a Russian noble, was stolen from the back of the coach. He returned immediately to Brunswick, and after having with the generous help of his patron, the Duke, obtained another good violin, though not comparable to his lost treasure, he started again on a tour to Leipzig, Dresden, and Berlin. Rochlitz, who heard him at the latter town, after praising in detail all the features of his technique, says that " he inclines to the grand as well as the gentle dreaming and emotional style. He combines fire with delicacy, refined taste with intensity of feeling. The deep entering into the ideas of a composition and rendering it in the spirit of the author, is what makes him the true artist." At his Berlin concert he was assisted by Meyerbeer, who, though only a boy of 13, was already a brilliant pianist. On Oct. 1, 1805, he was appointed concertmeister at the Court of Gotha, where he made the acquaintance of the harpist Dorette Scheidler, whom he married on Feb. 2, 1806, and they went on tour together, visiting Leipzig, Dresden, Prague, Munich and Stuttgart, where they met Weber, in 1807. At the latter place they had to stipulate that no loud conversation nor card-playing should take place during their performance, if they were to play at the Court, which was graciously conceded, though not extended to any other part of the concert! (*See* Spohr's Autobiography.) In 1809 Spohr and his wife toured in North Germany, and at Hamburg he was commissioned to write an opera, which was performed there in the following year. In 1809 he conducted the first musical festival in Germany, at Frankenhausen in Thuringia. In 1812 he went to Vienna, where he came into contact with Beethoven, whose greatest works he never understood, although he was an ardent admirer of his quartets, op. 18, which he was the first to perform at Berlin and Leipzig. He also met again with Rode, and an interesting incident in connexion with their meeting is told in his autobiography. It appears that Rode's violinistic powers had declined and he had fallen into bad mannerisms. After playing his famous variations in G, Spohr asked him if he remembered how he used to play them, offering to play them exactly in that manner, which he did forthwith, earning rapturous applause, in which Rode courteously joined, although he felt evidently hurt. Spohr says that he soon felt ashamed that he had allowed his artistic enthusiasm thus to obscure his better judgment. During this visit he was appointed leader in the orchestra of Theatre an der Wien, but left again in 1815 on account of differences with the director, Count Palffy. After spending the summer at the country seat of Prince Carolath, in Bohemia, afterwards conducting another music festival at Frankenhausen, he toured through South Germany, Switzerland, and thence through Italy. On his way there he composed his eighth concerto, the famous "Scena cantante." He played at all the principal Italian towns, and also met with Rossini, whose music he did not admire, as might be expected. He returned in 1817, and, after a visit to Holland, he became capellmeister at the theatre, Frankfort a/M., where in 1818 his opera "Faust" was performed for the first time. This was followed by "Zemire and Azor," which for a time became even more popular. At the end of two years, however, he left, again on account of dissensions with the management.

In 1820 he paid his first visit to London at the invitation of the Philharmonic Society, where both he and his wife met with an enthusiastic reception. At the first concert on Mar. 6 he played his eighth concerto, and at the second he led his solo quartet in E. The third concert, on Apr. 10, is memorable in the history of music in England, as on that occasion a baton was used for the first time in this country, in the face of a strong opposition, when Spohr conducted his symphony in d minor, specially written for this occasion. At the last concert another symphony of his was performed for the first time, as well as his nonet, op. 31. Both as virtuoso and as composer Spohr was henceforth firmly established in the favour of the English people. On his journey back he visited Paris, where he met with Viotti, Kreutzer, Habeneck, Cherubini and other eminent musicians, but his success was but qualified. The French could not understand the typical German soulful reserve, which was particularly appreciated by the kindred English spirit, and for his compositions they had no understanding except Cherubini, who made him play a quartet of his three times over, as he relates with some pride. In criticizing his playing, French vanity and spiteful jealousy went so far, that one leading critic said that "if he remained some time in Paris, he might improve his taste, and then return to form that of the good Germans." All they found to praise in his playing was purity of intonation and precision; to his greater qualities they were deaf and blind. In 1821 Spohr settled at Dresden so that his daughters might study under Miksch, a famous singing master. There he met Weber, whom he was no more able to understand than Beethoven, but when the former was offered the post of Court-capellmeister at Cassel he recommended Spohr instead, who was thereupon offered the appointment for life under very favourable conditions, and accepted. He entered upon his new duties on New Year's Day, 1822, and from that day he remained at Cassel to the end of his life, except for a few visits to England or to various German towns. For the rest he devoted himself, apart from his ordinary duties, chiefly to composing and teaching. His opera, "Jessonda," first performed at Cassel, soon made the round of all German theatres, and became a great popular favourite. In 1826 he conducted the Rhenish music festival at Düsseldorf and again in 1840 at Aix-la-Chapelle. In 1831 he finished his "Violin School," which deals with many individual traits of violin technique which appear in his concertos and other violin compositions, to which the work is chiefly preparatory. The elementary part is of less practical value as he had never taught beginners. It remained, however, for its advanced part a standard work until recent times. The politically troubled years which followed brought him many annoyances, as Spohr was a strong and independent character with definite radical leanings, while the new Elector was a ruthless despot. In 1834 he had the misfortune to lose his wife to whom he was greatly devoted. In 1836 he married the pianist Marianne Pfeifer. In the same year he conducted a Music Festival in his native town. In 1839 he produced his "Calvary" at the Norwich Festival, which proved a triumphant success in spite of the opposition to the text by some of the clergy, and soon after he received a libretto, "The Fall

of Babylon," by Prof. Edw. Taylor, with the request to compose it for the Norwich Festival of 1842. He was unable
to conduct the work on that occasion, as the Elector refused
the necessary leave, in spite of a monster petition from his
English admirers, and a special request from Lord Aberdeen,
the head of the Government. The work had an enormous
success, and during his summer vacation Spohr conducted it
twice in London and had an enthusiastic reception, also at a
Philharmonic concert chiefly devoted to his compositions, and
at another concert at the special request of Queen Victoria
and the Prince Consort.

In 1847 he came again to London, when the Sacred
Harmonic Society gave three concerts, at which his principal
sacred compositions were produced. In this year he received
the title of Director-General of Music with Court rank
(Hoffähigkeit) on the occasion of his 25 years jubilee as
capellmeister at Cassel. From 1850 his life was more and
more troubled by truculent behaviour of the Elector, who on
sundry occasions frustrated his plans without any rhyme or
reason. When he wanted to take his usual summer vacation
in this year the Elector refused to sign the leave of absence,
and after several attempts to obtain this, to which he was
entitled by contract, he left without it. This involved him
in a lawsuit and he was condemned to pay a fine of 350
thaler. He appealed, and after two of the higher courts
gave their verdict in his favour, he was in the last instance
condemned to pay the fine, after the suit had dragged on
for four years. In 1850 he played for the last time in public,
as leader of his quartet. London claimed him again, for the
season of 1852, when he conducted the Italian version of
his "Faust" at Covent Garden with great success on July 15.
In 1853 he produced Wagner's "Tannhäuser" at Cassel, after
several attempts had been thwarted by the Elector. It is
curious to find in the conservative Spohr, who failed to understand Beethoven and even Weber, a champion of Wagner,
whom he declared to be the greatest dramatic composer of
the time. He would also have produced "Lohengrin," but
for the intervention of the Elector. The season of that year
found him in London again, where he conducted not only
a number of his own works, including the symphony for 2
orchestras, but also Beethoven's choral symphony. A per-

formance of "Jessonda" was in preparation, but as his leave was expiring he could not conduct it himself. In 1857 he was pensioned, against his wish, with 1,500 thaler (£225) per annum, instead of his full salary, to which he was entitled by contract. He accepted his fate with philosophical resignation, pleased—as he wrote to his former pupil Bott—to be at last free to go wherever he liked. In the winter of that year he had the misfortune to break his left arm, and had to relinquish violin playing. On the occasion of the fiftieth anniversary of the Prague Conservatoire he conducted there, still with full vigour, his opera "Jessonda." That was his last appearance; in the following year he ended at Cassel a life rich in years and honours.

He had been decorated by most of the ruling monarchs and princes of his time. The King of Prussia had bestowed on him the order "Pour le Merite," one of the highest of that country, and the Academies of Arts of Brussels and of Vienna, of St. Cecilia at Rome, the Society Euterpe of Leipzig, etc., etc., had elected him as a corresponding member.

His compositions are throughout the expression of a noble, lofty mind, not without originality, but lacking in strength and vitality; as Schumann says: "Spohr is a mollusc, but a noble one." He inclined to mannerism, especially in the use of the chromatic element; this and an excessive use of harmonic complications tends to monotony. On the other hand, he raised the violin concerto to a much higher level. It took broader and more important forms. The cantabile element predominates, and his passage work, which is highly original, is always subservient to the expression of the poetical idea, it never descends to the conventional or mere virtuoso display, and this accounts for the fact that so severe a critic as Joachim delighted in playing the last three of his concertos, especially the "Scena cantante." Also his later violin duets, which make considerable demands upon the technical skill of the executant, are works of lasting merit, which by the frequent use of double stops for both instruments sometimes produce the effect of a quartet, and their subject matter is important and fascinating to the listener. His larger orchestral and choral works have not worn well, though now and again his "Last Judgment" is still performed by church choirs. For a full list of his works *see* the catalogue by H. M. Schletterer, Breitkopf and Härtel, Grove's Dictionary "Spohr," and Eitner.

Spohr was the founder of a new school of violin-playing in Germany, which adhered to a large extent to his principle of using long bows, wherever possible, thus cultivating a powerful and clear tone, but neglecting somewhat the spiccato and lighter kinds of bowing and excluding the spring bow and those which belonged essentially to the virtuoso style. The fullest development of the left hand technique, including the wide stretches necessary for the execution of his compositions, was self-understood. Of his pupils, 187 are enumerated in a sketch of his life by Malibran (Frankfort, Sauerländer); they came from all parts of Europe and even from America. Among the foremost were Ferd. David, Wassermann, Ries, St. Lubin, Pott, Kömpel, Bott, Schön, Blagrove, Hartmann, and Bargheer. A more detailed account of his varied and interesting life may be found in his autobiography (Engl. ed. by Longman's, 1864).

KARL WILHELM HENNING, b. Berlin, Jan. 31, 1784; d. there, Apr., 1867. Concertmeister in Berlin. Received his first lessons from his father, a military bandsman, which enabled him to earn a small livelihood by playing in taverns and at dances. By his zealous attempts at self-improvement he attracted Seidler's attention, who gave him lessons and made him acquainted with the best masters to take as models. Finally he studied for a time under P. Rode. In a short time he was able to join the orchestra of the Italian Opera as violinist, and, by studying composition under A. Gürlich, to appear as soloist in public, playing a concert piece of his own composition with great success. In 1807 he was appointed violinist at the National Theatre and 1811 chamber musician in the Court chapel, where he received the title of Royal Concertmeister in 1822. During 1823–6 he was conductor at the New Königstädter theatre, but soon after rejoined the Court chapel as actual concertmeister (leader). When the musical section of the Academy of Arts was created, he became a member. In 1836 he received the title of Royal Director of Music, and in 1840 King Frederick William IV nominated him Royal Capellmeister, soon afterwards decorating him with the Order of the Red Eagle. From 1841 to 1848 he was capellmeister at the Berlin Opera, where Nicolai succeeded him on his retirement. After fifty years' service he was pensioned, but he did not lose his interest in music and still practised the violin every day. He composed sonatas and solos for the violin and the violoncello; a string sextet and quartets, trios and duets, and opera, ballets, as well as incidental music for many plays, cantatas, songs, etc. Long list of compositions in Fétis.

ALBERT HENNING, b. Breslau, 1792; d. Berlin, 1832. Brother and pupil of Karl Wilhelm Henning; became, 1811, chamber musician and violinist at the Royal Opera, Berlin, afterwards conductor of the symphony performances. He was a talented violinist and teacher.

HERMANN HENNING, b. Berlin, ca. 1820. The son of Albert Henning, was brought up and educated by his uncle Karl Wilhelm, who was also his teacher of violin-playing. He entered the Royal Chapel as chamber musician in 1840 and was still a member ca. 1880.

LUDWIG WILHELM MAURER, b. Potsdam, Feb. 8, 1789; d. St. Petersburg, Oct. 25, 1878. Son of Georg Maurer, Royal chamber musician, pupil of Haack, who was a pupil of Franz Benda. He made his debut in Berlin at the age of 13 with great success. There he came into contact with many eminent artists, whereby he benefited considerably in his studies, and was after a time attached to the Royal chamber music. When the latter was dissolved after the Battle of Jena in 1806, Maurer went first to Königsberg, then to Riga, where he made the acquaintance of Rode and Baillot from both of whom he received much valuable advice. Then he went to Mitau and thence to St. Petersburg, where he gave a number of concerts which not only enhanced his reputation but also considerably increased his financial resources. He then went to Moscow, where he met Baillot again, on whose recommendation he became director of the chapel of the chamberlain, Wsogologski, whom he followed to his country seat on the Siberian frontier during the French invasion, returning with him afterwards to Moscow and remaining in his service till 1817. In 1818 he went to Berlin and thence to Paris, where he appeared in public with great success. In 1819 (Riemann, i, 24) he accepted the offer of the post of concertmeister at the Court of Hanover, which he occupied until 1832, when Wsogologski asked him to come to St. Petersburg as director of his chapel, which he accepted in 1833, conducted the French opera and there instituted symphony concerts. Became inspector of the Imperial theatre orchestra in 1841–62. This position he occupied to the time of his death, but in 1845 went for a longer period to Dresden. His still familiar work, the concertante for 4 violins, was first performed by himself, Spohr, Müller, and Wich, and again in Paris in 1838 at a concert given by Herz and Lafont, when also his "3 airs Russes Variés," op. 14, with orchestra, were played. He composed 8 violin concertos, a symphony concertante for 2 violins, op. 56, as well as the afore-mentioned one for 4 violins, op. 55; 2 concertinos; 2 fantasias with orchestra; variations for 2 violins; numerous fantasias, and airs with variations; also operas, symphonies, etc., which testify to excellent musicianship and noble and refined thought, but they lack the divine spark of true inspiration. As an executant he was a worthy representative of the Rode-Kreutzer school and stood in the front rank of early 19th-century violinists. His sons and pupils, WSEVOLOD MAURER (violinist) and ALEXIS MAURER (violoncellist), born in St. Petersburg, toured in Germany and then returned to St. Petersburg.

WILHELM SPEYER, b. Frankfort-on-Main, 1790. From his seventh year he studied music, and especially the violin; at first under an obscure teacher at Mayence, then under Fraenzl and finally under Thieriot, whom Fétis describes as "a very original violinist" and friend of the famous Jean Paul Richter. Having been sent as an apprentice to an important merchant at Offenbach, he studied composition under André, and at the age of 16 conducted the opera at that town as an amateur. The orchestra was an excellent one, and among the actors of the theatre were the parents of Henriette Sonntag. Afterwards Speyer became a merchant, first at Frankfort, then at Offenbach, but all his leisure hours were devoted to music, and apart from being a good violinist, he was a composer, many of his works being issued by the leading publishers of the time; they consist of 3 sets of violin duets, op. 1 (Bonn, Simrock), op. 4 and 15 (Offenbach, André); one quintet and several quartets for strings, duets for flute and violin; church music and songs.

CHRISTIAN URHAN, b. Montjoie, near Aix-la-Chapelle, Feb. 16, 1790; d. Paris, Nov. 2, 1845. His father instructed him in violin-playing but he studied the pianoforte and several other instruments without a master, and before he had reached his 12th year he had already composed variations for violin, waltzes and other little pieces. The Empress Josephine, who heard him on her visit to Aix-la-Chapelle in 1805, was so struck by his talent that she gave him the means of studying composition under Lesueur, while he perfected his violin playing by keen observation of the style of various famous masters, to whom he had frequent opportunity to listen. Very soon he began to attract public attention by his elegant and artistic performance of Mayseder's compositions, which he popularized in Paris. He revived the viol d'amour, which he played at several of Fétis' historical concerts. Meyerbeer wrote the viol d'amour solo in the first act of "The Huguenots" specially for him; he also played the violon-alto invented by Woldemar (*see* the latter), which was a violin with the addition of the viola "c" as fifth string. Fétis says that he played solos on this instrument at the Conservatoire concerts with charming effect. As a viola player he was unequalled in his time, especially in chamber music, and as such always took part in Baillot's chamber music performances. In 1816 (Riemann: 1814) he was appointed viola player at the Opera, but in 1823 he became one of the 1st violinists and later on succeeded Baillot as solo violinist. For a long time he filled also the post of organist at the church of St. Vincent of Paul. Fétis speaks of him as "a perfect musician, great lecturer and a man of good taste. . . . As a composer he was noted for the eccentric forms of his works." An instance of the latter is perhaps his quintet for 3 violas, violoncello, contrabass and timpani (Paris, Richault); the same pub. also his 2 "Quintettes Romantiques" for 2 violins, 2 violas and violoncello, as well as piano duets, other pianoforte pieces and songs. No violin compositions of his are pub.

HEINRICH JOSEPH WASSERMANN, b. Schwarzbach, near Fulda, Apr. 3, 1791; d. Richen, Baden, Sept. 3, 1838. The son of a musician, he began to play the violin in early childhood. His first systematic teaching on the violin and in harmony he received from the cantor Hankel at Fulda. Afterwards he became a pupil of Spohr, who procured him a position as violinist at the Court of Hechingen. In 1817 he accepted the post of musical director at Zürich, in the hope that the change of climate might improve his delicate health. In 1820 Conradin Kreutzer induced him to join the Court chapel at Donaueschingen as concertmeister. A few years later he went to Munich, then to Stuttgart, and afterwards for some time to Paris. In 1828 he went as concertmeister to Geneva and afterwards in the same capacity to Basle, but a nervous complaint compelled him to relinquish his career as a violinist and he retired to the village of Richen. He composed variations for violin with string quartet, op. 4; easy violin duets, a string quartet, op. 14; a quartet with flute, dances for orchestra, guitar pieces, etc.

KARL AUGUST PETERSEN, b. Hamburg, 1792. Studied first the flute under his father, and then devoted himself to the violin and the pianoforte. About 1825 he toured in Denmark, Sweden and part of Germany, and then settled in Hamburg where, according to Fétis, he was still in 1840 as teacher. He composed up to that time for violin: duos for 2 violins, op. 10; rondo with pianoforte, op. 12; sonata for pianoforte and violin, op. 5; divertissement do., op. 7; besides pianoforte pieces.

FERDINAND KESSLER, b. Frankfort a/M., Jan., 1793; d. there, Oct. 28, 1856. The son and violin pupil of a double-bass player, learned composition under Vollweiler. He became an esteemed violinist who also composed pianoforte sonatas, rondos, etc., which were pub. while larger works remained in MS.

IGNAZ PETER LÜSTNER, b. Poischwitz, near Jauer, Dec. 23, 1793; d. Breslau, Jan. 30, 1873. During 1819–26 concertmeister in the chapel of Prince Karolath, then held the same position at Breslau, where he founded a school for violin-playing in 1844. Of his five sons, two were violinists, two violoncellists, and one harp player.

MORITZ KLENGEL, b. 1793; d. Leipzig, Sept. 14, 1870. For many years concertmeister and later also leader of the 2nd violins at the Gewandhaus concerts. When the Leipzig Conservatoire was opened he was appointed as teacher of the violin, and pensioned in 1866.

*Louis Spohr* [signature]

LOUIS SPOHR
From an engraving in the possession of
Messrs. W. E. Hill & Sons.

FERDINAND DAVID

ADOLF WIELE, b. Oldenburg, June 18, 1794; d. Cassel, ca. 1853. Received his first lessons on the violin from his father and made such rapid progress that he appeared successfully in public at the age of 8. He then became a pupil of Maucourt at Brunswick and, when that chapel was merged with that of the King of Westphalia, at Cassel, King Jerome sent him to Paris, where he became a pupil of Baillot at the Conservatoire; there he gained the 2nd prize in 1812, and the first prize in the following year. In 1815 he entered the Royal chapel at Stuttgart as solo violinist. From 1819 to 1821 he gave concerts at Munich, Vienna, Leipzig, Berlin, Weimar, and Cassel; at the latter town the Prince Elector William II engaged him in 1821 for his chapel, and afterwards made him concertmeister. Fétis speaks highly of him as a composer, and mentions a Polonaise with orchestra and several sets of variations which were pub. before ca. 1840.

ELISABETH FILIPOWICZ, *née* MAYER, b. Rastadt, 1794; d. London, May 4, 1841. Received her final tuition on the violin from L. Spohr. She married and toured with great success in Germany as Mme Minelli. She settled in Poland, where she lost her husband, and afterwards married Fillipowicz, a Lithuanian, who shared the fate of his compatriots during the Polish Revolution of 1831. Obliged to leave the country, she went to Paris, where she gave concerts and was greatly admired. In 1835 she settled in London, where she was equally successful.

JOSEPH SCHMIDT, b. Bückeburg, Sept. 26, 1795; d. there, Mar. 15, 1865. Violinist and afterwards court-capellmeister at Bückeburg; composed songs, psalms, an oratorio, etc. (Riemann mentions no compositions for violin.) His son, VICTOR SCHMIDT, b. Bückeburg, July 6, 1833, was also a violinist, and an elder son, JULIUS CAESAR SCHMIDT, was an excellent violoncellist. He had 22 children.

ADOLPH GANZ, b. Mayence, Oct. 14, 1796; d. London, Nov. 11, 1869. The eldest of the three brothers; received his first instruction in violin playing and musical theory and further training in harmony and thorough-bass through Seb. Holbusch. He became musical director at the Mayence theatre in 1819, received the title of Grand Ducal Hessian capellmeister in 1825 and settled in London in 1845. His sons Eduard and Wilhelm were both pianists. The latter was well known in London, where he died Sept. 12, 1914.

JOHANN WILHELM MANGOLD, b. Darmstadt, Nov. 19, 1796; d. there, May 23, 1875. Son and pupil of Georg Mangold for the violin, while Rinck and Abbé Vogler taught him composition. In 1810 the 14-year-old boy was already violinist in the Court chapel with a salary of 160 florins per annum, plus an allowance of wood, corn, wheat, 6 chickens and a cock as well as a uniform consisting of a green tail coat with red facings, yellow knee-breeches, white silk stockings, buckled shoes, cocked hat, and a sword. Dressed up like that the boy felt bashful and slunk under the shadow of the walls through the park to the chapel, his violin under his arm. In 1815 he was sent to Paris. The difficulty of being a foreigner, which stood in the way of becoming a student at the Conservatoire, was, at the recommendation of Spontini and Méhul, overcome by making him an élève auditeur. He studied composition under Méhul, but also pursued his study of the violin. Afterwards he joined, together with Halévy, Batton and Leborne, the composition class under Cherubini, and as these four remained as the only pupils in that class, Cherubini gave them their lessons at his house, whereby they were all drawn together in a bond of lasting friendship. In 1818 Mangold returned to Darmstadt, where he rejoined the chapel as violinist, became concertmeister in 1819, Court capellmeister in 1825, and was pensioned in 1858. In friendly intercourse with Weber and afterwards also with Meyerbeer, he raised the efficiency of the orchestra as well as the artistic status of the opera to a high level. As a violinist he earned a high reputation in early youth for his beautiful tone and his soulful artistic playing. He toured most successfully in Holland and North Germany with his uncle, Aug. Dan. Mangold. He composed several operas, a cantata, overtures, chamber music, solo pieces for violin and other instruments, vocal music, etc.

KARL LUDWIG AMAND MANGOLD, b. Darmstadt, Oct. 8, 1813; d. Oberstdorf, Allgäu, Aug. 5, 1889, Wilhelm's younger brother, was a pupil of his father and his brother Wilhelm. He entered the Darmstadt chapel as violinist in 1831 and visited London with his brother Wilhelm in 1834. From

1836 to 1839 he studied at the Paris Conservatoire, the violin under Sauzay, singing under Bordogni and Berton, and composition under Neukomm. After his return he rejoined the Court chapel, became Court director of music in 1848 and was conductor of the Mozart Union from 1869 to 1873, after being pensioned from the Court chapel. He was a prolific composer in all branches of music, but his wider fame rested on his quartets for male chorus.

LUDWIG MANGOLD, b. Darmstadt, 1813, mentioned by Mendel as son of Karl F. Mangold, the fifth son of Joh. Heinrich, was a violinist in the Darmstadt Court chapel, and was pensioned in 1870.

Two sons of Joh. Wilhelm Mangold lived as eminent musicians in America: PAUL, b. 1835, was teacher of music in Philadelphia, and GEORG, b. 1836, was director of music and professor at the Ladies' Normal College in New York; a sister of Joh. W^m, Charlotte Mangold, b. Darmstadt, 1794, became an excellent operatic singer, and as such was a pupil first of C. M. v. Weber, then of Meyerbeer, both of whom were friends of the Mangold family. Already engaged for the Vienna Opera, she contracted a throat trouble and returned to Darmstadt, where for many years she was highly esteemed as a teacher of singing.

KARL NICOLA, b. Mannheim, 1797. Son of an oboist and singer at the Mannheim theatre; at the age of 10 he became a pupil of Wendling and afterwards of Gottfried Weber for composition. On the completion of his studies he was appointed as violinist in the Mannheim Court chapel, but in 1821 he received, according to Fétis, "an honourable position at Stuttgart, and in 1823 he was called to the Court of Hanover, where he was still in 1840." He composed an adagio and rondo for violin and orchestra, op. 11; 3 sonatas for pianoforte and violin, op. 5; an overture to the drama "Anne Boleyn," and a considerable number of Lieder, in which Fétis considered him most successful.

KARL MÜHLENFELDT, b. Brunswick, 1797. Son of a double-bass player in the Brunswick Court chapel, who died when Karl was only 11 years old. He was then already a good violinist and pianist. When he was 12 he gave successful concerts at Wolfenbüttel, Hildesheim and Quedlinburg. As his talents developed, his tours became more extended, and between 1820 and 1824 he toured in the double rôle of pianist and violinist with marked success in Germany and the Netherlands. In 1824 he settled at Rotterdam, where he became director of music. He composed sonatas and a polonaise for violin and pianoforte, chamber music, pianoforte pieces, etc. (*see* Fétis).

H. HERZ, b. Prenzlau, ca. 1797; d. Berlin. A German violinist; from 1821 Royal chamber musician at the Royal Opera, Berlin; entered the Dutch Court chapel at The Hague in 1827. Afterwards he went to Sumatra and Java and was for a larger period an officer in the Dutch Army and eventually in high Government offices in Java, whence he returned to Berlin with a pension from the Dutch Government.

HILDEBRANDT. A German violinist of the 18th-19th century who was a Royal chamber musician in Berlin, ca. 1815.

JOHANN HERMANN KUFFERATH, b. Mülheim on the Ruhr, May 12, 1797; d. Wiesbaden, July 28, 1864. A violin pupil of Alexander at Duisburg and Spohr at Cassel; he studied composition under Hauptmann, became in 1823 director of music at Bielefeld, and from 1830 until he retired in 1863, music director at Utrecht. Composed instrumental and vocal music.

HUBERT FERDINAND KUFFERATH, b. Mülheim on the Ruhr, June 10, 1808; d. Brussels, June 23, 1896. A violin pupil of his brother Joh. Herm.; studied pianoforte under his brother Louis; afterwards violin under Hartmann at Cologne, and, 1833–6, composition under Fried. Schneider at Dessau; finally he studied under Ferd. David and Mendelssohn. He turned to the pianoforte for his principal instrument and settled in 1844 at Brussels, where he became professor of composition at the Conservatoire in 1871.

KARL FRIEDRICH MÜLLER, b. Brunswick, Nov. 11, 1797; d. there, Apr. 4, 1873. Eldest son of A. Christ. Müller. He received his first music lessons from his mother, and in 1811 he became a pupil of Möser in Berlin, making such rapid progress that he was appointed as Royal chamber musician in 1812. Later he returned to Brunswick and toured in Germany several times with his father, being, like the latter, a chamber musician at the Court. Meanwhile he had formed, with three younger brothers, a string quartet, and by dint of zealous practice they arrived at such a degree of perfection in ensemble and rendering as had never been heard before. The despotism of the Duke prohibited any of his chamber musicians to play in the town, anywhere than at the Ducal theatre. The brothers therefore tendered their resignations, but after the Revolution of 1830, the new government immediately secured their services again. In 1831 they appeared at Hamburg with such success that they visited Berlin in 1832. Their reception there was at first indifferent, but the public soon waxed enthusiastic and from that time they toured in Germany, Holland, France, Belgium, Austria, and Russia with ever-increasing success, until the death of Gustav and Georg in 1855 ended their happy union. His four sons, KARL, HUGO, BERNHARD and WILHELM, formed the second Müller quartet. After the dissolution of his quartet, Karl Friedr. retained his post of concertmeister at Brunswick until 1872, when he was pensioned.

FRIEDRICH LINDNER, b. Dessau, July 5, 1798; d. there, Aug. 1, 1846. Began to play the violin at the age of 5 and later on became a pupil of Möser in Berlin. As he was also a good clarinet player he was appointed at first as such in the Royal chapel there in 1815. In 1817 he became a chamber musician for the violin in the Ducal chapel at Dessau, where in 1827 he rose to the position of concertmeister. He composed numerous pieces of various kinds for the violin as well as orchestral, vocal and chamber music. His son, R. AUGUST LINDNER, was an eminent violoncello virtuoso.

THEODOR HEINRICH GUSTAV MÜLLER, b. Brunswick, Dec. 3, 1799; d. there, Sept. 7, 1855. Second son of Aeg. Christoph Müller. He became the viola player in the first Müller quartet and director of symphony concerts at the Ducal Court.

LOUIS HAAS, b. Dessau, Dec. 25, 1799. Received his first music lessons from his father, a member of the Saxon Court chapel, and later on studied the violin under Dittmar; ca. 1808 he went to Dresden and studied under the concertmeisters Morgenroth and Polledro. About this time he devoted himself chiefly to the study of the horn, on which he eventually became a famous virtuoso, but later on he again

213

made a special study of the violin. In 1817 he entered the Royal Saxon chapel as horn player, and in 1823 he toured in Germany with his brother, also a horn player, when not only their duets for two horns were greatly admired but also the violin solos of Louis, whose tone and technique were equally excellent. When playing in Dessau in 1831 the reigning Duke was so much impressed by it that he made him a concert-meister at his Court. One knows of no compositions by him.

THOMAS TÄGLICHSBECK, b. Ansbach, Dec. 31, 1799; d. Baden-Baden, Oct. 5, 1867. Studied the violin under Rovelli and composition under Gratz at Munich, from 1816. In 1817 a mass of his, which was successfully performed, procured him an engagement as violinist in the Isarthor theatre. Lind-paintner, who was the conductor, noticed the ability of Thomas, and chose him as his deputy when, in 1819, he went on a year's leave. As he did not return, Täglichsbeck, who had given ample proof of his talent, was permanently engaged. In 1822 he accepted a place as violinist in the Royal chapel at Stuttgart, where he brought out his opera "Weber's Bild." Some time after that he toured successfully as violin virtuoso in Bavaria and Switzerland, thence visiting Frankfort, Mann-heim and Karlsruhe. His first violin compositions were published in 1825. In 1827 he became capellmeister of Prince Hohenlohe-Hechingen and after the mediatization of the Prince in 1848 he went to Strassburg as conductor at the theatre, but soon after, at the Prince's request, he followed him to Löwenberg in Silesia. In 1835 his first symphony met with so much success at a Paris Conservatoire concert that he was asked to write a second, which he did and conducted there in person in 1839. On the journey there he stayed some time at Brussels, but without giving a concert. He retired in 1854, living for some time at Dresden, at Munich and finally at Baden-Baden. He composed for the violin 1 concerto, sonatas, duets, fantasias, variations, etc.

CHRISTIAN FRIEDRICH NOHR, b. Langensalza, Thuringia, Oct. 7, 1800; d. Meiningen, Oct. 5, 1875. When a boy of 8 he and his father were wandering musicians, and had the good fortune to attract the attention of Princess Lobenstein, who granted Christ. Friedrich the means of studying music under the town musician Lindner. At the age of 15 he joined

a Saxe-Gotha regiment as oboist and served in this throughout
the wars against France. On account of his health he exchanged the oboe for the flute, but was pensioned in 1821.
He used his freedom to become one of the first pupils of
Spohr, studying at the same time harmony and counterpoint
under Hauptmann and Umbreit. After some successful
tours as violin virtuoso he became concertmeister at the Ducal
chapel of Saxe-Meiningen in 1830. He appeared with
acclaim in concerts at Frankfort, Munich, Leipzig and other
towns. He composed successful operas, oratorios, cantatas,
a symphony, orchestral pieces, quintets, quartets, violin pieces
and songs published at Leipzig, Offenbach, Berlin and
Munich. Before 1840 he composed two string quartets, 1
string quintet, a symphony, songs, etc., all pub. Leipzig,
Offenbach, Berlin and Munich.

KARL BARNEWITZ, b. Berlin, Nov. 12, 1800. Pupil of K.
Möser; entered the Royal chapel, Berlin, as violinist in 1821,
when Spontini was its conductor. Mendel praises him both
as musician and as composer, but says that up to ca. 1880 none
of his works had been pub.

LOUIS SCHLÖSSER, b. Darmstadt, Nov. 17, 1800; d. there,
Nov. 17, 1886. He lived in Vienna, ca. 1819, where he
became acquainted with Schubert, who took him to the house
of Count Esterhazy, where the amusing incident with regard
to Count Stefan occurred. (*See* Newman Flower: Schubert,
p. 68, etc.) In 1826-7 he was in Paris; afterwards he returned
to Darmstadt, where he became concertmeister in the chapel
and eventually Court capellmeister and conductor of the opera.
He was a strong opponent of Wagner, in spite of his otherwise
loving disposition, but he was too deeply rooted in the older
school. He composed a number of solos (pub. Vienna, Paris,
Mayence), 2 books of duets (Mayence, Schott); quartets,
concerto for horn, piano sonatas and pieces, symphonies,
overtures, operas, etc.

JOHANN NEPOMUK WANSKI, b. Posen (?), ca. 1800; d. Aix,
Provence, 184.. Son of the Polish violinist and popular
composer, Joh. Wanski (b. 1762), who died a few years after
the birth of his son. The latter studied the violin at Kalisch
and at Warsaw, toured as virtuoso and then finished his
studies under Baillot in Paris. His subsequent tours in

215

France, Spain, Italy, etc., gained for him more renown than material reward, and when on a tour in Switzerland he was attacked by a serious illness at St. Gall, his countryman Count Sobanski had to assist him to find the necessary medical aid at Winterthur (Wki.). After he had been nursed there through the winter, he was advised to go to the South of France, and consequently he settled in 1839 at Aix-en-Provence, where he married a Frenchwoman and devoted himself exclusively to teaching, composition and writing. His works include a concertino, fantasias, romances, variations, caprices, fugues, and many studies, etc., for violin; a "Grande Méthode" and a "Petite Méthode" for beginners; a tutor for the viola, "Gymnastique des Doigts et de l'Archet," and a harmony tutor.

SIMON GEORG SCHMIDT, b. Detmold, Mar. 21, 1801. A pupil of Spohr. He was for some time 1st violin and chamber musician at the Court of Saxe-Coburg and afterwards became capellmeister at the cathedral at Münster, Westphalia. In 1829 he accepted the position of concertmeister and solo violin at the society Felix Meritis at Amsterdam, where his wife was likewise engaged as a concert singer, but he left again in 1832 to go on a concert tour in Germany, and in 1834 he became director of music at Halle on the Saale, where he was still in 1842. He composed some violin concertos and variations, as well as an oratorio, a cantata, etc.; these remained mostly in MS.

FRIEDRICH BARNBECK, b. Cassel, ca. 1801. A pupil of his father, who was concertmeister at Cassel, and of Ludw. Spohr. Afterwards he became violinist in the Stuttgart Court chapel. He left there after a few years and settled at Halberstadt, where he wrote a tutor, "Theoretisch praktische Anleitung zum Violinspiel," Halberstadt, part i, 1845; part ii, 1846.

FRANZ XAVER HÖLLERER, b. Stuttgart, 1801. Became 1st violinist in the Stuttgart Court chapel, and composed ballets for the Court theatre; also songs.

J. C. CASPAR, d. Berlin, 1842. At the beginning of the 19th century a violinist chamber musician in the Royal chapel, Berlin. He distinguished himself by the production of important works, as, for instance, Haydn's "Seven Words" in 1801. Pensioned in 1818, he lived in retirement and died at an advanced age.

HEINRICH ROMBERG, b. Paris, Apr. 4, 1802; d. Hamburg, 1859. The eldest son and pupil of Andreas Romberg; from 1829 concertmeister at St. Petersburg, where for several years he was conductor of the Italian Opera. In 1847 he settled permanently at Hamburg.

HUBERT RIES, b. Berlin, Apr. 1, 1802; d. there, Sept. 14, 1886. The youngest son of Franz Anton Ries; pupil of his father, and from 1820 of Spohr and Hauptmann (composition) at Cassel. In 1824 violinist at the Königstadt theatre and 1825 at the Royal Opera; in 1830 he toured as far as Vienna, spreading his reputation as virtuoso and composer for the violin. On his return he became solo violinist and leader-conductor of the orchestra. On June 30, 1836–72, he was concertmeister in the Royal chapel; in 1839 he was nominated a member of the Royal Academy of Arts, and in 1851 he became teacher at and director of the instrumental school for the Royal theatres. He was also conductor of the Philharmonic Society orchestra in succession to Henning, until 1871. In 1833 he had already instituted public quartet performances with C. Böhmer, Maurer and Just, which did much to raise the standard of the public taste. As a teacher his merit was at least equally great, and his numerous works written for that purpose are still of some practical value. They comprise a tutor, several books of studies and instructive duets; he also composed 2 concertos. Of his three sons, all musicians, Louis Ries (q.v.) and Franz Ries (q.v.) were distinguished violinists.

WILHELM BERNHARD MOLIQUE, b. Nuremberg, Oct. 7, 1802; d. Cannstadt, near Stuttgart, May 10, 1869. Was at first a pupil of his father, a town musician at Nuremberg. At the age of 13 he received some lessons from Spohr, who wrote in his diary (Nov. 16, 1815): "In Nuremberg the ca. 14-year-old Molique introduced himself to me and asked me to give him some instruction during my stay there, to which I willingly acquiesced as the boy played already remarkably well for his years. As Molique has since that time, by the assiduous study of my works, more and more perfected himself in my style of playing and therefore calls himself a pupil of Spohr, I make an additional mention of the circumstances." King Maximilian I, whose attention had been drawn to the boy, caused him to be sent to Munich, where he studied for two years under P. Rovelli, after which he became a violinist at the Theatre on the Wien in Vienna. In 1817 he was recalled to Munich, and when Rovelli returned to Italy in 1820, Molique succeeded him as concertmeister in the Royal chapel. In the house of Peter von Winter, the Court capellmeister, he made the acquaintance of the niece of the latter, Marie Wanney, whom he married in 1825. In 1826 he became 1st violinist and director of music at Stuttgart, whence he made yearly extended tours through various countries. On at least one of these he visited Moscow, and on his return Schumann wrote: "Yesterday Molique returned to Germany, the Russian journey has barely covered his expenses; it serves him right, he grumbles about everything, and moreover he is such a dry stick." This does not give an attractive picture of the man. As a virtuoso, however, he was held in high esteem throughout Europe and also as a serious-minded composer, who followed in the footsteps of the classics and who produced symphonies, overtures, etc., as well as chamber music, concertos, sonatas which possess distinct merit, but lack the divine spark of genius. The turmoil of the Revolution drove him from Stuttgart in 1849. He went to London, where he remained greatly honoured until 1866, when he returned to Württemberg and settled at Cannstadt. In Sept., 1860, his oratorio "Abraham" was performed at the Norwich Musical Festival. Among his many pupils the most notable was Tiplady Carrodus. Molique possessed a Joseph Guarnerius which afterwards became the property of Wald. Meyer.

EDUARD RIETZ, b. Berlin, Oct. 17, 1802; d. there, Jan. 23, 1832. Son and pupil of Joh. Friedr. Rietz, Royal chamber musician (viola), and afterwards of Rode. He became in early youth a member of the Royal Chapel and was also an excellent concert soloist. As he had a very good tenor voice he became also a member of the Vocal Academy in 1821. From early boyhood he was an inseparable friend of Mendelssohn who, in accents of heartfelt grief, laments his untimely death in his letter from Paris of Feb. 4, 1832.

ERNST REITER, b. Würzburg, Mar. 30, 1804; d. Basle, July 14, 1875. A professor of violin at the Musical Institute at Würzburg. Appeared as soloist in concerts 1835–7; in 1839 he became musical director at Strassburg, and in 1841 at Basle; in 1843 he conducted at a musical festival at Lucerne. He composed an oratorio, string quartets (Vienna, Haslinger) and songs (Ib.).

GEORG WICHTL, b. Trostberg, Bavaria, Feb. 2, 1805; d. Bunzlau, Silesia, 1876. He learned in early youth to play all musical instruments then in use, and perfected himself at Munich on the violin. In 1826 he was appointed violinist and vice-capellmeister at the Court of Hechingen, and also became the founder and director of a school for singing in that town. He followed the Court chapel when it was removed to Löwenberg in Silesia, where he became also director of church music and in 1858 received the title of Royal Director of Music. After the dissolution of the chapel, Wichtl removed to Breslau in 1870 and to Bunzlau in 1876. He composed several books of studies and a tutor for violin, duets for 2 violins and violin and violoncello, violin concertos and solos, easy string trios, symphonies, overtures, masses, an oratorio, an opera, etc., etc. (*see* Mendel-Reissmann).

RUDOLPH WICHTL, b. Nov. 7, 1832; d. Löwenberg, 1857. The son of Georg Wichtl, was a good violinist and organist. After an appointment as organist at Seiss he succeeded his father in 1852 as conductor of the choral society at Hechingen, and after some time he went to Löwenberg as violinist in the Court chapel.

KARL MATHIAS KUDELSKI, b. Berlin, Nov. 17, 1805; d. Baden-Baden, Oct. 3, 1877. A pupil of Ed. Ritz in Berlin and Lafont in Paris for violin, and Urban for composition. His first appointment was as 1st violinist at the Königstädter theatre, Berlin, where he remained till 1830 when he went to Dorpat as leader of a string quartet. In 1839 he became capellmeister to a Russian Prince and in 1841 he was appointed concertmeister and conductor at the Imperial theatre in Moscow, from which he retired with a pension in 1851. From there he appears to have gone to Hamburg, and eventually he settled at Baden-Baden, devoting himself solely to composition. He wrote concertos for violin and for violoncello; duets for 2 violins and for violin and violoncello; violin, violoncello and pianoforte sonatas; pianforte trios, etc.; also a book on harmony, counterpoint and fugue.

ZEBELL. A German violinist of 1805 in the orchestra of the Vaudeville theatre, Paris, where he died in 1819. He composed 3 sonatas and 3 divertimentos for violin with bass, op. 1; 3 books of violin duets and variations ou études; 4 books of string trios, all pub. in Paris.

AUGUST POTT, b. Northeim, Hanover, Nov. 7, 1806; d. Graz, Aug. 27, 1883. He received his first instruction in the elements of music and the playing of several instruments from his father, a town musician, and from Kiesewetter. He soon conceived a predilection for the violin, and when Spohr was giving concerts at Göttingen, 1818 to 1820, he made several journeys there to hear him, and his father finally consented to his going to Cassel to study under that master. In 1824 he made his first public debut at the latter town with great success, and then toured in Denmark and all over Germany and Austria, renewing his successes wherever he appeared. He also visited Paris but Fétis says he is not sure whether he played in public there. In 1832 he became concertmeister at the Court of Oldenburg and afterwards Court capellmeister, and was pensioned 1861. He devoted the proceeds of a concert he gave at Salzburg in 1836 to start the Mozart Memorial Fund. He composed 2 violin concertos, duets, variations, etc.

KARL HENNING, b. Halberstadt, Feb. 26, 1807; d. Zeitz, 1866. Of a poor family, he had to utilize his musical talent, which showed itself at an early age, for the purpose of earning his living. He learned to play a number of instruments and served in various military bands with distinction until he was appointed musical director of the town of Zeitz in 1837, where he distinguished himself both as conductor and teacher. He wrote a useful tutor for violin and one for violoncello, as well as duets for 2 violins and easy violin pieces well adapted for beginners, also violoncello pieces, etc.

OTTO GERKE, b. Lüneburg, July 13, 1807; d. Paderborn, 1878. Pupil of Spohr. Mendel says he received his first instructions in violin-playing and harmony from his father. In 1822 he went to Cassel, where he studied the violin under Spohr and theory and composition under M. Hauptmann. Afterwards he toured as a violin virtuoso with great success, and in 1837 he went to Russia, where he remained for nine years. In 1847 he settled at Paderborn as teacher and composer. He composed a solo for violin with quartet; a quatuor brilliant pour le violon, op. 1 (Leipzig, Hoffmeister), a violin concerto and duets of important form and dimensions which are all described as of great merit.

HEINRICH PANOFKA, b. Breslau, Silesia, Oct. 3, 1807; d. Florence, Nov. 18, 1887. His father, a higher government official, intended him for the bar, but his eminent musical gifts showed themselves very early. At the age of 6 his talented sister taught him the violin, and the cantors Strauch and his successor Förster, singing and musical theory. At the age of 10 he made his public debut with great success. Concertmeister Karl Luge of Breslau trained in the school of Rode, then became his violin teacher and he appeared repeatedly at concerts as soloist. In 1824 his father sent him to Vienna to study under Mayseder, violin, and Hoffmann, composition, from 1824 to 1827. From the latter year to 1829 he gave some concerts in Vienna. In 1829 he played with great success at the Redoutensaal, and in the same year went to Munich, where during a sojourn of six months he gave a series of concerts. After this he went to Berlin, where he gave a number of concerts with the pianist Hauck, and became at A. B. Marx's request a contributor to the latter's musical periodical, and afterwards also to Schumann's *Neue Zeitschrift*, etc. In 1832 he went on tour with his friend Hauck, visiting Dresden, Prague and Vienna, whence after a sojourn of eight months he visited Silesia and Poland, returning to Berlin. After the death of his brother in that town he went to Paris, where, in 1834, he made his debut at a concert given by Berlioz at the Conservatoire, where he also gave a concert himself in 1837. In 1839 he visited London for the pub. of some of his compositions. Returned to Paris, he devoted himself chiefly to the study of singing under Bordogni, with whom he intended to found a vocal academy in Paris in 1842, which did not materialize. During that time he contributed articles to several Paris musical papers as well as to Schumann's. In the latter year he went to London, where he was soon in great request as a singing-master, and in 1847 Lumley engaged him as assistant conductor for the Italian Opera. In 1852 he returned to Paris, and in 1866 he went to Florence where he withdrew gradually from public life. He composed a number of variations for violin with orchestra, quartet, or pianoforte accompaniment; a grand morceau de concert, op. 23; numerous solos of the drawing-room order, duets concertante for violin, pianoforte studies and vocal compositions. He also made a German translation of Baillot's method for the violin.

FRANZ SCHUBERT, b. Dresden, July 22, 1808; d. there, Apr. 12, 1878. Son of the conductor and composer Franz Anton Schubert, who was his first master in musical theory, while the chamber musician A. Rottmeier, and afterwards Concertmeister Ludw. Haase, instructed him in violin-playing. On Apr. 23, 1823, he played in a chamber concert before the Queen, whereupon he was placed as Aspirant among the violins of the Royal chapel. In 1831 the King sent him to Paris at his expense to study the violin under Lafont. In that city he became acquainted with many great musicians, and a closer friendship sprang up between him, Chopin and Ernst. Returning to Dresden in 1833 he became Royal Concertist in 1834 and vice-concertmeister. After the death of Morgenroth in 1847 he succeeded the latter as concertmeister, and when Lipinsky was pensioned in 1861 he followed the latter as first concertmeister. In 1857 he received from the King the Cross of a Knight of the Order of Albrecht, and when he celebrated his 50 years' jubilee on May 1, 1873, he was decorated with the Order Pour le Mérite by the King and another order by the Duke of Mecklenburg-Strelitz, and then retired on a pension. He composed some solos and duos for the violin including the popular "L'Abeille," also called "The Bee's Wedding," and 2 duos concertante for violin and cello in collaboration with F. A. Kummer. Schubert was an outcome of the French school and combined with grace and elegance a brilliant technique of the left hand, but a rather small tone. It was of course the father, Franz Anton, who repudiated the authorship of the "Erl-King" in an indignant letter to Breitkopf of Apr. 18, 1817 (*see* O. E. Deutsch, ii, 39). His wife was a prima donna at the Dresden Opera and his son, FRANZ SCHUBERT, became a violinist in the Royal chapel.

FRANZ FERDINAND GEORG MÜLLER, b. Brunswick, July 29, 1808; d. there, May 22, 1855. The youngest son of Aegidius Christoph Müller; became 2nd violin in the first Müller quartet and capellmeister at the Ducal Court.

FRIEDRICH PACIUS, b. Hamburg, Mar. 19, 1809; d. Helsingfors, Jan. 9, 1891. A pupil of Spohr at Cassel, and an excellent violinist, who became director of music at Helsingfors University. He composed 2 operas and a Singspiel.

FRANZ HARTMANN, b. Ehrenbreitstein, July 29, 1809; d. Cologne, Apr. 6, 1855. Studied the violin at first under his father, a member of the Coblenz orchestra, and in 1824 and 1825 at Cassel under Spohr, who took a great interest in him. Wasielewski says that he went next to Hamburg and thence to Frankfort-on-the-Main, where C. Guhr appointed him as 1st violin in the town orchestra. Mason Clarke relates that he was for some time at Wolffenbüttel and then went to Brunswick (both belonging to the same Court), but gives no date. From 1833 to 1836 he had to serve in the Prussian Army. In 1836 he was, according to Wasielewski, appointed as concertmeister at the theatre and the Gesellschaft Konzerte (concert society) at Cologne, where he became also teacher of the violin at the Conservatoire, and did much for the cultivation of string quartet-playing until his untimely death from typhoid fever. Mason Clarke states that from 1839 to 1842 he was solo violinist at the theatre at Aix-la-Chapelle and thence went to Cologne.

FRIEDRICH WILHELM EICHLER, b. Leipzig, 1809. Received his final training as a violinist from Spohr and was accounted one of his best pupils. In 1832 he became concertmeister at the Königsberg theatre. From 1847 he lived for several years in London, and then went to Baden-Baden. Of his compositions only a few violin pieces were pub.

FRANZ LÖBMANN, b. Volschau, Lower Lusatia, 1809. A pupil of his father, town musician and organist at Muskau, who taught him the playing of various instruments, but especially the violin and the organ, while L. Schefer, a pupil of Salieri and Mich. Haydn, taught him harmony and counterpoint. In 1726 he became a violinist at the Königstadt theatre, Berlin, while continuing his violin studies under the chamber musician Dam and counterpoint under S. W. Dehn. In 1833 a place in the Royal chapel was offered to him, but he preferred that of concertmeister and choirmaster at the Riga theatre, from which he resigned under C. v. Holtey's management to devote himself to teaching and composition. He also conducted a choral society and, until the end of the fiftieth, often played as a soloist at the concerts given by this society, and here, as well as at Düsseldorf where he played at the Lower Rhenish Musical Festival in 1855, his powerful tone and exquisite rendering were greatly praised. He composed a number of large works, including a comic opera, which remained in MS., but some violin and pianoforte pieces and a book of songs were pub.

AUGUST ZIMMERMANN, b. Zinndorf, near Straussberg, Mar. 28, 1810; d. Steglitz, near Berlin, end of Dec., 1891. When he was 6 years old his father died and on the day he was buried the farmhouse in which the family lived was destroyed by a fire in the village. A childless clergyman adopted the boy, and as he showed signs of musical talent instructed him in violin-playing, later, as he made rapid progress, placing him under the town musician Lupin. At the age of 13 he was sent to the Werder Gymnasium (College) in Berlin, and after he had passed his final examination there, he entered C. Möser's school of music. He distinguished himself by his talent and zeal to such an extent that at the age of 17 he was awarded the Spontini scholarship, and in 1828 became a member of the Royal chapel. He also became 2nd violinist in Möser's quartet. In 1834 he founded his own quartet, which continued till 1860, with a break in 1835–6, and acquired a widespread reputation. Between 1830 and 1840 he toured frequently and successfully as a virtuoso. At Cologne he played at a concert for the Beethoven memorial fund, and as well as many German towns he also visited Paris, Brussels, and The Hague, where he played at the Court. About that time he had acquired a fine Stradivari violin for 150 francs. He was an excellent teacher and counted among his pupils his master's son, August Möser, before the father took over his final training; Rehfeld; Tomasini; J. Oertling; Rosalie Müller, and for quartet-playing Prince Leopold of Schwarzburg Sondershausen. In 1874 he retired from his artistic career to Steglitz.

FERDINAND DAVID, b. Hamburg, June 19, 1810; d. on a journey to Klosters, Switzerland, July 19, 1873. He commenced the study of the violin at an early age and appeared in public as a boy of 10 with great success. During 1823–5 he

224

JOSEPH JOACHIM
When a young man. From a photograph
by Julia Margaret Cameron, taken in 1868,
in the possession of Arthur Hill, Esq.

JOSEPH JOACHIM
From a photograph taken in 1894.

*Russell & Sons.*

was a pupil of Spohr at Cassel, receiving lessons in musical theory from M. Hauptmann. In 1825 he went on tour with his sister Louise, who, as Mme Dulcken, became the Court pianist of the Duchess of Kent, and made his debut at the Gewandhaus at Leipzig. In 1827 and 1828 he was a member of the Königstadt theatre orchestra in Berlin, where he first became acquainted with Mendelssohn. During 1829–35 he was leader of the string quartet of a Livonian nobleman, von Liphardt, whose daughter he subsequently married. During that time he toured in Russia and appeared with great success in St. Petersburg, Moscow, Riga, etc. When Mendelssohn became conductor of the Gewandhaus Concerts in 1836, David, who had already settled at Leipzig a few months before, was, on the former's recommendation, appointed as concertmeister in the Gewandhaus and Theatre orchestra at Leipzig on Mar. 1, as successor of H. A. Matthäi, and retained that position until he died. In 1843 he became, also, professor of violin at the newly founded Conservatorium, and his fame as an artist and teacher made this a centre for the study of violin-playing. With Mendelssohn, who was again instrumental in securing his appointment, David remained throughout the short life of the former on terms of the most intimate friendship, and he had no inconsiderable share in the writing of the passage work in the immortal E minor violin concerto, which he had the distinction to perform for the first time in public at a Gewandhaus Concert on Mar. 13, 1845. Although a pupil of Spohr, David did not follow in his great master's footsteps. He considered it better to absorb whatever appeared to him best in other eminent players, and thus create a style of his own. The result appears not to have been entirely good; Otto Jahn (article in *Der Grenzbote*, 1855) says that "unfortunately he developed an ever-increasing forced mannerism, which is opposed to the self-effacement which is indispensable in quartet-playing. Moreover, he introduced all sorts of cheap minauderies to give piquancy to the works of Haydn and Mozart. The manner in which Herr David coquets, especially in Haydn quartets, as if he wanted to show what *he* can make out of a Haydn quartet, how, for instance, he plays accompanying figures, as if he wanted to say: 'Thus accompanies the first violin,' is boastful and in bad taste." This is no doubt rather severe, but that it is not without justification, is evident from a letter of Feb. 1, 1844, in which David wrote to Mendelssohn: (trans.) "Yesterday we played the triple concerto by Beethoven with Hiller and Rietz. Curiously (!) it pleased very much; but then we played the last movement with all possible coquetry and chicane (lit. 'wir haben aber auch das letzte stück mit allen chikanen heraus-coquettirt!')." His mannerisms found sometimes expression even in his editions of the classics, in the over-abundant fingering, bowing, and expression marks.

For all his shortcomings, however, he was a great teacher, who took an intelligent and sympathetic interest in all his pupils, who could learn from him a great deal, if they did not imitate his mannerism, which all his best pupils avoided, foremost among them Joachim and Wilhelmj, as well as F. Hermann, R. Heckmann, A. Hilf, Japha and a large number of others. David was an excellent leader of the orchestra, for which his energetic attack, full tone and thorough musicianship particularly qualified him. His numerous compositions included 5 violin concertos, variations, rondos, caprices, solo pieces with pianoforte, concert pieces for various instruments, several symphonies, an opera, a sextet and several quartets for strings, songs, etc., though musicianly, effective, pleasing, and partly very popular in their time, lack those qualities which would make them of permanent value. His "Violinschule" (tutor), pub. 1863, is an excellent work of its kind, and far more systematic than its predecessors, containing many valuable and well-graduated exercises and études. A work of permanent practical value is his "Hohe Schule des Violinspiels" ("High School of Violin Playing"), a collection of violin sonatas and solos by masters of the 17th and 18th centuries, which he has arranged most effectively, although he has sometimes taken great liberties with the original versions.

LEOPOLD ALEXANDER GANZ, b. Mayence, Nov. 28, 1810; d. Berlin, June 15, 1869. Studied the violin under his father, his brother Adolph and under Spohr's pupil, F. Bärwolf. He became a member of the Mayence theatre orchestra, together with his brother MORITZ, violoncellist, with whom he played a great deal together in duets, etc. In 1827 he became a violinist in the Royal Chapel, Berlin, receiving the title of concertmeister in 1836, and taking Seidel's place as such in 1840. The two brothers appeared a great deal together in concerts, as duettists and chamber-music players, where, however, Moritz showed in many respects his superiority over Leopold.

WALTHER BRAND, b. Rudolstadt, 1811. Pupil of his father, then of Concertmeister Rettich, and finally for a year and a half of Spohr, through whose influence he was appointed as violinist in the Court chapel at Cassel. In 1831 he returned as Court musician to Rudolstadt, whence he toured with great success, but soon his health began to fail and he devoted himself to teaching and composition, in which he showed not only skill but also inspiration. His violin-playing was distinguished by power and beauty of tone and feeling.

EDUARD ELISSON, b. Frankenthal, 1811. Made his final studies in violin-playing under Baillot in Paris, and studied composition under Rinck. He was for a long period in London, where he was conductor of the opera at Drury Lane Theatre. In 1842 he went to Frankfort a/M., where he stood in high esteem as soloist, quartet player and conductor. He was also a composer of merit.

KARL APPEL, b. Dessau, Mar. 14, 1812; d. there, Dec. 9, 1895. A violin pupil of Concertmeister Lindner, in theory and composition of Friedr. Schneider. He entered the Ducal chapel at an early age and remained in it to his death, advancing successively to the positions of concertmeister and leader in 1880. He composed instructive violin pieces and vocal music, especially attractive quartets for male voices, also an opera which was performed in Dessau only.

EDOUARD RAYMOND, b. Breslau, Sept. 27, 1812. The son of a luthier. Studied the violin under Carl Luge from his seventh year, and made his public debut as a virtuoso at Breslau at the age of 14. In 1844 he became conductor of the Sunday Society there. He composed a number of violin solos, some with orchestra, all pub.; also operas, symphonies, overtures, etc., which remained in MS.

KARL WILHELM FERDINAND BRAUN, b. Berlin, ca. 1812; d. there, Dec. 12, 1851. An excellent violinist, good singer and composer who became chamber musician in the Royal chapel in 1835 and in the following year a member and soloist in the Berlin Vocal Academy. In his spare time he studied composition under Rungenhagen at the Royal Academy of Arts. In 1842 and 1844 he received the prize for composition at that institute. He died of scarlet fever contracted from his own children. The choir of the vocal academy sang at his obsequies his melodious setting of "Doch der Herr vergisst der Seinen nicht" ("The Lord does not forget His own").

HEINRICH WOLFF, b. Frankfort a/M., Jan. 1, 1813; d. Leipzig, July 24, 1898. Received his first instruction from the Dutch violinist Binger in London, where his family resided from 1815. Later on he became a pupil of Spagnoletti, at that time leader of the Italian Opera. At the age of 9 he made his successful debut at a Bath musical festival. In 1824 he returned to Frankfort, where he resumed his studies under François Fémy, a pupil of R. Kreutzer, and afterwards under Concertmeister Hoffmann; Schnyder von Wartensee was his master in composition. In 1828 he went to Vienna to perfect himself on the violin under Mayseder, while Seyfried gave him further instruction in the art of composition. From 1830 he began to tour all over Europe, including England and Russia, and from 1838 to 1878 he was concertmeister at Frankfort, where he was highly esteemed as an excellent violinist. Of his compositions little appears to have been pub. apart from Eight Studies for the Violin, op. 5 (Frankfort, Fischer), and a few songs. In 1835 he was nominated an honorary member of the Munich Philharmonic Society and in 1838 of the Royal Music Academy, Stockholm.

ANTON WALLERSTEIN, b. Dresden, Sept., 1813; d. Geneva, Mar. 26, 1892. Son of a well-to-do family; showed very early talent for music, especially for the violin. At the age of 10 he led a quartet by Rode in public. In 1827 he came to Berlin, where Spontini, Meyerbeer, Saphir and the Saxon Ambassador took an interest in him, and he met with an enthusiastic reception on his public appearance at the Court theatre. In 1828 he met with similar success at Leipzig. Returned to Dresden, he found a cordial reception in the family of Prince Gallitzin, the aged Prince becoming his pupil. Then he toured in Bohemia, where his playing was greatly appreciated. He excelled more by soulful expression than by sheer virtuosity. In 1829 he became a member of the Dresden Court chapel and in 1832 he received a similar position at the Court of Hanover, where his playing was greatly appreciated, especially by the art-loving Duke of Cambridge. In 1836 he became conductor of a French vaudeville company, and when they went to Copenhagen he obtained leave to accompany them at their request. On his return to Hanover he found circumstances less agreeable, and in 1841 he retired entirely from his career as virtuoso and devoted himself chiefly to composition of drawing-room pieces and dance music in which he became highly successful and immensely popular. In 1853 and 1855 he gave concerts of his dances, etc., in London and Paris. From 1858 he lived alternately in Dresden, Wiesbaden, Frankfort a/M., etc. For the violin he wrote some variations with orchestra.

FRANZ GÖTZE, b. Neustadt on the Orla, May 10, 1814; d. Leipzig, Apr. 2, 1888. A pupil of Spohr at Cassel, became 1st violinist in the Weimar Court chapel in 1831, but soon afterwards studied singing, becoming a distinguished operatic tenor in 1836 and professor of singing at the Leipzig Conservatoire, 1852–67.

CARL STÖR, b. Stolberg, Hartz Mountains, June 29, 1814; d. Weimar, Jan. 17, 1889. He received his first violin lessons from his father and played in his seventh year a concerto by Maurer in public. In his twelfth year he went to Vienna, where the Grand Duke Carl August became his patron and placed him under J. N. K. Götze. It was intended to send him, after his confirmation, to the Paris Conservatoire, but the death of the Grand Duke in 1828 frustrated that plan. He had in 1827 played solos between the acts at the Court theatre and was soon after, 1851 (Riemann: 1850) appointed as Court musician in the Imperial Chapel. Afterwards he studied composition under J. C. Lobe at Weimar where, in 1827 (Riemann: 1837), he became a member of the Court chapel and succeeded Listz as capellmeister in 1857, but had to resign that position a few years later on account of failing eyesight. In 1838 he appeared at Dresden, where he gained the friendship of Lipinski, who wanted to engage him for the Court chapel there, but he preferred to return to Weimar; neither would he accept an engagement offered to him for the Russian Imperial Chapel at St. Petersburg, where he appeared with great success together with the pianist A. Dreyschock.

Returning to Weimar, he devoted himself with zeal to composition, solo playing and leading the chamber-music concerts, and conducting the orchestral subscription concerts, both of which he had instituted.   He had proved himself an excellent conductor both at the Opera and of the concerts which he continued to conduct even after he resigned his position at the Opera.   His work was very beneficial to the musical life of Weimar and this was recognized by a public festival in honour of his fifty years' jubilee on May 28, 1877, when among many tokens of friendship and public appreciation from far and near the Grand Duke bestowed upon him the Order of the White Falcon.   He composed solo pieces for violin, a serenade for violoncello with orchestra, as well as music for the theatre, overtures, and symphonic pictures to Schiller's "Lay of the Bell," which became known in wider circles.

JULIUS WEISS, b. Berlin, July 19, 1814; d. there, June 30, 1898. A pupil of Henning and Rungenhagen.   Was held in great esteem as a teacher in Berlin, where in 1852 he took over his father's music pub. business.   He wrote a large number of elementary violin pieces, studies, duets, etc.

KARL WILHELM UHLRICH, b. Leipzig, Apr. 10, 1815; d. Stendal, Nov. 26, 1874.   A pupil of Matthäi; violinist in the Gewandhaus orchestra, concertmeister at Magdeburg, and finally for many years Court concertmeister at Sondershausen.   He was of a modest, homely nature, and although a virtuoso of high merit and a delightful chamber-music player, he did not thirst for fame, but found full satisfaction in the fulfilment of the duties of his office, only occasionally appearing in the towns of the surrounding country.   He died immediately before a concert at Stendal at which he was to appear.   The Lobconcerts at Sondershausen owed their success to a large extent to his energies.

HERMANN GEORG DAM, b. Berlin, Dec. 5, 1815; d. Nov. 27, 1858.   A son of Mads Gregers Dam.   Studied the violin under the chamber musician Hauck, against the wish of his parents, but finally received tuition from his relenting father, on the violin and in composition.   In 1830 he became assistant violinist in the Royal chapel and chamber musician in 1840.   He was esteemed as a composer and wrote numerous overtures and incidental music to the order of the Intendant-

General. His oratorio, "The Hallelujah of the Creation," was performed by Royal Command in 1847, and "The Flood" in 1849 and 1854. He also wrote 4 operas, cantatas and songs.

KARL LOTZE, b. Berlin, Dec. 25, 1815. About his earliest studies nothing is known, but in 1833 he became an advanced pupil of H. Ries and made his successful debut in Berlin in 1836. After this, he toured in Saxony, and in 1837 he became concertmeister at the Riga theatre and gave concerts in the German towns of the surrounding country. In 1849 he settled in Berlin as a private teacher, but in 1857 he was appointed a Royal chamber musician and 1st violinist in the Court chapel in Berlin.

JOHANN FERDINAND GÖBEL, b. Baumgarten, Silesia, 1817. A pupil of Pixis for violin and Dionys Weber for composition at the Prague Conservatoire. In 1840 he became 1st violinist, and 1844 musical director (conductor) at the Breslau theatre. He wrote several compositions for violin, overtures for orchestra and vocal music.

CHRISTOPH WOLFGANG HILF, b. Bad-Elster, Voigtland, Saxony, Sept. 6, 1818; d. there, Dec. 31, 1911. Studied the violin in early youth and at the age of 16 he had a few months' lessons from the town musician at Greiz, after which he returned to his father's business of linen weaver. His love for the violin, however, gaining the upper hand, he went in 1838 to Leipzig, where he studied for three years under David. His progress was such that it attracted the attention of Mendelssohn, and Schumann, who speaks about him in his letters ("Neue Folge," 173) and his collected writings ("Gesammelte Schriften, Aufl. II," ii, 189). After the first year under David he made his debut at the Gewandhaus concerts with great success, and at the end of his studies he toured in the Bohemian watering-places, being received everywhere with enthusiasm. At Carlsbad he met Spohr, through whom he was appointed as Hauptmann's successor in the Court orchestra at Cassel. In 1850 he became conductor of the Kur-orchestra at Bad-Elster, from which he retired into privacy in 1892. A. F. HILF, his nephew, was the well-known eminent violinist.

TRAUGOTT KRÄMER, b. Coburg, Nov. 19, 1818. Studied the violin at the Prague Conservatoire 1834-7 at the Duke of

Coburg's expense, and on his return entered the Court chapel there as 1st violinist. In 1854 he received the title of concert-meister. He formed a string quartet which became very popular both in Coburg and in Gotha. Later on he was appointed Ducal capellmeister and conducted the operas, with dialogue. He composed violin solos, symphonies, overtures, string quartets, cantatas, and songs which prove him an excellent musician.

HERMANN GUSTAV JÄSCHKE, b. Breslau, Dec. 12, 1818. An excellent violinist who enjoyed a high reputation as a soloist but never travelled beyond his native province. His compositions, violin solos and pianoforte pieces became known in wider circles.

KARL FRIEDRICH AUGUST HERING, b. Berlin, Sept. 2, 1819; d. Burg, near Magdeburg, Feb. 2, 1889. He received his first music lessons from his father, a painter. Some years later he studied the violin under Hub. Ries, and composition under Rungenhagen at the Royal Academy of Arts. In 1840 he studied the higher technique of violin-playing under Lipinski at Dresden, and finally he went to Prague as a pupil of Tomaschek for the pianoforte and singing. At the end of his studies he toured successfully as virtuoso in Austria and Germany. In 1844 he returned to Berlin, and in 1846 he became for some time a supernumerary violinist in the Royal chapel. In 1848 he founded the Sonatenverein (Sonata Union) fc. the cultivation of chamber music, which continued until 1851, when he opened a school for music, over which he presided until 1867, having meanwhile received the title of a Royal director of music. Hering was a fertile composer in all branches of music. For the violin he wrote pieces, elementary studies (op. 13), an elementary tutor, also 2 books: "Methodischer Leitfaden für Violin Lehrer" ("Methodical Guide for Violin Teachers") (Leipzig, 1857) and a guide for the teaching of R. Kreutzer's studies (Leipzig, 1858).

ADOLPH KÖTTLITZ, b. Treves, Sept. 27, 1820; d. Uralsk, Russia, Oct. 26, 1860. At the age of 5 he entered the music school of the cathedral teacher Fischer. At the age of 8 he was already admired as a violinist. In 1836 he appeared successfully at Cologne, where he lived for several years and then was taken by Lizst to Paris, remaining there for three years. On his return he settled at Breslau as a teacher, and married. In 1848 he was appointed concertmeister at Königsberg, where his wife died in 1851. In 1856 he married again, and in order to improve his financial position he went to Russia, leaving his family behind. He was engaged as director of music at Uralsk, where he was killed while out shooting. He is praised both as virtuoso and composer, but of his violin concertos, string quartets, songs, etc., very little was pub.

J. C. GULOMY, b. Pernau, June 22, 1821. An excellent violinist who toured very successfully until 1853, when he became concertmeister at the Court of Bückeburg, where he was still, ca. 1880.

ALWIN WIECK, b. Leipzig, Aug. 27, 1821; d. there, Oct. 21, 1885. A son of Friedr. Wieck by a first marriage. A violin pupil of Ferd. David at the Leipzig Conservatoire; 1849–59 violinist at the Italian Opera, St. Petersburg. Lived after that time at Dresden. He wrote "Materials to Friedr. Wieck's Method of Pianoforte Playing" (1875).

THEODOR UHLIG, b. Wurzen, near Leipzig, Feb. 15, 1822; d. Dresden, Jan. 3, 1853. A pupil of Fr. Schneider at Dessau, 1837–40; from 1841 violinist in the Dresden Court chapel; from a violent opponent of Wagner he became one of his most ardent admirers. He wrote the vocal score of "Lohengrin"; he composed symphonies, music for Singspiele, chamber music, but only a few pianoforte pieces and songs were pub. He devoted his later life to musical literary work. His works on musical subjects were pub. 1913 by L. Frankenstein.

JOHN BÖIE, b. Altona, Mar. 8, 1822; d. there, Mar. 19, 1900. An excellent violinist, pupil of Karl Müller at Brunswick; studied composition under J. C. Lobe at Leipzig and wrote many songs which became very popular. He was highly esteemed as orchestral player and teacher. His brother,

HEINRICH BÖIE, b. Altona, Sept. 16, 1825, d. there, June 18, 1879, devoted himself chiefly to composition, and after having served as an officer in the Schleswig-Holstein campaign against Denmark, founded a music shop at Altona in 1851 and composed operas, overtures, etc.; also Schiller's "Lay of the Bell" which became very popular (*see* Mendel).

JOSEPH WILHELM VON WASIELEWSKI, b. Grossleesen, near Danzig, June 17, 1822; d. Sondershausen, Dec. 13, 1896. He was the son of a Polish father and a German mother, both musically gifted. He showed early talent for music and became a pupil of the Leipzig Conservatoire when it was first opened on Apr. 2, 1843. There he studied the violin under Ferd. David, and musical theory and composition under Mendelssohn and Hauptmann. He continued his studies under David for several years after he left the Conservatoire in 1845. After touring with Carl Reinecke in the Baltic provinces he was, in 1846, appointed as a 1st violinist in the Leipzig "Gewandhaus" and the theatre orchestras and also as leader in Robert Franz's concerts at Halle and, 1848–9, at the Euterpe concerts, Leipzig. In 1850 Schumann called him to Düsseldorf as concertmeister and soloist, but in 1852 he became conductor of the newly founded choral society at Bonn, where he remained for three years. In 1855 he went to Dresden, where he commenced his literary career and only rarely played in public as a soloist. Between 1859 and 1869 he produced a number of important works of musical biography and history, including his valuable Schumann biography and the "History of the Violin." In 1869 he became musical director of the Bonn town orchestra, received the title of Royal Director of Music in 1873 and retired in 1884 to Sondershausen, where he continued his literary activity to the time of his death, producing a number of valuable works, including his "History of the Violoncello." His pub. compositions for violin consist only in a Notturno, 2 books of short pieces entitled "Herbstblumen," and a few patriotic choral songs.

JULIUS EICHBERG, b. Düsseldorf, June 13, 1824; d. Boston (Mass.), Jan. 18, 1893. The son of a musician, who showed such talent for the violin, which he studied first under Jos. Fröhlich at Würzburg while Julius Rietz instructed him in counterpoint and composition, that at the age of 7 he attracted the attention of Mendelssohn, who advised him to go to Brussels where, in 1843, he became a pupil of Meerts and de Bériot for violin and of Fétis for composition, in 1845 gaining the 1st prizes for violin-playing and composition. He then resided at Frankfort a/M. for some time as 2nd concertmeister at the theatre and in 1846 he became teacher of the violin at the Geneva Conservatoire. In 1857 he went to New York and accepted an engagement as director of the Museum concerts till 1866. He was at Boston (Mass.) in 1859, where in 1867 he founded a Conservatoire of music on European lines, which soon became famous throughout the United States. He was an excellent virtuoso and conductor, and always strove for the highest and noblest in his art. He wrote very useful studies and duets for violin, string trios and quartets, and 4 operettas, of which one or two at least became very popular. He was also appointed as superintendent of music in public schools.

PAUL CARL WIPPLINGER, b. Halle-on-the-Saale, July 7, 1824; d. Cassel, May 11, 1887. Pupil of Concertmeister G. Schmidt, a pupil of Spohr, and Ferd. Sturm. In 1844 he became concert-meister at Aix-la-Chapelle, and during his appointment there he renewed his studies for some time under Theodor Pixis at Cologne. From 1860 to the time of his death he was concert-meister at the Cassel Court theatre.

FERDINAND HÜLLWECK, b. Dessau, Oct. 8, 1824; d. Blasewitz, near Dresden, July 24, 1887. A pupil of Fr. Schneider in composition; became in 1844 2nd concertmeister in the Royal chapel at Dresden. Excellent soloist, quartet player and teacher at the Dresden Conservatoire; retired in 1886. He composed a number of instructive works for the violin, which are still of practical value.

OTTO FRIEDRICH VON KÖNIGSLÖW, b. Hamburg, Nov. 13 (14?), 1824; d. Bonn, Oct. 6, 1898. From the age of 7 pupil of his father, an excellent amateur pupil of Andreas Romberg; at the age of 14 he continued his studies under Spohr's pupil Fr. Pacius, and finally he was for some time a pupil of K. Hafner. During 1844–6 he was at Leipzig, where he continued his studies under Ferd. David, and Moritz Hauptmann (musical theory). From 1846 to 1858 he toured with marked success as a soloist. Although equipped with an excellent technique, he was not so much a virtuoso as a chamber-music player, and as such he distinguished himself by his dignified and refined rendering of the works of the classical masters. In 1858 he became professor of the violin at the Cologne Conservatoire and concertmeister in the Gürzenich orchestra, as well as leader of the Conservatoire quartet, which in its chamber con-

certs was joined by Ferd. Hiller as pianist. In 1881 he resigned his position as concertmeister on account of an affliction
in the arm, and in 1884 he retired, with the title of Royal
Professor, to Bonn.

HUGO BEYERLE, b. Minden, Prussia, May 31, 1825. A pupil
of L. Spohr in 1842; became at first supernumerary, and, in
1860, chamber musician in the Royal chapel, Berlin.

FRANCISKA FRIESE. A pupil of Ferdinand David.

# CHAPTER 53

# *Germany: to 1850*

JEAN JOSEPH BOTT, b. Cassel, Mar. 9, 1826; d. New York, Apr. 30, 1895. Son of Anton Bott, violinist in the Cassel Court chapel, and esteemed musician, who taught Jean the violin and pianoforte. At the age of 8 he gave very successful concerts. Spohr then took him in hand and he made such rapid progress that in 1840 he appeared as a virtuoso in Frankfort a/M.; Breslau, etc., etc. Under his great master he had also studied composition to such good purpose that in the same year he was the first to gain the Frankfort Mozart prize (founded 1838), by which he received an annuity of 400 florins from 1841 to 1845. He devoted himself now to serious theoretical studies under Moritz Hauptmann, and when the latter went to Leipzig in 1842, he continued them under Spohr, who gave him the most flattering credentials as virtuoso, composer and conductor. Equipped with these he went on tour again in Northern Germany, where he was everywhere received with applause and distinction. On his return in 1846 the Elector made him solo violinist of his chapel, and in 1849 court-concertmeister. When, two years later, he wanted to exchange this for a similar position at the Court of Hanover he was made capellmeister in 1852 at the Cassel Court theatre by the side of Spohr. In 1857 he went as first capellmeister to Meiningen and in 1865 in the same capacity to the Court of Hanover, where he also conducted the opera and the winter subscription concerts. All this time he did not neglect the violin and often appeared as a soloist. Two operas of his had been performed in various towns and one of his symphonies was acclaimed at Hanover in 1870. In 1878 he was pensioned and lived for some time at Magdeburg, whence he went to America. He wrote, among other pieces, a number of compositions for the violin which have not survived. As a violinist his style resembled that of his master perhaps more closely than that of any of Spohr's pupils. Breadth, dignity and beauty of tone were its outstanding characteristics. In 1894 his beautiful Strad., which he had just sold to Sr. Nicolini for £900, was stolen from Bott's New York residence and the grief over his loss hastened his death (particulars in *The Strad*, July, 1895).

JACOB BOTT, his younger brother, was also an estimable violinist in the Court chapel at Cassel.

KARL BRENDICKE, d. Berlin, 1832, while still young. He was a pupil of F. A. Henning, Berlin, made his successful debut there in 1826 and became Royal chamber musician in 1827.

AUGUST KÜNDIGER, b. Kitzingen, Feb. 13, 1827. Violinist in the Imperial Court orchestra, St. Petersburg, and composer for the violin.

EDUARD MOLLENHAUER, b. Erfurt, Apr. 12, 1827. Studied the violin in 1841 under Ernst, and 1843 under Spohr. In 1853 he went to New York, where he established a school for advanced violin students. He was one of the originators of the conservatoire system in America. He composed operas, symphonies, quartets, violin pieces, and songs.

FRIEDRICH MOLLENHAUER, b. Erfurt, 1818, d. Brooklyn, near New York, 1885. Eduard (as given above) was his elder brother.

LOUIS SCHUBERT, b. Dessau, Jan. 27, 1828; d. Dresden, Sept. 17, 1884. Went to St. Petersburg ca. 1845; then became concertmeister at Königsberg theatre, which, after six years, he left and devoted himself to concert playing and teaching there. In 1862 he left Königsberg and settled at Dresden as a teacher of singing. Composed some violin duos (transcribed from Bach), wrote a viola tutor, a singing tutor ("Gesangschule in Liedern") and 4 successful operettas.

FRIEDRICH HERMANN, b. Frankfort a/M., Feb. 1, 1828; d. Leipzig, Sept. 27, 1907. During 1843–6 a pupil at Leipzig Conservatoire, under David for violin, Hauptmann and Mendelssohn for composition. From 1846 to 1875 viola player in the Gewandhaus and theatre orchestras. In 1847 he became teacher of the violin at the Conservatoire, and in 1878 resigned from the former appointments to devote himself entirely to teaching, composing and the editing of Peter's and Augener's classical violin music. In 1883 he received the title of Royal Saxon Professor. He was very successful and greatly esteemed as a teacher. Apart from his excellent editions of numerous works he wrote a terzet for 3 violins, a duo for violin and violoncello, a quartet for wind instruments, a symphony, etc.

ADOLF KÖCKERT, b. Magdeburg, Oct. 27, 1828; d. Zürich, Aug. 27, 1911. Pupil of Mildner, Kittl and Gordigiani at the Prague Conservatoire 1843–9; then violinist at the Prague theatre, toured as a virtuoso in Europe from 1852 to 1857, when he married at Geneva and entered the business of his father-in-law. All his musical achievements during the next following years were the formation of a string quartet in 1859. After the death of his father-in-law in 1881 he returned to his musical career. He wrote compositions for violin, orchestra and songs; also wrote several books on musical subjects and articles for musical periodicals.

KARL MÜLLER-BERGHAUS, b. Brunswick, Apr. 14, 1829; d. Stuttgart, Nov. 11, 1907. Son and pupil of Karl Friedrich, the leader of the first Müller quartet. When this came to an end in 1855, Karl and his three brothers Hugo (2nd violin), Bernhard (viola) and Wilhelm (violoncello), founded the second Müller quartet at Meiningen, where they were all engaged as chamber musicians, Karl being also concertmeister, in which capacity he had previously been engaged for some time at the Court in Berlin. They toured chiefly in Northern and Middle Europe, and fully upheld the prestige of the elder quartet. When Karl married the excellent singer Elvira Berghaus he added her family name to his. In 1866 the quartet took its headquarters at Wiesbaden, but when, soon after Karl was appointed director of music at Rostock, his brothers followed him there, they were all engaged in the Court chapel. In 1867 the wanderlust awakened again in them, but as Karl could not forsake his duties at the Court his place was taken by L. von Auer. When Wilhelm, the violoncellist, however, became the successor of De Swert at the Berlin High School in 1873, the quartet was finally broken up. Karl was for some time conductor of the Kur-orchestra at Wiesbaden, then of the private chapel of the Russian Baron von Dervies at Nice, and in 1880 he went to Stuttgart, where his wife opened a school for singing and he took an engagement at Hamburg from 1881 to 1886.

LOUIS RIES, b. Berlin, Jan. 30, 1830; d. London, Oct. 3, 1913. He was the eldest son and pupil of his father, Hubert Ries, and afterwards pupil of Vieuxtemps. In 1852 he settled in London where, with Straus and Piatti, he was a member of the famous Monday and Saturday concerts quartet, mostly led by Joachim or Mme Norman-Neruda (Lady Hallé). He retired after thirty-eight years of active life, largely spent in teaching, for which he had a high reputation.

HORTENSIA SCHLETTERER, *née* Zirges, b. Mar. 19, 1830. Studied the violin at the Leipzig Conservatoire and after-wards toured successfully as a violin virtuoso.

ADOLPH LANG, b. Thorn, June 10, 1830; d. Oliva, near Danzig, May 15, 1912. Studied the violin under Ferd. David and composition under M. Hauptmann and Mendels-sohn at the Leipzig Conservatoire, 1844–7. In 1851 he became violinist in the Friedrich-Wilhelmstadt Theatre, Berlin. There he became first concertmeister and 1854–67 capellmeister. He composed operettas, overtures, marches, etc., which are musicianly written and melodious. In 1867 he took over a confectionery business of his father-in-law.

ALEXANDER CASORTI, b. Coburg, Nov. 27, 1830; d. Dresden, Sept. 28, 1867. The son of a Court dancing-master, living at Dresden. Studied the violin at the Brussels Conservatoire under Meerts and de Bériot and composition under Fétis; toured in Italy, where he became professor of the Academy of St. Cecilia in 1855, and was decorated with many orders, etc. He became concertmeister at a Venice theatre, but soon became ailing and returned to Dresden, where he died soon afterwards. He left 4 grand violin concertos with orchestra, string quartets and some overtures, also an opera. His compositions are very melodious and of good workmanship.

AUGUST KÖMPEL, b. Brückenau, Bavaria, Aug. 15, 1831; d. Weimar, Apr. 7, 1891. Son of a musician. Showing early

J. JOACHIM    L. RIES        L. STRAUS    A. PIATTI

## THE LONDON JOACHIM QUARTET
From an engraving after the painting by Bruck-Lajos, originally in the possession of
Mr. Arthur Chappell whose portrait is on the wall.

talent, he was sent to the music school at Würzburg in Dec., 1840. In Feb., 1844, he went to Cassel, where he found a patron in the Councillor Lüdner, who provided the means for his subsistence while Spohr instructed him gratuitously for three years. From 1849 to 1852 he was a member of the Court chapel at Cassel, employing his summer holidays by further studies under Ferd. David at Leipzig. From 1852 to 1861 he was solo violinist in the Court chapel at Hanover. During that time he went on a prolonged concert tour via Frankfort a/M. to Brussels, Paris and London, meeting everywhere with great success, which attended him also in occasional visits to other German towns. In 1861 he went to Holland, where he remained for a longer period, appearing as soloist in the principal towns; afterwards he toured on the lower Rhine and also gained laurels at the Leipzig Gewandhaus. At the beginning of 1863 (Mendel and others, 1867) he was called to Weimar as Court concert-meister, whence he toured from time to time in various parts of Europe, and also paid a second visit to Paris in the winter of 1866–7. He was also an excellent viola player, and, as such, a member of the Weimar string quartet. He was pensioned in the summer of 1884.

JOSEPH JOACHIM, b. Kittsee, near Pressburg, June 28, 1831; d. Berlin, Aug. 15, 1907. The greatest master of the violin of modern times; he was great as a virtuoso, great as musician, and great as the man. In the rendering of the works of the great masters he has not had his equal within a century. Even the works of composers of the second rank like Viotti, Rode, or Spohr gained a fresh lustre when played by him.

He began to play the violin at the age of 5, and soon showed such talent for music, and for the violin in particular, that his parents placed him under Serwaczynski, the leader at the Pesth Opera. At the age of 7 he played a duet in public with his master. In 1839 he went to Vienna, where he studied for a time under Miska Hauser and under Georg Hellmesberger, and in 1840 he played at a public concert Maurer's Concertante with three other boy violinists, two being the sons of Hellmesberger. Soon afterwards he became a private pupil of Böhm, and made such rapid progress that in 1843 his master declared his violinistic training as completed, and with his consent he was sent to Leipzig. He made his first public appearance there on Aug. 19, 1843, when he played a rondo by de Bériot at a concert given by Mme Viardot-Garcia. Mendelssohn, who felt attracted to the gifted boy, accompanied his solo. On Nov. 16 he played Ernst's Othello fantasia at a Gewandhaus Concert and roused the audience to the utmost enthusiasm. Musicians were astounded by the perfection in every detail of his marvellous technique, which also testified to the thoroughness and excellence of Böhm's teaching. His parents thereupon resolved to leave him in the care of his uncle, a Leipzig merchant, and he received now and again advice from Ferd. David, while M. Hauptmann became his master in counterpoint and composition, and he pursued with great zeal his general education. In 1844 he accompanied Mendelssohn to London, where he played first at a benefit concert of Bunn the impresario, at Drury Lane Theatre, on Mar. 28; then at a concert of Jul. Benedict on May 19, and at the Philharmonic Concert on May 27, he played for the first time the Beethoven concerto in public, Mendelssohn conducting the orchestra. This work he made particularly his own, and nobody else has played it with that soulfulness and noble grandeur. On Dec. 4 of that year he played an adagio and rondo with orchestra at a Gewandhaus Concert at Leipzig with great success. Apart from frequent visits to many of the principal German towns and two more visits to England, he remained for the following years at Leipzig, where he had become a teacher at the Conservatoire, as well as member, and eventually vice-concertmeister, of the orchestra. In the latter part of 1849, Liszt, who had settled there, induced him to accept the post of concertmeister at the Court of Weimar. He felt, however, out of his element in musical circles which were bound up with the "New German School," and therefore accepted readily the post as concertmeister, and Royal chamber virtuoso at the Court of Hanover in 1853. For some years he remained still in touch with Liszt and the circle of musicians surrounding him, but when these became openly antagonistic to Mendelssohn, Schumann, and Brahms, to whom he was bound by a spiritual relationship and the ties of sincerest friendship and veneration, he severed his connexion with the former by the letter of Aug. 27, 1857, published in Moser's "Joseph Joachim." In 1853 he played the Beethoven concerto at the Lower Rhenish Music Festival at Düsseldorf, conducted by Schumann and—for the first time—by Ferd. Hiller. He received many ovations; his playing of the concerto had deeply moved his hearers and it was said that he was destined to reach the highest pinnacle of his art. In 1862 he visited London for the seventh time, and from that year he appeared annually at many of the principal London and provincial concerts and as leader of the quartet at the Monday and Saturday Popular Concerts. In 1863 he married the celebrated contralto singer Amalie Weiss, who was then engaged at the Hanover Court opera. When Hanover became a Prussian province in 1866, Joachim settled in Berlin, where, in 1868, he was appointed Director of the newly founded High School for Music, and in 1869 member of the Senate of the Royal Academy of Arts, with the title of Royal Professor. In the same year he founded also in Berlin a permanent string quartet with E. Schiever, H. de Ahna, and Wm. Müller; the 2nd violin was afterwards successively taken by de Ahna, Joh. Kruse, and Carl Halíř, while the viola devolved in succession upon Ed. Rappoldi and Em. Wirth, R. Hausmann succeeding Müller as violoncellist. The Joachim quartet was unequalled in the rendering of the classics as well as the classic-romanticists, and their visits were always hailed with enthusiasm over the whole of Europe. At the Popular Concerts in London, Piatti was the violoncellist, while the 2nd violin was in the capable hands of Louis Ries and the viola was played successively by C. W. Doyle, J. B. Zerbini, L. Straus, and B. Hollander. In Joachim's absence Mme Norman-Neruda generally took his place. Apart from many concert performances in various Continental and English towns, he devoted himself chiefly to teaching, and the total number of his pupils from all parts of the world amounted to round about 500. He also conducted at many important musical festivals, as for instance in 1875, within a few weeks at the Lower Rhenish Music Festival, and the first music festival at Kiel. The Universities of Cambridge (1877), Oxford, and Glasgow, each conferred upon him the honorary degree of Doctor of Music, and orders of Knighthood were conferred upon him by the sovereigns of various countries. In the spring of 1889 he celebrated the jubilee of his first appearance in public, when he received a purse of £5,000, of which £1,000 went to the starting of a Joseph Joachim Foundation. On Apr. 22, 1899, a concert was given at the rooms of the Berlin Philharmonic Society, to commemorate the sixtieth anniversary of his artistic career. The concert had been arranged by his former pupil, A. Moser, and all the string players, except the double basses, in the orchestra, were chosen from his former pupils. On May 16, 1904, the sixtieth anniversary of his first appearance in England was celebrated by a festival concert at the Queen's Hall when he conducted his overture to "Henry IV," and, as well as on the former occasion, played the Beethoven concerto. On that occasion he was presented with his portrait painted by J. Sargent, R.A. His English friends and admirers presented him with a magnificent Stradivari violin of the best period. In 1905 he visited Rome with his Berlin quartet, where they played all the 16 Beethoven quartets in the Farnese Palace. Early in 1907 he had an attack of influenza, from which however he recovered so far, after a few weeks rest on the shores of Lake Geneva, that he was able at the end of May to play at the third Festival of the new Bach Society. This was his last appearance in public, for in June he was attacked by actinomycosis, a very uncommon disease, to which he succumbed about two months later. Only the minor part of his compositions has been pub., viz. 3 violin concertos of which the Hungarian concerto has proved of lasting value; Andantino and allegro scherzoso, Notturno, Variations in E minor, all for violin with orchestra; Romance, and 6 pieces for violin and pianoforte; pieces for viola and pianoforte; 5 overtures and 2 marches for orchestra; Scena for contralto and orchestra; songs; cadenzas for the concertos of Beethoven and Brahms. As a composer Joachim was strongly influenced by Schumann, as well as by his friend Brahms, but if he lacked originality, a lofty nobility of thought gave his work the mark of distinction. In his latter years he expended much labour and thought upon the tutor which he wrote in conjunction with Moser, and in which he laid down the principles of his art. Together with the latter, he prepared also a carefully phrased and fingered edition of Beethoven's quartets, although he never bound himself to a rigidly fixed system with regard to these, as he justly considered a certain amount of freedom in their case, subject to momentary inspiration, essential for true artistic rendering. His faultless technique only served him as an aid to a perfect rendering of the works of the great masters whose mode of thinking and feeling he strove to penetrate, sinking his own individuality in theirs as far as possible, with the result that his rendering, especially of the works of Beethoven and Bach, as well as of all the other masters, served as a model for all who heard him. An excellent analysis of his playing, as far as an idea can be given of it in words, is to be found in the *Musical Gazette* for Mar. and July, 1900, under the title "Performance and Personality." A fuller account of his life has been given by A. Moser, "Joseph Joachim, ein Lebensbild," 2 vols., 1907–10. An English translation of the earlier ed. of 1898 has been made by L. Durham, 1901.

JOSEPH WALTER, b. Neuburg on the Danube, Dec. 30, 1831; d. Munich, July 15, 1875. Received his first instruction on the violin from his father and made his public debut at the age of 11. In 1848 he toured as a soloist. From 1847 to 1850 he was a pupil at the Munich Conservatoire and after that he studied for a short time under de Bériot at Brussels. He was violinist in the Court orchestras of Vienna (1851) and Hanover (1853), and from 1859 concertmeister at Munich and professor of violin at the Royal Conservatoire there. He was praised for his technique and tone as well as artistic style and temperament.

CARL LOUIS BARGHEER, b. Bückeburg, Dec. 31, 1831; d. Hamburg, May 19, 1902. The son of an oboist in the Court chapel who began to teach him violin-playing from his seventh year, after Campagnoli's method. In 1848 he became a pupil of Spohr at Cassel, on whose recommendation he was, in 1850, appointed as violinist in the Court chapel of Detmold. The Prince of Lippe Detmold became interested in the young artist and gave him the means for further studies, first under Ferd. David at Leipzig, then under Joachim at Hanover. In 1860 the Prince appointed him as concertmeister and 1863 as Court capellmeister. After the dissolution of the chapel in 1876 he became concertmeister of the Philharmonic Society and teacher at the Conservatoire at Hamburg until 1889. He was also leader of the subscription concerts under H. von Bülow from 1883 to 1891.

JOHANN CHRISTOPH LAUTERBACH, b. Kulmbach, July 24, 1832; d. Dresden, Apr., 1918. Although not originally intended to become a musician, he began to play the violin at an early age, and while at school at Würzburg and afterwards at the college (Gymnasium) there he studied the violin under Fröhlich and Spohr's pupil J. G. Bratsch at the music institute. But, Fröhlich having no thorough knowledge of violin technics, he was left largely to his own devices. His progress by dint of study supported by remarkable natural talent, was such that he soon decided to devote himself entirely to the violin. In 1850 he went to the Brussels Conservatoire as a pupil of de Beriot (and Fétis for composition); in 1851 he gained the prize of honour and soon after he was appointed as deputy teacher during the temporary absence of Léonard. In 1852 he toured in Belgium, Holland, and Germany, and in 1853 he went to Munich as concertmeister at the Royal Chapel and teacher of the violin at the Conservatoire. In 1861 he succeeded Franz Schubert as second concertmeister at the Court and teacher of the highest violin class at the Conservatoire, Dresden. When Schubert was pensioned in 1873 Lauterbach followed him as 1st concertmeister; meanwhile he continued his tours, and during the season of 1864 and 1865 he appeared before enthusiastic audiences in England. He also played at the last concert in the Tuileries on Apr. 23, 1870, and received from Napoleon a golden box set with diamonds. Also 1872 in Vienna and 1875 at Copenhagen he met with triumphal successes, which continued everywhere until he retired in 1889. As a soloist he ranks among the great masters who carried on the classical traditions. He combined the grace and elegance of de Bériot's with the breadth and power of the German school, and above all he was a true artist, and this documented itself not least in his thought- and soulful quartet performances, in which he was worthily supported by Ferd. Hüllweck, Louis Göhring and Friedr. Grützmacher, sen. He trained many excellent pupils at the Dresden Conservatoire, from which he retired in 1877. His compositions consist mainly of concert and salon pieces for violin. An artist of great refinement and amiable personality he was a great favourite at the Court, as well as with his brother artists and all those of the public with whom he came into personal contact. He had received the title of a Royal Professor, and in 1902 the King of Saxony made him a Court Councillor, he being the first violinist upon whom that honour was ever bestowed. He had also been decorated with high orders by various Courts of Europe.

FR. WILHELM LANGHANS, b. Hamburg, Sept. 21, 1832; d. Berlin, June 9, 1892. Studied the violin under good teachers while at the grammar school. In 1849 he entered the Leipzig Conservatoire as a pupil of Ferd. David (violin) and Hauptmann and Richter (composition), and completed his studies under Alard in Paris, after playing for some time in the Gewandhaus and theatre orchestras, to which he returned after his sojourn in Paris and to which he belonged from 1852 to 1856. During 1857–60 he was concertmeister at Düsseldorf, where he married, in 1858, the pianist Louise Japha, a former pupil of Mme Schumann. In 1860 he was concertmeister and teacher at Hamburg, and 1863 in Paris. In both cities he and his wife did much to popularize the then modern chamber music (Schumann, Mendelssohn, etc.). In Paris he also commenced his literary activity chiefly as reporter for the *Neue Zeitschrift für Musik*. In 1869 he went to Heidelberg, where he took his degree of Dr.Phil., and from that time he devoted himself chiefly to the theoretical side of his art. In 1871 he settled in Berlin, where in 1873 he became a teacher of musical history at Kullack's Academy, and in 1881 he joined Scharwenka's Conservatoire. In 1864 he obtained at Florence a prize for a string quartet. For the violin he composed: a concert allegro with orchestra, a violin sonata, solos, and studies, also a symphony, an overture, and songs. The most important of his literary works are his continuation of Ambros's "History of Music," entitled "Die Geschichte der Musik des 17. 18. und 19. Jahrhunderts" (2 vols.) and "Musikgeschichte in 12 Vorträgen" (1878, Dutch trans. by J. Hartog, 1885). Langhans was an honorary member of several Italian, etc., Academies and other important music literary societies.

HUGO MÜLLER, b. Brunswick, Sept. 21, 1832; d. there, June 26, 1886. A son and pupil of Karl Friedrich Müller. He was 2nd violinist in the second Müller quartet, 1855–73, and Court musician in the chapel at Meiningen.

LEOPOLD DAMROSCH, b. Posen, Oct. 22, 1832; d. New York, Feb. 15, 1885.   He showed musical talent and studied the violin in early youth, but was destined for a medical career and visited the University at Berlin.   At the same time he continued his musical studies under Hubert Ries and composition under Dehn.   After acquiring his degree of M.D. he practised at Posen in 1854.   In 1855 he took up music professionally and played as violin virtuoso in several North German towns.   In Berlin he received recommendations to Weimar where, towards the end of 1856, he became a violinist in the Court chapel, and a member of the inner Liszt circle, the artistic ideals of which he defended enthusiastically in the *Neue Zeitschrift für Musik*.   Next he became musical director of the theatre at Posen, and in 1866 he occupied a similar position at the Breslau theatre, but after the winter season he took over the conductorship of the orchestral society of that town and remained there until 1871.   During that time he carried on a vigorous Wagner-Liszt propaganda, but meeting with much opposition and unpleasantness, he accepted a favourable offer of the choral society Arion, New York, and went there in the summer of 1871.   Henceforward, although still playing as soloist on many occasions, he devoted himself chiefly to conducting. He also edited a musical paper, which he conducted in the spirit of the young-German school.   By untiring zeal and excellent performances he was the pioneer who first introduced and popularized Wagner's works in America.   Damrosch composed an overture, violin pieces, and songs which show talent but lack originality.

JEAN BECKER, b. Mannheim, May 11, 1833; d. there, Oct. 10, 1884.   Studied the violin first under his father, then under Hildebrand and Hartmann, but his chief teacher became Kettenus, who had received his training in the Belgian school.   All these were members of the Mannheim Court orchestra.   Vincenz Lachner was his master in musical theory.   At the age of 11 he appeared at Mannheim with such success that he was awarded a Mozart medal.   After the completion of his studies at Mannheim he went to Paris, where he studied still with Alard, chiefly the latter's brilliant virtuoso pieces. After a short time he was recalled to Mannheim to succeed Kettenus as concertmeister, where he was so much admired that the Grand Duchess Stephanie of Baden bestowed upon him the title of Chamber Virtuoso. In 1858 he resigned his position at Mannheim and went to Paris, where he gave three concerts with the greatest success. There he received an invitation to play at the Monday Popular Concerts in London. In 1860 he re-visited Paris and then toured in Germany. After that he was leader at the old Philharmonic Society in London, but only for one season, then he toured again all over Europe. So far he had appeared as a virtuoso of exceptional brilliancy, but he felt the emptiness of this career and decided to serve the higher ends of his art. He had already attempted at Mannheim and Strassburg to infuse new life into quartet-playing in connexion with which his name was to become pre-eminent in the history of violin-playing. His chance came in 1865, when he was called upon to lead ten subscription concerts of a society for the study of chamber music founded by Baseri, a wealthy professor at Florence. He reconstructed the quartet with E. Masi for the 2nd violin, L. Chiostri for the viola, and the German violoncellist, F. R. Hilpert. Masi had so far but little experience in quartet-playing, but soon became efficient under Becker's tuition, who moreover presented him with a Stradivari violin, as his own was but a poor specimen. Becker himself had a fine Guarnerius. By dint of untiring practice they reached a degree of perfection in their ensemble which has rarely been equalled and never surpassed. In 1875 Louis Hegyesi took Hilpert's place in the quartet which, as the Florentine quartet, visited between 1866–80 all the principal towns of Germany, with phenomenal success. It was by their delightful rendering that the now famous Menuet by Boccherini attained its wide popularity. In 1880 the Florentine quartet was dissolved and Becker formed a new combination with his own children, his daughter JEANNE as pianist, his elder son HANS (afterwards professor at the Leipzig Conservatoire) as viola, and his younger son HUGO as violoncello. They toured successfully in Germany, but Becker's health soon began to fail and he died at the comparatively early age of 51. His charming and talented daughter died in 1893, at the early age of 34.

FRIEDRICH WILHELM DIETZ, b. Marburg-on-the-Lahn, June 15, 1833; d. Soden, Taunus, Dec. 16, 1897. A pupil of Spohr and Kraushaar at Cassel; lived as an esteemed teacher at Frankfort a/M.; composed violin, violoncello, and pianoforte pieces, chamber-music works, etc.

ALOYS BALDENECKER, b. Frankfort a/M., 1833; d. Wiesbaden, Nov. 28, 1869. The son of the pianist Jean Baptist Baldenecker, and nephew of Joh. Bernh. Baldenecker. He commenced to study the violin as a child and appeared as a virtuoso at the age of 10. In 1847 he became a violinist at the Frankfort theatre, and in 1852 he was appointed as concertmeister at the Ducal theatre at Wiesbaden, where he had exercised a beneficial influence on the musical life of that town by his musical soirées and chamber-music concerts. He was an excellent artist, his style was broad and full of expression. Unfortunately his mind became affected in 1868 and he died in an asylum the following year. He was beloved for his simple modesty.

LUDWIG ABEL, b. Eckartsberga, Thüringen, Jan. 14, 1834; d. Pasing, near Munich, Aug. 13, 1895. Received his first musical education at Weimar, and afterwards studied the violin under Ferd. David at the Leipzig Conservatoire. Was appointed concertmeister at Basle, where he remained till 1866, and went in 1867 in the same capacity to Munich, where for many years he was one of the chief professors (violin, score reading, etc.) at the Conservatoire. He composed solo pieces and a tutor for the violin.

FRIEDHOLD FLEISCHHAUER, b. Weimar, July 24, 1834; d. Meiningen, Dec. 11, 1896. Some time between 1850–4 he was a pupil of Joachim at Weimar, and afterwards finished his studies under Ferd. Laub. Later he became a member of the Weimar Court chapel and in 1860 solo violinist at Aix-la-Chapelle, and in 1864 he was appointed in the Meiningen Court chapel, where he remained.

RUDOLPH BIAL, b. Habelshwerdt, Silesia, Aug. 26, 1834; d. New York, Nov. 13, 1881 (Riemann: Nov. 23). Studied the

violin at Breslau, where he was first violinist at the theatre till
1853, when he went to Berlin. Then he toured with his
brother Karl, the pianist, in Africa, Australia, England, returning to Berlin, where he became concertmeister in, and afterwards conductor of, Kroll's band. After a period of work as
private teacher he became capellmeister at the Wallner theatre
in 1864, for which he composed many amusing and successful
farces and operettas; afterwards he became director of the
Italian Opera in Berlin, and 1878 he went to New York as an
impresario.

CARL RUNDNAGEL, b. Hersfeld, Apr. 4, 1835; d. Cassel, Feb. 2,
1911. Received his first music lessons from his father, a
music teacher at a grammar school, and played a violin solo in
public in his ninth year with great success. After successfully
passing a severe examination by Spohr, that master accepted
him as his pupil and always retained a great interest in his
career. At the end of his studies he became a 1st violinist at
the Cologne town theatre, but shortly after, he went to Cassel
as a member of the Court orchestra. As he had also made a
thorough study of organ-playing, he was in 1866 appointed
Court organist apart from his post as violinist in the Court
orchestra. He became a distinguished organist and wrote
many compositions for that instrument, as well as violin pieces,
chamber music, etc.; he also arranged and ed. many of Spohr's
works.

GEORG JOSEPH JAPHA, b. Königsberg, Aug. 28, 1835; d.
Cologne, Feb. 25, 1892. During 1850–3 a pupil at the
Leipzig Conservatoire under Ferd. David and Rain. Dreyschock. In 1853 he studied under Edm. Singer at Königsberg, and afterwards under Alard in Paris. During 1855–7
he was in the Leipzig Gewandhaus orchestra, where he played
repeatedly as soloist. In the winter 1857–8 he went to
Russia, and on his return he settled at Königsberg as a private
teacher, giving also chamber-music concerts, in 1863, with
Ad. Jensen. In the latter year he visited London as soloist
and quartet player, and then went to Cologne as concertmeister at the Gürzenich concerts, teacher at the Conservatoire and 2nd violin in the professor's quartet, of which he
became the leader after the retirement of von Königslöw.
Japha was highly esteemed as a teacher, counting many

prominent violinists among his pupils, who revered him also for his amiable personality.

KARL HERNER, b. Rendsburg, Jan. 23, 1836; d. Hanover, July 16, 1906. He studied, 1852–5, at the Prague Conservatoire and afterwards under Joachim at Hanover; was violinist successively in the orchestras of Hamburg, Kiel, Copenhagen, Brussels, Brunswick and, 1858, at Hanover where, with Bach and Bargiel, he was a member of the first Joachim quartet. He toured as pianist with Vieuxtemps and Carlotta Patti; became 1865 accompanist at the Hanover Court theatre, 1869 chorus master, 1877 conductor, 1887 capellmeister, and was pensioned in 1900. He composed a ballet, overtures, songs, etc.

JOSEPH HUBER, b. Sigmaringen, Apr. 17, 1837; d. Stuttgart, Apr. 23, 1886. Entered the Stern Conservatoire, Berlin, 1854, as pupil of L. Ganz for violin and B. Marx for composition; afterwards he studied at Weimar, whither he was attracted by Liszt, violin under Singer and composition under P. Cornelius. He then went as violinist in the chapel of the Prince of Hechingen to Löwenberg, where he composed 2 symphonic poems, violin pieces, songs, etc., which were successfully performed there. In 1864 he became concert-meister of the Euterpe concerts, Leipzig, where he made the acquaintance of the poet Peter Lohmann, who encouraged his revolutionary ideas with regard to musical form, and supplied him with a book to an opera "The Rose of Lebanon," the score of which was pub. in 1870. This was followed by another opera, "Irene," also on a book by Lohmann. Meanwhile he had in 1865 been appointed to the Court chapel at Stuttgart, where he remained to the end. He composed also 4 one-movement symphonies, instrumental solos, etc. (About his musical theories *see* Riemann's "Musik Lexikon," also Mendel, Reissmann.)

AUGUST SCHULTZ, b. Lehre, near Brunswick, June 15, 1837; d. there, Feb. 12, 1909. Received his first violin lessons from the music-director Zinkeisen, studied composition under Leibrock and became a chamber musician in the Brunswick Court chapel in 1855. He was sent to Hanover at the expense of the Intendant of the theatre for further study under Joachim. Afterwards he became concertmeister at Lippe-

Detmold and eventually returned to Brunswick as leader and conductor of the symphony orchestra. He composed songs for male chorus which became very popular, also an opera.

ALBERT KARL TOTTMANN, b. Zittau, July 31, 1837; d. Leipzig-Gohlis, Feb. 26, 1917. A violin pupil at the Leipzig Conservatoire, afterwards violinist in the Gewandhaus orchestra, and 1868–70 conductor at the Old Theatre. From that time onward he was chiefly writer on musical subjects and pub. among others a "Critical Repertory of the Violin and Viola Literature" (in German), which in its third ed. (1900) appeared as "Guide" (Führer) through the violin literature, and is still a valuable book of reference; he also wrote "Büchlein von der Geige" (Little Book of the Violin) (1904).

RAPHAEL MASZKOWSKI, b. Lemberg, 1838; d. Breslau (?), Mar. 14, 1901. He was intended for the career of an engineer and went to the Vienna Polytechnic in 1854; at the same time studied the violin at the Conservatoire under Hellmesberger. He then decided to devote himself entirely to music and in 1859 he went to the Leipzig Conservatoire as a pupil of Ferd. David and of Richter and Hauptmann for theory. During 1863–4 he conducted the Philharmonic Society and Vocal Academy at Hamburg. In 1865 he was director of the Imthurneum at Schaffhausen, and 1869 director of the Royal Musical Institute at Koblenz. In 1890 (1891?) he succeeded Max Bruch as conductor at Breslau. A nervous complaint of the left hand compelled him to abandon his violinistic career.

FRIEDRICH FERDINAND LISTEMANN, b. Schlotheim, Thuringia, Mar. 25, 1839; d. Boston, Mass., Dec. 28, 1909. Brother of Bernhard Listemann; pupil of his uncle, Concertmeister Uhlrich of Sondershausen, and Ferd. David at the Leipzig Conservatoire, 1856–7. In 1858–67 he was chamber virtuoso at the Court of Rudolstadt. In 1867 he went to Boston, Mass., and in 1871 he became 1st violin in the Thomas orchestra. In 1874 he went on tour in America with the Boston Philharmonic Club (a sextet), and in 1878 he became 1st violinist in the Philharmonic orchestra, and 1881 to 1885 he held that position in the symphony orchestra; since then he has devoted himself chiefly to teaching and occasional tours with the Listemann Concert Co. He composed 2 concertos (MS.) and a few solo pieces for violin and songs (pub.).

OTTO LÜSTNER, b. Breslau, Apr. 9, 1839; d. Barmen, Sept. 8, 1889. Son and pupil of the violinist, Ignaz Peter Lüstner; was violinist successively in the orchestras of Schwerin and Breslau; 1867–72, leader of Count Stolberg's quartet at Werningerode; 1873–5, concertmeister in Bilse's orchestra, Berlin; 1875–7, Court concertmeister and Ducal Sax. chamber virtuoso at Sondershausen; from thence onward municipal director of music at Barmen.

WILHELM HELLMICH, b. Berlin, June 30, 1839. A pupil of Ferd. Laub; 1st violinist in the Prussian Royal chapel from Aug. 1, 1868. Leader of several chamber-music enterprises.

SIMON E. JACOBSOHN, b. Mitau, Dec. 24, 1839; d. Chicago, Oct. 3, 1902. He showed very early talent for the violin, which on account of the poverty of the family he had to exercise in early boyhood as a dance musician, but eventually he became a pupil of Concertmeister Weller at Riga. In 1858 he entered the Leipzig Conservatoire as a pupil of Ferd. David. In 1859 he was able to appear as a successful soloist at the Gewandhaus Concert. Next he toured in Northern Europe as far as St. Petersburg, and in 1860 he was appointed concertmeister at Bremen. In 1872 he joined the Thomas orchestra in New York in a similar capacity. Afterwards he became teacher of the violin at the Cincinnati Conservatoire and thence he went to Chicago. He excelled both as player and teacher.

GEORGES JACOBY, b. Berlin, Feb. 13, 1840; d. London, Sept. 13, 1906. Studied under E. Ganz (piano) and the violin under L. Ganz, Berlin, de Bériot at Brussels, Massart in Paris, and composition under Gevaert, Chéri and Réber. 1861 solo violinist at the Grand Opera, Paris; 1869 conductor at the Bouffes Parisiens. At the outbreak of the Franco-Prussian War he went to London, where in 1871 he became conductor at the Alhambra theatre, and 1896 also professor at the Royal Academy of Music. He composed 7 operas and operettas for various theatres and over 100 ballets for the Alhambra.

MAX SCHEREK, b. Posen, Mar. 6, 1840. He showed remarkable talent for the violin at a very early age and played

Beethoven's G major sonata with Hans von Bülow in public when he was only 9 years old. At the age of 14 he entered the Leipzig Conservatoire, and after finishing his studies there he became concertmeister at Hamburg. From there he went to Angers as violin teacher at the Conservatoire, and afterwards as capellmeister to San Sebastian, Spain. Some time before 1880 he returned to his native town.

LOUIS LÜSTNER, b. Breslau, June 30, 1840; d. Wiesbaden, Jan. 24, 1918. A son and pupil of Ignaz Peter Lüstner. Was town capellmeister at Wiesbaden from 1874 to 1905, when he retired. He received the title of Royal Director of Music in 1899, and became conductor of the Vocal Academy in 1902.

PETER PAUL DAVID, b. Leipzig, Aug. 4, 1840. Brother and pupil of Ferd. David. 1862–5 member of the Karlsruhe orchestra; from 1865 to the time of his death principal music master at Uppingham School. The University of Cambridge bestowed upon him the honorary degree of Mus.Mag.

GUSTAV ADOLPH BARGHEER, b. Bückeburg, Oct. 21, 1840; d. Basle, Mar. 10, 1901. Brother of Karl Louis Bargheer and, like the latter, pupil of his father from his seventh year. He was the last pupil of Spohr (1857–8) and finished his studies under Joachim, after which he was for two years violinist in the Detmold Court chapel, and then concertmeister at Münster, Westphalia, until 1866, when he was appointed concertmeister and teacher at the Conservatoire of Basle.

BERNHARD FRIEDRICH WILHELM LISTEMANN, b. Schlotheim, Thuringia, Aug. 28, 1841; d. Chicago, Feb. 11, 1917. Brother of Ferdinand F. Listemann. Pupil of his uncle Uhlrich at Sondershausen, and of David at the Leipzig Conservatoire 1856 to 1857. During 1859–67 he was concertmeister in the Court orchestra at Rudolstadt and during that period he studied under Vieuxtemps (1861) and under Joachim (1862). In 1867 he went with his brother Friedr. to America, where he toured with Leopold de Meyer, and spent two years at Boston. From 1871 to 1874 he was first concertmeister of the Thomas orchestra, New York. In the latter year he returned to Boston, where he founded and conducted the Philharmonic Club, which in 1879 became the Philharmonic orchestra. In 1881 he founded the Listemann quartet and at the same time he became concertmeister of the Boston

Symphony Orchestra, in both of which he remained until 1885. During 1885–93 he was engaged in teaching in Boston, occasionally touring with the Listemann Concert Company. In 1893 he became head of the violin department of the Chicago College of Music. From 1909 to 1911, when he retired from active life, he resided in Boston again. He composed a method and solo pieces for the violin; also a symphony.

GEORGE SAINT-GEORGE, b. Dresden, Nov. 6, 1841, d. London Jan. 5, 1924. Studied the violin under Mildner, at the Prague conservatoire, where he also studied the pianoforte and composition. Soon after completing his studies he came to London, where he settled as teacher of the violin and pianoforte. At Prague he had taken a great interest in the viol d'amour, which he played with great perfection, and also in the old viol music and learned to play the viol da gamba. He then studied the art of making viols and produced a number of excellent viols d'amour, gambas and lutes. One of his viols d'amour, richly inlaid with designs in purfling, called the Dragon, from a carved dragon's head, and designs symbolic of the legend of St. George, was played by Miss Kate Chaplin at the revival of "The Beggar's Opera." He was a fertile and melodious composer, especially of violin pieces. His little suite "L'Ancien Régime" (Augener) is still a great favourite with amateur orchestras. He also edited Ariosti's Sonatas for Viol d'amour in an arrangement for violin. Composed also for viols, songs, etc. HENRY SAINT-GEORGE, his son and pupil, was also a violinist, and for several years examiner for Trinity College of Music, London. He wrote "The Bow, its History, Manufacture and Use" (*Strad* Library, 1896).

GUSTAV ADOLF NIEMANN, b. Wesselburen, Holstein, Dec. 6, 1841; d. Helsingfors, Dec. 5, 1881. Studied the violin at first under his father, then for a short time in Paris, and 1862–4 under Ferd. David at the Leipzig Conservatoire. In 1865 he was induced by the violoncellist, A. Meissner, to go to Helsingfors, where he became concertmeister in the concert orchestra, soloist, and chamber-music player, in which latter capacity he developed a meritorious activity in introducing the chamber-music works of the German masters.

FABIAN REHFELD, b. Tuchel, Prussia, Jan. 23, 1842; d. Berlin, Nov. 11, 1920. A pupil of Zimmermann and Grünwald in

AUGUST WILHELMJ
From a photograph in the possession of Messrs. W. E. Hill & Sons.

Berlin. In 1868 Royal chamber musician, 1873 to 1898 concertmeister, 1903 Royal professor. An excellent violinist and composer of violin pieces, also ed. of the very popular collection of pieces "Sang und Klang" (several books).

JOSEPH VENZL, b. Munich, Mar. 26, 1842. Studied at the Royal School of Music, 1852–8; was a member of the Court orchestra there. Wrote instructive violin music (*see* Hoffmeister cat.).

CARLO ROSA (KARL AUGUST NIKOLAS ROSE), b. Hamburg, Mar. 21, 1842; d. Paris, Apr. 30, 1889. Toured as a violinist at the age of 12 in Germany, England and Denmark. In 1859 he resumed his studies at the Leipzig Conservatoire under Ferd. David and afterwards studied for some time at the Paris Conservatoire. During 1863–5 he was concertmeister at Hamburg, and in Mar. 1866, he appeared with success at the Crystal Palace, London. He then went on a concert tour with C. Ratenau, vocalist, in the United States of America, where he met with the prima donna Euphrosine Parepa, whom he married in Feb., 1867, in New York. They formed an English opera company with which they toured successfully in the United States until 1871, when they returned to London, where they continued giving operas. Mme Parepa Rosa died there in 1874, when her husband continued the operatic enterprise which at his death became the still flourishing Carl Rosa Opera Company.

RICHARD HIMMELSTOSS, b. Sondershausen, June 17, 1843. Son of a violoncellist in the Court chapel, he commenced to play the violin under Concertmeister Uhlrich at the age of 8, and at 14 he entered the chapel of the Prince as a Court musician. On the recommendation of the capellmeister, he was sent by the Prince to Hanover in 1863–4 to study for five months under Joachim, who took a great interest in him. After that time he returned to Sondershausen where, in 1867, Max Bruch was appointed capellmeister and he induced him to go to Berlin for further studies at the High School for Music. There he studied once more under Joachim, and after nine months obtained the final certificate (Zeugnis der Reife). In the autumn of 1871 Bernh. Scholz engaged him as concertmeister for the orchestral union at Breslau, where he was also leader of the chamber-music soirées founded in 1873 for thirty-six years. At the orchestral concerts he played as soloist for twenty-five years. Apart from Berlin and Leipzig he appeared as soloist only in Silesia. He excelled both in that capacity and as chamber-music player.

PAUL JAPSEN, b. Berlin, Sept. 9, 1843. After a good preliminary training he made his higher studies in violin-playing under Ferd. Laub, while Fr. Kiel was his master in composition. He specialized in the art of teaching and contributed during 1870 and 1871 some valuable articles on violin-technics to the Berlin musical periodical *Echo* and the *Deutsche Musiker Zeitung*. On Apr. 1, 1872, he became chamber musician and violinist in the Royal chapel in Berlin, continuing his activity as a teacher.

HERMANN SCHRÖDER, b. Quedlinburg, July 28, 1843; d. Berlin, Jan. 31, 1901. Son and pupil of the town musician Karl Schröder and pupil of A. Ritter at Magdeburg. Founded in 1873 an institute for music in Berlin and was from 1885 concurrently also violin teacher at the Royal Institute for Church Music. He composed orchestral and chamber-music works and wrote a tutor for the violin, as well as a book on violin playing and scientific works on musical subjects.

GUSTAV JENSEN, b. Königsberg, Dec. 25, 1843; d. Cologne, Nov. 26, 1895. Brother of the famous composer, Adolph J. A pupil of S. Dehn, J. Joachim and F. Laub; from 1872 teacher of counterpoint at the Cologne Conservatoire. He was viola player in the Königslöw (the professor's) quartet; occasionally he played his own arrangements of violin sonatas by older masters (Handel, etc., mostly pub. by Augener) at the Saturday evening concerts of the Cologne Musical Society at the Conservatoire. He combined a good technique and beauty of tone, with great refinement of rendering. He composed 3 suites and 1 sonata, pieces, op. 15, and 18 for violin and pianoforte; two violoncello sonatas, chamber music, orchestral and choral compositions, pianoforte pieces, songs, and edited "Classical Violin Music" (sonatas and pieces by older masters—Augener).

RUDOLPH HERFURTH, b. Eisenberg, Altenburg, Feb. 9, 1844. A pupil of his father, the town director of music at Eisenberg. At the end of his primary school time his father died, and as he had consequently no means to enter the Leipzig Conservatoire he joined a local band as a violinist to enable him to pursue his studies. After that he was engaged successively as solo violinist in the orchestras of various German towns until he was in 1865 appointed as director of music at Freiburg i/B., and conductor of the band at the watering-place of Badenweiler. From 1871 he was capellmeister at the Imperial theatre, Strassburg, conjointly with Weissheimer.

HUGO HEERMANN, b. Heilbronn, Mar. 3, 1844. His musically talented mother fostered his early propensity for that art. He inclined from the beginning to the violin which he began to study seriously under a violinist named Marschek from the age of 8, and at 9 he appeared as a prodigy. When he was 10 Rossini heard him at Wildbad and, recognizing his talent, recommended him to Fétis at Brussels, where he studied at the Conservatoire the violin under Meerts and theory under Fétis. After three years he gained the 1st prize which enabled him to pursue his studies still further, in which the hearing of artists like de Bériot, Léonard, Vieuxtemps and Joachim was of great advantage to him. He went to Paris, where he studied for another period (of three years—Riemann), after which he returned to his native land. Although trained entirely in the Franco-Belgian school, he combined the grace and elegance with the strength and depth of the Germans. In 1865 he went to Frankfort a/M., as leader of the Museum Quartet, and later on he became concertmeister in the town orchestra. In 1878 he was appointed first teacher of the violin at the Hoch Conservatoire, where with Bassermann, Naret-Koning and Hugo Becker he formed a string quartet which ranked among the foremost of its time. He also toured a great deal as soloist, meeting with a particularly enthusiastic reception at the Lamoureux concerts, Paris, in 1894, as well as on his sundry visits to London, notably at Sir Augustus Mann's concerts at the Crystal Palace and the Henschel symphony concerts. In 1907 he succeeded E. Sauret at the Musical College, Chicago, but went to Berlin at the beginning of 1910 as soloist, quartet player and teacher. After a time he accepted an engagement at Geneva which he did not hold for very long before he retired to enjoy his life in peace and quietness on the borders of the lake. He composed solos, studies, etc., and edited a number of works by older violinist composers.

EMIL HEERMANN, son of Hugo, is concertmeister in Cincinnati, U.S.A.

JOSEPH LUDWIG, b. Bonn, Apr. 6, 1844; d. London, Jan. 29, 1924. Studied the violin from Apr., 1859, to Sept., 1863, at the Cologne Conservatoire, then during the following two winters under Joachim at Hanover. In 1869 he went to London as successor of L. Jansa at the London Academy of Music and eventually became a naturalized Englishman. He had already appeared at Leipzig and other German towns with great success as a soloist, but he devoted himself chiefly to chamber music, in which he showed himself a true artist in the highest sense, and his refined rendering of the classics, as well as his sympathetic personality, made him a great favourite everywhere. For many years he gave successful Chamber Concerts in London, including several seasons of Hampstead Popular Concerts with Collins, Alfred Gibson and Whitehouse. For twenty years he was leader of the Bath Quartet Society. He enjoyed a great reputation as a teacher, one of his most eminent pupils being Beatrice Langley. One of his pupils bought from Mr. W. E. Hill the twin instrument of Paganini's Guarnerius del Guesu, which he lent him for his lifetime. Ludwig composed two symphonies, the first of which was performed in London in 1894, and also a number of Solos for violin and for 'cello. PAUL LUDWIG, his son, is the well-known 'cellist.

RICHARD HOFMANN, b. Delitzsch, Apr. 30, 1844; d. Leipzig, Nov. 13, 1918. Son of the town musical director; pupil of R. Dreyschock and Ellsig at Leipzig; became violinist in several Berlin orchestras and, 1866, in the Euterpe orchestra at Leipzig, where he then studied under Jadassohn and settled there as teacher. During 1880–3 he conducted the vocal academy and received the title of Royal professor in 1904, when he was also appointed teacher of orchestration at the Conservatoire. He wrote a violin tutor, "Grosse Violin-technik," op. 93–5; a new guide through the violin and viola literature (1909); instructive compositions and numerous arrangements for violin (Augener); tutors for various instruments and a valuable work on orchestration (Engl. R. H. Segge, 1898).

GERHARD BRASSIN, b. Aix-la-Chapelle, June 10, 1844. Pupil of David at the Leipzig Conservatoire. In 1863 violin teacher

at the music school at Berne; then concertmeister at Gothenburg, Sweden.   In 1874 he was teacher at the Stern Conservatoire, Berlin; 1875–80 conductor of the Tonkünstlerverein at
Breslau; then he went to St. Petersburg, and thence to Constantinople, where he was still in 1909 as teacher at the
Imperial Conservatoire, and leader of the chamber-music
society.   He composed some pieces for violin solo which are
described (Riemann) as valuable.   His brother LEOPOLD,
Court pianist, died at Constantinople, 1890, and Gerhard
probably went there before that time.   A third brother,
LOUIS, was the famous pianist, professor at the Brussels Conservatoire 1869–79, who died at St. Petersburg in 1884 at the
early age of 44.

KARL WILHELM FRIEDRICH FEININGER, b. Durlach, 1844.
Received his first violin lessons in his parental home.   From
1861 to 1863 he studied the violin under F. David and composition under E. F. Richter at the Leipzig Conservatoire,
and became an excellent violinist and composer.   He wrote
orchestral works, which however remained in MS.

AUGUST EMIL DANIEL FRIEDRICH VICTOR WILHELMJ, b. Usingen,
Nassau, Sept. 21, 1845; d. Hampstead, London, Jan. 22,
1908.   His father, Dr. jur. Aug. Wilhelmj, was an owner of
numerous important vineyards at Hattenheim, and his mother,
*née* Charlotte Petry, was an excellent pianist and singer, pupil
of André at Offenbach, Chopin and Bordogni in Paris, and it
was she who nurtured the early signs of talent in her son.   In
1849 he began to study the violin under the Court concertmeister, Conrad Fischer, of Wiesbaden.   His progress was so
rapid that when Henriette Sonntag heard him play, with
absolute purity of intonation, facility and expression, she
kissed the barely 7-year-old boy, exclaiming: "You will be the
German Paganini one day!"   He not only had the sense of
absolute pitch but also a very fine ear.   In 1853 he took part
for the first time in a quartet by Haydn, when he played his
part like an experienced musician.   On Jan. 8, 1854, he made
his first public appearance at a charity concert at Limburg-on-
the-Lahn, and on Mar. 17, 1856, he played at the Court
Theatre at Wiesbaden, on both occasions creating quite a
sensation.   His father, however, did not wish him to choose
music for his career, and only gave way to the boy's insistent

entreaties on condition that a competent judge should decide if such a step would be justified. In the spring of 1861 Prince Emil von Wittgenstein therefore sent him with a letter of recommendation to Liszt, to whom he played Spohr's Scena cantante and Ernst's Hungarian airs, and after he had also played something at first sight, Liszt said: "You are so much predestined for the violin, that if it had not been in existence already, it would have to be invented for you," with other complimentary remarks. He took him personally to Leipzig and introduced him to Ferd. David with the words: "Here I bring you the future second Paganini—take care of him." During 1861–4 he studied at the Leipzig Conservatoire, his masters in counterpoint and composition being Moritz Hauptmann and E. F. Richter, and afterwards still J. Raff at Wiesbaden. David's work was merely to guide him on classical lines; technically the pupil surpassed the master.

David became so fond of his favourite pupil that he looked upon him as a member of his family. At his house Wilhelmj made the acquaintance of David's art-loving niece, Baroness Sophie von Liphart, who became his wife on May 29, 1866. On Nov. 24, 1862, Wilhelmj made his debut at the Gewandhaus Concert with Joachim's Hungarian concerto. Soon after leaving the Conservatoire in 1864 Wilhelmj was attacked by a severe illness which prevented him from pursuing his studies for a time, but as soon as his recovery would permit, he took them up with redoubled energy, and in the autumn of 1865 he started on his first tour in Switzerland; early in 1866 he toured in Holland, and thence he went to England, where, through Jenny Lind's influence, he made his debut at one of Alfred Mellon's concerts at Covent Garden, where he achieved a perfect triumph. He was equally successful at a Monday Popular Concert on Nov. 26, and at the Crystal Palace on Dec. 1. In 1867 he was in Paris where, through Joachim's recommendation, he played on Jan. 20 at one of Pasdeloup's concerts at the Cirque Napoleon, and the press hailed him as "the new Paganini"; thence he returned to the Rhineland, and in the autumn he went to Florence, where on Dec. 15 he played at the Società del Quartetto, and at the fourth concert of the Society on Dec. 29 he was elected protector of the Society. In Jan., 1868, he followed an invitation of the Grand Duchess Helena Pavlovna to St. Petersburg, where with Hector Berlioz and other famous musicians he stayed at the Palais Michel. It was there that Berlioz said: "Never have I heard a violinist with such an eminent, enchanting, and noble tone as August Wilhelmj—his whole manner has something phenomenal." On Jan. 27 he made his first public appearance in St. Petersburg—the people were in ecstasy. During 1868–9 he revisited Switzerland, France and Belgium, and in the following year he toured all through Great Britain with Santley. In 1871 he went again to Holland, where the enthusiasm of the people grew to such proportions that at Leyden a torchlight procession was given in his honour. Then he went to Scandinavia, where he received the grand medal of arts and sciences and was made a member of the Royal Academy of Stockholm as well as a Knight of the Order of Gustav Vasa. On Oct. 22, 1872, he appeared for the first time in Berlin, at a concert of the Sing-Akademie, and on Mar. 22 he made his debut in Vienna. His success in both towns was epoch-making. He spent 1875 in England, playing in London and the provinces, and making propaganda for Wagner, and in 1876 he was leader of the Bayreuth Festival orchestra. In 1877 he induced Wagner to come to London and conduct the Albert Hall Festival, Wilhelmj was leader of the orchestra, and organized two extra concerts on May 28 and 29. His restless activity had overtaxed his strength and he passed through a serious illness. In Mar., 1878, he gave a series of soirées for German chamber music at Milan, where he was made an honorary member of the Società del Quartetto. He then started on a tour round the world, which brought him back to London again in 1882 on the way to his villa at Mosbach-Bieberich. Next he founded a school for violin-playing at Wiesbaden, but in 1885 he toured again, and at the invitation of the Sultan he visited Constantinople, where he had the unique experience of playing to the ladies of the Harem, being rewarded with the Medjidie Order of the second class and some fine diamonds. During 1886–93 he lived at Blasewitz, near Dresden, and in 1894 he settled in London as principal professor for the violin at the Guildhall School of Music. In 1895 he married Miss Martella Mansch-Jerret, a distinguished Dresden pianist. His son ADOLF, b. Mar. 31, 1872, was appointed violin professor at the Belfast Conservatoire in the same year. The writer knew Wilhelmj, as a comparatively young man, and heard him play at the height of his fame. He stood on the platform like a Greek statue come to life again. Tall, broad-shouldered, with a massive forehead, surrounded by a mass of long wavy hair, the picture of dignified repose, and as he looked, so he played. Whether he played a simple air or a Paganini concerto, his quiet pose remained the same. His notes issued from his violin like clarion notes, scintillating, with extraordinary brilliance, always beautiful, never forced, and rarely equalled in purity of intonation. Difficulties did not seem to exist for him, the most terrifying passages he overcame with such facility, as if they were exercises for beginners. A well-known London instrument dealer once said: "You just missed Wilhelmj, he tried some violins—I think he could make a cigar box sound like a Cremona fiddle." He had perhaps the biggest, and at the same time beautiful tone of any violinist past or present. His own compositions, a concerto, solo pieces, a cantata and songs are not important, but he has written some excellent arrangements of various pieces by Wagner, etc., and a most useful tutor, together with James Brown (Novello & Co.) which is one of the best graduated methods in existence.

FRANZ RIES, b. Berlin, Apr. 7, 1846; d. Naumburg, June 20, 1932. Youngest and most talented son of Hubert Ries; violin pupil of his father and in composition of Friedr. Kiel. From 1866 to 1868 he was a pupil of Massart at the Paris Conservatoire, where he gained the 1st prize; thence he went to London, where he met with great success both as virtuoso and composer, but a nervous complaint forced him in 1873 to abandon his career as a soloist. He went to Dresden, where he acquired the music-seller's business of Hoffarth, but still took part occasionally in public performances as virtuoso as well as composer. In 1876 he was appointed music seller to the Saxon Court, but afterwards he removed to Berlin where, from 1881 until Apr. 1, 1924, he was partner in and head of the firm of Ries & Erler. He composed a violin concerto, 4 suites for violin and pianoforte, numerous pieces for do. do., 2 string quartets, 1 string quintet; orchestral works, numerous songs, etc. His violin pieces in particular occupy a high artistic level and are still deservedly popular. As the nephew of Beethoven's pupil and friend,

Ferdinand Ries, he formed one of the last links with the great classical period.

HENRY SCHRADIECK, b. Hamburg, Apr. 29, 1846; d. Brooklyn, Mar. 25, 1918. Received his first tuition in violin playing from his father, a noted teacher of that instrument, at Hamburg. At the age of five and a half Henry played a Beethoven violin sonata in public, and after that he appeared repeatedly in concerts. When Theresa Milanollo visited Hamburg in the winter 1853–4, she was so impressed with the boy's talent that she sent him at her expense to the Brussels Conservatoire, where for four years he studied under Léonard; the first two years at the expense of Theresa Milanollo; for the latter two years friends at Hamburg had provided the means. In 1858 he gained the 1st prize at the Conservatoire and returned to Hamburg, where his playing was greatly admired. In 1859 he went to Leipzig, where he studied for some time under Ferd. David, but with little success as his whole being was steeped in the traditions of the Belgian school. He studied composition chiefly under E. F. Richter at Leipzig and Grädner and Marxsen at Hamburg. He lacked the spirit of enterprise, with the result that he never went on tour and consequently became but slowly known in wider circles. In the winter of 1863–4 he was engaged as leader and soloist for the Bremen "Privat Concerte." In 1864 a Russian merchant persuaded him to go to Moscow, where he became a teacher, together with Laub, at the newly founded Conservatoire and also 1st violinist in the orchestra. In 1867 he gave a very successful concert and also played at the concerts of the Russian Musical Society. In 1868 he returned to Hamburg and succeeded Auer as concertmeister in the Philharmonic concerts. He also played at concerts in various German towns and at Brussels. When David died in 1874 Schradieck succeeded him at the Conservatoire and at the Gewandhaus concerts, where he was until 1882 co-ordinated with Röntgen. He was overworked there and left when in 1883 he was appointed teacher at the Conservatoire at Cincinnati. In 1889 he returned to Hamburg as concertmeister of the Philharmonic Society. He also played at concerts in neighbouring towns, but he did not occupy the position as a virtuoso to which his uncommon powers entitled him, and when the opportunity came in

1898 he accepted the post as violin professor at the National Conservatoire, New York, and 1899 at Broad St. Conservatoire, Philadelphia. In 1912 he returned to New York as teacher at the America Institute of Applied Music. He composed a number of valuable studies for the violin; he also interested himself in the art of violin-making and tried to found a special school for the purpose of furthering this.

BENNO WALTER, b. Munich, June 17, 1847; d. Konstanz, Oct. 23, 1901. A younger brother of Joseph Walter; studied the violin from the age of 4 under his father. He made such rapid progress that at 8 he was able to tour as a violin prodigy with great success in South Germany. At the age of 11 he was presented with a Guarnerius violin by the Queen of Bavaria, who greatly admired his talent. In 1863 he became a member of the Munich Court orchestra, where he succeeded his brother on the death of the latter in 1875, as concertmeister. He always strove for the highest ideals in art, and his remarkable technique and excellent style were essentially due to his unaided efforts as he never studied under any of the great masters of his time. He toured as a virtuoso in Austria, Switzerland and America, and was greatly esteemed as a chamber-music player, his quartet attaining a wide reputation for its excellence.

HUGO WEHRLE, b. Donaueschingen, July 19, 1847; d. Freiburg i.B., Mar. 29, 1919. A pupil of a Court musician at Donaueschingen, where he played as a small boy in Kalliwoda's quartet. During 1859–61 he was a violin pupil of David at the Leipzig Conservatoire, and 1862–3 of Alard at that of Paris. He toured after that and became a violinist in the Weimar Court chapel in 1865, and in 1868 second concertmeister (by the side of Singer) at Stuttgart, where until 1880 he played in Singer's quartet. A nervous complaint of the hand compelled him to resign in 1898 when he went to live at Freiburg as teacher. He composed pieces for the violin and ed. pieces by older masters (Aus alten Zeiten, Melodia) including an Allemande by Thomas Baltzer from "The Division Violin"; songs for male voice chorus, also for single voices.

FRITZ STRUSS, b. Hamburg, Nov. 28, 1847. He studied the violin under Unruh, Auer (1865) and Joachim (1866).

In the latter year he was for a short time violinist in the Schwerin Court chapel. In 1870 he became a member in the Court chapel in Berlin, where in 1885 he rose to the position of chamber virtuoso, and in 1887 to that of Royal concert-meister. At the same time he became also a teacher at the Scharwenka-Klindworth Conservatoire. In these positions he was still in 1900.

RUDOLPH SACHSE, d. young at Leipzig, Apr. 17, 1848. A teacher of the violin at the Leipzig Conservatoire. Composed 3 elegies for violin and pianoforte, op. 4 (Leipzig, Kistner); introduction and variations for violin and orchestra, op. 5 (Ib.).

FRITZ SEITZ, b. Güntersleben, near Gotha, June 12, 1848; d. Dessau, May 22, 1918. A pupil of Uhlrich at Sondershausen, whose daughter he afterwards married. In 1874 he studied under Lauterbach at Dresden; afterwards he was concertmeister at Magdeburg and from 1884 at Dessau. He composed violin pieces; 3 children's trios, and concertos for teaching purposes with pianoforte.

GEORG JULIUS ROBERT HECKMANN, b. Mannheim, Nov. 3, 1848; d. Glasgow, Nov. 29, 1891. His first masters were Jean Becker and Naret-Koning, and at the age of 14 he became a violinist in the Mannheim orchestra. In 1865 the Grand Duke enabled him to resume his studies for two years at the Leipzig Conservatoire under Ferd. David, Vincent Lachner and Hauptmann being his masters in composition; in 1867 to 1870 he was concertmeister at the Euterpe concerts. In 1869 he studied for about one year under Léonard and Alard, and in 1870 he went to Berlin and thence toured in Germany. In 1872 he was called to Cologne as concertmeister at the opera and the Gürzenich concerts, which position he held till 1875. In 1873 he married Marie Hertwig, pupil of Moscheles and Wenzel, a brilliant pianist, who became his worthy partner in the performance of chamber music, to which he devoted himself more and more, although he was also an excellent soloist and as such the first to play Bruch's beautiful romance in public, which is dedicated to him. About that time he formed a quartet with O. Forberg (2nd violin), Th. Allekotte (viola) and Rich. Bellmann (violoncello), which for its beauty of tone and ensemble became famous throughout Europe. Although at that time still an amateur, the writer had the privilege from 1877 to 1879 (when he left Cologne) to fill sometimes the place of 2nd violoncellist, notably in the Brahms Sextet. Heckmann championed the then living composers, apart from Brahms, especially Svendsen and Grieg, whose sonatas he was the first to play, the first Grieg sonata in F major being dedicated to him. The writer remembers Grieg and Heckmann rehearsing it ca. 1877 at Cologne, where they played it with immense success before going on tour together in Scandinavia. His quartet soirées at that time were immensely popular with the young musicians who were ardent worshippers of Brahms, and when the latter's third pianoforte quartet in C min. appeared, Heckmann announced its first public performance in the *Cologne Gazette*. Thereupon he received a letter from Ferd. Hiller, director of the Conservatoire, with a peremptory demand to take the quartet off his programme as the quartet of the Conservatoire professors considered it their privilege to perform the work first. Heckmann pointed out to him that it was the work of a modern composer and that he could not comply with his request. This elicited a wrathful letter from Hiller, ending with the words: "Ich bitte mich nicht mehr zu grüssen" ("Please do not salute me any more"). The letter appeared in the *Cologne Gazette* a few days before Carnival, and when that came the Cologne people seized upon the incident as a great joke and walked about with ribbons round their hats with the above words printed on them. The Heckmann quartet became more popular than ever, their ensemble was unequalled at that time and they toured far and wide with unabated success, which was due largely also to their exquisite rendering of the later Beethoven quartets which were still but little known. In 1881 he was once more for a short time concertmeister in the Cologne orchestra, and in 1891, shortly before his death, he had been appointed in the same capacity at Dresden. In 1891 they came to England, and after being greeted with enthusiasm in London they toured through the provinces and came to Glasgow, where Heckmann was attacked with influenza, which turned to pneumonia, and he died within about a week.

JOSEF SCHWARTZ, b. Gohr, Nov. 25, 1848. Studied the violin at the Cologne Conservatoire. In 1872 he became concertmeister at the theatre, and 1879 teacher at the Conservatoire; he succeeded Japha in the Gürzenich quartet; he was also conductor of the Cologne male choir (Männergesangverein) 1892–1924, which he brought to a high state of excellence; since 1925 honorary conductor. He received the title of Professor and Royal Director of Music. He composed very effective choral songs for male voices.

EMIL KARL SEIFERT, b. Berlin, Feb. 6, 1849. Appeared in public in his ninth year as a remarkable violin virtuoso. Afterwards he toured extensively, ever increasing his reputation as a distinguished player. In 1874 he was appointed violin teacher at Peabody Conservatoire of Music at Baltimore; afterwards he became conductor in New York, and writer on musical subjects. He composed an overture, a march for orchestra, songs and pianoforte pieces.

ADALBERT BLACHA, d. Breslau, Jan. 13, 1870. A 19th-century violinist of merit who was successively violinist, concertmeister, and conductor at the Breslau theatre.

LOUIS ABEL, d. Munich, Aug. 13, 1895. A pupil of Ferd. David, highly esteemed as teacher at the Munich Conservatoire.

OERTLING. Mentioned by Wasielewski as a noteworthy pupil of Aug. Zimmermann, Berlin, in the mid-19th century.

HEINRICH DITTMAR, b. Cassel, 18..; d. in Yorkshire, Oct. 10, 1910. Began to study the violin under Ellenberger, a pupil of Spohr, at Cassel; at the age of 16 he became a pupil of Kömpel at Weimar. At the end of his studies there he was for some time a member in the Hallé and Richter orchestras in England, but went for further studies to Rappoldi at Dresden, and in 1901 he became a pupil of Ševčik at Prague. In May, 1903, he went to London to spread that famous master's system, and after a time he settled in Yorkshire, where he was in great demand as a very successful teacher when he died in the flower of manhood.

# CHAPTER 54

## Germany: to 1875

RICHARD BARTH, b. Grosswanzleben, Province of Saxony, June 5, 1850; d. Marburg, Dec. 25, 1923. He had already received instruction in violin-playing from his grandfather when, through an accident, he hurt the second finger of his left hand so badly that it remained permanently stiff. As the boy was determined to play the violin, his grandfather taught him to use the right hand for fingering and the left hand for bowing. He succeeded so well that he was sent for further tuition to Concertmeister Beck of Magdeburg, and finally he studied under Joachim from 1863 to 1867, when he became concertmeister at Münster, and in 1882 he went in the same capacity to Crefeld, and afterwards became director of music at the University of Marburg. In 1895 he succeeded von Bernuth as conductor of the Hamburg Philharmonic concerts as well as the Vocal Academy and the United Male Choirs. The latter position he resigned in 1908 when he was appointed principal of the Hamburg Conservatoire. Until 1913 he conducted also the Teachers Choral Union with which he toured most successfully. In 1904 the University of Marburg bestowed on him the hon. Dr.Ph., and appointed him as director of music at the University. He composed 3 violin sonatas, partita and a ciacona for violin solo, 1 pianoforte trio, and 1 string quartet. He also ed. Brahms' correspondence with J. O. Grimm, and wrote "Brahms und seine Musik." In spite of his physical handicap he had a remarkable technique and a beautiful tone. The writer remembers his playing in the orchestra at a Nether Rhenish Music Festival at Cologne, and the curious effect of his bow moving in the opposite direction of all the rest, which was quite conspicuous even in that large orchestra.

MAX BRODE, b. Berlin, Feb. 25, 1850; d. Königsberg, Dec. 29/30, 1917. Violin pupil of Ganz and Zimmermann. Played at the age of 10 at the Hotel Arnim where Paul Mendessohn-Bartholdy heard him, and took him into his house, charging himself with his scientific and artistic education. During 1863–7 he studied under de Ahna at the Stern Conservatoire and finally at the Leipzig Conservatoire until 1869. Afterwards he was the leader of a string quartet at Mitau and then renewed his studies under Joachim at the Berlin High School of Music from 1870–3. 1874–6 he was teacher at the Augsburg Conservatoire. In the latter year a nervous complaint in the fingers caused him to abandon the career of a virtuoso. For three years from 1876 he was concertmeister at the Königsberg theatre. He instituted symphony concerts there and was in great request as a teacher. In 1891 he became conductor at the Philharmonic Society and in 1894 musical director at the University, where he also lectured on theory of music and history. In 1897 he received the title of Royal Professor. In 1898 he added to the foregoing the post of conductor of the Vocal Academy and teacher of singing at the Gymnasium in the old town.

FELIX MEYER, b. Berlin, Feb. 5, 1850; d. there, Oct. 3, 1914. Brother of Waldemar Meyer. Pupil of Ferd. David at the Leipzig Conservatoire; member and afterwards soloist at Bilse's orchestra; 1878 violinist and afterwards chamber virtuoso in the Royal chapel.

LUDWIG MAXIM. ADOLPH STIEHLE, b. Frankfort a/M., Aug. 19, 1850; d. Mülhausen, Alsace, July 6, 1896. Son of a good violinist; pupil of Vieuxtemps and Heermann at Frankfort, and of Joachim, 1867, at Hanover, and 1869–71 in Berlin. In 1872 member of Alard's quartet in Paris; 1873 in that of Baron von Dervies, Nice; 1875 member of the Hochberg quartet. Settled afterwards at Mülhausen and gave chamber-music soirées with Hans Huber. He possessed a large collection of chamber-music works by the older masters.

CARL SCHATZ, b. Hamburg, Sept. 23, 1850. A pupil of Schradieck; violin teacher at Hamburg; wrote a number of instructive violin pieces.

HEINRICH JACOBSEN, b. Hadersleben, Jan. 10, 1851; d. Berlin, 1901. A pupil of F. David at the Leipzig Conservatoire.

In 1869 he became a 1st violinist in the Gewandhaus and theatre orchestras and in 1872 he entered the service of the Duchess of Anhalt-Bernburg as soloist and leader of the chamber music, touring at intervals to Denmark, etc. In 1873 he went to Berlin for further studies under Joachim, and was accorded a two years' scholarship by the Government. In 1876 he was appointed as teacher of the violin at Berlin High School of Music and occupied that position to the time of his death.

GUSTAV HILLE, b. Jerichow on the Elbe, May 31, 1851. From 1864 to 1868 pupil at Kullak's Academy, and 1869–74 of Joachim at the High School of Music, Berlin. In 1879 he became a member of the Mendelssohn Quintet Club, Boston, Mass.; 1880 violin teacher at the Philadelphia Academy for Music, and co-founder of the Leefson-Hille Conservatoire there, of which he was the principal until 1910, when he returned to Germany. He composed 5 violin concertos, 1 double concerto for 2 violins, 1 canonic suite for violin, 2 suites for solo violin, 2 sonatas for violin and pianoforte, pianoforte pieces and songs.

EMIL MAHR, b. Wiesbaden, 1851; d. Boston, Mass., 1914. A pupil of Joachim; from 1877 concertmeister in Richter's London orchestra and from 1885 also in the Henschel orchestra. In 1876 and 1885 he played in the Bayreuth orchestra; in 1887 he became professor of violin at the New England Conservatoire, Boston, Mass.

E. GOBY EBERHARDT, b. Hallersheim, near Frankfort a/M., Mar. 29, 1852; d. Lübeck, Sept. 13, 1926. A pupil of J. Diety, H. Heermann and of Wilhelmj. At 14 he played in the Frankfort Orchestra; afterwards he was leader successively in the Berne and Bremen symphony orchestras, and for a time he was at Hamburg, where H. von Bülow took a kindly interest in him. He toured as a soloist successfully in Germany, Switzerland, Italy and Russia, but a stroke paralysed his left side and for many years he was unable to play. For the benefit of his health he went to Braunlage in the Hartz Mountains, where he studied Schottky's biography of Paganini, which gave him the idea of evolving upon the basis of ideas contained therein, a new system for the study of the violin, which he tried first on himself and found that thereby he was gradually

EDUARD RAPPOLDI

Jean Becker

JEAN BECKER
By kindness of Prof. Hugo Becker.

HUGO HEERMANN

ROBERT
HECKMANN

regaining the use of his left hand. He next tried it on a young amateur pupil, who after one year played at a concert at Hanover with such success that he received a brilliant notice in the *Berliner Tageblatt*. Since then he has laid down the principles of his system in a tutor and books of studies, and pupils have gone to Braunlage from all parts of Europe to study under him during the summer, while during the rest of the year he teaches in Berlin. At the beginning of the war he settled at Lübeck. He wrote a violin tutor, system of seconds, Virtuoso school; Melody school, op. 86; 5 books and several other didactic works which were, and partly are still, widely used. He also wrote "Erinnerungen an bedeutende Männer unserer Epoche" ("Reminiscences of Famous Men of our Epoch") (1926).

FRITZ SCHEEL, b. Lübeck, Nov. 7, 1852; d. Philadelphia, Mar. 12, 1907. Pupil of Ferd. David at the Leipzig Conservatoire; concertmeister successively at Bremerhaven, Chemnitz and Hamburg. He went to San Francisco in 1894 and in 1900 to Philadelphia as conductor of the symphony orchestra and of the choral union Euridice.

CARL EMIL MAX GRÜNBERG, b. Berlin, Dec. 5, 1852. Was solo violin in the Meininger Court chapel, then concertmeister at Sondershausen, after that at the Landestheater, Prague, and living (1928) as teacher in Berlin. Wrote "A Little Guide through the Literature of Stringed Instruments" (1913); "Masters of the Violin" (1925); "Method of Violin Playing" (2nd ed., 1926) (all in German).

WALDEMAR MEYER, b. Berlin, Feb. 4, 1853. Brother of Felix Meyer. His early talent for the violin attracted the attention of Joachim, who for four years instructed him gratuitously and then procured for him in 1873 a place in the Berlin Royal chapel. Later on he toured in Germany with Pauline Lucca. In 1881 he left the Royal chapel to tour as soloist in Germany, England (1888–90?), France, Belgium and Russia. He also formed a permanent quartet which acquired European fame. His tone was powerful, his style broad and dignified, and he subjected his brilliant technique to the service of higher artistic aims. Since 1922 he has lived at Berchtesgaden.

OTTO HOHLFELD, b. Zeulenroda, Saxony, Mar. 10, 1854; d. (?) May 10, 1895. Destined to follow his father's trade as a weaver. He showed very early talent for music and at first played the flute, but soon exchanged it for the violin, on which he received his first instruction from the cantor Solle, author of a violin tutor. After studying from 1868 at the teachers' seminary at Greiz under Music-Director Regener for violin, and Cantor Urhan for musical theory, he entered the Dresden Conservatoire in 1872, where he studied for three years under Lauterbach. After that he became a violinist in the Royal Court chapel. He had by that time become an excellent soloist, and in Nov., 1877, he was appointed as Court concert-meister in the Grand Ducal chapel at Darmstadt, and from there he toured periodically in Germany, Russia and Poland until his untimely death. He was an eminent representative of what might be termed the German classical school and excelled both as soloist and chamber-music player. He composed an elegy for violin and orchestra, op. 4, and a string quartet, etc.

GUSTAV HOLLÄNDER, b. Leobschütz, Silesia, Feb. 15, 1855; d. Berlin, Dec. 4, 1915. From his sixth to his twelfth year he received violin and music lessons from his father, a musical amateur, and appeared as soloist in public before he entered the Leipzig Conservatoire. There, 1867–9, he was a pupil of Ferd. David; 1869–74 he studied under Joachim, and Fr. Kiel (composition) at the High School for Music, Berlin. In 1874 he became Royal chamber musician at the Court opera and, 1875, teacher at Kullak's Academy. In 1874 he toured with Carlotta Patti in Austria and 1878–81 he gave subscription chamber-music concerts with X. Scharwenka and H. Grünfeld in Berlin. In 1881 he succeeded O. von Königs-slöw as concertmeister at the Gürzenich concerts and teacher at the Cologne Conservatoire, where he also succeeded Japha as leader of the Cologne string quartet. In 1884 he became also leader at the Cologne theatre, and when the new Municipal orchestra was formed he was chosen as second conductor. In 1893 he became Royal professor. From 1895 he was director of the Stern Conservatoire, Berlin. In 1911–12 he conducted the first part of the performances of Humperdinck's "The Miracle," at Olympia, London. He composed 4 concertos, a suite, a sonata, pieces, and studies for violin, also pieces for string orchestra.

MORITZ KÖHLER, b. Altenburg, Nov. 29, 1855. A pupil of his father, Stamm, and Müller-Berghaus at Chemnitz. In 1873, member of the Bilse orchestra, Berlin; went, 1880, to St. Petersburg, where he rose to the position of second concert-meister, and 1898 to that of capellmeister, at the Imperial Opera. He composed a concerto and pieces, with pianoforte, for violin, also for violoncello, string quartets, and suites, seranades, etc., for orchestra.

RICHARD KADEN, b. Dresden, Feb. 10, 1856; d. there, July 9, 1923. Studied at the Dresden Conservatoire under Lauter-bach, Hüllweck, Rietz and Döring; also at the Polytechnic. During 1872–96 viola player in the Court orchestra, and at the same time, 1872–83, teacher of violin and ensemble playing at the Conservatoire; from 1883 director of the Pedagogic School of Music founded by Fräulein von Mertschinska, whom he married in 1900. He made a new revised ed. of the Baillot-Rode violin tutor; pub. 50 violin duets with poetical explana-tions, 100 violin pieces phrased and fingered, etc. Composed a symphony, a sinfonietta, a concert overture, etc. He was also a public lecturer on musical subjects; some of his lectures were afterwards published.

FRIEDRICH WILHELM ROHDA, b. Altona, Dec. 11, 1856. A pupil of J. P. Rud. Reinecke. 1873–6 pupil of David, Röntgen, Schradieck for violin, Richter and Kretschmar for composition at the Leipzig Conservatoire; 1878–86 member of the Balatka Quintet, Chicago, then member of the Boston Symphony Orchestra and teacher at the Boston Conservatoire. He returned to Hamburg, and was afterwards at Schwerin, and since 1914 has been at Copenhagen. A distinguished composer of important orchestral and choral works, a string quartet, a pianoforte trio, pianoforte pieces and songs.

FRÄULEIN KUMMLER. A German violinist who carried off the 2nd prize at the Paris Conservatoire in 1857 (Pougin).

ARNO FRANZ HILF, b. Bad Elster, Saxony, Mar. 15, 1858 (Riemann: Mar. 14); d. there, Aug. 2, 1909. The pupil at first of his father, the concertmeister at Bad Elster, then of his uncle, Christian Wolfgang Hilf (q.v.). During 1871–5 he studied at the Leipzig Conservatoire under David, Jul. Röntgen and Schradieck. In 1878–88 he was teacher at the Moscow Conservatoire and second concertmeister. Returned to Germany, he played Joachim's Hungarian concerto at a music festival at Dessau with such great success that he was immediately appointed as concertmeister at the Court of Sondershausen, but in 1889 he was called to Leipzig as concertmeister in the Gewandhaus and theatre orchestra, which position he relinquished in 1892 for that of 1st violin teacher at the Conservatoire as successor of Brodsky, taking also the latter's place as leader of the famous quartet. He died suddenly from a stroke on a visit to Bad Elster. He had a brilliant technique combined with purity of intonation, artistic temperament and taste, and he was an excellent teacher.

RICHARD GOMPERTZ, b. Cologne, Apr. 27, 1859; d. Dresden, Nov., 1921. At an early age he studied the violin and harmony under J. Jansa at Cologne. During that time he made his debut in Cologne at the Gürzenich concerts. In 1875 he went to Berlin, where he completed his studies under Joachim at the Hochschule until 1878. After touring successfully in Germany for some time he was, in 1880, invited by Stanford, on Joachim's recommendation, to become teacher and leader at the Cambridge University Musical Society, and while there formed the Cambridge String Quartet. In 1883 he became teacher, and in 1895 professor for violin at the newly founded Royal College of Music, where he carried on Joachim's traditions and formed a large number of pupils who afterwards came to prominence. In 1884 and 1886 he appeared successfully at the Crystal Palace Concerts, and in the winter of the latter year took part with Mme Haas and Signori Piatti in Beethoven's "Triple Concerto" at the first of Henschel's London Symphony Concerts. He also formed a permanent quartet with Ch. Ould as 'cellist, and for a number of years he gave very successful chamber music concerts. In 1899 he resigned his position at the College and retired to Dresden. He was an artist of high and noble aims and a lovable personality. He composed a sonata for pianoforte and violin and a number of songs.

WILLY HESS, b. Mannheim, July 14, 1859. Received his first violin lessons at an early age from his father and after touring for some years as soloist he studied from 1875 to 1878 under Joachim. At the early age of 19 he became concertmeister at Frankfort a/M. and held a similar position at Rotterdam from 1886 to 1888 when he went to England as leader in the Hallé orchestra. In 1895 he returned to Germany as 1st violin teacher at the Cologne Conservatoire, concert-meister at the Gürzenich concerts and leader of the Conservatoire quartets. On May 1, 1900, he received the title of Royal Prussian Professor. In Sept., 1903, he succeeded Sauret as professor at the Royal Academy of Music, London; in 1904 he became leader of the Boston, Mass., Symphony Orchestra, and in the summer 1910 he went as professor of violin to the Berlin High School for Music (as successor to Halíř), where he became also conductor of the orchestra, leader of the Halíř Quartet and of a trio with H. Dechert and G. Schumann. He is a distinguished representative of the Joachim school both as soloist and chamber-music player. He retired in 1928.

RUDOLF ARTHUR RÖSEL, b. Münchenbernsdorf, Thuringia, Aug. 23, 1859. Studied at the Grand Ducal School of Music at Weimar 1873–7, and after playing successively in the orchestras of Hamburg, Lugano, Nizza, Weimar, Rotterdam, Bilse-Berlin and Pavlovsk he was, 1887–1925, Court concert-meister at Weimar and teacher at the Grand Ducal School of Music. He composed 2 violin concertos and pieces for the violin, a viola and a clarinet concerto, 2 string quartets, various orchestral works, songs and 2 operas.

ANDREAS MOSER, b. Semlin on the Danube, Nov. 29, 1859; d. Berlin, Oct. 7, 1925. Studied engineering at Zürich and Stuttgart, but decided to become a violinist and entered the Berlin High School of Music in 1878 as a pupil of Joachim. A nervous complaint of the arm made the career of a virtuoso impossible, and he specialized in the art of teaching so success-fully that Joachim made him his assistant teacher. In 1888 he became a regular teacher at the High School. In 1900 he received the title of Royal Professor, and in 1925 the Honorary Doctor degree. He lived towards the end of his life in retirement at Heidelberg. He wrote the important life of Joachim (English by J. Pulver); the correspondence between Brahms and Joachim; a violin tutor in 3 volumes, together with Joachim (English by Alfr. Moffat); Methodik des Violinspiels (Method of Violin-playing), 2 vols. (Leipzig, 1920); Technik des Violinspiels (Technic of Violin-playing),

2 vols. (Leipzig, 1925); also a number of editions of classical sonatas and chamber music (quartets, etc.).

KARL VENTH, b. Cologne, Feb. 10, 1860. Pupil at the Cologne Conservatoire, and of Wieniawski at the Brussels Conservatoire. In 1880 concertmeister in the Metropolitan Orchestra, New York. Founded a school of music at Brooklyn in 1888; and after various other enterprises he settled in Texas. Composed "Schiller's Lay of the Bell" for chorus and orchestra, pianoforte pieces, songs, etc.

BERNHARD DESSAU, b. Hamburg, Mar. 1, 1861; d. Berlin, Apr. 28, 1923. In early childhood and youth studied the violin under Schradieck, Joachim and Wieniawski; he was concertmeister successively at Görlitz, Gand, Königsberg, Brünn, Prague, Rotterdam, where he was also teacher at the Conservatoire, then at the Bremen Philharmonic Society, from 1898 at the Berlin Royal Opera. For a time he was also teacher at the Stern Conservatoire, and in 1906 he received the title of Royal Professor. He composed a violin concerto in the olden style, op. 55, and a considerable number of pieces with pianoforte.

CARL HEINRICH PAUL STOEVING, b. Leipzig, May 7, 1861. A pupil of Schradieck at the Leipzig Conservatoire, and of Léonard in Paris. During 1882–3 concertmeister at the Hamburg Symphony Orchestra; went, 1884, to America and 1886 to London, where in 1898 he became teacher at the Guildhall School of Music, and 1907 also at Trinity College of Music. In 1914 he returned to America, where he taught partly at New York, partly at the New Haven School of Music, of which he was the principal 1914–18. He wrote "The Story of the Violin and the Art of Bowing" (1902).

OTTO SINGER, JUN., b. Dresden, Sept. 14, 1863. Studied the violin first in Paris, afterwards under Joachim (composition under Kiel) in Berlin, then under Léonard in Paris, and composition under Rheinberger at Munich. Although an excellent violinist, he devoted himself chiefly to conducting and composition. His Concertstück for violin and orchestra is praised as of particular merit; besides this he has written a violin concerto, violin and pianoforte pieces, various chamber-music works, and made very good pianoforte scores of Strauss' operas.

HEINRICH DESSAUER, b. Würzburg, 1863; d. Linz, Apr. 9, 1917. Studied the violin at Würzburg, Munich, and finally under Joachim and Sauret in Berlin. He was for some time teacher at Beslaur's Conservatoire, and eventually settled at Linz. He tried to solve the problem of how to enlarge the viola without exceeding the dimensions of violin stopping. He published a book on the subject in 1912, also a Universal Violin Tutor (1907).

KARL PRILL, b. Berlin, Oct. 22, 1864. A violin pupil of his father, musical director, Berlin, and for pianoforte of music-director Handwerg. When he was 9 years old his father took him and his brothers PAUL (violoncello) and EMIL (flute) on tour through Germany, Russia, Denmark, Sweden, Holland, etc. After this he studied again under Hellmich, Wirth and Joachim at the High School for Music, and during the latter part of his studies he was also solo violinist in the orchestras of Brenner and Laube; 1883–5 concertmeister in Bilse's orchestra. In 1885–6 he was in a similar position in the Hlawacz orchestra, Pawlowsk; 1886–91 leader, conductor and teacher at Magdeburg, where he also had a permanent string quartet. In 1891 he became concertmeister in the Gewandhaus orchestra and leader of the quartet founded by Petri, a successor to A. Hilf. In 1897 he went to Vienna as concertmeister at the Imperial Opera and the Philharmonic Society, Professor of Violin at the Imperial Academy and founder of a string quartet. He also continued to appear at many German and Austrian towns as a successful soloist. In 1897, 1899 and 1901 he was leader of the Wagner Festival Orchestra, Bayreuth.

HERMANN GÄRTNER, b. Salzwedel, Aug. 24, 1865, is chiefly autodidact as he had, apart from three month's instruction from Schradieck, very little schooling. This made it difficult for him to obtain a permanent position, and he spent the earlier part of his career in touring in Germany, England, Portugal, etc. During 1890–5 he was concertmeister at Altona, and from then until 1905 or 1907 he was in a similar position at the Nuremberg theatre. Since then he has lived at Nuremberg, where he is in great demand as an excellent teacher. He has the reputation of possessing a brilliant technique combined with a full tone and artistic style. He has edited a considerable number of standard violin compositions for Breitkopf & Härtel.

CARL ALEX. JOH. MIERSCH, b. Dresden, 1865; d. Cincinnati, Sept. 8, 1916. Studied the violin under Rappoldi at Dresden, Abel at Munich and Massart in Paris; 1887 concertmeister at Graz; 1880–90 teacher at Aberdeen; 1892–3 violinist in the Boston symphony orchestra; 1894–8 principal of the Athens Conservatoire and violinist to the Greek Court. He toured in Europe from 1898 to 1902, when he returned to the United States of America. He composed a concert polonaise for violin and orchestra, op. 4.

MAX HENNING, b. Rosslau, Anhalt, Apr. 10, 1866. He entered the Magdeburg Conservatoire in 1881 and on its dissolution continued his violin studies under Zeitz. He was afterwards engaged as a violinist in various orchestras and lived as a teacher in Colmar from 1888 to 1895, studying concurrently at the Strassburg Conservatoire under C. Lomborn, Schuster and Münch from 1892 to 1896. During 1897–9 he continued his studies at the Berlin High School for Music. After that he was for three years conductor at Upsala and during one season at the German theatre, London. Since 1904 he has lived in Berlin-West-end as teacher and composer. Compositions: Chamber music; orchestral works; songs; works for the theatre.

LUDWIG VOLLNHALS, b. Munich, Mar. 6, 1867. A pupil of Benno Walter at the Academy of Music there. In 1886 viola player in the Walter quartet, succeeded the latter as second concertmeister in 1901, and 1906–26 he was first concertmeister in the Munich orchestra in succession to Miroslav Weber; Royal Professor, teacher at the Academy of Music and, 1928–9, member of the Berber quartet.

KARL CORBACH, b. Lütgendortmund, near Dortmund, Mar. 16, 1867. Pupil of O. von Königslöw and G. Holländer, at the Cologne Conservatoire; violinist in the Laube orchestra at Hamburg in 1890; became Court concertmeister and teacher at the Conservatoire at Sondershausen in 1891; Professor in 1910, and Court capellmeister and director of the Conservatoire there in 1911.

ADOLF WEIDIG, b. Hamburg, Nov. 28, 1867. Son of a musician; pupil of Bargheer (violin) and Riemann (com-

FRIEDRICH ERNST FESCA
By kindness of Prof. O. E. Deutsch.

FRANZ RIES
By courtesy of Messrs. Ries & Erler.

JOHANN CHRISTOPH LAUTERBACH
By courtesy of Herrn Kammervirtuos Theo Bauer, of Dresden.

FERDINAND LAUB

HENRI PETRI

GOBY EBERHARDT

*Goby Eberhardt* (signature)

RICHARD GOMPERTZ

ANTONIO BAZZINI

E.N.A.

position) at the Hamburg Conservatoire. He gained the Mozart scholarship, which enabled him to continue his studies, 1888–91, at the Munich Conservatoire under Abel and Rheinberger; since 1892 he has lived at Chicago where, 1892–6, he was member of the Chicago Orchestra; 1892–1901 viola in the Spiering quartet; 1898 co-director of the American Conservatoire, council member of the Federated musical clubs of the United States. Composed an Italian suite for violin and pianoforte, op. 40; a considerable number of chamber-music works; orchestral and choral compositions, songs, etc.

ARTHUR SEYBOLD, b. Hamburg, Jan. 6, 1868. Pupil of Bargheer and Bott at the Conservatoire there (also pianoforte and composition under various masters). In 1888 he went with Laube's orchestra to Russia, and afterwards played as violinist in a theatrical touring company in Germany. In 1890 he became violinist in the Bülow orchestra at Hamburg and remained there as teacher of the violin and conductor of male choirs. He wrote numerous grateful pieces for violin and pianoforte, some with orchestra, pupils' concertos; Melody and Rhythm, op. 204; a method for violin; tutor for positions, op. 184; school for studies, op. 182; choruses for male voices, and songs.

FRANZ DRDLA, b. Saar, Moravia, Nov. 28, 1868. Pupil of Hellmesberger at the Vienna Conservatoire. An excellent violin virtuoso and composer of violin concertos and concertinos as well as a large number of solo pieces which, apart from being very melodious, are so well written in the nature of the instrument that they have become very popular, especially a Serenade in A major, No. 1; Souvenir, Vision, etc. He is now living at New York. He has also written 2 operas.

WILLY BURMESTER, b. Hamburg, Mar. 16, 1869; d. there Jan. 16, 1933. A son of a musician who taught him violin-playing from his fourth year. When 6 he made his successful public debut, but his father wisely refrained from exploiting his early talent and continued his tuition, while Hans von Bülow, who had taken an interest in the talented boy, often played with him, which was of incalculable advantage for the development of his musical faculties. From 1882 to 1885 he studied under Joachim at the Berlin High School of Music, and from that time he followed his own intuition in his studies. His only concert tour so far had been one to Portugal in 1881. But from 1886 he toured frequently. In 1888 he visited St. Petersburg, and on his return he became, still in that year, solo violinist and concertmeister at Helsingfors: it was during that time that, by dint of indefatigable study, he arrived at artistic maturity. In 1890 he was for a short time concertmeister at Sondershausen, then at Bremen, Weimar, and at Bülow's request 1st violinist in the latter's Hamburg orchestra. About the end of Oct., 1894, he gave a Paganini evening at the Singacademy in Berlin which created a sensation among the public and the critics. It was acknowledged on all sides that he had succeeded in imbuing the works of the great Italian with fresh life and to prove himself a complete master over their technical as well as their musical problems. A week later he gave another concert where he played the seventh concerto by Spohr in a manner which proved him equally a great musician as the previous one had shown him to be a great virtuoso. In 1895 he was hailed with equal enthusiasm in London, where he made his first appearance at a Henschel symphony concert on Mar. 14, with Paganini's D major concerto and "Nel cor più" variations. *The Strad* (July, 1895) in an article on Burmester said: ". . . not only has he played it (the concerto), but in a number of cases he has added technical difficulties of a kind that has no equal in violin literature." He settled at Charlottenburg, whence he undertook frequent and extended concert tours which went so far as America. He also made a speciality of the study of Bach's works which he played with such perfection that the Bach society of Harlem, Holland, elected him to their honorary membership. He composed a serenade in D major for strings, and edited a number of solo pieces by the older masters. He also published a book of memoirs, "Fünfzig Jahre Künstlerleben."

FRANZ SAGEBIEL, b. Otterndorf, Hanover, June 9, 1869; violin pupil of K. Bargheer, and E. Rappoldi at the Dresden Conservatoire, afterwards of Aug. Wilhelmj; after touring in Germany as virtuoso he became a member of the Weimar Court chapel. In 1900 he went to Coblenz where he often played as soloist, and in chamber concerts with the founders of the Conservatoire: Heubner, Ebert, and J. F. Ritter; afterwards he appeared frequently together with the pianist Jos. Pembaur. Since 1906 he is director of the Conservatoire at Coblenz.

FERDINAND KÜCHLER. He wrote a "Praktische Violinschule" (practical violin tutor) (Basle, Hug & Co., 1910) based on Steinhausen's "Physiology of Bowing," which Wasielewski and Carl Flesch describe as the best modern tutor, free from the want of clearness and faults of older schools. He studied the violin under W. Hess, H. Heermann, Naret-Koning, singing and theory under Stockhausen, Egidi and Knorr at the Hoch Conservatoire, Frankfort a/M. During 1869–98 he was engaged at Basle; after that he was teacher at the Hoch Conservatoire and viola player in the Heermann quartet, with which he toured in France, Italy and Spain. In 1910 he was solo viola player in the Basle symphony orchestra, and principal of a private school of music. Since the autumn of 1927 he has been teacher at the Landes-Conservatoire, Leipzig. He wrote a violin tutor which appeared in its 9th ed. in 1927 (also in English and French); "Daily studies for the Left Hand," and a tutor for choir singing.

JOHANN KRAL. A viola player at the opera, Vienna, ca. 1870. An excellent viol d'amour player who did much to revive that instrument, and trained pupils on it. He wrote "Anleitung zum Spiele der Va. d'am. für Violinspieler" ("Viol d'Amour for Violinists").

GUSTAV STRUBE, b. Ballenstedt on the Hartz. The son of the cantor there; pupil of Brodsky, Reckendorf, Reinecke and Jadassohn at the Leipzig Conservatoire; teacher at the Mannheim Conservatoire; 1891 violinist in the symphony orchestra, Boston, Mass.; conductor of the summer concerts and second conductor of the Musical Festivals at Worcester (Co.); from 1913 violin teacher at the Peabody Conservatoire, Baltimore; 1916 conductor at the Baltimore Symphony Orchestra. He composed for violin 2 concertos, suite for pianoforte and violin; also sonata for pianoforte and viola; 1 string quartet; 1 opera, 2 symphonies and other orchestra works, some with solo voice or chorus.

FRANZ SCHÖRG, b. Munich, Nov. 15, 1871; d. Würzburg, Apr. 5, 1923. He studied the violin first at the Munich

School of Music, then at the Brussels Conservatoire, as a pupil of Ysaÿe, where he carried off the 1st prize; after that he founded there the famous Brussels string quartet which he led until the beginning of the War.   After the War he succeeded Schulze-Prisca at the Würzburg Conservatoire and formed again a string quartet with Wyrott, Kunkel and Cahnbley.   He toured in Europe with Mme Albani and the pianist Éthel Sharpe.   At the end of the tour he resided for two years at Geneva, where he devoted much time to the cultivation of chamber music, together with Gaillard the violoncellist, who had also been a member of the touring party.   Finally they both went to Brussels, where they founded the Brussels quartet with Miry and Daucher, both pupils and friends of Ysaÿe.   They toured all over Europe, Russia and Mexico with great and ever-increasing success, which followed them also on their tour in England in 1908.

FELIX BERBER, b. Jena, Mar. 11, 1871; d. Munich, Dec. (?), 1930.   At Dresden, to where his family had moved, he received regular violin lessons from the age of 7.   Soon afterwards he played in public, while studying at the Dresden Conservatoire. In 1884 his father died, and on the advice of Bülow he went to the Leipzig Conservatoire, where he studied under Brodsky until 1889, when he played Joachim's Hungarian concerto at the pupils' concert.   He then went to London, where he gave among others, a very successful chamber concert with Ries, Strauss and Piatti (members of the famous Joachim quartet). Two years later, 1891, he went to Magdeburg as concert-meister; but in 1896 he resigned and toured in Germany, Switzerland, England and Russia.   In 1898 he became concertmeister at the Leipzig theatre and Gewandhaus, but differences arose concerning the artistic management of the latter, and he resigned on Apr. 1, 1903, and accepted the professorship for violin at the Royal Academy for Music at Munich.   He succeeded Hermann as professor at the Hoch Conservatoire, Frankfort a/M., in 1907, and in 1908 he became Marteau's successor at Geneva, where he formed also a permanent string quartet.   In 1912 he lived as private teacher and from 1920 has been professor at the Academy of Music, where he formed again a quartet with Huber, Härtel and Hegar, but later on with Milly B. (his wife), Härtel and Köhler.

HERMANN LANG, b. Grossvoigtsberg, near Freiberg, Saxony, Mar. 29, 1872. A violin pupil of Rapoldi, Dresden, Draeseke (composition), Ed. Engel (singing), and P. Janssen (organ). During 1893–5 violinist in the Royal chapel, Dresden; 1895–1920 teacher of violin, viola, theory and ear training at the Dresden Conservatoire where, 1913–17, he was also a member of the committee; since 1918 chamber musician in the State chapel. Has composed violin pieces and studies, chamber-music works and songs.

ALFRED KRASSELT, b. Glauchau, Saxony, June 3, 1872; d. Eisenach, Sept. 27, 1908. Received his first instruction on the violin from his father, who was concertmeister in the Kur orchestra at Baden-Baden; afterwards he went to Dresden, where he studied under Petri, then at the Leipzig Conservatoire under Brodsky. In 1893 he became concertmeister in the Kaim orchestra at Munich, 1896 Court concertmeister at Weimar, and afterwards concertmeister at Baden-Baden.

FRIEDRICH A. STOCK, b. Jülich, Nov. 11, 1872. The son of a military bandmaster. During 1886–90 a pupil of Japha, Zöllner, Humperdinck and Wüllner at the Cologne Conservatoire; violinist in Cologne orchestra, afterwards in the Thomas orchestra, now symphony orchestra, Chicago, where in 1901 he became deputy conductor and in 1905 succeeded Thomas as conductor. In 1915 he was made an honorary Mus.Doc. of the North Western University. He composed a symphony and overture, symphonic variations, chamber-music works, solo pieces and songs.

AUGUST LEOPOLD SASS, b. Bredow-Stettin, Nov. 9, 1874. From 1888 to 1892 a pupil of the town musician, Wulkow, at Frauendorf, then he was a military bandsman, 1st violinist and concertmeister at the Stettin theatre; from 1901 a pupil of Sitt, Quasdorff and Klesse at Leipzig; afterwards in the orchestra again till 1906, and until 1909 violin teacher at the Löwe-Riemann Conservatoire at Stettin. In 1909 he founded the "German Violin School Sass-Stettin" (Deutsche Geigerschule Sass-Stettin). Since 1907 he has written a number of pamphlets and articles on violin technique, also books of studies. He has also composed violin pieces, chamber music, and an opera.

# CHAPTER 55

# Germany: to Present Day

CARL WENDLING, b. Strassburg, Aug. 10, 1875. A pupil of his brother at the Strassburg Conservatoire, then of Zajic (1886–9); after that of Heinr. Schuster (pupil of Joachim) till 1894, and finally of Joachim and Halíř till 1896. After that he became a teacher at the Strassburg Conservatoire and served his obligatory year in the German army in 1897–8. In 1898–9 he took a further course of lessons from Joachim. From the latter year until 1903 he was concertmeister in the Court chapel at Meiningen, with which he toured a great deal and appeared as a soloist with great success in many of the concerts of the chapel. He also formed a string quartet during that time which was often joined by the famous clarinet player Rich. Mühlfeld. In 1903 he succeeded E. Singer as concertmeister in the Stuttgart Court orchestra, where he received the title of Royal Professor. In 1903 and 1905 he was also leader under Richter during the London Season, at the Royal Opera, Covent Garden. In 1907–9 he held the same position in the Boston orchestra under C. Muck, and also at the Bayreuth Festivals of 1902, 1904 and 1906. The Wendling quartet (H. Michaelis, (now Hubel), 2nd violin; Ph. Neeter (now Natterer), viola; Alfr. Saal ('cello) toured a great deal, visiting many countries, and meeting everywhere with marked success. They made a speciality of the works of Max Reger, who was an intimate friend of Wendling, to whom he dedicated his piano quintet, op. 146, which was finished only a short while before his death. Wendling is also a teacher at the Stuttgart Conservatoire.

WALTER HANSMANN, b. Köslin, Prussia, Dec. 4, 1875. A violin pupil of Hans Becker at the Leipzig Conservatoire; 1896–1902 assistant teacher of his master, 1st violinist in the Gewandhaus orchestra, soloist and chamber-music player. In 1911 teacher of violin at the Conservatoire; since 1912 director of the Thuringian State Conservatoire at Erfurt. In 1925 he founded and became conductor of the Erfurt Bach Union (Bachgemeinde) and of the higher public school concerts there.

CAMILLO RITTER, b. Coblenz on the Rhine, 1875. His parents settled at Glasgow when he was a child and there he received his first violin lessons and played at minor concerts from 1882 to 1888; studied under Hy. Holmes at the Royal College of Music, London, 1888–90, and 1890–3 under Joachim at the Berlin High School, where he gained a scholarship. He then returned to Glasgow, afterwards studying for a few months during each of three years under Ševčik at Prague, where in 1905 he played at a concert with great success, and on his return to Glasgow also with the Scottish orchestra. In 1906 he gave very successful concerts at Vienna and Graz.

ERNST WENDEL, b. Breslau, Mar. 26, 1876. A violin pupil of E. Wirth and Joachim; composition of Succo and Bargiel at the Berlin High School of Music. In 1896, at Joachim's recommendation, he was appointed first concertmeister in the Thomas orchestra, Chicago, and in 1898, also on Joachim's advice, conductor of the musical society's concerts, and leader of the Wendel quartet at Königsberg. In 1909 he became conductor of the Philharmonic Society at Bremen; 1913 professor; 1922 Director-General of Music. Toured as virtuoso before the War in Belgium and Russia: after the War in Italy. Since 1913, in addition to his activities at Bremen, he conducts concerts at Frankfort a/M. and at Nuremberg. The most important of his compositions are choruses for male voices with orchestra.

JOSEPH LEDERER, b. Dresden, Dec. 16, 1877. Pupil of Rappoldi for violin and F. Draesecke for composition. Since 1897 violinist in the Dresden State chapel. Composed a violin concerto, pieces for violin and pianoforte; violoncello concerto, string sextet, pianoforte quintet; pianoforte music; operas and orchestral compositions, songs, etc.

ADRIAN RAPPOLDI, b. Berlin, Sept. 13, 1878. A pupil of his father, Eduard Rappoldi, and of L. von Auer (composition under Draeseke). He became concertmeister in Bilse's orchestra, afterwards successively in Chemnitz, Teplitz and Helsingfors, and since 1910 violin teacher at the Dresden Conservatoire, of which, since 1915, he is one of the directors.

KARL KLINGLER, b. Strassburg, Dec. 7, 1879. He was a pupil first of his father, making his debut at a charity concert at the age of 5, and then of Concertmeister Schuster there, till, in 1897, he became a pupil of Joachim at the Berlin High School, which he left in 1900 with the Mendelssohn prize. During 1901–2 he was second concertmeister of the Berlin Philharmonic orchestra. In 1903 he became teacher at the Berlin High School for Music and at Easter, 1910, he received the title of Royal Professor. From the spring of 1906 till Mar., 1907, he deputized for Prof. Wirth in the Joachim quartet, and in the winter 1905–6 he formed, with Jos. Rywkind (a Russian), Fridolin Klingler, and Arthur Williams (an Englishman), a string quartet which visited with marked success Germany, the Netherlands, England, France, Spain and Norway, Austria and Switzerland. At the outbreak of the Great War, Alphonse Brun (pupil of Klingler) supplanted Rywkind and Hugo Dechert took the place of A. Williams. When Klingler himself had to join the army there was a pause in the quartet's activities, but after it had been completed again in 1916 by the addition of Rich. Heber and Max Baldner, a number of performances were given to the troops at the front. After the death of Joachim, Robert von Mendelssohn placed that master's violin at Klingler's disposal for life. In 1926 Francesco v. Mendelssohn took Baldner's place in the famous quartet. Klingler composed a violin concerto, 2 sonatas for violin and pianoforte and do. each for viola and violoncello, 3 string quartets, 1 string trio, 1 pianoforte trio, 1 violoncello duet, 1 symphony. He also wrote "The Foundations of Violin Playing." The Klingler quartet is well and favourably known in England.

HANS NEUMANN, b. Dresden, 1879. He received his first training as a violinist, as well as his general musical education from an early age until he was 14, from his father, Concertmeister Neumann, and after that he was for two years with Arno Hilf at Leipzig. He had already appeared frequently in public from the age of 8; but his real career began when he left Leipzig and toured successfully in Germany and Holland. On several occasions he deputized as 2nd violinist in the Joachim quartet, and at a subscription concert in the Dresden Opera House he played the Bach double concerto with Ysaÿe. About 1900 he settled in London as soloist and teacher. In 1908 he gave five sonata recitals with Septimus Webb, and in 1911 he gave a similar series of recitals with Willibald Richter. Neumann himself is also an excellent pianist with a remarkable facility for playing from full score at first sight.

WALTER SCHULZE, b. Halle a/S., May 18, 1880. He began to study the violin at a very early age, and when he was 8 years old and the family had settled at Chicago, he played at dancing parties. At 14 he studied at the Chicago College of Music under J. F. Ohleiser for three years. Then followed a period of touring in the United States, and two years' engagement as teacher at the Quincy Conservatoire, Illinois, after which he resumed his studies under Ohleiser, and, at the latter's recommendation, under E. Jacobson, a pupil of Ferd. David, who on his death in 1902 was succeeded by E. Lauret, under whom Schulze gained a scholarship at the Chicago College, and filled at the same time the post of 1st violinist in the Theo. Thomas orchestra. In 1903 he went to Prague and studied under Ševčik until Mar. 24, 1906, when he gave a most successful concert with the Bohemian Philharmonic Orchestra, and also appeared on several occasions together with his famous master. On May 8, 1906, he gave a successful concert in the Queen's Hall, London, and in the summer of that year he resumed his studies under Ysaÿe.

EDGAR WOLLGANDT, b. Wiesbaden, July 18, 1880. Was a pupil of the Conservatoire there, and afterwards for three years of H. Heermann at the Hoch Conservatoire, Frankfort a/M. In 1900 violinist in the Royal orchestra, Hanover; 1903 concertmeister in the Gewandhaus orchestra and leader of the Gewandhaus quartet (with C. Hermann, K. Wolschke, Jul. Klengel, now H. Münch-Holland). In 1914 he was offered the vacancy caused by the death of Petri at Dresden, but declined. He is the son-in-law of A. Nikisch. For four years he was also first concertmeister at Bayreuth. In 1928 he received the title of Professor.

MAX MENGE, b. Hamburg, June 13, 1881. A pupil of Corbach at Sondershausen and of Heermann at the Hoch Conservatoire, Frankfort a/M., and during 1900–2 at the Basle Conservatoire. He lives at Hamburg, as virtuoso and teacher.

GUSTAV HAVEMANN, b. Güstrow, Mar. 15, 1882. Pupil of his father, director of music, his brother-in-law, E. Parlow, and Concertmeister Bruno Abner. At the age of 6 he played a violin solo in public at Rostock. During 1899–1901 he studied under Joachim and Markees at the Berlin High School. He was concertmeister at Lübeck 1901–3, Darmstadt 1903–9, Hamburg 1909–11, and from 1911 to 1915 he was violin teacher at the Leipzig Conservatoire. In autumn, 1915, he went to Dresden as first concertmeister at the Opera, and received the title of Royal Professor in 1917. At present he is professor at the Berlin High School of Music, where he has also a string quartet with Kniestädt, Mahlke and St. Steiner. He has also been a pioneer of the more modern school, and Reger, in recognition of the fact, dedicated to him his Chaconne in G minor, op. 117. He has written a violin concertino and a considerable number of solo pieces, many of which possess distinct merit and are popular with amateurs as well as with artists. He also composed a string quartet.

SIEGFRIED EBERHARDT, b. Frankfort a/M., Mar. 19, 1883. Son of Goby Eberhardt; studied the violin under B. Dessau, and theory under M. Loewengard at Stern's Conservatoire, Berlin. He is the pioneer of a technical method of movements, intended to divert the pupil systematically from the mechanical exercise of the fingers to the causal movements of the body, and which culminates in the formulating of a law of the corporeal disposition as the condition of the creative spontaneity of expression on the part of the artist. He collaborated in the working-out of his ideas with Carl Flesh, and their united efforts resulted in various works which are listed in Riemann.

VACLAV TALICH, b. Kremsier, Moravia, May 28, 1883. He studied the violin first at the Prague Conservatoire, then at Leipzig (composition and conducting, Reger, Nikisch) and at

Milan. Became violinist in the Berlin Philharmonic orchestra; concertmeister at Odessa; professor at Tiflis, where he commenced his career as conductor, to which henceforth he devoted himself entirely; since 1918 he is capellmeister of the Czeskian Philharmonic orchestra of Prague, with which he has toured extensively.

ROBERT REITZ, b. Burgdorf, June 17, 1884. Son and pupil of music director Fritz Reitz. He appeared in public as a violinist at the age of 8. From 1900 to 1904 he was a pupil of Hans Sitt at the Leipzig Conservatoire and violinist in the Gewandhaus orchestra; afterwards he studied under Berber, Flesch and Heermann. In 1904 he was concertmeister of the symphony orchestra at Majorenhof near Riga; 1904–6 he held also a similar position at Görlitz, where he was also leader of a string quartet and took the place of conductor. In 1907 he was concertmeister in the Philharmonic orchestra at Breslau; 1907–9 first concertmeister in the newly founded orchestra of the Society of Friends of Music at Kiel and at the same time conductor at the theatre and church orchestra at Westerland. Since 1909 he has been first concertmeister at the National Theatre, Weimar, where until 1926 he was also teacher at the State School of Music; professor there since 1919 and leader of a quartet. He has ed. and arranged concertos by older masters.

WALTHER DAVISSON, b. Frankfort a/M., Dec. 15, 1885. During 1900–6 pupil of Naret-Koning, Knorr and Rebner at the Hoch Conservatoire. During 1906–13 he was 2nd violin in the Rebner quartet; 1908–18 teacher at the Hoch Conservatoire. On Oct. 1, 1918, he succeeded Becker as teacher at the Leipzig Conservatoire, of which, in 1924, he became vice-principal, and in 1926 he received the title of Professor. Together with Paul Klengel he ed. the two violin concertos by Bach.

HEINRICH SCHACHTEBECK, b. Diemarden, near Göttingen, Aug. 6, 1887. Made his first studies in the Göttingen town chapel. From 1905 pupil of Arno Hilf at the Leipzig Conservatoire and privately of Walter Hansmann; 1909 violinist in the Gewandhaus orchestra; 1909 first concertmeister in the second Municipal Theatre orchestra; 1911–14 in the Philharmonic (Winderstein) orchestra. He also appeared frequently as soloist and, 1915, he formed a permanent quartet with Albert Patzak, A. Witter (now E. Waetzold) and Alfr. Patzak; his wife, Augusta Sch.-Sorocker, is connected with the quartet as pianist.

CATHARINA VAN DEN BOSCH, b. Tiel, Feb. 24, 1888. Teacher at Zürich Conservatoire, 1912; since 1922 at Stuttgart. Married the pianist P. O. Möckel.

ALPHONSE AIMÉ BRUN, b. Frankfort a/M., Oct. 25, 1888. A son of the concertmeister Alph. Brun, and pupil of K. Klingler at the Berlin High School from 1908. In 1912 concertmeister of the Music Society, Berne. From 1914 to 1915 temporary 2nd violinist in the Klingler quartet. In 1915 he formed the Berne string quartet with B. W. Garraux, H. Blume and L. Lehr.

ADOLF BUSCH, b. Siegen, Westphalia, Aug. 8, 1891. Received his first violin lessons from his father, who settled as musical instrument-maker at Cologne, then from Concertmeister Anders. In 1902 he entered the Cologne Conservatoire where he studied, first under Hess, then under Eldering, while Fritz Steinbach gave special attention to his musical education. He left the Conservatoire in 1908 and studied composition under Hugo Grüters at Bonn, whose daughter he married in 1913. Since 1907 he had become an intimate friend of Max Reger, who played his chamber music preferably with Busch. In 1912 he became concertmeister at the Vienna Konzertverein and toured in Holland, Sweden, Switzerland, England and Russia; and when Marteau left Berlin, he succeeded him in 1918 as violin professor at the Berlin High School of Music. In 1919 he formed a permanent quartet with K. Reitz, E. Bohnke, and P. Grümmer; Reitz and Bohnke were afterwards replaced by G. Andreasson and R. Doktor. He has also a trio with the pianist Rud. Serkin, and his brother Hermann Busch; since 1926 he has settled at Basle. Busch is a fertile composer with a strong leaning to the style of Reger, but is gradually freeing himself from that influence and developing greater individuality. His compositions for violin consist of a solo piece with orchestra; a sonata with pianoforte; a sonata for violin solo; and a Prelude and Passacagia for pianoforte and 2 violins, duet for violin and violoncello, op. 6b. His other works include a choral work, a symphony, overture, orchestral variations, serenade for strings, and various chamber-music works (for list, *see* Riemann).

FRANZ ERNST ARANYI, b. Cologne, Mar. 21, 1893. Son of the Hungarian violin teacher, Prof. Fritz Aranyi; pupil of H. Marteau and W. Hess at the Berlin High School for Music and of Hubay at the Budapest High School, where he studied composition under Antal Molnár. In 1912 he became concertmeister in the Vienna Tonkünstler orchestra; after the War he held similar positions at Wiesbaden and Stockholm. Since 1922 he has been touring as a virtuoso, and as such has made a considerable name for himself.

BERNARD WAGENAAR, b. Aix-la-Chapelle, Aug. 18, 1894. A violin pupil of G. Veerman, theory G. Wagenaar. In 1920 he became violinist in the Philharmonic orchestra, New York. He has composed a sonata and pieces for violin and pianoforte; a string quartet, serenade for strings and pianoforte; a trio, a Concertstück with orchestra and sonata for violoncello; orchestral and choral works, many songs.

GEORG KUHLENKAMPFF, b. Bremen, Jan. 23, 1898. A pupil of Hess at the Berlin High School of Music. In 1916 first concertmeister of the Bremen Philharmonia, and touring as violin virtuoso. He went to Berlin in 1919, where he was teacher at the High School from 1923 to 1926. Since then he has toured as soloist. Technically as well as musically he ranks among the foremost living German violinists.

KARL WASSERMANN, d. Schöneberg, Black Forest, Sept. 15, 1902. For many years a violinist in the Court chapel, and a teacher at the Conservatoire at Karlsruhe, Baden. He wrote: "Entdeckungen zur Erleichterung und Erweiterung der Violintechnik" ("Discoveries for the Facilitation and Enlargement of Violin Technics," 2nd ed., 1901); "Complete New Violin Method," based upon the former book (double-fifths system, German text only), 2 parts; "Criticism of the Marking of Positions" (against F. Hermann and Herm. Schröder, in German).

AUSSAUER. A pupil of Corbach. Early 20th-century concertmeister of the Breslau Philharmonic Society.

GEORG HEROLD. A pupil of Bennewitz at the Prague Conservatoire. After finishing his studies he became concertmeister at the Prague Philharmonic Society. He founded a string quartet which had but a short existence, but in 1908 he succeeded Nedbal as viola player in the Bohemian quartet.

ERNST HEIM. A pupil of Cologne Conservatoire, latterly director of music at Davos. Author of "Gradus at Parnassum," etc.

SCHULZE-PRISCA. A contemporary German-American violinist and pupil of Ševčik; was concertmeister at Dortmund, then at Würzburg.

WEINMANN. Quoted by Wasielewski as a pupil of Marteau, without further particulars.

PALMA VON PASZTHORY. Violinist. Gave concerts with M. Reger (ca. 1918).

BORIS KROYT. A pupil of A. Friedemann, now in Berlin.

GESTERKAMP. A pupil of Em. Wirth and of Joachim. About 1919 or 1920 he was concertmeister in the Berlin Philharmonic orchestra.

PAUL MORALT. Living at Munich in 1920 as concertmeister and solo violinist of the former Court chapel; belongs to the same family as the four brothers of the Moralt quartet.

STEFFI GEYER. An eminently talented lady pupil of Hubay; married Walther Schulthes in 1921.

EDITH VON VOIGTLÄNDER, b. Weimar. She showed uncommon talent for the violin from her fourth year, and at the age of 11 she went to Berlin on Joachim's advice, and studied for two years under Barmas. Since then she has toured far and wide, and by her brilliant technique, artistic temperament and refined style, she ranks high among living violinists, and gathered laurels also on her appearance in London.

# CHAPTER 56

## *Great Britain: to 1850*

DURING the 18th century the art of violin playing, as well as the cultivation of music in general, although patronized by the Court and by some members of the nobility, was practised chiefly by Continental musicians; Italians mostly in the earlier part of the century, and Germans in the latter part. The active occupation with music on the part of a man was considered a sign of effeminacy right into the 19th century, although a very small minority disregarded that prejudice. The advent of Viotti, who wrote the second series of his concertos for the Salomon concerts, where he played them himself, created a great deal of enthusiasm for the violin, the effects whereof did not become patent until much later; he was, however, together with Salomon, and other musicians and music patrons, a founder of the Royal Philharmonic Society in 1813, which marked an epoch in the musical life of England. In 1822 the Royal Academy of Music was founded, where Nic. Mori, for a short time Viotti's pupil, was appointed as first professor of violin, and proved himself a very capable teacher, and the same may be said of Prosper Sainton, who occupied that position from 1844, and trained many good violinists, but none of outstanding merit. About the middle of the century Molique came from Stuttgart to London, remaining till 1866. He was greatly admired as a soloist, and counted among his pupils one of the first English virtuosos, J. T. Carrodus, who shone, however, chiefly as leader in the principal orchestras. English violinists of importance begin to increase in number from this period. In 1880 the Guildhall School of Music opened its doors in Aldermanbury in the City of London, and Viotti Collins was one of the first teachers for the violin. The school soon grew to such proportions that the original premises proved inadequate and the present sumptuous building with a spacious concert-room was erected in John Carpenter Street, Victoria Embankment, and opened in 1886. Since then it has produced many good pupils under such eminent teachers as A. Wilhelmj, etc., and the present professor Louis Pecskai, who is also a professor at Trinity College of Music, which, founded in 1872, has also done good work for the advancement of violin-playing and of music in general. Then there is the very important Royal College of Music, founded in 1883, of which R. Gompertz and Hy. Holmes were the first professors, and among the eminent teachers who followed were A. Rivarde and F. Arbos. A large number of violinists who have since appeared as successful soloists at London and provincial concerts received their training at the Royal College and the Royal Academy of Music. The latter counted among its teachers E. Sauret, who succeeded Sainton in 1890, and H. Wessely, who was appointed in the same year.

F. J. KLOSE, b. London (bapt. ca. 1790), towards the end of the 18th century; d. there, Mar. 8, 1830. Studied music at first under his father, then under various masters, especially under Francis Tomisch. He became one of the good London violinists and played in various orchestras, especially at the King's theatre and the Concert of Antient Music; but from about 1821 he devoted himself chiefly to teaching and composition. He wrote many ballads, some of which became very popular, also ballets and melodramas, sonatas, etc., for various instruments, but apparently nothing for violin.

NICHOLAS MORI, b. London, 1793 (Wki. and Clarke, 1796); d. there, June 14, 1839. When he was already recognized as an excellent violinist he received for some months finishing lessons from Viotti. He combined a powerful tone of great richness and beauty with a remarkable technique of the left hand. When the Royal Academy of Music was founded, 1822, he became professor of violin, together with F. Cramer. In 1813 he became a director of the Philharmonic Society and remained so for several years. In 1819 he married the widow of Lavenu, the music publisher, and became interested in the business. From 1836 to the time of his death he gave regularly classical chamber concerts.

NICHOLAS MORI, b. London, 1822, second son of Nicholas Mori, was also a violinist and viola player but of mediocre talent; he died there in poor circumstances, ca. 1900.

MICHAEL ROPHINO LACY, b. Bilbao, July 19, 1795; d. Pentonville, Sept. 20, 1867. The son of an English merchant, he began to study the violin at the age of 5 and by 1802 he was a player of generally recognized ability. He then began his studies at a college at Bordeaux and afterwards at one in Paris, where at the same time he continued his study of the violin under R. Kreutzer. After appearing at the French Court as well as at public concerts with great success, his father took him to London in 1805, where he became a pupil of Viotti. After touring as a violin virtuoso with marked success throughout Great Britain he suddenly went on the stage as a comedian. In 1818 he resumed the violin and became conductor of the Liverpool concerts. In 1820 he was engaged in London as ballet composer for the Italian Opera, but in 1824 he resumed his former position at Liverpool. He composed violin and pianoforte pieces, a pianoforte quintet and English songs, and gave great assistance to Schölcher for his "Life of Handel."

ISAAC COLLINS, b. 1797; d. London, Nov. 24, 1871. For many years solo violinist at the Crystal Palace concerts.

VIOTTI COLLINS, his son, was also an excellent violinist and for many years professor of violin at the Guildhall School of Music. He possessed a remarkable technique, and was a good musician and chamber-music player.

JOHN ELLA, b. Thirsk, Yorks, Dec. 19, 1802; d. London, Oct. 2, 1888. Intended for the law. In 1821 he came to London. Studied the violin under Femy, harmony under Attwood. In 1822 he became a violinist at the King's theatre, the concerts of Antient Music, and the Philharmonic Society. In 1845 he studied counterpoint and composition under Fétis at Brussels, and in the same year he founded the Musical Union, which continued until his retirement in 1880, and in 1850 also the "Musical Winter Evenings," which came to an end in 1859. For these concerts he wrote analytical programmes which were an improvement on those written by John Thompson for the Edinburgh Professional Society in 1837. In 1855 he was appointed Lecturer on Music at the London Institution. Some of these lectures were published.

He also contributed articles to various London papers, wrote a "Personal Memoir of Meyerbeer," etc., and "Musical Sketches Abroad and at Home" (three eds.: 1861, 1869, 1878).

JOSEPH HAYDON BOURNE DANDO, b. Somers Town, London, May 11, 1806; d. Godalming, Surrey, May 9, 1894. A pupil of N. Mori and became a member of the Philharmonic Orchestra. He devoted himself chiefly to the cultivation of chamber music, and in 1835 instituted the first chamber-music concerts in the strict sense of the word. Only string quartets and trios by the classical masters were performed, and those in great perfection; his associates were Loder, Blagrove, Gattie, and Lucas.

ROBERT MACKINTOSH, d. London, Feb., 1807; had, some time before, settled there as teacher. Composed pieces for stringed instruments several of which appeared towards the end of the 18th century at Edinburgh.

RICHARD MICHAEL LEVEY, b. Dublin, Oct. 2 (Riemann: 25), 1811; d. there, June 28, 1899. An esteemed violinist; his son, Wm. Chs. Levey, was conductor at the Covent Garden Opera, 1868–74, afterwards at the Haymarket Theatre, London.

HENRY GAMBLE BLAGROVE, b. Nottingham, Oct. 20, 1811; d. Nottingham, Dec. 15, 1872. He was a prodigy who began to study the violin under his father, on a small violin specially made for him when he was only 4 years old, and first played in public at the age of 5. In 1817 he made his debut at Drury Lane Theatre, London, and soon after he performed daily at the Exhibition rooms in Spring Gardens. In 1821 Spagnoletti took an interest in him, and with him he remained until 1823, when he entered the recently opened Academy of Music as a pupil of Franz Cramer. In 1830 he was appointed as violinist in the Queen's private band; but in 1833 he went to Cassel to study for one year under L. Spohr. When that great master came to England in 1839 he played with his former pupil a duet (double concerto) at the Norwich Festival. About 1836 Blagrove appears to have toured on the Continent, for Hanslick records his successful appearance in Vienna about that time. He was one of the best English violinists of his time and excelled as a quartet player. He died after a long illness.

GEORGE HADDOCK, b. Leeds, 1823; d. there, 19... A pupil of Spagnoletti's pupil Bywater of Leeds, of Vieuxtemps (1846–50) and from 1850 for some years of Molique; he was an excellent violinist who did much to foster musical life at Leeds, and was personally acquainted with all the greatest musicians of the Victorian era, of whom he has many interesting things to relate in his "Musical Recollections." He composed some solos and made many transcriptions of Classical pieces for the violin. His collection of about 80 violins included the "Emperor" Strad of 1715, several by Joseph Guarnerius del Jesu, Joseph Guarnerius filius Andrae, some of the finest Amatis, etc.

DR. JOHN DAY, b. London, Mar. 7, 1830; d. there, Nov. 4, 1905; studied the violin under de Bériot in 1843–5. In 1845 he made his debut with his master's second concerto at a Philharmonic Concert in London. He also appeared as violinist at the Norwich and Birmingham Festivals. In 1847 he became a member of the Queen's band and for many years played as soloist to Queen Victoria. He also was a clever violin-maker, as well as organist at Upton and at All Saints', Fulham.

JOHN TIPLADY CARRODUS, b. Keighley, Yorks, Jan. 20, 1836; d. London, July 13, 1895. Received his first violin lessons from his father, and at the age of 12 he became a pupil of Molique at Stuttgart and in London, 1848–57. He then became leader of the Glasgow orchestra. He was engaged for the first Bradford Musical Festival under Costa, who was so pleased with his playing that he engaged him for his orchestra at the Royal Italian Opera in London. His first appearance as a soloist in London was at a concert of the Musical Society on Apr. 22, 1863. Later he was leader at Her Majesty's Theatre, under Arditi, until it was burnt down. When Sainton retired, he succeeded him as leader at Covent Garden, where, eventually, he died at his post. As a soloist he appeared frequently at the Crystal Palace and many London and Provincial Concerts, and the writer remembers a remarkably fine performance by him of Bach's Ciaconna, at the old St. James's Hall, remarkable for his powerful tone, perfect technique, and purity of intonation. His precision of attack made him an orchestral leader of the very first order. He was

principal professor at Trinity College, London, and the first
president of the College of Violinists. A short time before his
death he was honoured by the bestowal upon him of the freedom of his native town. He composed some solo pieces and
wrote "Chats with Students of the Violin" and "How to Study
the Violin," both pub. in *The Strad* Library.

JOHN FARMER, b. Nottingham, Aug. 16, 1836; d. Oxford,
July 17, 1901. Studied the violin first at the Leipzig Conservatoire and then under Späth at Coburg. After that he
was teacher at the Zürich Conservatoire. In 1862 he became
violin teacher at Harrow School, and 1885 organist at Balliol
College, Oxford, where he instituted regular concerts. He
composed an oratorio, a requiem, an operetta and minor vocal
compositions. HENRY FARMER, b. Nottingham, 1819; d.
there, June 25, 1891; nephew; self-taught violinist, wrote a
violin tutor which became very popular.

THE HOLMES BROTHERS: ALFRED, b. London, Nov. 9, 1837; d.
Paris, Mar. 4, 1876, and HENRY, b. London, Nov. 7, 1839;
d. San Francisco, Dec. 9, 1905. Received their instruction on
the violin from their father (a self-taught musician) on the lines
of Spohr's violin school and the works of Rode, Baillot and
Kreutzer; afterwards they were for some time pupils of Spohr,
who speaks of them in his autobiography, and dedicated to
them one of his last duets. They both showed remarkable
talent at a very early age and made their debut as duet players
at the Haymarket Theatre in 1847, after which they withdrew
from the public for renewed studies. In 1853 they made
another appearance in London, and in 1855 they started on a
prolonged tour on the Continent. They remained for a longer
period in Brussels, where they gave a number of concerts with
great success and in 1856 they toured in Germany and Austria
as far as Vienna, afterwards going to Sweden, where they
remained for two years. In 1860 they went to Copenhagen,
in 1861 to Amsterdam and 1864 to Paris, where ALFRED
settled permanently, making occasional tours by himself.
He composed 6 symphonies, 2 overtures, and an opera.
HENRY left Paris in 1865 and returned to London after another
tour through Scandinavia. In 1883 he was appointed as
teacher of the violin at the Royal College of Music and was
highly esteemed both in that capacity and as soloist, but in

1893 he was dismissed on account of notorious conduct toward pupils, which he defended in a book of such questionable tone which was suppressed by the authorities. Henry went to California, from which time until his death further particulars are wanting. He composed a violin concerto, duets (dedicated to Spohr) which testify to his great technique, solo pieces, 5 symphonies, a concert overture, 2 string quintets, 2 cantatas and songs. He also edited a number of violin sonatas by Corelli, Tartini, Bach and Handel.

GILBERT HENRY BETJEMANN, b. London (?), Nov. 17, 1840; d. London. A pupil of Chas. Doyle. In 1858 was 2nd, from 1859 was 1st violin at Covent Garden Opera; 1884 conductor of Italian Opera at Her Majesty's Theatre; 1886–1907 conductor of Highbury Philharmonic Society. From 1895 he was leader of the Royal Opera, Covent Garden; leader at Provincial Festivals; examiner at R.A.M. and R.C.M.; Musician in ordinary to Queen Victoria, King Edward, etc.

GEORGE ALFRED GIBSON, b. Nottingham, Oct. 27, 1849; d. Mentone, May 21, 1924. Showed early talent, and received violin lessons from his father until the age of 9, when he studied for two years under Hy. Farmer, after which he toured successfully as a prodigy, continuing his studies, without a master, by observation only. In 1870 he became 1st violinist at Drury Lane Theatre and in 1871 at the Royal Opera, Covent Garden. He devoted himself chiefly to the playing of chamber music and played in quartets, etc., with Joachim, Lady Hallé and other eminent musicians of the time, making his first appearance at the Monday Popular Concerts, Jan. 28, 1882. He succeeded Zerbini as 2nd viola and, in 1893, Straus as 1st viola at the Monday and Saturday Popular Concerts. He also was Straus' successor as leader of the Queen's private band in that year, and teacher of the violin at the Royal Academy of Music and the Guildhall School of Music. He was the fortunate possessor of a Guarnerius del Jesu violin, a beautiful Guadagnini and a very fine Stradivari viola, the latter fulfilling Joachim's long-cherished wish that the "Pops" Quartet might be composed entirely of instruments by Stradivari.

ISAAC COOPER. A Scottish violinist, end of 18th to beginning of 19th century.

## CHAPTER 57

## *Great Britain: to Present Day*

W. FRYE PARKER, b. Dunmow, Essex, 1855. Made his debut at the age of 7 as a boy violinist. In 1866 he entered the Royal Academy of Music, London, where he studied under Sainton. After being the leader at some theatres and at the Queen's Hall Sunday Concerts, he became a professor of the Violin at the R.A.M. and the Guildhall School of Music in 1881, and from 1896 he was principal violin in the Philharmonic orchestra, the Leeds Festival, etc. He has also appeared successfully as soloist, but he is chiefly esteemed as teacher, orchestral leader, and conductor of some of the more important amateur orchestras.

JOHANN SECUNDUS KRUSE, b. Melbourne, Mar. 23, 1859. The son of a chemist who emigrated from Hanover to Australia. He began to study the violin from the age of 9 and in a short time he was able to appear in public. In 1876 he studied under Joachim at Berlin and afterwards became concertmeister in the Philharmonic orchestra there. In 1892 he was appointed concertmeister at Bremen, later on he became for some time teacher of the violin at the Berlin Hochschule and 2nd violin in the Joachim quartet. He settled in London in 1897, where he formed a quartet with which he gave concerts at the old St. James's Hall. In 1902 he took over the Saturday and Monday Popular Concerts into which he brought fresh life, and in the same year he gave a series of orchestral concerts under the conductorship of Felix Weingartner. In 1903 he gave a Beethoven Festival of eight concerts, which he followed up by another Festival of seven concerts. In 1921 he gave a series of chamber concerts with Mathilde Verne and others, and in 1926 he again formed a quartet bearing his name. He paid two visits to Australia in 1885 and 1895.

EMILY SHINNER (MRS. LIDDELL), b. Cheltenham, July 7, 1862; d. July 17, 1901. Began the study of the violin at the age of 7. From 1874 to 1876 she studied under Joachim's pupil H. Jacobsen, female pupils not being admissible to the Hochschule. In 1874 the ban was lifted and she became a pupil of Joachim, under whom she studied for three years. In Feb., 1881, she came to London, and after playing in several private concerts, she made her debut at a concert given by H. R. Bird at the Kensington Town Hall. At the London Musical Society's concert, June 29, 1882, she played David's E minor concerto with great success. On Feb. 9, 1884, she played at the Popular Concert, and on the following Mar. 8 at the Crystal Palace. She held a high position among English artists both by reason of her excellent technique and her interpretative powers. In 1887 she formed a permanent quartet with female players, which acquired a high reputation. In 1889 she married Capt. A. F. Liddell. In 1894 Emily Shinner appeared in London as a soloist and also gave a series of concerts with her quartet. In July, 1894, she gave one Schumann and one Brahms recital with Leonard Borwick.

EDMUND SEVERN, b. Nottingham, Dec. 10, 1862. Violinist; composition pupil of G. W. Chadwick and Scharwenka; commenced his career at Springfield, U.S.A., in 1890. A member of several quartet and trio unions; choirmaster at Westfield and Warren; soloist of the Springfield concert society; since 1907 in New York; 1914 teacher at the Board of Education; since then private teacher and composer. He composed a violin concerto; a sonata and 2 suites for violin and pianoforte; a suite for 2 violins and pianoforte; a string quartet; choral and orchestral works, etc.

BASIL ALTHAUS, b. London, 1865; d. there, Dec. 28, 1910. Studied the violin under Geo. Palmer at the Guildhall School of Music, where he held a four years' scholarship. In 1885, two years before leaving that school, he started the Tavistock Violin Academy, which proved so successful that it was after a short time removed to larger premises in Maida Vale, where it numbered over 200 pupils, and had a full orchestra with professional leaders. In 1898 he disposed of the school, took up teaching in Brussels and became a

member of the Ostend Kursaal Orchestra. In 1901 he
returned to London as director of the College of Violinists,
which under him attained to a flourishing condition. He
composed a number of pieces for violin and pianoforte and
wrote a violin method and a treatise on the seven positions.
He died suddenly from a stroke, greatly lamented by numerous friends and pupils, among whom he was greatly beloved
on account of his genial personality. At the time of his
death he was preparing for a three weeks' engagement in
the South of France. His portrait published in *The Strad*
of Feb., 1911, is from a photograph taken three hours before
his death.

JOHN DUNN, b. Hull, Feb. 16, 1866. Received his first
instructions on the violin from his brother, and in 1878 he
went to study at the Leipzig Conservatoire, violin under
Schradieck, theory and composition under Richter and
Jadassohn. He made his debut at Hull in 1875, and at
the Covent Garden Promenade Concerts in Oct., 1882;
since then he has played at most of the leading concerts in
London and the Provinces, and by his exceptionally brilliant
technique and fine powerful tone he has raised himself to
the rank of one of the foremost English violinists. He was
the first to play the concertos by Gade (1887), Tschaikovsky
(1900), and Elgar (1911) in London. Since then he has
toured with great success on the Continent and in America
(U.S.A. and Canada). He is a brilliant exponent of Paganini's
works. He composed a number of solo pieces, also cadenzas
to the Beethoven concerto, etc.; and a violin concerto (still
MS.); he also wrote a manual on "Violin Playing," which
is included in *The Strad* Library.

JOHN SAUNDERS, b. London (?), 1867; d. there, Oct. 7, 1919.
Pupil of J. T. Carrodus and Benoit Hollander at the Guildhall School of Music; chiefly chamber-music and orchestral
violinist. He formed a permanent quartet which for twenty-
eight years took a prominent part in the South Place Sunday
Concerts and toured also successfully in the provinces. In
1910 he became leader of the Philharmonic, and ca. 1915
of the New Symphony, orchestra, and in the summer of
1919 he filled a similar post in Diaghileff's Russian Ballet
orchestra. In 1916 his fellow musicians gave a dinner in

NICHOLAS MORI
By kind permission of Messrs. W. E. Hill
& Sons, owners of the portrait painted
from life.

CHARLES AUGUSTE DE BERIOT

his honour as artist and confrère, at which they presented him with a Stradivari violin. He was for a number of years teacher at the Guildhall School of Music.

HENRY SUCH, b. London, 18... A pupil of Jos. Ludwig, then of Joachim at the Berlin High School. In 1893 he made his successful debut with the Berlin Philharmonic orchestra and in the same year he toured in Germany with the celebrated pianist Clotilde Kleeberg. Subsequently he resumed his studies under Wilhelmj and afterwards toured with great success in Germany, Denmark and Sweden. From Oct. to Nov., 1908, he gave 3 recitals at the old St. James's Hall which further enhanced his reputation. He eventually settled in the United States of America.

CHRISTOPHER RAWDON BRIGGS, b. near Wakefield, Yorks, 1870. In 1877 the family went to Geneva, where he received his first violin lessons from a local woman teacher; after many changes of locality he came to stay at Florence in the house of a good violinist, Bicchierai, who advised the then 10-year-old boy to adopt the musical profession. From ca. 1889 he was for four years a pupil of Singer at Stuttgart, and afterwards of Joachim and de Ahna at the Berlin Hoch-schule, where he remained for two years. He then made a successful debut in London. In the following year he was for one season 1st violin in the orchestra of the Glasgow Choral Union; whence he was called to Manchester as second teacher of the violin at the Royal Manchester College of Music, on the retirement of Risegari he became leader of the Hallé orchestra, and in 1907 he became leader of the Liverpool Philharmonic Society. He was 2nd violin in the Brodsky quartet and he also formed the Rawdon Briggs quartet with J. Bridge, Mrs. Rawdon Briggs (a former pupil of his) and W. Hutton. They have toured with great success in the north of England, Scotland and Ireland. He has been frequently heard as a soloist, but devotes a great deal of his time to teaching, in which he has done excellent work.

WILLIAM HENLEY, b. West Bromwich, 1874. A pupil of his father from the age of 6 and five years later of T. M. Abbott of Birmingham. In 1886 he made his first concert tour through Gloucestershire and was hailed as "the boy Paga-nini." In 1887 he toured in France as leader of the D'Oyley

Carte No. 1 Company.   On his return to England he toured
with sensational success in the provinces.   An enthusiastic
Birmingham admirer enabled him to study for two years
under Hy. Holmes in London, afterwards taking a course
of lessons from Willy Hess.   In 1893 he studied under
Sauret, but soon after he placed himself under Wilhelmj,
who bestowed upon him that loving and fatherly care which
made him the idol of all his pupils.   He trained him in
chamber-music playing, by letting him lead a quartet at his
house while he took the 2nd violin; and when Henley
appeared in 1896 as soloist at one of Stockley's concerts in
Birmingham, Wilhelmj attended in person to lend him his
countenance.   Since then Henley has toured with great
success both in England and on the Continent, especially
Germany.   He has a considerable number of effective
compositions to his credit, and established a considerable
reputation as a teacher.   His experiences as such are
embodied in his "School for the Violin" in 12 books, and
his book on "Solo Playing," etc., in *The Strad* Library.   In
1906 he formed a permanent string quartet with Gertrude
Compton, a pupil of Singer and Henley (2nd violin), James
Lockyer (viola), and Gertrude Ess (violoncello), whose early
death was a loss to music.   They gave their first series of
four concerts in June that year, which met with great praise,
as did Henley's quartet, op. 47, performed at the fourth
concert.

WILLIAM HENRY REED, b. Frome, July 29, 1876.   A member
of a family of musicians, and a violin pupil of Sauret, in theory
and composition of E. Prout, F. Corder, MacEwan and
Stewart Macpherson; teacher at the Royal College of Music;
leader of the Philharmonic and London Symphony concerts
and at Musical Festivals.   Composed a violin concerto,
violin pieces, 5 string quartets, also orchestral works, songs,
etc.

DETTMAR DRESSEL, b. London, 1878.   His father was a
professor at the Guildhall School of Music, and his mother
a singer.   He began to study the violin under Alexander
von Czeke at the age of 5, and at 10 he appeared occasionally
at public concerts and private musical soirées.   Soon afterwards he went to school at Weimar, where he often played

before the Grand Duke. In 1895 he became a pupil of Wilhelmj, who was so pleased with him that he presented him with the bow he generally used. In Nov., 1897, he made his successful debut at the old St. James's Hall, and after that he played at all the principal halls in London. In 1901 he started on a successful tour throughout Germany; while spending a holiday in Belgium he met with Ysaÿe, who befriended him and gave him much valuable advice. Early in 1905 he lost his father, but in the spring he repeated his successes at Dresden and other German towns. Since then he has been largely occupied in teaching, and on Jan. 22, 1913, he gave a successful pupils' concert at the Steinway Hall, London.

HAYDN WOOD, b. London (?), 18... His first teacher was his brother Harry, a conductor in the Isle of Man, but in 1897 he gained a three years' open scholarship at the Royal College of Music, and later on the Morley scholarship for a further three years' tuition. During the whole of that time he studied the violin under Arbos and composition under Stanford. After gaining the Dove and Hill prizes for violin-playing and the Sullivan prize for composition, he went to Brussels, where from 1903 to 1904 he studied under César Thomson, from whom he acquired that art of bowing for which the Belgian school of violin-playing is famous. On his return, Mme Albani engaged him for her tours, for eight years he toured all over Great Britain, Canada, Australia, New Zealand and India, and in the intervals he appeared successfully at many of the important concerts in England and Scotland, including Mme Albani's farewell concert at the Albert Hall. In 1914 he went on tour with his wife, a singer, on the variety stage. He has acquired a great reputation as a composer; some of his violin pieces have become very popular, and he has also written orchestral and chamber works, besides songs.

BEATRICE LANGLEY (MRS. BASIL TOZER), b. in Devonshire, as the eldest daughter of a Colonel of the Royal Artillery. In her eighth year she led a private performance of Beethoven's Septet. She studied in London under Jos. Ludwig and Aug. Wilhelmj, and made her public debut at one of the Henschel symphony concerts, in the nineties of the last century, which led to an engagement at the Crystal Palace, and she became a favourite at the Promenade concerts, and the Queen's Hall Sunday afternoon concerts. Afterwards she toured with Mme Albani in North America, which tour proved so successful that it was thrice repeated. She also visited South Africa. With Mathilde Verne she started the "Twelve o'clock Concerts," which led to the formation of the Langley-Mukle quartet, and to this she devoted her whole energies for a period of five years. In the winter of 1912 she came forward again as a soloist at her concert in the Bechstein Hall, which was followed by other concerts in London and the provinces.

SPENCER DYKE, b. St. Austell, Cornwall, July 22, 1880. After preliminary violin lessons from John Parden he gained, when 10, the silver medal awarded by the late Duke of Edinburgh. He then entered the Royal Academy of music as a pupil of H. Wessely and at 17 obtained the Dove scholarship, which on account of his exceptional abilities was extended from three to four years; he also carried off the Sauret prize and the R.A.M. Club prize. After completing his studies he became a professor at the Royal Academy in 1907. During the Great War he served in the London Electrical Engineers. Since then he has resumed his activities at the Royal Academy. In 1920 he formed a permanent quartet with E. Quaife (2nd violin), E. Tomlinson (viola), and B. Patterson Parker (violoncello), which has become one of the best quartets of modern times, and has been touring far and wide. They have also played on several occasions for the B.B.C. (British Broadcasting Co.). Although he gives a great deal of his time to his quartet, Mr. Spencer Dyke appears not unfrequently as an eminent soloist. He composed violin pieces, studies, wrote a book of scales and ed. works of the classics (Boosey, Bosworth, J. Williams).

PERCIVAL HODGSON, b. Bury, Lancs, Dec. 7, 1882. Violin pupil of A. Brodsky and of Dr. H. Hiles and Dr. W. Carroll for harmony, etc., at the Royal Manchester College of Music. In 1917 he toured the Somme Front with a Lena Ashwell Firing Line Party. In 1918 he became a member of Sir Thomas Beecham's Birmingham orchestra. Later on he founded the Birmingham String Quartet which toured successfully in the British Isles. In 1922 he married Miss Joan Willis, the violoncellist of the quartet, and 1923 they both received posts at Cardiff University College. Mr. Hodgson has become a most successful teacher of his instrument, and has relinquished his position at the College to devote himself to the study of modern teaching methods, the result of which is an extremely unconventional violin school. He intends shortly to publish his system. He is also a frequent contributor to *The Strad*.

ARTHUR CATTERALL, b. Preston, Lancs, 1883. Studied the violin at first under his father and toured for three years as a prodigy from the age of 6. From 1892 he studied under Willy Hess and after that from 1895 under Brodsky. At the age of 14 he played to Joachim, who predicted that he would become one of the greatest English violinists. In 1901 he became a member of the Hallé orchestra and accompanied Richter to Bayreuth in 1902, where he played in the Festival orchestra, as well as in all the soirées of Cosima Wagner. In 1904 he made his London debut at the Queen's Hall with the Tschaikovsky concerto; a great success. In 1909 he was appointed leader of the Queen's Hall Promenade Concerts, in 1913 at the Liverpool Philharmonic Society, in 1914 of the Hallé orchestra, and, on its formation in 1929, of the British Broadcasting Co. orchestra. He is also a professor at the Royal Manchester College of Music. In 1910–11 he founded the Catterall Quartet with O'Malley, Reggel and Hock. In 1914–15, J. S. Bridge succeeded O'Malley and F. S. Park took the place of Reggel. Their repertoire is composed chiefly of works by the classical masters, but includes also those by modern composers of all nationalities. The ensemble ranks among the best of the present time and often appears in B.B.C. programmes.

JOHN PEEBLES CONN, b. Penicuik, Midlothian, Sept. 15, 1883. A pupil of MacKenzie, Townsend, and Prof. Niecks at Edinburgh; gained the Bucher scholarship in 1902, which enabled him to study, 1902–6, under W. Hess and Bram Eldering at the Cologne Conservatoire, where Steinbach was his teacher of composition. After that he studied under Ševčík at Prague. His first appointment was as concertmeister in the Philharmonic Orchestra at Dortmund,

Westphalia, 1909. In 1914 he became leader and assistant conductor of the town orchestra at Bielefeld. During
the War he was interned at Ruhleben. From 1919 to 1922
he was second leader in the Scottish orchestra; since then,
teacher of violin at the Glasgow Athenæum and conductor
of the orchestral societies of Glasgow, Greenock and Dun-
fermline.

MARY HALL-BARING, b. Newcastle-on-Tyne, Apr. 8, 1884.
She received her first lessons on the violin from her father,
a poor harpist and violinist, who accompanied the child
with his harp as a street musician. When she was about
10 she attracted the attention of Mr. (now Sir Edward)
Elgar, who taught her for about a year, after which she had
three years' tuition from Max Mossel, Birmingham. At
that time she appeared in public as a prodigy. In 1899 she
lived with her parents at Bristol, where she found a circle
of influential friends who paid for her further tuition, first
under Joh. Kruse in London and after one year, on the advice
of Kubelik, under Ševčik, where she made such rapid progress that in 1902 she was ranked among the first virtuosos.
In 1903 she gave some highly successful concerts at Prague,
Vienna and Dresden, whence she returned to London,
being there received with acclamation. In 1905 she
toured in America, 1907 in Australia, 1910 in South Africa.
In 1911 she married her impresario, Baring, with whom she
visited the East Indies in 1913. She is the fortunate owner
of a very fine Strad. In her more recent appearances she
has brought forward many works by modern British composers, to wit, Vaughan Williams, Rutland Boughton, Percy
Sherwood, Gordon Bryan.

FREDERIC JAMES FALCONER, b. Edinburgh, May 2, 1885.
In 1904 a pupil of Wünsch at Brunswick, then studied,
1905–6 at the Prague Conservatoire, and 1906–8 at the
Royal Academy of Music, London; leader of a string quartet
and teacher of the violin at Edinburgh. Composed: Fantasia
for 4 violins; violin pieces, pianoforte pieces, orchestral suite,
songs.

EVANGELINE ANTHONY, b. Hereford, Nov. 28, 1885. A
pupil of D. Heins, before he went to Ottawa, and of Aug.
Wilhelmj, who had a high opinion of her talent. In Mar.,

1903, she played the Mendelssohn concerto with great success at the Hereford Orchestral Society, where she appeared repeatedly and also played the Kreutzer Sonata with Adela Verne at the Triennial Festival chamber concert in that year. She has also composed a number of effective solo pieces. On Nov. 5, 1904, she made her successful London debut with the London Symphony Orchestra at the old St. James's Hall, and afterwards she played with equal success in various provincial towns. In Oct. and Nov., 1905, she gave two successful recitals in London and in the latter month appeared with the London Symphony under Elgar at Cheltenham.

MARJORIE HAYWARD, b. Greenwich, 1885 (?). In early childhood she showed the sense of absolute pitch, and soon began to study the violin under Miss Jessie Grimson. Afterwards she entered Sauret's class at the Royal Academy of Music where, during the seven years she studied there, she gained the Sainton Scholarship and many important prizes. On the termination of her studies at the Academy, Sauret left for America, and she went to Prague, where she studied for a little over two years under Ševčik, and appeared during that time at one of his public pupils' concerts, also playing Ernst's F sharp minor concerto at one of the Bohemian Philharmonic Society's concerts with such success that a brilliant future was predicted for her. On her return to England she made a most successful debut with the same concerto and Saint-Saëns' in B minor at an orchestral concert with the London Symphony Orchestra under Dr. (now Sir Fr.) Cowen, which she gave at the Queen's Hall. After that she toured in Southern England. In 1908–9 she played at the "Twelve o'clocks" as a soloist and a member of the Beatrice Langley quartet. In the last few years she has devoted herself chiefly to chamber music, and has been frequently heard from the B.B.C. studios in sonata recitals and as leader of the Virtuoso string quartet.

ALBERT EDWARD SAMMONS, b. London, Feb. 23, 1886. His father and his elder brother taught him the rudiments of violin-playing. Afterwards he had about thirty lessons from John Saunders and Weist-Hill, and that finished all the instruction he ever had. About 1901 he began to earn his own living by playing at theatres and during the summer in a hotel band at Harrogate. When Thomas Beecham started his orchestra, he engaged Sammons as 1st violinist and in 1906 made him leader, and this position he held for eight years. In 1910 he formed the "new string quartet" with Thomas W. Petre, H. Waldo Warner, and C. Warwick Evans, which soon changed its name to the London String Quartet, which has since become famous for precision, beauty of tone and thoughtful artistic rendering. His career as a virtuoso began with a fine performance of Bruch's G minor concerto at a concert of a Patron's Fund at the Queen's Hall in 1911. In 1912 he played in the same hall Saint-Saëns' B minor concerto in the presence of the aged composer and the King and Queen. In 1913 he was leader in the Dieppe Symphony Orchestra. In 1914, after the outbreak of the War, he played the Elgar concerto, conducted by the composer, and gave so beautiful a rendering of it that he found himself literally famous overnight, and for three years his triumph was followed up by success after success until he was called upon in 1917 to join the army as a clarinet player in the Grenadier Guards. Since the end of the War he has resumed both his solo and quartet-playing with unabated success. His playing belongs to the school of the classics of the violin. Although equipped with a faultless technique he is no friend of mere technical display. Sammons has composed a number of very effective solo pieces and also edited and arranged pieces by older masters. In 1914 he played the difficult solo part in Strauss's Heldenleben at a Philharmonic Concert under Mengelberg, who not only insisted on Sammons sharing the applause, but also wrote a charming letter in his praise to the directors of the Philharmonic Society. He was leader of Monteux's Russian Ballet, touring in Germany and later in the summer at the Dieppe Casino, where he played a number of important concertos with such success that he was re-engaged in 1914. In Jan., 1925, he played the Elgar concerto at a concert of the B.B.C., London, where he has appeared frequently in recent years both as soloist and in chamber music. He has written a number of effective solo pieces as well as arrangements for violin.

ARTHUR BECKWITH, b. Croydon, 1887; d. London, Nov. 9, 1928. Studied the violin from the age of 5 under his father, and at the age of 15 gained a scholarship at the Royal College of Music, where he studied under Achille Rivarde and after four years carried off the Tagore Gold Medal which was presented to him by the King at Marlborough House. After leaving the College he became a 1st violinist in Sir Henry Wood's orchestra where, during the first season, he played the Brahms double concerto with Warwick Evans with such success that he was promoted to the first desk with M. Sons. Afterwards he was second leader at Covent Garden, leader of the Beecham concerts, and 1st violin in the Philharmonic quartet. In 1916 he joined the army, in which he served during the last years of the Great War. In 1919 he became musical director at the Grand Hotel, Eastbourne, where he remained for three years. In 1923 he went to America to take the place of the leader of the London String Quartet who had fallen ill. From July, 1923, he was for three years concertmeister of the Cleveland Orchestra, afterwards returning to London, where he died suddenly of pneumonia in the prime of life. He was very highly esteemed as a chamber-music player and quartet leader.

ELSIE SOUTHGATE, b. London, 1889. Studied at the Royal Academy of Music, London, under Sauret, 1899–1906; made her debut under Sir H. J. Wood at the Queen's Hall Promenade Concerts and afterwards played at the Ballad and Crystal Palace Concerts; then she made a successful tour in Germany and also played at the Lamoureux Concerts, Paris. After marrying, she retired for a few years from the concert platform, but when her husband died and left her with two children, she went on the music-hall stage, where, chiefly by the playing of simple melodies, with feeling and beauty of tone, she has met with unvaried success all over Great Britain. She has played before many crowned heads and received valuable tokens of their favour, one of the most welcome and precious being a fine Joseph Guarnerius from the late Shah of Persia.

OTIE CHEW, b. London, in the 'eighties of the last century. Studied the violin under Rich. Gompertz at the Royal College of Music, then under E. Sauret, and finally for three years at the Berlin High School for Music, where for one year she was a pupil of Joachim. Ysaÿe expressed his admiration of her talent. She made her London debut in 1904 with a Bach concerto at the last Richter concert of the season, and a few days later she gave a successful recital at the Bechstein (now Wigmore) Hall, London.

MIRAN LUCAS, b. London, 188?. Studied the violin first at the Royal College of Music, London, as did also her sisters JANET (violin) and PATIENCE (viola), while the youngest studied the violoncello under Paul Ludwig. In the latter part of the 'nineties the four sisters went to Prague, where the former three became private pupils of Ševčik for three years, and, with their youngest sister, played quartets to him. During the latter part of that time they also gave successful public concerts at Prague and other Bohemian towns. They then went to Vienna where for a period of four years they studied chamber music under A. Rosé and together with the famous Rosé quartet they played there a number of octets; during that time the Lucas quartet fulfilled many private engagements at notable Viennese houses, among others that of the Duchess of Teck, Princess Schönberg, etc. They made their successful London debut at the Bechstein Hall in 1909, where they gave three concerts, after which they were engaged for the Broadwood concerts at one of which they played the Svendsen octet with the Rosé quartet, when Rosé insisted that they should take the leading part.

IRENE PENSO, b. London, 188?; of Anglo-Italian parents. A pupil for a short time of Sauret, but chiefly of Achille Rivarde. She made a very successful debut with an orchestral concert at St. James's Hall in 1903, conducted by Sir Henry J. Wood, who engaged her for several Promenade and Sunday afternoon concerts at the Queen's Hall. Afterwards she toured on the Continent, where she played with many famous orchestras as well as pianists. In Berlin she gave a series of chamber concerts with X. Scharwenka.

SARAH FENNINGS, b. in Essex, 18... Came to London in early childhood; at the age of about 10 she began to study the violin at the Kensington School of Music, now the Royal College. Her family was a musical one and had formed a quartet among the members. After a short time at the school she studied for eighteen months under Hollander and then became a pupil of Wilhelmj, of whom she speaks with gratitude and admiration. After playing as a soloist in London and the provinces, she heard Kubelik and Marie Hall, and through Sir Fred. Cowen's recommendation she became a pupil of Ševčik, under whom she studied for a year and a half. On her return she re-appeared at Bechstein Hall with great success and has since been heard frequently in London and the provinces, holding a high reputation.

MAY HARRISON, b. Roorkee, N.W. India, 1890, and came to England in early childhood. At the age of 10 she gained the Gold Medal of the Associated Board, and she was also awarded an Exhibition in the Royal College of Music, London, where she studied under Arbos and Rivarde and finally under Auer at Petrograd. At the age of 18 she took Kreisler's place at a Mendelssohn Festival at Helsingfors, and in 1909 she appeared successfully in Berlin with the Philharmonic Orchestra. She has since toured in all parts of the world, frequently with her sister BEATRICE, the well-known violoncellist, with whom she has played the double concertos by Brahms and Delius. She has also proved herself a thoughtful and intelligent interpreter of the works of the classical school in a number of sonata recitals and at various concerts. At her recital in the Wigmore Hall, Oct., 1930, she played the new Delius sonata. Her younger sister MARGARET is also a very talented violinist who made her successful London debut in 1918. Since then she has appeared at a number of important concerts, and given recitals from time to time.

VIVIEN CHARTRES, b. in Italy, ca. 1896, of an English father and an Italian mother, a famous authoress. Studied first for a few months under Sauret in London; then under Ševčik at Prague, where she made her debut on Jan. 11, 1905. On May 15, 1905, she made her debut in London with the Queen's Hall Symphony Orchestra under Dr. Cowen, playing Bruch's G minor concerto, Paganini's Moïse Fantasy, Vieuxtemps' Fantasia Appassionata, and Grieg's Berceuse, and achieved a triumphant success. In 1906 she toured in Scandinavia and Germany, Austria and Italy, and was honoured by many Royal personages. She has a brilliant technique as well as musical feeling. Before the age of 12 she had composed a number of songs, some pub. by Ricordi, and she has a perfect command of English, German and French.

SYBIL EATON, b. Ketton, Rutland, 1897; related to Elizabeth Browning on her father's side. She began to study the pianoforte at the age of 6 and the violin at 8 under Kienle, and at 13 for some time under Oliver Williams. In May, 1914, she attended von Auer's summer school at Loschwitz. The War prevented her from continuing her studies under that famous professor, but on her return to England she continued for six years to study under his assistant, Miss Editha Knocker. She made her public debut in 1917 by giving three recitals which proved a great success, and soon after that she appeared at the Promenade Concerts and the Albert Hall. A breakdown in health caused her retirement from public work from 1920 to 1923 and she used that time to enrich her repertoire. She is an enthusiastic champion of modern British composers, many of whose works she played for the first time in public, and Stanford's Irish Rhapsody, No. 6, Herbert Howell's first sonata, and Armstrong Gibb's violin sonata were specially written for her. She has formed a string quartet which gives fortnightly recitals for schools at the B.B.C. She acquired from Conus, head teacher at the Moscow Conservatoire, a Maggini violin, formerly the property of Lvoff, with his coat of arms painted on the back.

EDITH KNOCKER, one of the numerous pupils, and assistant teacher in England of von Auer, for some time teacher of Miss Sybil Eaton. We have so far no further particulars.

ISOLDE MENGES, b. Brighton, 1894. Received her first instruction on the violin from her father, and gave a recital playing pieces from memory at the age of three and a half years; later on she studied under Sametini and from 1909 under von Auer at St. Petersburg. On Feb. 4, 1913, she made a very successful debut in London with the Brighton Municipal Orchestra; in 1916 she appeared for the first time in New York and in 1921 she paid another visit to America, returning in Sept., when she played the Glazounov violin concerto at the Queen's Hall. Since then she has become a great favourite of the musical public by her noble and dignified style, which is reminiscent of the great classical violinists of the 19th-century German school, by its breadth and intelligence, and she ranks unquestionably amongst the foremost women violinists of the present time.  She married in or before 1923 the composer Tod Boyd, who wrote some solo pieces for her which met with a favourable reception at her concerts.  Her repertoire includes all the classical concertos as well as some of the romantic and modern schools. In Sept., 1929, she played the Bach double concerto with Orrea Pernel, and in Nov., 1930, Mozart's symphony concertante for violin and viola with L. Tertis.  Her recitals met with great success and she has also become a great favourite with the B.B.C. audiences.

WINIFRED SMALL (MRS. M. COLE), b. London, Mar. 29, 1896. Showed musical talent in early childhood, and received instruction from her father, an enthusiastic amateur.  She began by playing the pianoforte, but at the age of 7 she took up the violin and at 13 she gained the Campbell Clarke Scholarship at the Royal Academy of Music, where she studied under Rowsby Woof.  After three years she carried off the Broughton Packer Bath Scholarship tenable for another three years, during the latter part of which she became a sub-professor for chamber music at the Royal Academy.  She made her debut by giving a recital in London with Harriet Cohen, the pianist.  Besides playing at a number of concerts and recitals, she made her debut at the Winter Gardens, Bournemouth, that year with the Mendelssohn concerto.  Recitals followed in 1917 and 1920, the latter being an All-British Recital assisted by Myra Hess.  In Aug., 1920, she played at a Queen's Hall Promenade concert and in 1921 she toured for six months in India, Burma, Malay Straits and Ceylon. In 1923 she was one of the first violinists to broadcast from Marconi House, afterwards toured frequently for the B.B.C. and also broadcast from some German stations.  In 1927 she married the well-known pianist Maurice Cole, with whom she is frequently heard at concerts, recitals and on the wireless.  In Apr., 1931, she gave six short recitals of Corelli sonatas for the B.B.C.—"Foundations of Music"— which were distinguished by a fine understanding of the old master, as well as by a perfect technique and full, singing tone. Her violin is a J. B. Guadagnini dated 1739.

TESSIE THOMAS, b. Neath, Wales, 1899. She began to study the violin at a very early age, and at the age of 6 she appeared at local concerts; at the age of 12 she was sent to Hubay on the advice of eminent musicians, and remained his pupil at the Budapest Conservatoire for five years. Returned to London in 1917, she made her debut with the London Symphony Orchestra, playing the Mendelssohn and Elgar concertos, Sir Edward Elgar himself conducting the orchestra. She was greatly praised by the press as "a player of very rare quality" whose reading of the Elgar concerto was "full of individuality and poetic instinct." At her second concert she played the concertos by Tschaikovsky and Brahms with equal success. In the following season she played in the provinces with the Hallé orchestra.

MARGERY BENTWICH, b. London, 189?. Began to learn the piano when quite young, but Wilhelmj induced her to change for the violin, and after six months' lessons from him she appeared in the concert room, and during the five years she studied under him she played frequently at the students' concerts at the Hampstead Conservatoire. She then had some lessons from Sauret until he went to America in 1903, after which she became one of the few pupils of Fritz Kreisler, who advised her to beware of over-practising, and to devote some time to literature and subjects which develop the intellectual and æsthetical faculties. When Kreisler also went to America, she resumed her studies under von Auer in London, and followed him to Germany, where she made a successful appearance at the fashionable seaside place of Norderney, when von Auer conducted the orchestra and even lent her his own violin. After her return to London she gave two successful concerts at the Bechstein Hall.

MARY LAW, b. London (?), 189?; d. there, Apr. 1919. She began to play the violin at the age of 6 and studied under Johannes Wolff from the age of 8 till she was 13; she then went to Sauret, and at the end of 1903 went with him and his family to Chicago, where she won the 1st prize, a diamond medal, at the Conservatoire, twice in two successive years, and returned to London two years later. She then resumed her studies under A. Rivarde, and finally for some time under Mossel. While studying under Rivarde she played with

318

great success at a Patrons' Fund Concert, afterwards she made her debut with a concert at the Bechstein Hall, and in 1914–15 she gave a sonata recital with the pianist Norman Wilks. On a previous occasion the manager of the Tivoli who heard her play at a concert engaged her for a trial week at that (then) music-hall; it resulted in a five years' contract for the Tivoli, the Oxford and the Pavilion, which did not debar her from extra concert work. During that time she proved that good music was fully appreciated by the music-hall public by playing to them the works of Bach, Beethoven, Mozart, Brahms, etc. Unfortunately the career of this talented and promising young artist was cut short by pneumonia supervening on an attack of influenza.

KATE CHAPLIN, b. London, 18... At the age of 9 she began to study the violin at the instigation of her elder sister NELLIE, the pianist and harpsichord player. Kate was for some years a pupil of Pollitzer and then she became a private pupil of Ysaÿe at Brussels, who was very encouraging to her. At the end of her studies she played successfully in many concerts, and when the youngest sister Mabel returned from her studies of the violoncello at the Brussels Conservatoire, they formed the Chaplin Trio, which became favourably known in the widest circles. Meanwhile Miss Nellie had trained a troup of girls for the performance of ancient dances, which proved immensely successful. Miss Nellie played the harpsichord to these and the writer persuaded Miss Kate to study the viol d'amour under George Saint George, while he taught Miss Mabel the viol da gamba. Since then they gave a number of successful concerts of ancient music and also supplied the music for the revival of the "Beggar's Opera" and of "Polly." They gave a series of delightful concerts for children at Steinway (now Grotrian) Hall, and played on various occasions at the South Place Popular Sunday Concerts, where they made their first appearance in 1888.

MARIE DU CHASTAIN, b. London, 18... Of French parents who settled in Brussels, where she received her first violin lessons from local teachers and afterwards became a pupil of Ysaÿe. At the age of 18 she made her debut at the Gürzenich concert at Cologne under Steinbach, when she met with a very favourable reception; after that she toured in France,

Belgium and Germany; she has also given many recitals with her brother Jean, a talented pianist. She makes a special study of the works by Bach.

MARIAN JAY, b. London, 18... She came from a violinists' family as both her grandfather, Dr. J. G. H. Jay, and her father, John Jay, were good English violinists. She was a pupil of E. Sauret at the Royal Academy of Music, London, where she gained the Sauret prize and had the degree of Associate bestowed upon her. She appeared on several occasions at the Queen's Hall Promenade Concerts, and toured in the provinces, meeting everywhere with great success. In 1907 she visited India in the company of some eminent artists, and on her return she gave a concert at the Bechstein Hall, where she played, for the first time in England, Busoni's violin concerto. Since then she has appeared successfully at many concerts and given recitals in London and all parts of Great Britain.

MARGARET FAIRLESS, b. Newcastle-on-Tyne, 18... Pupil of Ševčik, she gained a scholarship at the Meister Schule of the Royal Academy of Music, Vienna, also at the Guildhall School of Music, London, where she also gained the Silver and the Gold Medal, and was made an Hon. Fellow G.S.M. She also gained the Silver Medal of the Worshipful Company of Musicians. She made her first public debut in Vienna at the age of 13, and her first appearance in London at the age of 15, at the Albert Hall Sunday Concerts, conducted by Sir Landon Ronald. Since then she has played at many of the principal London and provincial concerts, and also toured in South and East Africa.

DOROTHY BRIDSON, b. 18..; d. London, Dec. 31, 1917. Younger daughter of John Bridson, a well-known baritone. She studied the violin first at the Cologne Conservatoire, where she carried off conspicuous honours and finished her studies under Ševčik at Prague, where she made her debut with the Bohemian Philharmonic Orchestra in Apr., 1903, with Saint-Saëns' B minor Concerto. Afterwards she played frequently at concerts at Prague and in Vienna with such success that she was looked upon as one of the coming violinists. She made her debut at the old St. James's Hall, London, in 1903, where she made a deep impression, and

GIUSEPPE, COUNT CONTIN DE CASTEL SZEPRIO
From an original photograph.

HENRY HOLMES

JOHN TIPLADY CARRODUS

FRANZ PECHATSCHEK
By kindness of Professor O. E. Deutsch.

from that time to her untimely death she was a favourite with concert audiences both on account of her excellent technique and artistic rendering as well as her personal charm and sympathetic personality.

JESSIE GRIMSON, b. London. A scholarship student under Gompertz and Holmes at the R.C.M. and afterwards studied with Wilhelmj. She belonged to a family, eight of whom performed the Mendelssohn Octet at the Queen's Hall, Jan. 21, 1896. Jessie made her debut at the Crystal Palace under Sir Aug. Manns. She founded the Grimson Quartet which played in London and toured successfully in the Provinces and on the Continent. She is also a successful teacher.

FERDINAND WEIST-HILL, b. London, 18... Studied the violin from the age of 7 under his father, the late Principal of the Guildhall School of Music. After a few years he was sent to the Brussels Conservatoire as a pupil of Ysaÿe, in whose house he lived. After three years he carried off the Grand Prix at the Conservatoire and returned to England, where he made his debut at a concert of the Westminster Orchestral Society. His first engagement was in the Monte Carlo Opera and Symphony Orchestra. Early in this century he played the Mendelssohn and Beethoven concertos at the Queen's Hall Promenade Concerts under Sir Henry Wood with great success. After playing for some time in Gottlieb's String Band, which was engaged by the Court, he toured with Sir Thomas Beecham's Russian Ballet orchestra on the Continent; since then he has been engaged in hotel work and is now musical director at Claridge's. He possesses a remarkable technique as well as sound musicianship.

WILLIAM PRIMROSE, b. Glasgow. He began to study the violin before he was 5 years old under his father, John Primrose, and then became a pupil of Camillo Ritter. At the age of 12 he made a successful appearance at the Musicians' Union, playing the first movement of the Mendelssohn concerto. When he was 15 Sir Landon Ronald offered him a scholarship at the Guildhall School of Music, where he became a pupil of Max Mossel, and gained the Basil Althaus memorial, the Gold Medal, an ensemble prize and the Silver Medal of the Worshipful Company of Musicians. In 1922 he appeared twice at Glasgow with the Scottish orchestra and afterwards at Eastbourne and other towns. On Nov. 28, 1922, he played the 1st and 2nd movement of the Elgar concerto at an Elgar students' concert of the Guildhall School, at the Queen's Hall, receiving flattering notices in the press. In June, 1923, he played the whole of that concerto with the London Symphony Orchestra at the Queen's Hall. He has since appeared with signal success at many London and provincial concerts, and in 1930 he gave a week's "Foundations of Music" recitals for the B.B.C., when he played the whole of the Bach solo sonatas, a remarkably fine rendering, which marked him as a true artist, for they form a severer test than any concerto. He has composed a number of effective solo pieces for the violin.

ALBERT SANDLER, b. London, 1906. A pupil of Hans Wessely and Kalman Ronay. He commenced his career by playing at a small cinema, thence he went first to Lyons' Corner House, then to the Trocadero as director and solo violinist, and thence as musical director and solo violinist at the Grand Hotel, Eastbourne, his performances being broadcast by the B.B.C. In Apr., 1928, he became musical director at the Park Lane Hotel. At the beginning of 1929 he formed a trio with his pianist, E. ffoulkes, and his violoncellist, F. Léonard, and visited the provinces with signal success. He has an excellent technique, a strong and full tone, intelligence and temperament.

FRANK THISTLETON. Pupil of Wilhelmj and Arbos. Has played successfully in London; has a considerable reputation as a teacher of the violin, and has written "The Art of Violin Playing," "Modern Violin Technique," etc.

ORREA PERNEL. Since her London debut, 1928, has played at many important concerts, including the Delius concerto at Queen's Hall, Aug., 1930. Occupies a high place among women violinists.

CHAPTER 58

# *Hungary*

THE Hungarians are naturally a very musical people, but their musical talent showed itself chiefly in their folk music. At the end of the 18th century we encounter Böhm as the first Hungarian violinist, though evidently of German origin, who devoted himself to more serious studies, and the foundation of a Landesmusik Akademie (State Academy of Music) and a National Conservatoire in Pesth and Ofen soon attracted national talent and produced a number of eminent violinists, one of the foremost being Jenö Hubay.

MÁRK RÓZSAVÖLGYI, b. in Hungary, 1790; d. 1848. Hungarian national fiddler and composer; for a short period concertmeister at the old National Theatre, Budapest. Generally he wandered throughout his native country delighting the people by playing unaccompanied his original fantasias, czárdás, etc. His son was the founder of the famous music publishing house at Budapest which bears his name.

JOSEPH BÖHM, b. Pesth, Mar. 4, 1795; d. Vienna, Mar. 28, 1876. Received his first instruction in violin-playing from his father and afterwards became a pupil of Rode, whom he met in Poland on his return from Russia ca. 1808. In 1815 he evoked great enthusiasm in Vienna when he played between the acts at the Burg theatre. He then toured in Italy with the pianist, P. Pixis. On his return to Vienna in 1819 he appeared frequently as soloist and instituted regular quartet soirées. In the same year he was also appointed violin professor at the Vienna Conservatoire, and in 1821 he became a member of the Imperial Chapel. About this time he took over from Schuppanzigh the quartet matinées (Quartett Unterhaltungen) which took place at the Erste Kaffeehaus

323

(The First Coffeehouse) in the Prater at eight o'clock in the morning. During 1823–5 he toured as a virtuoso in Germany and France. From 1827 he retired more and more from the concert platform and devoted himself almost entirely to teaching. At Schubert's one and only concert on Mar. 26, 1828, however, Böhm, with Holz, Weiss and Linke, played the first movement of the D minor quartet, and with K. M. von Bocklet and Linke the great E flat major trio. He resigned from his position at the Conservatoire in 1848, but remained in the Imperial Chapel until 1868. Wasielewski reproduces an appreciation of his playing from the *Wiener Musik Zeitung* of 1820, in which, after giving the fullest praises to his technique, tone and style, it says that the use of more light and shade would be advisable. If one knows that paper, however, one will not attach too much importance to its criticism. If a tree is best known by its fruit it will suffice to enumerate some of his pupils, viz. Joachim, Ernst, Rémenyi, Singer, Grün, Hellmesberger, sen., Rappoldi, L. Straus, J. Dont, etc. He was a great teacher and therein lies his chief claim to remembrance. P. Stefan ("Franz Schubert," p. 57) says that Böhm was the "first violinist who played his solos by heart" (except Paganini, *see* p. 347). A few compositions for violin which he published are of no account.

SIGISMUND OTTO, BARON VON PRAUN, b. Tyrnau, Hungary, June 1, 1811; d. Cracow, Jan. 5, 1830. Was a musical prodigy. In May, 1815, when barely 3 years old, he played in a trio of Pleyel, but at the performance at the Burgtheatre in Vienna he became frightened at the large audience and cried while playing, in the next year however he led in a quartet by Rode and astounded the audience by his technique and the comparatively powerful tone. He then became a pupil of Mayseder, and three years later he started touring all over Europe, but did not quite fulfil the promise of his early childhood. At the end of 1829 he contracted pneumonia, which his constitution, weakened by overwork from childhood, was unable to withstand, and died in his nineteenth year.

AUGUST BIRNBACH, b. Pesth, Nov. 3, 1817. Grandson of the violinist Karl Joseph Birnbach, and son of the violoncellist Heinr. Aug. Birnbach, with whom he went to Berlin in 1824, where he studied the violin under K. W. Henning, after he had made his debut at a concert of the brothers Bliesener. In 1839 he entered the Royal Chapel as violinist and was pensioned in 1868. He composed chamber music and a sextet of his was publicly performed.

BÉLA KÉLER (ALBERT VON KÉLER), b. Bartfeld, Hungary, Feb. 13, 1820; d. Wiesbaden, Nov. 30, 1882. He began to play the violin at an early age, and although originally intended for the law, then for agriculture, he resolved to become a musician. In 1845 he went to Vienna and studied composition under Schlesinger and Sechter, while at the same time playing the violin in the orchestra of the Theatre on the Wien. In 1854 he became Gungl's successor as conductor of Sommer's band in Berlin, where he became very popular as solo violinist, conductor and composer of dances, marches, etc. Towards the end of 1855 he returned to Vienna to take over the band of Aug. Lanner, who had just died, but on Aug. 1, 1856, he became military bandmaster there, and in 1863 went to Wiesbaden in a similar capacity, where, in 1867, he became conductor of the Kur-orchestra, resigning in 1873 on account of ill-health. His violin concertos, fantasias, etc., in spite of their brilliant violinistic qualities, are mostly forgotten, while some of his overtures and dances (csardas, etc.) are still favourites.

MISKA HAUSER, b. Pressburg, 1822; d. Vienna, Dec. 8, 1887. A pupil of K. Kreutzer, Mayseder, Böhm (for a shorter period) and Sechter (for composition) in Vienna. From 1840 he toured practically all over the world, meeting everywhere with unbounded enthusiasm on account of his brilliant technique, which he knew how to amplify by effects cleverly conceived to meet the taste of his respective audience, which never failed to tell. His intonation was absolutely flawless, and his playing was full of feeling. He made his last public appearance at Cologne in 1874. He wrote a considerable number of solo pieces, mostly of the virtuoso and drawing-room type. The best were his songs without words, many of which were deservedly popular, especially his charming little cradle song which even the severe Joachim disdained not to play as an encore, to the writer's personal recollection.

KARL HUBAY (real name HUBER), b. Varjas, Hungary, July 1, 1828; d. Budapest, Dec. 20, 1885. A professor of violin at the Pesth Conservatoire and conductor at the National theatre there. He composed 3 operas which were performed between 1858 and 1875. His son, Jenö (q.v.), was the more famous.

EDMUND SINGER, b. Totis, Hungary, Oct. 14, 1830; d. Stuttgart, Jan. 23, 1912. His parents moved to Budapest where, at the age of 6, Edmund began to study the violin under Professor Ellinger, and on Apr. 10, 1840, he made his public debut with the first concerto by de Bériot. He then entered the Pesth Conservatoire, where he became a pupil of Professor Ridley Kohne, a pupil of Böhm, with whom he toured in 1842 in Hungary and Transylvania with such success that both the Conservatoires of Hermannstadt and Klausenburg made him an honorary member. Next he went to Vienna, where he studied under Böhm, the master of Joachim, Hauser, Ernst and other great violinists, at the same time studying composition under Preyer, the organist of St. Stephen's Cathedral. A year later he left the Conservatoire as a finished artist, being able to play the caprices by Paganini with technical perfection. After a highly successful concert at Budapest he went to Paris, where he benefited (in 1844) greatly by his personal and friendly intercourse with many eminent artists. In 1846 he returned to Budapest as leader of the orchestra and solo violinist at the German theatre, where in 1847 he became also conductor. In 1851 he started on a prolonged tour through Europe, going first to Dresden, where Lipinski introduced him at the Court theatre. In Weimar he appeared under the patronage of Liszt, and in Leipzig on Dec. 18, 1851, where he played Lipinski's popular "Military Concerto" at the Gewandhaus with such success that Rietz, who conducted—full of enthusiasm—embraced the young artist amid the applause of the audience. In 1853 he succeeded Laub, through Liszt's influence, as Court concertmeister at Weimar. He married there in 1859, and remained until 1861 when, at Meyerbeer's recommendation, he went to Stuttgart as Court concertmeister and teacher at the Conservatoire, and a little later the King bestowed upon him the title of Professor. In 1878 he founded, in conjunction with Seifriz, the Stuttgart Tonal Artists' Society. By this and his very successful chamber music concerts he did a great deal for the advancement of music in Stuttgart. He continued to make frequent tours,

chiefly in Germany. He took part in the first performance of
Liszt's Graner mass at Gran, played at the laying of the
foundation-stone of Wagner's opera house at Bayreuth, and
various festivals, etc. He also gave concerts together with
Liszt, Bülow, Cossmann, Grützmacher and other eminent
artists. He resigned from the Royal chapel in 1903, but
remained at Stuttgart. He wrote numerous compositions for
the violin, including concertos, solos, duets, etc., also a complete tutor in conjunction with Seifritz and valuable eds. of
works by older masters, including two of the still sadly
neglected solo sonatas by F. W. Rust. As a teacher he occupied a high rank. His technique was perfect, his tone full
and of noble quality, his playing full of life and feeling without
sickly sentimentality. He was the fortunate possessor of one
of the finest Maggini violins, which he had acquired from his
former teacher Ridley Kohne, the tone of which was considered
equal to that of the best Strads.

EDUARD REMÉNYI (real name HOFFMANN), b. Heves, Hungary,
1830; d. San Francisco, May 15, 1898. He was of a German
family but Magyarized his name during the Hungarian Revolution. He studied the violin at the Vienna Conservatoire,
1842–5; at the outbreak of the Hungarian Revolution he
joined the ranks of the revolutionaries and became the adjutant
of Görgey. On the submission of Hungary he went to
America, where he renewed his studies of the violin and toured
most successfully in the States as a virtuoso from 1849 to 1852,
when he returned to Europe and lived with Liszt at Weimar.
He toured, 1852–3, in Germany with Brahms as a pianist.
This was one of the earliest opportunities which Brahms had
to become known in wider circles. In 1854 Reményi became
solo violinist to Queen Victoria of England. Later on he
toured again, but in 1857 he returned to England and played
during the season at a concert of the Philharmonic Society.
In 1860 he was permitted to return to his native country and
became concertmeister at Budapest and afterwards solo
violinist in the Court chapel in Vienna. For some time he
lived in retirement on his estate in Hungary; but in 1865 he
paid his first visit to Paris, which he took by storm. In 1877
he revisited London, where he repeated his success and played
a "Huguenot Fantasia" at Mapleson's benefit concert at the
Crystal Palace. In 1878 he played at the Popular Concerts

when passing through London on his journey to America, where he remained for some years. In 1888–90 he toured again, visiting also Cape Colony. His last visit to London was in 1891, again on his way to America. On that occasion he appeared at the house of the late Colonel North at Eltham, and at the old Lyric Club. Soon afterwards he went to America where he remained. He had a brilliant, faultless technique and a full and luscious tone; his playing was full of poetical feeling but somewhat erratic. His compositions are of a superficial type but his Hungarian melodies became very popular.

ADOLF POLLITZER, b. Budapest, July 23, 1832; d. London, Nov. 14, 1900. Pupil of Böhm (violin) and Preyer (composition) at the Vienna Conservatoire, which he left in 1846 after gaining the 1st prize. He went on tour for some time and then renewed his studies under Alard in Paris. In 1851 he became leader at Her Majesty's Theatre, London, afterwards at the New Philharmonic Society and teacher at the London Academy of Music. He composed 10 caprices and some pieces for violin which were pub.; a violin concerto, and some concert pieces remained in MS.

KARL GRAFF, b. Alsó Eor, Hungary, May 20, 1833. On Liszt's advice he studied the violin at the Vienna Conservatoire, where he obtained, after three years, his master's diploma and became solo violinist at the Theatre on the Wien, continuing his study under Böhm (violin) and Sechter (composition). Afterwards he toured for a longer period in Hungary; meeting F. Servais at Jassy, they joined forces and continued their tour together through Hungary and part of Turkey. After his return he went to Paris where, in order further to perfect himself, he studied for some time under Vieuxtemps, whom he then accompanied as 2nd violin during a tour extending over two years. He appeared as soloist in London and Paris and then continued his tour alone as far as Cassel, where Spohr engaged him as 1st solo violinist in 1858. Partly from reasons of health he went to Marseilles in 1863 as 1st violinist at the theatre and afterwards as teacher. In 1864 he instituted chamber-music soirées there with Turner and A. Tolbecque. In 1870 he settled at Mentone. He composed a concert piece and fantasias for violin and pianoforte; string quartets, orchestral and choral (church) works, and pieces for various instruments.

LUDWIG STRAUS, b. Pressburg, Mar. 28, 1835; d. Cambridge, Oct. 23, 1899. The son of a school teacher. He began to play the violin at a very early age, and while he was still a pupil at the Academic Grammar School in Vienna, he studied at the same time at the Conservatoire, 1842–4, under Hellmesberger, and then under Böhm until 1848, and composition under Preyer and Nottebohm. When through the Revolution the Conservatoire existed for some time only in name, Böhm continued to teach Straus as a private pupil, and in 1850 he made his debut as a soloist with such success that he felt encouraged to give in 1853 a series of quartet evenings at the hotel Zum römischen Kaiser where, before him, Schuppanzigh gave his quartet concerts and which for some time was the meeting-place of Schubert and his famous circle of friends. In 1855 he started on his first prolonged tour through Southern Austria and Upper Italy, first with Anton Door, then with Arabella Goddard as pianists. In Vienna he came into contact with nearly all the great violinists of his time, his friendship with Mayseder proving particularly fruitful for his studies. He always praised that master's delicacy of style and humour in the playing of Haydn quartets, his pellucid tone and lightness of the bow. Straus took part in the performance of Mayseder's quartet at the house of Baron Heintl during 1856 and 1857. In 1858 he made the acquaintance of Piatti in Vienna and they toured together in Germany, Belgium and Holland and Sweden. From Aug., 1859, to 1862, he was concertmeister of the Museums concerts and at the theatre. In the latter year he relinquished his position at the theatre but retained that at the Museums concerts until 1864, when he went to London, where he played at the Popular Concerts and the Musical Union. He returned again in 1865, when he was appointed leader at the Philharmonic Society and settled 1888 at Manchester, where he led the Hallé orchestra. He was for many years viola player in the Popular Concerts quartet, and violin teacher at the London Academy of Music. In 1894 he retired from all public engagements. He had a faultless technique, perfect intonation, and above all he was an artist of great intelligence

329

and temperament, whose amiable personality made him beloved by all with whom he came into closer contact.

JACOB M. GRÜN, b. Budapest, Mar. 13, 1837; d. Baden, near Vienna, Oct. 1, 1916. Studied the violin successively under Ellinger at Pesth and Böhm in Vienna. From 1858 to 1861 he was in the Weimar Court chapel and 1861 to 1865 in the Royal chapel at Hanover. After that he toured in Germany, England, Holland, and Hungary until 1868, when he became concertmeister at the Imperial Opera in Vienna, teaching in his free time. In 1877 he became also professor of the highest violin class at the Vienna Conservatoire, where he became very popular as an eminent teacher, as well as on account of his refined and amiable personality. His kindheartedness, especially towards the younger pupils, was almost proverbial. He was also violin examiner for the Teachers' Training Institute in Vienna. After a long and fruitful activity he retired to Baden in 1909.

LEOPOLD VON AUER, b. Veszprém, Hungary, May 28, 1845; d. Dresden, July 16, 1930. He received his first instruction on the violin by Ridley Kohne at the Conservatoire at Pesth, continuing his studies under J. Dont at the Vienna Conservatoire 1857 and 1858, and finally under J. Joachim at Hanover. In 1863 he became concertmeister at Düsseldorf, where he had a trio with Mme Schumann and J. de Swert, and 1866 he went to Hamburg as concertmeister. In 1886 he joined the famous Müller quartet as leader and at the end of that year he received a call to St. Petersburg as solo violinist of the Imperial Chapel and professor at the Conservatoire. During 1887–92 he was conductor of the Imperial Music Society, where he brought out Berlioz's Requiem and Schumann's Manfred for the first time in St. Petersburg. There he also founded the St. Petersburg quartet, with S. Korgneff, E. Krüger and A. Werzbilovicz, which was one of the most perfect ensembles of its time. In 1894 the Tsar raised him to the rank of nobility and appointed him a councillor of State in 1903. In 1911 he lived near Dresden but returned to St. Petersburg in 1914. In 1917 the unsettled conditions caused by the war drove him to Oslö, and in Feb., 1918, he went to New York, where he founded an academy for violin playing. He wrote "Violin Playing as I Teach It" (1921); "My Long

330

Life in Music" (1923); "Violin Master Works and their Interpretation" (Boston, 1925). He has been for many years one of the greatest teachers of the violin, counting among his pupils a large number of prominent virtuosos—Elman, Zimbalist, Kathleen Parlow, May Harrison, etc., and Menuhin, the latest prodigy (ii, 437). He combined all the qualities of a virtuoso of the first rank with those of a thoughtful and soulful artist.

CHARLOTTE DEKNER, b. Nagi Bittse, Hungary, 1846; d. Luyos, Hungary, 1887. Studied the violin at first under her father at Luyos, to where the family had removed. Showing extraordinary talent, she was placed under Jaborsky, director of the orchestra at Temesvar. Eight months later, in 1856, she appeared with great success at the Temesvar Theatre. In 1860 she became a pupil of Hellmesberger, who taught her gratuitously. Illness and material losses compelled her father to recall her after only one year, but some time after she went to Concertmeister Ridley-Kohne at Pesth, under whom she became a finished artist. Before she was 18 she appeared at the National theatre there, where she received an enthusiastic ovation. After that she started with her father on a tour of constant successes through the whole of the Austrian Empire, Prussia, Saxony, Italy, Sweden, Holland, and Denmark, remaining over a year at Leipzig, where she studied the works of the classical masters under Ferd. David. Afterwards she went to England and appeared with great success in London and the provinces. Thence she returned home. In 1872 she went on tour in Spain and France and finally she settled as teacher at Marseilles. In 1887 she went to visit her parents at Luyos and died there at the early age of a little over 40. She combined with a brilliant technique a soulful tone of almost masculine power.

VICTOR VON HERZFELD, b. Pressburg, Oct. 8, 1856; d. Budapest, Feb. 20, 1920. At first a law student in Vienna, where at the same time he studied violin and composition, gaining prizes for both in 1880. In 1884 he gained the Beethoven prize of the Society of the Friends of Music and then continued his theoretical studies under Ed. Grell in Berlin. In 1886 he returned to Budapest as professor of musical theory at the National Academy and became 2nd violinist in the Hubay-

Popper quartet. He composed some orchestral and chamber music works which are favourably spoken of.

JENÖ HUBAY (EUGEN HUBER), b. Budapest, Sept. 14, 1858; d. Lodz, late in 1925. Studied the violin for five years under his father Karl at the National Conservatoire at Budapest and at 11 he played a Viotti concerto in public. During 1871–5 he studied under Joachim at the Berlin High School for Music, and in 1876 he toured with immense success in Germany. Liszt, who took a great interest in him, gave him letters of recommendation for Paris, where he played at a Pasdeloup concert and won the admiration and friendship of Vieuxtemps. At the beginning of 1881 Vieuxtemps asked him to come to Algiers and on his arrival Hubay found the concertos Nos. 6 and 7 waiting for him to arrange the orchestral scores, which he did, and after studying them under the composer he played No. 6 at the last soirée given before Vieuxtemps' death. No. 7, which Hubay considers a very fine work, is dedicated to him. After the master's death Hubay remained at the request of the family for three weeks longer in Algiers to put in order Vieuxtemps' last works. Hubay was appointed, on the recommendation of Gevaert, as his successor at the Brussels Conservatoire, in 1882, without having to pass through the customary year of trial. In 1886 he succeeded his father as first professor for violin to the National Academy at Budapest and founded the famous quartet, with Popper as violoncellist. Until 1898 he continued his occasional concert tours, but from that time he retired more and more from the virtuoso career and devoted himself to teaching, composing and the activities of his quartet. He had a highly developed technique, a beautiful tone and fine artistic feeling. In 1894 he married the Countess Rosa Cebrian. He composed 4 violin concertos and a large number of violin pieces of which many are still great favourites, also 7 operas, a symphony, etc., and songs.

TIVADAR NACHEZ (real name THEODOR NASCHITZ), b. Budapest, May 1, 1859; d. 1932. He showed talent for the violin at a very early age, but being very delicate his parents hesitated to allow him to choose music as a profession. While at the Grammar School he studied the violin under Sabatil, a pupil of Mildner. He became, however, more and more determined in his object and secretly obtained certificates with regard to his talent from Liszt and Rob. Volkmann. With these he obtained a state scholarship which secured him the consent of his parents, and he went to Berlin to study under Joachim, but his leaning towards the virtuoso element induced him, three years later, to place himself under Léonard in Paris. He studied there for several years, after which he settled in London. From there he undertook successful tours, visiting practically all European countries, including Russia. He composed a violin concerto, op. 30, and a number of solo pieces of the drawing-room kind, one of the best known being Danse Tzigane, a virtuoso piece; he also ed. two violin concertos by Vivaldi (Augener, 1913).

JOSEF BLOCH, b. Budapest, Jan. 5, 1862; d. there, May 6, 1922. A pupil there of Al. Gobby, K. Huber and Rob. Volkmann, and at the Paris Conservatoire of Ch. Dancla. For six years he was 2nd violin in the Hubay-Popper quartet; 1889 violin teacher at the Hungarian National Academy of Music; 1890–1900 teacher at the National Conservatoire, Budapest; from 1908 director of a violin teachers' class at the Royal Hungarian Academy of Music. Composed concerto op. 64, solo pieces, studies and a tutor for violin, a string quartet and a number of orchestral works.

ARNOLD JOSEF ROSÉ, b. Jassy, Oct. 24, 1863. A pupil of Carl Heissler at the Vienna Conservatoire where, during three years' study, 1873–6, he carried off three prizes, the Silver Medal of the Society of the Friends of Music, and the Artists' Diploma (Künstlerische Reife). In the spring of 1881 he played the Goldmark concerto at a Vienna Philharmonic Concert with such success that although only in his eighteenth year he was appointed 1st solo violinist and concertmeister at the Imperial Opera. Ed. Hanslick, in his notice of the concert in the *Neue freie Presse* (reproduced in Wasielewski's "Die Violine," etc., p. 480), says that he combined the musicianship of a ripe artist with a faultless technique and intonation, and that he belonged already to the best virtuosos of his instrument. In 1888 he toured with great success in his native Rumania and took part also as concertmeister in the Bayreuth festivals from this time onward. In 1889 he toured in Germany, and until 1924 he was professor at the Vienna State Academy. He formed a quartet with E. P. Fischer, A. Ruzitska and F. Buxbaum (the latter replaced in 1922 by J. Walter), which by its perfect ensemble, delicacy and beauty of tone, and above all the high artistic standard of its rendering of both classical and modern works, has acquired fame both in and beyond Europe.   Rosé has edited a number of classical violin compositions.

OTTOKAR NOVÁČEK, b. Ungarisch (Hungarian), Weisskirchen, May 13, 1866; d. New York, Feb. 3, 1900.   A violin pupil of Dont at the Vienna Conservatoire and of Schradieck and Brodsky at the Leipzig Conservatoire.   In 1889 he gained the Mendelssohn prize and was a member of the Brodsky quartet until 1891, when he became a member of the Boston, Mass., Symphony Orchestra.   In 1892 he joined the Damrosch orchestra as principal viola player; afterwards he rejoined the Brodsky quartet, but had to retire in 1899 from all activities on account of failing health.   He was also a composer of rare promise who wrote 3 string quartets, a Perpetuum Mobile for violin and orchestra, Bulgarian dances for pianoforte and violin, violin pieces, a pianoforte concerto, and pianoforte pieces.   Brodsky, who had a great affection for him, often played one or other of his delightful quartets, or his Perpetuum Mobile, in public, with great success.

ALEXANDER SEBALD, b. Budapest, Apr. 29, 1869.   Pupil of Saphir at the Conservatoire there, and of C. Thomson at the Brussels Conservatoire.   Until 1903 a member of the Leipzig Gewandhaus orchestra and quartet; toured then as virtuoso in various countries, and opened in 1907 a school for violin-playing in Berlin, where, in 1913, he received the title of Royal Professor; since then he has lived in Paris.   He composed a romance for violin and pianoforte, 2 military marches, and wrote "Violin Technics" in 3 parts.

KÁLMAN RONAY (ROTH), b. Veszprém, July 20, 1869; d. Jan. 4, 1933.   A nephew of Prof. L. v. Auer; studied the violin at an early age under F. Raczek, solo violinist at the Cathedral; from 1881–4 under Grün at the Vienna Conservatoire, where he gained the gold medal; 1884–6 he studied at the Leipzig Conservatoire under Brodsky, and finally, 1886–8, at the Berlin Hochschule under Joachim.   After finishing his studies he toured in Austro-Hungary and in Germany.   In 1892 Sir Augustus Harris heard him there and induced him to come to London as leader at the Covent Garden Opera.   Soon

334

afterwards he toured again on the Continent, where he was decorated by several sovereigns and knighted by Carmen Sylva, Queen of Rumania. On his return to London after his prolonged tour he was for several years teacher of the violin at the Hampstead Conservatoire, and eventually he went in the same capacity (1900–18) to the Guildhall School of Music, being highly esteemed as an excellent teacher.

CARL FLESCH, b. Moson, Hungary, Oct. 9, 1873. Began to study the violin at the age of 6. In 1883 he was sent to a High School (Gymnasium) in Vienna and in 1886 he entered the Conservatoire there as a pupil of J. Grün. His final studies he made at the Paris Conservatoire, first under Sauzay in 1890, but soon after, under Marsick. In 1894 he gained the 1st prize, and commenced touring in 1895. In 1896 he gave three concerts in Berlin which established his reputation not only as an eminent virtuoso but also as a great artist. Next he became teacher of the violin at the Bukarest Conservatoire and leader of the string quartet of the Queen of Rumania. In 1902 he received the title of a chamber virtuoso but left soon after and toured very successfully until he became the successor of Bram Eldering at the Amsterdam Conservatoire in 1903. In 1905 he gave five recitals in Berlin, illustrative of the evolution of violin literature from Corelli to Reger, which awakened a wide interest in violinistic circles, and earned for him the praises of the grand master Joachim. In 1908 he left Amsterdam and settled in Berlin, where, apart from many concert tours, he formed a permanent trio with the pianist Schnabel and the violoncellist J. Gerardy, which acquired a widespread reputation. At the outbreak of the War Hugo Becker took Gerardy's place. He toured frequently, also in England where in 1911–12 he gave a series of very successful orchestral concerts. In 1914 he visited America for the first time. During 1921–2 he gave special courses for violin-playing at the Berlin High School for Music, which he resumed after a lapse of about six years in 1928. In 1921 he received the Government title of Professor. Since 1924 he has been principal of the violin classes of the Curtis Institute, Philadelphia, and since then divides his activities between America and Europe. In 1926 he removed his private residence to Baden-Baden. He is a virtuoso of the highest order, who uses his almost unlimited technical resources in the service of the highest ideals of true art. He published a book of studies (1911) and "The Art of Violin Playing," vol. i (1923), vol. ii (1928). He arranged and ed. a long series of pieces by older masters, and Paganini's 24 caprices, Dont's studies, as well as the concertos by Beethoven, Mendelssohn, Brahms, and Paganini, and, with A. Schnabel, Mozart's violin sonatas. Among his European pupils are Willem de Beer, Jos. Wolfsthal, and Anna Moodie.

PETER LAZAR STOJANOWITS, b. Budapest, Sept. 6, 1877. A pupil there of J. Hubay at the National Conservatoire, and of Jac. Grün (violin), Rob. Fuchs, and R. Heuberger (composition) at the Vienna Conservatoire; 1909 to 1910 teacher at the New Vienna Conservatoire and member of the Ondriček quartet; 1911 inspector of the Budapest Municipal Music Schools. In 1913 he founded a school for advanced violin-playing in Vienna; since 1925 he is director, 1st teacher of violin and composition at the Stankovič Conservatoire, Belgrade. He composed for the violin 2 concertos, a sonata and pieces, also a quintet, quartet and trio all for pianoforte and strings; operas and orchestral works.

LOUIS PECSKAI, b. Budapest, July 20, 1880. Began the study of the violin under Baldini at Fiume at the age of 5 and a year later he gave his first concert. By special dispensation of the Minister of Education he entered the Budapest Conservatoire at the age of 7, where he studied under Popper (the violinist), Hubay and Kössler until 1895, when he went on tour through Hungary, Germany, Austria and Italy, meeting everywhere with great success. He made his debut in London at a concert of Mme Grimaldi on May 19, 1896, and on the 29th of that month he gave his first recital, enthusiastic-ally acclaimed by the audience, and unanimously praised by the Press. After that he was frequently heard in London and the provinces. He eventually settled in London where, in 1912, he succeeded Simonetti as leader of the London trio (*see* Grove). In 1917 he joined the British Army but took up his place in the trio again after demobilization in 1919. Since then he has been for many years a highly esteemed teacher at the Trinity College of Music, London, and for some years also at the Guildhall School of Music. He continues to appear with great success as a soloist, combining the qualities of an excellent and thoughtful musician with a brilliant technique, beauty of tone and faultless intonation.

GEZA VON KRESZ, b. Budapest, June 11, 1882. Studied the violin under Hubay, then under Ševčik at Prague, 1900–2, and finally under Yasÿe. 1908–9 concertmeister in the Vienna (Tonkünstler) orchestra; 1909–15 professor at Bukarest orchestra and leader of the Queen of Rumania's string quartet; 1916 he went to Berlin where, 1917–21, he was first concertmeister in the Philharmonic orchestra, and 1920–3 head of the highest violin class at the Stern Conservatoire. In 1923 he settled at Toronto, Canada, where he is teacher at the Hambourg Conservatoire, leader of the Hart House string quartet founded by him, and soloist at concerts. He married the pianist Norah Drewett.

FERENCZ HEGEDÜS, b. Fünfkirchen, Hungary, 1885. Showed very early talent for the violin and at the age of 8 he studied at the Fünfkirchen Academy of Music. Three years later Count Geza Zizsy brought him to the notice of Archduke Joseph, who procured his admission to the Budapest Conservatoire, although he had not yet reached the stipulated age. There he studied under Gobby and Hubay and carried off the special diploma at the age of 18. He made his debut in London in 1901 with great success and afterwards appeared at the most important Continental towns with equal success, which fortunately only stirred him to renewed studies, at the end of which he has toured all over Europe and America, ever gathering fresh laurels, not only for his brilliant technique, but also for his intelligent and soulful rendering of the classics. He has since paid frequent visits to England. In 1907 some of his friends and admirers presented him with the famous "Gillot Joseph," one of the finest Guarnerius del Jesu known, an excellent reproduction and description of which appeared in *The Strad*, Sept., 1911, see also the sumptuous and most thorough work on the Guarnerius family by A. F. and A. E. Hill.

NÁNDOR ZSOLT, b. Esztergom, Hungary, May 12, 1887. A pupil of Hubay and H. Koessler at the Budapest High School for Music. From 1908 he was for some years second leader in the Queen's Hall orchestra; since 1920 he has been teacher at the Budapest High School. He has composed pieces for violin and pianoforte; a pianoforte quintet; symphony and Toccata for pianoforte.

EMIL TELMÁNYI, b. Arad, Hungary, June 22, 1892. From 1899 a pupil of Moritz Unger there; 1905–11 pupil of Hubay (violin), Koessler and Herzfeld (composition) at the Budapest Royal Academy of Music, where he gained several diplomas. Since then he has been touring as virtuoso in Europe and America; and is, from 1919, also active as conductor. In the latter year he married the daughter of C. Nielsen, the composer, and settled at Copenhagen.

JOSEPH SZIGETI, b. Budapest, Sept. 5, 1892. He began to study the violin from the age of 6 and afterwards became a pupil of Hubay at the Budapest Royal Academy, where he made his first public appearance at the age of 13. This was followed by appearances in Berlin and Dresden. He made his London debut in 1907 at Bechstein (now Wigmore) Hall with such success that he remained in London for nearly seven years, touring also in the provinces with Busoni, Backhaus and Melba. During 1917–24 he was professor at the Geneva Conservatoire, as successor to Marteau. During that time and in the following year he played in all the principal towns of Europe, including Scandinavia and England. In 1925 he played at the Philharmonic Society in London, and in the same year he visited America, where he toured also in the following years. In later years he has frequently appeared in London and in the provinces and on several occasions his performances have been broadcast. Many of the most eminent modern composers have dedicated concertos, rhapsodies and sonatas to him, and although he is an excellent exponent of the classics, he has done a great deal to bring the works of modern composers to the fore wherever he went. Szigeti has not only a perfect command over all the intricacies of modern violin technique, but he possesses likewise all the qualities which ensoul his performance. He has arranged a number of pieces for violin and pianoforte, pub. in the Universal ed., Vienna.

FRANZ VON VECSEY, b. Budapest, Mar. 23, 1893. He received his first instruction on the violin from his father. When he was 2 years old Hubay, who was a friend of the family, recognized his talent and took him under his care, which continued when in the following year he visited the Budapest Conservatoire. In 1903 he was taken to Joachim at Berlin. The latter, who was suspicious of all prodigies, accepted him as a pupil after hearing him play a Bach sonata. On Oct. 17, 1903, he made his first public appearance in Berlin, where he met with an enthusiastic reception which was repeated when in 1904 he played the Beethoven concerto there with the Philharmonic Orchestra, Joachim himself conducting. He made his debut in London at the old St. James's Hall, and has since paid repeated visits to London between his tours in America and on the Continent of Europe.

EUGEN LEHNER (LÉNER), b. Szabadka, Hungary, June 24, 1894. Studied violin and music theory at the Budapest High School; formed with J. L. Smilovitz, A. Roth and E. Hartmann, the well-known string quartet bearing his name.

JULIUS (DUCI) VON KERÉKJARTO, b. Budapest, 1898; pupil of Gust. Szerémi and E. Hubay at the Budapest Conservatoire; cultivated the purely virtuoso side of his art, acquiring an astounding technique. He toured as a virtuoso from early youth and went to America ca. 1922, where he was still in 1928.

ERNA RUBINSTEIN, b. Nagyszeben, Hungary, Mar. 2, 1903. Pupil of Hubay at the Budapest Conservatoire.

ZOLTÁN SZÉKELY, b. Kocs, Dec. 8, 1903. Pupil of J. Hubay and Kodaly (composition) at the National Academy of Music, Budapest, where he gained the Master Diploma; since 1922 he has lived in Holland. Has composed a sonata for violin solos, duo for violin and violoncello, and arranged some dances by Béla Bartok for violin and pianoforte.

MAGDA WEIL, b. Arad, Hungary. Pupil of Ševčik; appeared as virtuoso with great success in Berlin.

ADILA and JELLY VON ARANYI, b. Budapest of a Hungarian father and a French mother. They are great-nieces of Jos. Joachim, who showed very early musical talent. ADILA VON ARANYI, the elder sister, at first studied the pianoforte, which, however, she soon forsook for the violin and became a pupil of Hubay at the Budapest Conservatoire, where she gained the diploma for the most advanced pupils with such distinction that the examiners presented her with a violin. Joachim then

339

undertook the personal supervision of her studies, and she stayed the last few months before his death at his house in Berlin, receiving daily lessons, hearing him play and meeting all the great musicians who visited him. And when Joachim died he bequeathed to her a fine Stradivari violin. At that time JELLY VON ARANYI was still studying the violin under Hubay at the Budapest Conservatoire, where she also displayed remarkable talent. About 1908 the two sisters decided to make duet playing a feature of their artistic work, and in this they met with great success, without however relinquishing solo playing. They have settled permanently in London, where Adila is now married and known as MADAME FACCHIRI. Both are frequently heard in public and greatly appreciated. They are notably fine exponents of J. S. Bach's double concerto.

## CHAPTER 59

# Italy: to 1850

TOWARDS the end of the 18th century the great, sublime old Italian school fell into a state of rapid decline; it had fulfilled its mission and run its course. The immense productive power of the country had exhausted itself. Nearly all the great masters of the violin were dead; Viotti, the last of their number, had left his native country without leaving any impress of his individuality behind. The oppression of the people by despotic princes and a degenerate priesthood, who no longer supported the great and sublime in art, but merely looked to it for sensuous enjoyment, had changed the mentality of the whole people. The traditions of the great masters of the violin soon faded away, a new epoch began which pursued different ideals, substituting pleasing superficiality for true greatness.

At that point, Paganini appeared like a meteor from the sky. He belonged to no school, and he stood too far above the technical standard of violin-playing of his time to become the founder of a school. Although a few benefited by his example and advice, he had only one real pupil, who at least received his higher schooling from him, and this was C. Sivori, who inherited much of his technique, but not his genius. Among those who at least partly enjoyed the advantage of Sivori's teaching was Henry Marteau, who followed, however, more serious lines. Paganini himself became indirectly a teacher, as his works formed, and still form, the most valuable material for the study of the highest technical degree of violin-playing.

More important than Sivori for the advancement of the art of violin-playing in Italy was Antonio Bazzini, through his activity as teacher and director of the Milan Conservatoire. Among those who excelled chiefly as teachers among Italian violinists Pietro Rovelli, Ettore Pinelli, E. Polo and Guido

341

Papini deserve special mention, although the latter was chiefly active in London. Among the outstanding Italian violinists of the 19th century were the sisters Milanollo and Teresina Tua.

NICOLO PAGANINI, b. Genoa, Oct. 27, 1782; d. Nice, May 27, 1840. Antonio Paganini, his father, kept a small shop near the port. He was an avaricious man of a hard and brutal nature, his only redeeming feature being his love for music. He was a skilled mandoline player and gave his younger son Nicolo elementary violin lessons. Discovering the child's aptitude he kept him to his practice from morning till night, which undoubtedly undermined his frail constitution. This might have created a distaste for music in the boy, but the sacred fire was burning within him, and he was determined to gain distinction. In this he was further encouraged by his mother, who told him that in a dream she saw an angel, who told her that her little son would become the greatest violinist in the world. His father placed him under Servetto, a violinist at the theatre, and two years later he received for about six months lessons from Giacomo Costa, capellmeister at the Church of St. Lorenzo, on condition that he should play a new concerto every Sunday at one of the churches, which greatly helped to develop his extraordinary powers of playing at sight. His father still continued his tyrannical oversight, and, as Dubourg says, "the sickly child, incapable of attaining a healthy maturity, was merged into a suffering man." In 1793 he played at a concert given by two eminent singers, Luigi Marchesi and Signora Bertinotti, and chose for his solo, variations on "La Carmagnole" of his own composition, which he repeated at his own benefit concert soon after, when he was assisted by the forenamed singers as a mark of their gratitude. His success was such that the audience was roused to the utmost enthusiasm. After leaving Costa he worked for a time by himself and ca. 1795 his father, at Costa's advice, took him to Parma to study under Alessandro Rolla. The latter, indisposed and still in bed, refused to receive them. In the room where he waited with his father, the boy noticed on the table a violin and a manuscript concerto, which Rolla had just finished; he took the violin and played the concerto right through. Rolla, who heard this, asked who the virtuoso was.

When told that it was the boy he called him to his bedside and said to him: "I can teach you nothing," but advised the father to take him to Paër for lessons in theory and composition. Paër being absent at the time, he studied under Ghiretti, the master of Paër, and devoted himself assiduously not only to harmony and counterpoint but also to a close study of instrumentation. At the beginning of 1797 his father took him on a tour of the principal towns of Lombardy, where his fame spread with every successive appearance, and the father foresaw the realization of his golden dreams. On the return to Genoa Paganini finished the composition of his 24 Caprices, op. 1, which inspired both Schumann and Brahms to very beautiful sets of variations. He then practised for ten or eleven hours a day, to overcome their difficulties, until he collapsed from sheer exhaustion. His moral and general education was utterly neglected, and he chafed under the continued goading of his avaricious father. But the time of his deliverance was at hand. In Nov., 1798, he persuaded his father, with much difficulty, to allow him to visit the festival of St. Martin at Lucca in company of his elder brother. His playing there was received with such enthusiasm that he felt encouraged to extend his tour to Pisa and the neighbouring towns. By threats and imprecations the father obtained a large part of his earnings, but Nicolo refused to return under his iron rule. Having thrown off his fetters, without having obtained that moral foundation which is necessary to restrain unruly passions and desires, he mistook licence for liberty, and welcomed every form of excitement, including to his misfortune that of gambling. Once his gambling debts had compelled him to pawn his violin when he was due to play at a concert at Leghorn; in that dilemma a French merchant, Livron, came to his rescue by lending him his fine Joseph Guarnerius. When after the concert he wanted to return the instrument, Livron presented it to him with the words: "My fingers shall never profane the violin which your fingers have touched; it now belongs to you." On a later occasion he obtained a Stradivari violin from Sigr. Pasini, a painter, an amateur violinist of Parma, who having heard of Paganini's extraordinary powers of sight reading, placed before him a MS. concerto in which difficulties of every description were brought together. He gave him a Stradivari violin and told him that if he could play the concerto without

343

studying it first, the violin would be his,—and it was, but the Guarneri always remained his favourite. At one time when gambling once more had reduced him to dire straits, he was sorely tried to accept an offer of 2,000 francs for it, but as a last resource he resolved to risk his last 30 francs at the gaming tables. At first he lost all but 3 francs, but with these his luck turned and he won 160 francs. This helped him over his momentary difficulties, and saved his violin. It also cured him of gambling; "convinced that a gambler is universally despised, I renounced for ever that fatal passion," to use his own words.

In 1800 Napoleon crossed the Alps, Italy became the scene of wars, and Paganini retired for over three years to the château of a Tuscan lady who was a good amateur guitar player, whereby the former was induced likewise to take up that instrument, on which he soon acquired a high degree of virtuosity, and composed a good deal of music for it. Fétis says he occupied himself there also with the study of agriculture. At last, tired of this time of dalliance, which in after-years gave rise to the prison story, he returned invigorated to Genoa, where he resumed his study of the violin with redoubled energy, and it was during that time that he occupied himself with the Caprices by Locatelli. In 1805 he began touring again, and at an evening festival at a convent church at Lucca his playing aroused the congregation to such a pitch of enthusiasm that the monks had to stop the applause. He was then offered and accepted the position as leader of the Court orchestra and solo violinist to Prince Bacciochi, whose wife was a sister of Napoleon. There he fell in love with a lady of the Court, who returned his affection, and this led him to compose a love scene for the G and A strings only, taking off the first and third strings. He played this piece before the Court, and it so pleased the Princess, who was unaware of its true import, that she suggested, since he could perform such wonders on two strings, it might be possible for him to express his ideas even on only one string. A few weeks later, on the Emperor's birthday (Aug. 15) he played before the Court a sonata for the G string, which he entitled "Napoleon," and which awakened such enthusiasm that a cantata by Cimarosa which followed fell quite flat. The success of that sonata encouraged him to compose several more compositions for the G string, for which he developed a predilection and made it the object of special study.   In 1808 he obtained leave to travel.   He went first to Leghorn, where he gave a concert; but having run a nail into his heel, he came on to the platform limping, which caused laughter in the audience.   As he was starting to play the candles dropped from his desk, which increased the laughter, but when after playing a few bars a string broke the hilarity reached its climax.   This was soon hushed, however, when without stopping he continued to play his solo on three strings, and at the end was greeted with thunders of applause.   The breaking of a string happened to him afterwards not infrequently, and it is said that it was probably not always quite accidental, but a trick to show his extraordinary powers in a sensational way.   The exclusive use of the G string for a whole piece was, however, not Paganini's invention, and although the famous air by Bach was originally not written for the G string only, nor even as a solo, yet of Mich. von Esser (b. 1736) Leopold Mozart tells us that he played on the G string alone with the greatest ease, and Fr. Wm. Rust wrote in 1796 a whole sonata for the E string with the advice to practise it on each of the other strings as well, and this sonata anticipates several of Paganini's boldest devices, but it remained in MS. till after his death and was unknown to him.   In 1809 the Princess Bacciochi became Grand Duchess of Tuscany, the Court moved to Florence, and Paganini became Court capellmeister with the rank of a captain of the Guard, the brilliant uniform of which he was entitled to wear.   When in 1813 he appeared in it at a State function for which ordinary dress had been commanded, he was told to change, but he took this as an insult and refused compliance, which led to his instant dismissal.

Lafont, who had looked upon Paganini as a charlatan, visited Milan in 1813 (Wasielewski says 1812 and Grove 1816) and invited Paganini to play together with him at a concert at La Scala.   Rossini, whose account of it is given by Ferd. Hiller (Künstlerleben, ii, 53), persuaded Paganini to accept.   It resulted in the discomfiture of Lafont.   Paganini's success at Milan was so great that he remained there right into 1814, giving 37 concerts in all.   Later in that year he was ill for several months at Ancona, from an internal malady, which had already attacked him once before at Turin in 1808.   In 1815 he met Antonia Bianchi, a dancer, at Venice, with whom he fell in love, and who bore him a son, Achillo, born at

Palermo in 1826; she was very devoted to Paganini, but her jealous temperament caused them to separate in 1828, their child remaining with the father.

He kept touring the length and breadth of Italy with ever-increasing enthusiasm on the part of the people. In 1828 he visited Germany for the first time, arriving in Vienna on Mar. 16, and on the 29th of that month he gave his first concert at the Redoutensaal. Schubert, who had just met with the, for him, extraordinary good fortune of receiving a small sum of money, went to hear Paganini, and was so filled with enthusiasm, that he took his friend Bauernfeld, the playwright, to the next concert, whose amusing account thereof may be found in Newman Flower's "Franz Schubert," pp. 138–9. Vienna went into ecstasies, everything in the shops and restaurants was "à la Paganini." His cabdriver painted on his vehicle the words "Cabriolet de Paganini," and earned enough money in consequence to become a hotelkeeper (S. Stratton's "Paganini," p. 37). Paganini gave 12 concerts, the last by command of the Emperor, who attended in person, and showed his appreciation of his genius by nominating him an Imperial chamber musician and presenting him with a gold snuff-box set with diamonds. The city of Vienna presented him with the Gold Medal of St. Salvator, and a medal was struck in his honour. From Vienna he went to Prague, accompanied by Bianchi and his little son. There he was afflicted with an abscess in the face which prevented him from playing for several weeks. His first concert was a great success, but his second concert was not very well attended; one of the reasons were the absurd stories about his personality, and he had even to publish a letter from his mother to prove that he was not the son of the devil. At Cassel he gave two concerts which were attended by Spohr, who, while admiring his faultless intonation, wonderful technique and flashes of genius, was repelled by his tricks, and probably by much of what more progressive musicians would have admired. For three years he toured in Germany, and then went to Paris, where he gave his first concert at the Opera on Mar. 9, 1831, met with his usual success and remained till May. On the 21st of that month he was announced to appear at the King's Theatre, London, but the prices of admission were fixed so high that they met with a storm of indignation in the Press. Laporte, his manager, was accused of attempting to rob the public. Meanwhile Paganini fell ill and the concert did not take place till June 3; after all, the sordid money matters had found a satisfactory solution. The result was the same as everywhere else: people were perplexed, for what they heard went beyond anything that seemed possible. Mori declared that if he could not sell his fiddle, he would burn it. Lindley, Cramer, Dragonetti were in ecstasies. He was the first who played everything from memory (except Böhm (q.v.)), a feature which the *Athenæum* hoped to see imitated. It is not generally known that memory-playing, now the rule, originated with Paganini and Böhm. On June 10 he gave his second concerto, where Lablache was again the vocalist and also struck the silver bell in the Rondo of his C minor concerto. The receipts on that occasion amounted to £1,200.

The financial as well as artistic success of his sojourn in London induced him to prolong it as long as possible. On July 4 he played at the King's Theatre a new concerto in E major, which made a great impression on his audience, and was declared the best he had played so far. Eventually, however, he imposed too much on the good nature of the public by the number of his "Final Concerts," with fatal results to their attendance. He also gave two concerts at the London Tavern, in the city. The first was a great success, but when at the second concert he tried to reduce expenses by replacing the orchestra by a pianist, and engaged only an indifferent singer, it proved a failure. In the provinces he met with similar experiences at additional concerts. At charity concerts in London he demanded one-third of the gross receipts, and the consequence was that Lablache and Rubini refused to sing wherever he played. In Aug., 1831, he went to Dublin, where he played at the first Musical Festival, and Stratton ("Paganini," pp. 61 *et seq.*) relates several interesting and amusing incidents, the most typically Irish being, that when he played his famous Rondo from the C minor concerto, an excited voice was heard above the storm of applause, shouting: "Arrah now, Signor Paganini, have a drop of whiskey, darlin', and ring the bell again!" On his return he toured the English provinces with varying success, the high prices and charges of avarice sometimes threatening to result in riots. In Mar., 1832, he paid a short visit to Paris and gave a concert

347

for the poor on Mar. 18. On his way back to London he gave a concert at Boulogne which was again accompanied by untoward incidents, from which, however, he emerged triumphant. In 1833 he was again in London, but was out of favour because he had refused to play for the distressed English actors in Paris, and his concerts were poorly attended. On Dec. 22 he heard Berlioz's Symphonie Fantastique in Paris which fascinated him, and he asked Berlioz to write him a solo for his Stradivari viola, which resulted in the symphony "Harold in Italy," performed for the first time at the Paris Conservatoire on Nov. 23, 1834, Paganini playing the viola part.

In 1834 he came to London once more and gave a successful concert at the Adelphi Theatre on Apr. 7, and a second concert on the following day at the Hanover Square Rooms, which was poorly attended. After this he fell ill and the third concert was postponed. At his last concert he played a viola solo of which the critic of the *Athenæum* said: ". . . his precision and brilliancy upon the former (viola), as displayed in double stop passages, harmonics and arpeggi, of extraordinary difficulty, were most amazing. . . ." He had separated from Bianchi, and fallen in love with a young English girl, who had been singing at some of his concerts, but this romance (told at length by Schilling in his Encyclopædia, and by Stratton, "Paganini," p. 70) came to an early end by the intervention of the father, with whom Paganini had lodged. The latter returned to Paris and after the performance of Berlioz's symphony, in Nov. (*see* above), to Italy. On the 12th of Dec. he played at the Court of the Duchess of Parma and was decorated with the Imperial Order of St. George. About that time he bought the villa Gajona, near Parma, which he made his home, and invested also in other landed property. He intended now to publish his complete works, but the price he demanded prevented the project from materializing. In 1836 French speculators involved him in the foundation of the "Casino Paganini" in Paris, ostensibly for musical purposes but in reality a gambling den. The Government, informed of its real character, refused to license it, and failure was the consequence. This involved him in a lawsuit which dragged on for some time, and eventually ended in condemning him to an indemnity of 50,000 francs or imprisonment, but by that time he was beyond the power of earthly law. Between 1837 and the earlier part of 1839 he paid several visits to Paris, and on Dec. 16, 1838, after a performance of some of Berlioz's works, Paganini led him to the platform and kneeling down kissed his hand. On his way home Berlioz met Armand Bertin, the publisher, and told him of the occurrence, caught a chill and was laid up for some days. On the 18th little Achillo appeared by his bedside with a letter from Paganini, informing him that on presentation thereof at Rothschild's he would receive 20,000 francs in token of the writer's homage. This was a godsend to poor Berlioz; but it has been said that Bertin was the real donor, who asked Paganini to be his agent, enjoining him to observe strictest secrecy.

In 1839 Paganini's health was declining rapidly. On June 21 he still took part, according to Fétis, in a performance of Beethoven's mass in C at one of the Paris churches, but very soon after he went, on the doctor's advice, to Marseilles, where he rallied somewhat, and on one occasion even led a Beethoven quartet. Soon, however, a relapse set in and he went to Genoa, where he was prostrated by a violent nervous attack. Hoping to benefit by the sea air he went by ship to Nice, where he died not long after from a disease of the larynx. On the last night of his life he was perfectly tranquil, took up his violin, and according to those who were listening, his playing during those last hours surpassed all he ever achieved before. As he had not received the last sacraments, not believing his end so near, the Bishop refused his burial in consecrated ground and the body, after being embalmed, was moved from place to place until it finally found its last resting-place in 1845 in the village churchyard adjoining his villa Gajona, near Parma. He left to his son a fortune of two million francs (£80,000), subject to legacies of 110,000 francs for his brothers, and an annuity of 1,200 francs for Antonia Bianchi.

Paganini was a meteor in the firmament of music; apart from a little rudimentary teaching and some hints from Durand he had no master, and he left no school, and only few pupils, including Catterina Calcagno whom, as a little girl, he instructed at Genoa for a few months in 1804 and who died young, Chiaudelli (Ciaudelli), who had lessons from him for a short time, and E. C. Sivori, a great virtuoso, but lacking the divine spark of his master's genius, and therefore quite incapable to convey an idea of Paganini's playing. Yet Paganini completely revolutionized violin-playing, and many of the orthodox rules of his predecessors and contemporaries went by the board. Many technical features, like the use of artificial harmonics, the playing of two independent parts together, alternate pizzicato and bowed notes, etc., had been used before him; but they would not have found their way into the higher technique of all modern violin-playing but for Paganini, as, for instance, the accompaniment of a melody by left-hand pizzicato, the chromatic glides with one finger, and the guitar-like treatment, used by Sarasate with so much effect, must be credited entirely to him. The only musician who had much in common with him was Liszt, who also sprang into existence as a complete virtuoso, and revolutionized pianoforte playing, but he was by far the greater artist. Both had to compromise with the taste of their audiences, and on account of that both were blamed for a certain amount of mere firework display which at least in Paganini's case was in a considerable measure indigenous to his nature. His individuality was so strong that it imprinted itself upon any work by other composers, and although he played sometimes concertos by Viotti and Kreutzer and even works by Mozart and Beethoven, yet they always took the personality of Paganini, who "had to restrain himself not to embellish them with brilliant passages and trills," as C. Guhr tells us in his "Ueber Paganini's Kunst die Violine zu spielen," the best, most authentic and detailed account of the latter's playing. The anecdotes and interesting incidents in Paganini's life, and his meeting, and intercourse, with artists and noted people of his time would fill a book by themselves. There are numerous biographies and biographical sketches in various languages, *see* list in Grove, to which we can add S. S. Stratton, "Nicolo Paganini" (*The Strad* Library). For list of his works *see* Eitner, and Grove. His 24 caprices, and 2 Concertos in E flat and b minor, are the most important.

FERDINANDO GIORGETTI, b. Florence, June 25, 1796; d. there, Mar. 23, 1867. He had to renounce solo playing on account of a nervous complaint, but was highly esteemed as teacher at the Liceo (1839) and as composer; Concerto dramatico, trios for 2 violins and violoncello; 2 quartets, 1 quintet, 2 sextets, all for strings; also church music: full list in Fétis.

GIUSEPPE GHEBART, b. Piedmont, Nov. 20, 1796; d. Milan, Jan. 22, 1870. A pupil of F. de Radicati at Turin, where, 1814, he became a violinist in the Royal chapel. In 1817 he conducted also the concerts of the Philharmonic Academy and in 1839 succeeded Polledro as conductor at the theatre; 1846 he became director-general of the instrumental and chamber music. He declined tempting offers of important posts from Paris and Dresden, and he was the first to introduce German instrumental music in Turin. Composed several violin concertos, duos and studies for string quintets and quartets, overtures, masses, a miserere, etc.

PAOLO CORONINI, b. Vicenza, 1796; d. Trieste, Jan. 14, 1875. He was 1st violinist and conductor at the Opera and the chapel of St. Just at Trieste, and composed a number of pieces and studies for the violin.

CATTERINA CALCAGNO, b. Genoa, 1797. The only girl pupil of Paganini, who in Italy rivalled the fame of the sisters Milanollo (A. Niggli, "Paganini," 289). In the spring of 1814 she appeared at Milan with great success, to the great joy of Paganini, who was giving concerts at the Teatro del Ré about the same time, and who gave her lessons for several months.

STANISLAUS RONZI, b. Florence (?), ca. 1800. The son of an Italian balletmaster and the eldest of a family of four talented musicians; Antonio was a tenor singer and composer; Josephine, a famous operatic singer; Luigi, a pianist and composer. In 1820 Stanislaus accompanied his sister to Paris and afterwards lived at Rome. There he gave successful concerts and became solo violinist at the Valle theatre, where on one or more occasions he played with his brother Luigi a symphony concertante of the latter's composition.

NICOLA DA GIOVANNI, b. Genoa, 1802; d. Parma, May 14, 1856. Was conductor at the Parma theatre there; an excellent violinist.

BERNARDO FERRARA, b. Vercelli, Apr. 7, 1810. Entered the Milan Conservatoire in 1821 to study violin under Rolla, and composition. By 1830 he was 1st violinist at the Carcano theatre, Milan, and in 1835 director of the Ducal chapel at Parma. In 1836 he succeeded Rolla as professor of the violin

351

at the Milan Conservatoire. Failing health caused his retirement into private life in 1861.

ERNESTO CAMILLO SIVORI, b. Genoa, Oct. 25, 1815; d. there, Feb. 18, 1894. At the age of 5 he received his first violin lessons from the guitar teacher of his sisters and showed such remarkable talent that a year later he became a pupil of Costa, who (according to Mendel) was then the representative of the classical Italian school of violin-playing. Paganini, who heard the boy play, then took him under his personal care and he acquired a technique which, apart from his master, was unequalled and combined with a limpid tone of exquisite quality (but *see* Paganini, *ante*). Unfortunately he used his talent chiefly for the mere display of virtuoso acrobatics, although it is said that in private circles he would sometimes lead Haydn, Mozart and Beethoven quartets, not only with great intelligence, but also with refinement and feeling, and there is no doubt that it was the taste of the general public that drove him to specialize in firework displays, just as it did in the case of Liszt and other great virtuosos. Paganini wrote for him 6 sonatas with guitar, viola, and violoncello, in which he himself used to play the guitar, and a concertino, the MSS. of which Sivori preserved as his most precious treasures. In 1827 he visited Paris in company of Paganini, and by his success showed that he had a great future before him. After a brief stay he returned to Genoa to resume his studies. When he had completed these he toured in Germany, Russia, Belgium, Holland and France. In 1843 he played in Paris with such immense success that he was presented with a medal of honour. From Paris he went to England and also toured Scotland and Ireland. In 1846 he went to America and visited all principal towns of the United States, where in several instances the populace turned out to meet him, strewing roses in his path. In Valparaiso he took a boat to Rio de Janeiro, but there he had an attack of yellow fever. When he had recovered he travelled to Montevideo, then on to Buenos Aires, where he met his first teacher, the guitarist Rostono. Everywhere he was fêted like a monarch. He met with many adventures which were sometimes not unconnected with danger; as, for instance, when on his journey over the Isthmus of Panama he had to cross a river in a boat which was rowed by four natives. To try the effect of his

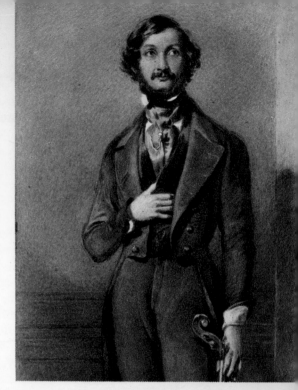

CAMILLO SIVORI

HEINRICH WILHELM ERNST
From an original painting in the possession of Messrs.
W. E. Hill & Sons

JOHANN STRAUSS

CARL HALIR

art on these he took out his violin and began to play. But scarcely had he started when his black audience became terrified. With unearthly howls they threatened to throw him overboard and only by presents could they be pacified. In 1850 he returned to Genoa with a considerable fortune, the greater part of which he lost in bad investments; so that he was obliged to tour again. After revisiting the British Isles he went in 1853 to Switzerland, where, in a carriage accident, he broke his arm, which fortunately healed perfectly, but delayed him for a considerable time. In 1862 he revisited Paris where he met with unabated enthusiasm, and on one occasion played at the same concert (for the benefit of the poor) with Alard, the latter playing the Mendelssohn concerto and Sivori Paganini's b minor concerto. The writer heard him in this and "Le Streghe" at Cologne in the latter part of the 'seventies of last century, and still remembers the wonderful impression his superb technique, faultless intonation and beauty of tone made upon him. He had previously toured in Germany in 1863. He was the first to play the Mendelssohn concerto in England in 1846 and also the first who was allowed by the municipal authorities of Genoa to play on Paganini's "Joseph." He composed 2 concertos, 2 duos concertante for violin and pianoforte, and a number of solos which are entirely of the virtuoso order and possess no greater value.

ANTONIO BAZZINI, b. Brescia, Mar. 11, 1818; d. Milan, Feb. 10, 1897. A pupil of the capellmeister Faustino Camisani, Brescia. At the age of 17 he became capellmeister of the church of St. Filippo, Brescia, for which he wrote masses and vespers, also 6 oratorios, and some overtures for the theatre. In 1836 Paganini advised him to tour as a violin virtuoso. In 1837 he gave successful concerts at Milan, then he went to Venice, Trieste, Vienna and Budapest. During 1841–5 he travelled in Germany, Poland and Denmark, and stayed for four years at Leipzig to study the German masters, especially Bach and Beethoven. He was essentially virtuoso, combining a perfect technique with beauty of tone and faultless intonation. The great admiration which he found everywhere was, however, due to the fact that apart from his virtuosity he possessed higher artistic qualities, although Wasielewski states that his playing was not altogether free from mannerism and over-emotionalism. In 1848 he toured in Spain and settled in Paris in 1852. In 1864 he returned to Brescia and devoted himself entirely to composition, and in 1873 he was appointed professor of musical theory and composition at the Milan Conservatoire, of which he became the director in 1882. His numerous compositions include many solos for the violin, some of which, especially the Ronde des lutins, are still favourites with both artists and amateurs; 6 string quartets and a quintet; important choral and orchestral works including an opera. Although his melody is typically Italian in its grace and suavity, he shows in the treatment thereof, and particularly in his chamber music, that he has studied the German masters to good purpose. His harmony is of German depth and richness, his counterpoint pure and varied, his form perfect and as elegant as it is strict; this shows itself particularly in his string quintet, which is his masterpiece, but also his six string quartets are attractive and may still be heard with pleasure. His opera, "Turandot," was unsuccessful; his symphonic poem, "Francesco da Rimini," and his symphonic cantata, "Senacheribbo," were well received.

COSTA. According to H. Mendel (in his dictionary in an article on Sivori), Costa flourished, ca. 1820. He was a representative of the classical school of Italy, and first violin teacher of Sivori (perhaps related to Sir Michael Costa).

GIUSEPPE ROMAGGI, b. Genoa; d. Dec., 1820, at Lucca. A violin pupil of Filippo Manfredi. In 1773 violinist at the Opera, Lucca; sometimes he disappears from the list but always appears again, as on Oct. 2, 1778. Afterwards he became leader and musical director (*see* Nerici, 211, 301, 341). Among the autographs of the Masseangeli there is a letter by him dated Lucca, May 16, 1791.

LUIGI ARDITI, b. Crescentino, Piedmont, July 16 (according to his autobiography, Riemann: July 22), 1822; d. Hove, Brighton, May 1, 1903. A pupil of Milan Conservatoire, who toured as violin virtuoso in Italy. His playing was characterized by elegance, a full and noble yet sweet and singing tone, and perfect legato and staccato. In 1841 at the Conservatoire he produced his first opera, which was well received. He was successively conductor of the Opera at

Vercelli (1843), Milan and Turin, whence he went on tour with the famous double-bass player, Bottesini. Then he went to Havana as conductor and solo violinist at the theatre, and with that company he visited New York in 1847, 1848, 1850, etc., and in 1852–6 was conductor of the Italian Opera there. In 1857 he conducted an operatic star company, visiting, under the impresario Lumley, Hamburg, Berlin, Dresden and Warsaw. There he left the company and went to Constantinople, but after a short time he accepted Lumley's engagement for London, where he arrived in 1858 as conductor at Her Majesty's Theatre. From that time onward he resided in London, paying occasional visits to Germany, Russia and Austria. He conducted also Promenade Concerts at Covent Garden, and the first performance of Humperdinck's "Hansel und Gretel" at Daly's Theatre in 1894. He composed operas, various instrumental works (including scherzo for 2 violins) and songs, the best known being the still popular vocal waltz, "Il Bacio." His "Reminiscences" appeared in 1896.

THE MILANOLLO SISTERS: TERESA MILANOLLO, b. Savighiano, Piedmont, Aug. 28, 1827; d. Paris, Oct. 25, 1904; MARIA MILANOLLO, b. Savighiano, July 19, 1832; d. Paris, Oct. 21, 1848. They were the daughters of a spinning machinery manufacturer. TERESA began to play the violin at an early age under Ferrero, a local violinist, and later on studied at Turin under Caldera and Giov. Morra. In 1836 her father took her to Paris, where she studied under Lafont, and in 1840 for some time under Habeneck. In 1841 she became a pupil of de Bériot at Brussels. From her ninth year she appeared in public concerts. When MARIA also took up the violin Teresa became her teacher, and in 1840 the two young sisters began touring in Germany, France, England, Belgium, Holland, etc., everywhere meeting with enthusiastic receptions. Their technique was smooth, well developed and suited to the virtuoso literature of their time. Teresa, however, the more important of the two sisters, was more serious and thoughtful, while Maria was of a lively, merry temperament. Unfortunately she fell into consumption and died at the early age of 16. Teresa continued touring until 1857, when she married General Théodore Parmentier, after which she lived at Toulouse and later in Paris, and appeared in public only on rare occasions. She was at the zenith of her powers between 1853 and 1856. Even the severe Berlioz speaks at some length in enthusiastic terms about her faultless technique, purity of intonation, and full, round tone, especially on the G string, when she performed a concerto by her master, Habeneck, at a Conservatoire concert on Apr. 18, 1841, in the presence of the composer, who was enchanted by the performance of his pupil: while both the audience and the orchestra clapped and shouted with never-ending hurrahs, the modest little girl, meanwhile smiling but, showing no more emotion than if she had been complimented in a drawing-room, went to embrace her mother, who appreciated more fully the importance of such a success before such a terrible Areopagus.

STEFANO TEMPIA, b. Racconigi, Piedmont, Dec. 5, 1832; d. Turin, Nov. 25, 1878. An excellent violinist, who, in 1859, became capellmeister at the Turin theatre, and from 1868 violin teacher at the theatre there. He composed instructive violin music, orchestral works, masses, and wrote on various musical subjects.

TOMASINI. Fétis mentions him as a concertmeister at Neu-Strelitz in 1834, who appeared as soloist at the Hague in 1840, and at Düsseldorf in 1845. Wasielewski suggests that this may have been a son of Antonio Tomasini. He is probably also identical with the pupil of A. Zimmermann, mentioned by H. Mendel, as Neu-Strelitz, where Tomasini had apparently his first appointment, is not a very great distance north of Berlin.

GIUSEPPE, COUNT CONTIN DE CASTEL SZEPRIO, b. Venice, 1835; d. London, Dec. 30, 1899. His mother was an eminent Austrian pianist. He began the study of the violin early and made his public debut at the age of 11; at 15 he played a concerto in B major of his own composition at Trieste. At the same time he studied law at Padua University, where he took his degree of Doctor of Law. He then went to Vienna, there studying the violin under Mayseder and composition under Eckert. After returning to Venice for a time, he went to Paris in 1863, where he made the acquaintance of de Bériot, Alard and Vieuxtemps, and was on terms of intimate friendship with Rossini. Returning to Venice, he became president of the principal musical institutions, including the Liceo Benedetto Marcello, of which he also was a founder, and the hall of which he lent to Wagner for the private performance of the latter's symphony in C on Christmas Eve, 1882, about six weeks before Wagner's death. Contin had the honour of being accompanied in some of his compositions by the Queen of Italy and also by Liszt. The King of Italy made him a knight of the Order of Maurizio and Lazzaro. A few years later, misfortunes deprived him of practically the whole of his fortune. He went to London, where he became a 1st violinist at Drury Lane in 1887, and after several other engagements he became the leader and solo violinist at the Empire, a post which he held for five years until he was attacked by his last and fatal illness. He composed an opera, a cantata, 6 violin concertos: one of those being a concerto for 4 violins which was performed with great success at "King Cole Club," London, ca. 1894, the composer leading, and Victor Buziau playing the 2nd violin. Contin also composed a number of very effective solo pieces, some pub. in Paris and some in the Edition Chanot, London. A berceuse, among the latter, became a great favourite.

FILIPPA. The *Musical World* of Dec. 20, 1838, p. 250, thus refers: "Among the distinguished solo violin players who are to be heard this winter in Paris, honourable mention is made of young Filippa (Filippo?) aged three years. He is accompanied by his sister, Mlle. Ninetta, who has a pure and flexible voice."

ETTORE PINELLI, b. Rome, Oct. 18, 1843; d. there, Sept. 17, 1915. A pupil of Ramacciotti in Rome, who later studied for some time under Joachim. Returning to Rome in 1866, he worked with great zeal to familiarize his countrymen with the works of the German masters. He was a co-founder of the Liceo Musicale at Rome in connexion with the Academy di Sta Cecilia, where he became professor for the violin in 1877. He formed with Sgambati a society for classical chamber music and with him he conducted alternately the concerts at the Italian Court. He composed a string quartet, an overture, an Italian rhapsody, etc. He performed "St. Paul," the "Creation" and the "Seasons" with the orchestral society which he founded in 1874.

VIRGINIA and CAROLINA FERNI, sisters, b. Como, ca. 1845. In their childhood they played at the fairs in Upper Italy, where their father, Luigi Ferni, showed his marionette theatre. Gradually they won their way into the better cafés of Milan and Venice and then to the concert platforms. In 1858 they began to tour all through Germany and part of Russia, meeting everywhere with an enthusiastic reception which was only equalled by that accorded to the sisters Milanollo, and although the Ferni sisters had a very pretty talent, their personal beauty and charm contributed considerably to their success. Their violinistic career was of comparatively short duration, as Carolina, the younger and more talented, became a successful operatic singer and as such was still active, ca. 1880.

ANGELO and TERESA FERNI, brother and sister, appeared as young violin virtuosi with great success in Paris in 1859, where they obtained the patronage of the French Court. Angelo Ferni became teacher of the violin at the Conservatorio di Pietro, Naples, where he was still in 1896 (*see* R. Tagliacozzo).

GUIDO PAPINI, b. Camagiore, near Lucca, Aug. 1, 1847; d. London, 1912. A pupil of Giorgetti at Florence. At 13 he made his debut there with a concerto by Spohr, but in spite of his success it was only through the insistent advice of influential friends that he was prevented from following an impulse to throw up his musical career. Dr. Basevi asked him to become leader at his famous quartet soirées (Società del Quartetto) and this caused him to continue. He toured successfully in Italy, France and England and was for several years leader of the Società del Quartetto at Florence. In 1874 he appeared in London, where he played the viola at the Musical Union. As a violin virtuoso he achieved great success at the old and new Philharmonic concerts, and in 1876 at the Pasdeloup concerts in Paris. During 1893–6 he was violin teacher at the Irish Academy at Dublin. In the latter year he returned to London on account of ill-health. For several years he was president of the College of Violinists in London, in which he took an active interest. He excelled both as soloist and chamber-music player. He composed a large quantity of very effective solo pieces, as well as a tutor for violin, op. 57 (mostly pub. in the Edition Chanot, London).

GAËTANO CHIAUDELLI (CIAUDELLI).   Lived in the early 19th century; mentioned by H. Mendel as a distinguished violinist and violoncellist, pupil of Paganini, who lived as teacher at Naples.

# CHAPTER 60

# Italy: to Present Day

ACHILLE SIMONETTI, b. Turin, June 12, 1859; d. London, Nov. 19, 1928. In early youth he studied under Fr. Bianchi and Polledro (son of G. B. P. (?), d. 1853); 1872 under Cavallini at the Milan Conservatoire; 1873, violin, under Gius. Gamba at Turin, and composition under C. Pedrotti at Pesaro; then he became a pupil of Sivori, and after some successful concerts at Marseilles and Lyons—at Lyons also violinist at the theatre—he studied further under Dancla (violin) and Massenet (composition) at the Paris Conservatoire, at the same time (1881) playing in the Pasdeloup Orchestra. In 1883–7 he was engaged at Nice, where he formed a quartet, and afterwards he toured in England with the Marie Roze Company and the pianist B. Schönberger. In 1891 he settled in London as soloist and leader of the London Trio (Amina Goodwin, pianoforte, Edm. Whitehouse, violoncello), paying occasional visits to the principal Continental cities. During 1912–19 he was violin teacher at the Dublin Conservatoire, and in the latter year he went for some time to France, afterwards returning to London again. He composed 2 sonatas for violin and pianoforte, a number of solo pieces for violin, some of which have become very popular, and 2 string quartets.

EMILIO PENTE, b. Padua, Oct. 16, 1860. Pupil of Bazzini and Corbellini at the Milan Conservatoire. For a time editor of a musical periodical at Padua; 1894–1904, violin teacher at Florence; toured as soloist until 1909, when he became teacher at the Guildhall School of Music, London. He has prepared a new ed. of the works by Tartini.

ERNESTO CENTOLA, b. Salerno, Mar. 2, 1862. Studied the violin at the Naples Conservatoire, and in 1884 became principal for the violin of the school at Corfu. In 1887 he made renewed studies in Berlin; toured as soloist; was teacher at the Lyceum for music at Turin in 1889; and during 1893–7 violinist at S. Carlo Theatre, Naples. Later he was principal of a school of music at Constantinople, afterwards living at Naples. Composed a number of good solos, etc., for violin and pianoforte, as well as studies.

TERESINA TUA (real Christian names: MARIA FELICITA), b. Turin, Apr. 23, 1866 (according to Riemann's Lexikon of 1929; Wasielewski, Baker and Legge give the date as May 22, 1867). The child of poor musicians; at first pupil of her father. She appeared in public at the age of 7, and when playing at Nice, a wealthy Russian lady became interested in her and provided her with the means to study at the Paris Conservatoire under Massart. During that time she made many friends who took a practical interest in her career, among others Queen Isabella of Spain and the wife of President MacMahon. In 1880 she gained the 1st prize at the Conservatoire, and in 1881 started on her first concert tour through France, Spain and Italy as a fully equipped artist; technical difficulties she overcomes with perfect ease, her intonation is faultless, her tone is velvety and sweet though not powerful, and her style is like that of most representatives of the French school, leaning strongly towards the virtuoso element. Wherever she appeared she met with unbounded enthusiasm which may have been enhanced by her youth and personal charm. In 1882 she appeared for the first time in Vienna, and on May 5, 1883, at the Crystal Palace, London, which she visited on many subsequent occasions. In 1887 she went to America, where unabated success accompanied her everywhere; it continued also after her return to Europe, although the German critics said that she had not matured as much in depth of feeling and musical spiritualization as one might have hoped for. About 1891 she married Count Franchi Verney della Valletta, a distinguished critic, and only appeared occasionally at concerts in Italy. In Jan., 1897, however, she gave a concert at St. James's Hall in London. Since then one has unfortunately heard very little of this admirable artist. She was married a second time in 1914 to Count Emilio Quadrio de Maria Pontaschielli. In the same year she became titular professor of the Milan Conservatoire and in 1924 the same honour was bestowed upon her by the Liceo di S. Cecilia in Rome.

MARCO ANZOLETTI, b. Triente, June 4, 1866.   Studied at the Milan Conservatoire and commenced his career as a virtuoso in Rome.   In 1890 he became professor of the Milan Conservatoire and devoted himself henceforward to composition and music-literary work.   Wrote violin concertos in one movement; concertos for 4 violins; violin sonatas; solos, studies, trios, quartets, operas, orchestral works; biographical essays, and a book on the teaching of the violin in Italy.

FRANCESCO DE GUARNERI, b. Adria, June 5, 1867; d. Venice, Sept. 16, 1927.   Studied the violin under Frontali at the Liceo Benedetto Marcello, and under Ch. Dancla at the Paris Conservatoire, afterwards composition under C. Franck and V. d'Indy.   During 1886–8 he was violinist in the Lamoureux orchestra and later toured as virtuoso and chamber-music player in Germany, Russia and England.   He founded the International Society for Chamber Music in Paris, where he brought out Debussy's string quartet.   From 1896 he was teacher at the Liceo Benedetto Marcello, Venice.   He composed a sonata and pieces for violin, 2 string quartets, a violoncello sonata, and edited classical violin compositions. His brother, ANTONIO DE GUARNERI, a violoncellist, is capellmeister at La Scala, Milan.

ENRICO POLO, b. Parma, 1868.   Began to study the violin at the Royal Conservatoire at Parma.   Was a pupil of Joachim at the Berlin High School of Music in 1893–5.   In 1896 he competed successfully for the posts of concertmeister at the Royal theatre and of teacher for the violin at the Liceo Musicale, Turin, where he founded a permanent trio. In 1903 he gained, again in a competition, the violin professorship at the Royal Conservatoire Giuseppe Verdi at Milan.   He has formed a permanent string quartet and as an enthusiastic chamber-music player he has done a great deal to familiarize his countrymen with the works of the German masters, especially those of Beethoven and Brahms. He has also been engaged in bringing to light again many works by Italian 18th-century masters which had sunk into oblivion, and among others has been fortunate enough to discover 8 hitherto unknown string quartets by Boccherini.

His own compositions comprise a number of solo pieces and studies as well as songs.

NATALE ROSARIO SCALERO, b. Moncalieri, near Turin, Dec. 24, 1870. Studied the violin at a very early age under Pietro Bertazzi, teacher at the Conservatorio S. Cecilia at Turin; then he was for three years a pupil of Luigi Avalle, a pupil of Polledro, at the Liceo Musicale, Turin. Ca. 1885 he met César Thomson, who, attracted by his talent, instructed him in playing the Beethoven concerto, which soon after he played with great success; but, feeling that he could do better, he retired into the country, where he practised so much that he impaired his health. He then returned to Turin where he studied for a considerable time under Sivori, in whose quartet he frequently played the 2nd violin until 1889. In 1891 he appeared at Leipzig, where the critics praised his good tone and sound technique. Next he played on Bazzini's invitation at a Conservatorium concert at Milan, and during the next two years he appeared frequently at Rome, where, especially, his rendering of Joachim's Hungarian concerto was greatly praised. During the following years he toured with great success on the Continent and in 1895 he gave some recitals at the Queen's Hall, where he played also an effective little romance of his own composition. Some of his solos and a violin sonata have been pub. by Peters, Leipzig. In 1896 he lived as a teacher at Lyons, and then went to Vienna, where he studied composition for seven years under Mandyczewski, after which he became teacher of musical form at the Academy S. Cecilia at Rome. In 1919 he went to New York as teacher of composition at the David Maune School of Music, a position which he exchanged in 1928 for a similar but more important one at the Curtice Institute of Music at Philadelphia. He composed a violin concerto, a sonata for violin and pianoforte, op. 12; suite in the olden style, op. 15; 14 variations, pieces and Neapolitan dances, all for violin and pianoforte; a string quartet with a voice, orchestral and choral works (motets, etc.).

ALFREDO D' AMBROSIO, b. Naples, June 13, 1871; d. Nice, Dec. 29, 1914. He studied at Naples Conservatoire under Pinto, Bossi and Camillo de Nardis and gained 1st prizes as violinist and as composer. His melodious and brilliant compositions, which were played by Sarasate, Kubelik, Kocian, Heermann, Serato, Thibaut and many others of note, became general favourites. They comprise chiefly violin solo pieces, as well as 2 concertos and a string quintet. The second concerto, op. 51, in G minor, dedicated to Thibaut, who first played it in Paris in 1913, is a work which has a claim to more serious consideration than most of his solos, but all are thoroughly "violinistic" and hence grateful for the instrument. His career was prematurely brought to an end by an attack of appendicitis.

ARRIGO SERATO, b. Bologna, Feb. 7, 1877. Son of the celebrated violoncellist Franc. Serato; pupil of Frederigo Sarti at the Bologna Conservatoire, where he passed his final examination at the age of 17, playing a Paganini concerto and Bach's Chaconne so well that Martucci, director of the Conservatoire, presented him with his autographed photograph. After a successful tour in Italy he went to Germany to acquaint himself with the music of that country, and at the same time he gave most successful concerts in the principal towns and then toured nearly all European countries and even visited Egypt. He has devoted himself chiefly to the interpretation of the works of the classics of which he is not only by his perfect technique, but also by his intellectual rendering, an excellent exponent. Serato is a great bibliophile and member of several literary societies, possessing a library of 6,000 volumes in his flat in Berlin. In 1914 Serato was appointed teacher at the Conservatoire of S. Cecilia at Rome, but according to an agreement of 1926 is bound only for four months in the year to hold master-classes, touring for the rest of the time.

RICCARDO TAGLIACOZZO, b. Naples, Dec. 28, 1878. Until 1896 violin pupil of Angelo Ferni at the Conservatoire di Pietro there, afterwards of Joachim at the Berlin High School of Music. Toured extensively as virtuoso and was then for four years violin and viola teacher at the Palermo Conservatoire; he also founded there the Quartetto Siciliano. Since 1910 he has been teacher at the Musical Institute at Florence. He has composed pieces for violin and pianoforte, 1 gavotte and scherzo for string quartet, and ed. sonatas by Tartini and Veracini.

ADOLFO BETTI, b. Florence, 188?. A pupil of C. Thomson at the Liège Conservatoire, where he gained the gold medal. With two other pupils of Thomson, Alfred Pochon (b. Lausanne), Ugo Ara, an Italian, and the violoncellist Iwan d'Archambeau (b. Brussels), he formed, at the instigation of E. J. Coppet, at the latter's villa Flonzaley on the lake of Geneva in 1903, the Flonzaley quartet, which has since been touring all over Europe and America and won for itself the golden opinions of the public. They also revived with great success a sonata by W. Friedemann Bach for 2 violins and violoncello.

EMILIO COLOMBO, b. 18??. Studied at first under his father, in whose orchestra he played as a 1st violinist at the age of 7. On their tour in Russia, Tschaikowsky took an interest in the boy, and on his advice he went to Brussels to study at the Conservatoire under César Thomson. After gaining the 1st prize and the gold medal he toured through Germany, Scandinavia and Finland to Russia, where he became violinist to the Tsar. On the outbreak of the Revolution he was on a tour in Siberia with a singer and a pianist. They succeeded after many adventures to make their way to Tokio, where they were received by the Imperial family and gave concerts at the Imperial theatre. Afterwards they visited Hongkong, Singapore, the Indies, and then sailed for America, where his companions were not allowed to land because of their Russian nationality. Colombo toured through the States and Canada, whence he proceeded to England in 1920. He gave his first recital at the Aeolian Hall in 1921 and toured in the Provinces and in Scotland with great success. In London he played also at the Sunday League and other concerts. At the Italian Embassy he played to the King and Queen of Italy, and was decorated with the Cross of the Cavaliere d'Italia. He also played before members of the English Royal Family. He has been for some time past director of the music at one of the principal hotels in the West End.

ANTONIO DE GRASSI, b. 188?. Descended of an ancient North Italian noble family. He made his debut at Trieste at the age of 7 with concertos by Viotti and Spohr, but as his parents insisted upon his studying medicine, he ran away and joined a travelling orchestra. After that the parents gave in to his wishes and sent him to the Milan Conservatoire, where he obtained a diploma for violin and composition and then studied composition under Jadassohn; next he studied at the Berlin Hochschule under Joachim, who took a great interest in him and even chose him as 2nd violin in his quartet at the memorial concert for the painter Menzel, at the German Court. After the death of Joachim he went to Prague as a pupil of Ševčik, who after six months made him an assistant teacher and his deputy when he had to undergo an operation. Here he made the acquaintance of Miss Winifred June Morgan, an American pupil of Ševčik, who was also a good singer and became a chief interpreter of his songs. After a successful American tour he made his debut in London in 1910, when he received most flattering notices as an "artist of marked thought and individuality," and since then he has appeared here repeatedly and also toured in Russia and the greater part of Europe and America.

CONRADO MOSCHETTO, b. Biella, near Turin, 18... Began to study the violin from the age of 5. When he was 9 the family moved to Lyons, where he entered the Conservatoire and after four years carried off the 1st prize for violin-playing. Afterwards he studied under Lucien Capet, the late leader of the Capet quartet. He then gave recitals, started to teach and became a member of a symphony orchestra. During the War he served in the Italian army, afterwards rejoining the symphony orchestra; he also played for a time under Toscanini, who soon after offered him the post as leader, but he preferred an offer from the Café de Paris at Monte Carlo, which had the attraction of the beautiful climate and country, with easier work and approximately the same remuneration. In 1923, however, he received an engagement at the Savoy Hotel, London, and in the spring of 1928 he became musical director of the Mayfair Hotel, where he gained a high reputation for his orchestra and as a soloist. In Oct., 1932, he became musical director at the Dorchester Hotel.

MELANI, b. Naples, 1818; d. Buenos Aires, latter part of 19th century. A pupil of Joachim and an eminent violinist who excelled in the interpretation of works of the classical and romantic schools.

# CHAPTER 61

## *Netherlands*

JAKOB DAHMEN, b. Amsterdam, May 4, 1798; d. London, 18... Brother of Wilh. Heinr. Dahmen, and pupil of his father, Hermann Dahmen. He lived as violinist at Harlingen, Amsterdam, Rotterdam, and finally in London.

JEAN ARNOLD DAHMEN, b. Rotterdam, 1807; d. The Hague, May 5, 1853. Violin virtuoso and excellent hornplayer; 1827 teacher for horn at the Hague Conservatoire, afterwards member and then concertmeister in the Royal Chapel.

JEAN HERMANN DAHMEN, b. Rotterdam, 1807. The twin brother of Jean Arnold. Lived ca. 1883 at Utrecht as concertmeister. The twins were brothers of Wilh. Heinrich Dahmen and pupils of their father, Hermann Dahmen.

THEODOR HAUMANN (HANMANN), b. Ghent, July 3, 1808; d. Brussels, Aug. 21, 1878. Of Jewish parentage, and destined for the study of the law, but his love for the violin, which he studied under Snel at Brussels, gained the upper hand and after two years' study of law at Louvain University he played as supernumerary at the theatre of that town. Against the wishes of his family he went to Paris in 1827 and played in a number of concerts with varying success. He had a powerful tone and a broad style combined with artistic temperament, but he showed the lack of systematic technical as well as musical training and played in an erratic emotional manner without regard to time, which exasperated his accompanists. At the beginning of 1829 he obtained, however, decided success at the Théâtre Italienne with his playing of Rode's 7th concerto. Rode, who was present, expressed his astonishment and admiration and Haumann seemed to have reached the rank of a distinguished virtuoso. He went to London next, where he played at the Philharmonic Society but failed to show any of his brilliant qualities, nor was he more successful on subsequent occasions. This so discouraged him that he returned to the University, where he obtained the degree of Doctor of Law in 1830, but his love for the violin soon prevailed again. He underwent a course of two years' severe training, studying for ten hours a day. In Dec., 1832, he appeared once more in Paris with far greater success than before. It was evident that he had vastly improved technically as well as musically, touring afterwards in the South of France and then in Germany and Russia, meeting everywhere with great success. Recognizing that his power of tone and breadth of style proved the chief attraction in his playing he took all movements too slowly, using constantly a rubato style which became a mannerism. His want of true musicianship prevented him, in spite of his excellent technique, from ever ranking with the great violinists.

JOSEPH BATTA, b. Maestricht, Apr. 24, 1820. A violin pupil of the Brussels Conservatoire, where he received the Grand Prix for composition in 1845. He entered the orchestra of the Opéra-Comique, Paris, in 1846. As a composer he is said to have surpassed his brothers ALEXANDRE, the famous violoncellist, and JEAN LAURENT, the pianist; but of his more important works for orchestra, also cantatas, etc., nothing has apparently been pub.

FRANZ A. DUPONT, b. Rotterdam, 1822; d. Nuremberg, Mar. 21, 1875. Made his first musical studies at Rotterdam, and went in 1843 to the newly opened Conservatoire at Leipzig, where he studied under Ferd. David and Mendelssohn. After that he appeared in his native country as composer of important instrumental and vocal works. In 1856 he was capellmeister at the theatre at Linz, where an opera, "Bianca Siffradi," was successfully performed. During 1857–8 he was for a longer period at Hamburg, and in 1862 he became capellmeister at the Nuremberg theatre, where, as well as later on at Warsaw and at Moscow, he earned the reputation of an eminent conductor. Mendel praises his compositions, especially a pianoforte trio and a quartet.

FRANZ COENEN, b. Rotterdam, Dec. 26, 1826; d. Leyden, Jan. 24, 1904. Received his first music lessons from his father, an organist. He studied the violin under Molique

HENRY WIENIAWSKY

ADOLF BRODSKY

*Lafayette, Ltd.*

and Vieuxtemps; toured with the pianists Henri Herz and afterwards with Ernst Lübeck successfully in North and South America, and the East Indies. He cultivated the highest and noblest form of his art and was not only an excellent virtuoso, but also highly esteemed as leader of a quartet. He was solo violinist to the King of Holland and professor for violin and composition at, and director of, the Amsterdam Conservatoire until his retirement in 1895. His compositions include violin pieces, quartets, a symphony and sacred music.

ENGELBERT RÖNTGEN, b. Deventer, Sept. 30, 1829; d. Leipzig, Dec. 12, 1897. He showed early talent for the violin and played at the age of 8 years in local concerts; he also visited the art school where he gained the 1st prize for painting and drawing. Soon afterwards he decided to devote himself entirely to the study of the violin and became a pupil of Ferd. David at the Leipzig Conservatoire, where Hauptmann was his master in composition. At the end of his studies he became 2nd concertmeister at the Gewandhaus concerts and teacher of the violin at the Conservatoire, which positions he occupied to the time of his death. His wife, *née* Klengel, was a distinguished pianist and his son, Julius Röntgen, is the well-known pianist and composer.

MAURICE GERARD HUBERT LEENDERS, b. Venloo, Mar. 9, 1833. A pupil of his father until ca. 1844, when he became a pupil of Meerts and Léonard. He toured with success in Holland, Germany, Denmark, Sweden and Poland. After returning to Belgium he devoted himself to teaching and became director of the Conservatoire at Tournai. He composed a concerto and fantasias for violin and songs.

JOHANN JOSEPH DAVID NARET-KONING, b. Amsterdam, Feb. 25, 1838; d. Frankfort a/M., Feb. 29 (Riemann: Feb. 28), 1905. Pupil of Bunten at Amsterdam and Ferd. David at Leipzig. From 1859 to 1870 he was concertmeister at Mannheim, whence he went to Frankfort a/M. in 1871 in a similar capacity, receiving the title of Royal Professor in 1896. After leaving Mannheim he remained conductor of the Musical Union and of the Choral Society (Sängerbund) there until 1878. He was an excellent teacher, who trained a number of distinguished violinists.

BERTHOLD TOURS, b. Rotterdam, Dec. 17, 1838; d. London, Mar. 11, 1897. A pupil of his father, of Verhulst and of the Conservatoires of Brussels and of Leipzig. He went to London, 1861, where he was esteemed as an orchestral violinist and teacher. In 1872 he became musical adviser and ed. to Novello & Co., for whom he wrote a Primer for the Violin. He composed church music, and made arrangements of classical compositions.

CORNELIUS COENEN, b. The Hague, 1838. A violin virtuoso who as such toured extensively. In 1859 he became conductor at the Amsterdam theatre and, 1860, bandmaster of the National Guard at Utrecht. Composed overtures, choral songs with orchestra, etc.

JOSEPH HUBERT CRAMER, b. Warlingen, German province of Geldern, Feb. 29, 1844. A pupil of van Bree, Léonard at Brussels, and Ferd. David at the Leipzig Conservatoire. He appeared as virtuoso at Brussels and toured in Germany. In 1862 he settled at Groningen, where he instituted quartet soirées which enjoyed great popularity. Later he became concertmeister at the Palais vor Volksvlyt at Amsterdam, which position he occupied still in ca. 1883.

SIMON SPEELMAN, b. Amsterdam, 1851. Played an air-varié by de Bériot in public at the age of 10, and then became a pupil of Franz Coenen. The death of his father compelled him to earn his own living from the age of 13, thus cutting short his studies, but at 14 he was already principal 2nd violin in the Municipal orchestra. In 1870 he went to Manchester as 1st violin at de Jong's popular concerts, but from the following season he occupied the post of leader of the violas in the Hallé orchestra. In 1873 he became also 2nd violin in the newly formed Risegari quartet. In 1877 he went to Blackpool as principal viola in the North Pier orchestra, of which afterwards he became the leader and finally conductor as successor of de Jong. When Brodsky formed his quartet at Manchester, Speelman joined it as viola player.

JEAN DE GRAAN, b. Amsterdam, Sept. 9, 1852; d. The Hague, Jan. 8, 1874. Was a pupil of Joachim of quite exceptional talent, who unfortunately died in his twenty-second year.

BENOIT HOLLANDER, b. Amsterdam, June 8, 1853. He studied the violin at the Paris Conservatoire (and composition under Massenet and Saint-Saëns) and received the 1st prize. After touring as a virtuoso for some time, he went to London, where he appeared at chamber-music concerts and in the principal orchestras as an excellent viola player, but soon afterwards became leader at the Opera under Hans Richter, and in 1887 he was appointed as teacher of the violin at the Guildhall School of Music. In 1903 he conducted symphony concerts with an orchestra which he had formed partly from his pupils. He composed 2 concertos, and 2 sonatas for violin, a septet for string and wind instruments, a string trio, a pianoforte trio, a symphony, etc.

WILLEM KES, b. Dordrecht, Feb. 16, 1856. A pupil from 1867 of Nothdurft, Tyssen, and capellmeister Ferd. Böhm, a pupil of Spohr, on whose recommendation he was in 1871 sent to the Leipzig Conservatoire, where he became Ferd. David's pupil, studying composition under Reinecke and pianoforte under Wenzel and Jadassohn. In 1873 he received a scholarship from the King of Holland to study under Wieniawski at Brussels, and finally he went for one year to the Berlin High School as a pupil of Joachim for violin, and Bargiel and Kiel for composition. After that he toured for some time in Holland, and in the autumn of 1877 (Riemann says 1876) he became first concertmeister of the Park orchestra and the society Felix Meritis at Amsterdam. In the following year he also became conductor of the Choral Society Mozart in Dordrecht. In 1880 he became first capellmeister of the Park orchestra at Amsterdam, but accepted in the same year the post of musical director at Dordrecht. In 1883 he formed the famous orchestra and instituted concerts at the Concertgebouw, Amsterdam. In 1888 he was appointed director of a newly formed orchestra at Dordrecht, and 1895 he succeeded Geo. Henschel (now Sir George H.) as conductor of the Glasgow orchestra, with which he went on tour. In 1898 he went to Moscow as Director General of the Philharmonic Society and the Conservatoire. In 1904 he went to Dresden, and was director of the Musical Union at Coblenz, 1905–26. Since then he lives at Ober-Audorf on the Inn. He has composed several violin and violoncello concertos, a violin sonata and pieces with pianoforte, a symphony, a choral ballad, overtures, pianoforte pieces, songs, etc.

HENRI WILHELM PETRI, b. Zeyst, near Utrecht, Apr. 5, 1856; d. Dresden, Apr. 7, 1914. The son of an oboist in the town orchestra, who gave him his first lessons on the violin, but died when his son was still very young, after which Concertmeister Dahmen became his teacher. As he made considerable progress Dahmen took him to Joachim in 1871, under whom he studied for three years on a scholarship from the King of Holland, who then sent him to Brussels to study for eighteen months at the Conservatoire. During the season of 1877 he played in London, where Joachim had introduced him, and later in the same year he went as concertmeister to Sondershausen, remaining there for three and a half years. In 1881 he went in the same capacity to Hanover, and in Oct., 1883, he succeeded Schradieck in the Leipzig Gewandhaus and theatre orchestras until 1889, when he succeeded Lauterbach in the Dresden Court chapel and at the same time became teacher of the violin at the Conservatoire there until 1912. He also formed a string quartet, and with this and as soloist he toured most successfully over the greater part of Europe as well as in Russia. He composed violin pieces and songs, also ed. Kreutzer's studies and other works and pieces by old masters.

CHRISTIAN TIMNER, b. Den Helder, Holland, Apr. 18, 1859. Pupil at the Royal School of Music at the Hague, then until 1874 at the Brussels Conservatoire, and finally for three years of E. Wirth at Rotterdam. By 1879 he was concertmeister in the Bilse orchestra, Berlin; and in 1883 went to Amsterdam, where, 1888–90, then again in 1891 and 1907–10, he held a similar position in the Concertgebouw orchestra, and was periodically concertmeister at the Netherlandish opera. From 1910 he was at Los Angeles (U.S.A.).

ISIDOR SCHNITZLER, b. Rotterdam, June 2, 1859. Entered the Cologne Conservatoire in his twelfth year. Afterwards he studied under Emanuel Wirth at the Rotterdam Conservatoire, then with a scholarship from the King of Holland for one year under Wieniawski, and finally, in 1875 to 1876, under Joachim. After that he toured with Mme Désirée Artot and her husband, the singer Padilla y Ramos, in Rumania.

On his return he played at a Gewandhaus concert at Leipzig and then toured in Holland. In 1880 he was engaged by the Mendelssohn Quintet Club at Boston, Mass., and with that organization he toured in America and in Australia. He made a further tour through the United States with that club in conjunction with Christine Nielson.

JOHANNES WOLF, b. The Hague, May, 1862. His father was an official at the Dutch Court, who destined him for the career of a lawyer, but after much opposition allowed him to take up the study of his beloved violin and placed him under Prof. Wirth at Rotterdam, where he gained a scholarship offered by the King. This enabled him to study under Rappoldi at Dresden, where he again gained distinction at the annual examination; he then went to Paris, where he studied in 1880 at the Conservatoire under Maurin and carried off the 1st prize. Soon after that he made his debut at the Pasdeloup Concerts with Vieuxtemps' fourth concerto and achieved a marked success. During the following years he toured all over Europe and was honoured by many Orders from ruling sovereigns and other marks of distinction. In 1892 he went on a tour through the United States of America and through Canada with the violoncellist Jos. Hollmann. About the middle of 1894 he revived the "Musical Union" in London, which became famous under Ella. Wolff, gave the first concert of the New Series at the Old James's Hall on May 21, 1894, and the second concert with a Saint-Saëns programme on June 7. The last concert, in July, was with the assistance of the wind quartet of the Paris Opera. He was a favourite of Queen Victoria and in the autumn of 1893 he spent more than a month at Balmoral, which he visited again in Sept., 1894, at the Queen's command. In Nov., 1894, he gave the first concert of a new series of Musical Union Concerts. He was appointed additional teacher, together with Wilhelmj, at the Guildhall School of Music in that year. At the beginning of 1895 he played at the Court of Darmstadt, Carl Fuchs the violoncellist appearing at the same concert. In the early part of this century he was leading a quartet with D. Kordy as violoncellist at the house of Mrs. Lewis-Hill.

JAN SMIT, b. Utrecht, May 23, 1862. Studied the violin first at the Hague Conservatoire and then under Léonard in

Paris. During 1882–3 he was concertmeister in Bilse's orchestra, Berlin. Afterwards he toured as virtuoso for several years and became teacher at the Gand Conservatoire in 1889.

BRAM ELDERING, b. Groningen, Holland, July 8, 1865. He received his first instruction there from Chr. Poortman, and during 1882–6 he studied under J. Hubay, whom he followed in the latter year to Budapest as viola player in the Hubay-Popper quartet, and teacher of the violin. From 1888 to 1891 he renewed his studies, under Joachim, at the Berlin High School of Music. During 1891–4 he was concert-meister in the Philharmonic orchestra, Berlin, and 1894–9 he was in the same capacity in the Meiningen Court chapel; then 1899–1903, he was first professor at the Amsterdam Conservatoire. In the latter year he went to Cologne as professor at the Conservatoire as well as concertmeister in the Gürzenich orchestra and leader of the Gürzenich quartet.

MAX MOSSEL, b. Rotterdam, 1871. At the age of 5 he made his public debut with a concerto by Rode and then toured as a prodigy with his brother, a clever violoncellist. When only 8 he entered the Rotterdam Conservatoire, where he obtained the 1st prize; and then became leader at the Grand Theatre. Two years later he held a similar position in the Concertgebouw orchestra at Amsterdam, and during the four years he was there he made several concert tours in Holland and Belgium. In 1892 he made a very successful debut at the Crystal Palace under Sir Augustus Manns, to whom he had been introduced by Albert Fransella. This led to an engagement as leader of the Glasgow orchestra for the season. A similar engagement at Llandudno resulted in an engagement for Birmingham, which he made his home, and arranged highly successful drawing-room concerts. With the aid of an influential committee he founded the Birmingham Promenade concerts, for which he engaged Sir Landon Ronald as con-ductor, and when the latter became Principal of the Guildhall School of Music he placed Mossel on the staff of teachers. He is also principal violin professor at the Midland Institute, where he also founded a permanent quartet bearing his name. As a change from his many strenuous duties he undertook in

1909 a concert tour in the Dutch Indies, which proved a great success.

LOUIS ZIMMERMANN, b. Groningen, Holland, July 19, 1873. A pupil at the Leipzig Conservatoire and of Ysaÿe at Brussels; he began his violinistic career at Hamburg, was engaged 1896–9 at Darmstadt, 1899–1904 at the Concertgebouw, Amsterdam. During 1904–11 he was in London as teacher at the Royal Academy of Music, soloist and orchestral leader. Since then he has been first concertmeister of the orchestra, leader of the quartet and violinist of the trio at the Concertgebouw, Amsterdam, and second conductor at the Cecilia Union. He composed a violin concerto (1921). Introduction and Rondo for violin and orchestra; pieces for violin and pianoforte; cadenzas for concertos by Mozart, Beethoven and Brahms; a string quartet and songs.

JAN VAN OORDT, b. in India, Dec. 13, 1874, of Dutch parents. At the age of 5 he made a sensational public debut in Holland as an accordion player. Two years later he commenced the study of the violin and at 12 he entered the Hague Conservatoire under J. G. Mulder, and after gaining the gold medal there four years later, he became a private pupil of César Thomson. In 1896 he made his London debut at the Queen's Hall, proving himself in possession of a remarkable technique. He then toured in America and Russia, and revisited London a few years later.

LEON SAMETINI, b. Rotterdam, Mar. 16, 1886. He received his first musical education from his uncle, de Groot, who remained his master for six years, after which he became a pupil of Concertmeister van der Bruyn. After a few years he went to Togni for a time and then to Bram Eldering, whom he holds in high esteem, and for whom he composed a Fantasia for violin and pianoforte, at the age of 15, as a souvenir on his departure for Prague where he studied two years under Ševčik. He made his public debut at the age of 12 with the Mendelssohn concerto and Saint-Saëns' "Rondo Capriccioso," after which he toured for some time in Holland, when several eminent violinists predicted a brilliant future for him, and Joachim recommended him to the Queen of Holland, who presented him with a violin and a scholarship which enabled him to study under Ševičk until 1903. After that he played at a Philharmonic concert in Prague, where he met with an enthusiastic reception, and then toured again in Holland. He was fascinated by the compositions of Wieniawski, whose daughter recommended him to go to London, where he made his debut in 1904 with two recitals and an orchestral concert which were so successful that he received numerous engagements for the principal London concerts; then he toured in the provinces with equal success. After a fortnight's service in the Dutch army, he toured for some time in Holland and returned to England in Apr., 1906. He then toured with Ada Crossley in Australia 1908–9 and afterwards in the U.S.A. of America and was ca. 1919 in Chicago.

DE GROOT, b. Rotterdam, 18... Son of a double-bass player. He began to study the violin at the age of 8, and had various masters until he was 14, when it was decided that he should go to Berlin to study under Joachim, but sudden family misfortunes compelled him to take an engagement in Holland to assist the family. He then continued his studies under Prof. Joseph Cramer, and a few years later he went to Paris as a restaurant player. About 1900 he came to London and a few years later he became leader at the Piccadilly Hotel, where he soon attracted the attention of the visitors by the careful arrangement of his programmes, the excellent performances of his little orchestra and particularly by his solos, which included many violin concertos and other important compositions. He never descended to jazz playing, but even for his popular items he chose good music of the lighter kind. He remained there for twenty-five years as a great popular favourite, who received many practical marks of appreciation, taking in one case the form of a Stradivari violin from a Sheffield admirer, one of his broadcasting audience. An illness in 1928 caused him to resign his position at least temporarily, and forming a trio with two members of his orchestra, he has recently toured in London and the provinces, appearing at the principal concert and music halls.

GODEFROID DE VREESE, b. Kortrijk, 1893. Studied music at first at Kortrijk, then under César Thomson, Gilson, Lunssens and Rasse at the Brussels Conservatoire; became 1st violinist in the Kursaal orchestra, Ostend; then conductor at the Lyric Schouwburg, Antwerp; after that conductor of Park theatre Waux-hall, Brussels, opened 1924; since then conductor and solo violinist at Monaco. He has composed a sonata for violin and pianoforte orchestral and choral works, songs, and gained the Prix de Rome with a cantata "Beatrÿs" in 1922.

WILLEM TEN HAVE. One of the last pupils of Chas. Dancla. An excellent violinist who lived in Paris ca. 1902. He composed a large number of brilliant and melodious pieces for violin, including a concerto, op. 30, and many drawing-room and concert pieces (London, Laudy & Co.).

ANTON MAASKOFF. A pupil of Brodsky who gave some successful recitals at the Wigmore Hall in 1930 and has been before the public on many occasions for some years, with the reputation of an excellent violinist.

# CHAPTER 62

# *Poland*

THE Poles share with all Slavonic nations the love and talent for music, but the unsettled condition of their country was not favourable for a systematic cultivation of musical art, notwithstanding that early in the 19th century a musical society was formed at Warsaw, where in 1821 also a Conservatoire was founded. Although Poland produced in Lipinski, Lotto and Wieniawski some of the greatest violinists of their time, these sought a field for their activity in other countries. Since then, however, the Warsaw Conservatoire has gained in importance.

CARL JOSEF LIPINSKI, b. Radzyn, Poland, Oct. 30, according to the official certificate, but Nov. 4, 1790, according to his family record (perhaps a difference between Russian and Polish style); d. at his estate, Urlow, near Lemberg, Dec. 16, 1861. His father was a self-taught violinist, who gave him his first lessons, after which he followed his own instinct, which fortunately led him in the right direction. In his tenth year he felt attracted by the more sonorous tones of the violoncello, which henceforth he practised with such assiduity that eventually he could play the concertos by Romberg. Arrived at that stage he bethought himself that a violinist had greater chances, and returned to that instrument; he felt convinced, however, that the study of the violoncello not only strengthened the fingers of his left hand, but also accounted for the richness and great power of his tone on the violin. In 1810 he had progressed so far in his studies that he was appointed concertmeister at the Lemberg theatre, where in 1812 he became conductor, and trained both orchestra and chorus in the most painstaking manner, resulting in excellent performances of German, French and Italian operas. Not

378

being a pianist, he used his violin at rehearsals, and often played two parts in double stopping, and chords to indicate changes of harmony, and in that manner he acquired that facility in polyphone playing which was an outstanding feature of his technique. In 1814 he retired from the theatre and devoted himself with redoubled energy to the study of the violin, using the works by Tartini and Viotti for that purpose as well as solos written by himself. He also began at that time to compose overtures and operettas. He continued in this manner until 1817, when suddenly the fame of Paganini resounded throughout Europe, and awakened in him an unconquerable desire to see and hear for himself the wonders which were reported of this Italian. He arrived at Piacenza just in time for a concert by Paganini. He watched and listened in breathless wonder, while the public cheered and shouted in frenzied ecstasies over the brilliant fireworks of that violin-sorcerer; when, however, Paganini had finished an adagio in that wonderful singing style, entirely his own, Lipinski was the only person who applauded. This attracted the attention of those around him, and when he told them of the long journey he had undertaken to hear Paganini they took him straightway and introduced him to the Maëstro. On the following day they made closer acquaintance, and after Paganini had heard his admirer, they played together every day, and in the former's public concerts on Apr. 17 and 30, 1818, they played duets by Kreutzer and Pleyel. Paganini at that time proposed to Lipinski that they should tour together throughout Italy, but this the latter declined as it would keep him away too long from his family and his native town. Towards the end of 1818 Lipinski, on his homeward journey, visited Trieste, where he found a still surviving pupil of Tartini, in the person of Dr. Mazzurana, who was then upwards of ninety years old, though still a sturdy old man, and to him he applied for information about Tartini's manner of playing. The Doctor told him that he no longer played the violin, but that if Lipinski would play to him an adagio by Tartini, he would explain to him as far as possible Tartini's method. When Lipinski had played it, he shook his head, told him to read carefully the lines under the movement, and explained that Tartini often sought inspiration from some lines from his favourite poets which he indicated at the foot of the violin part. After having done this, Lipinski played the adagio again to the entire satisfaction of Tartini's old pupil. After that incident Lipinski endeavoured more and more to imbue himself with the poetical idea of a composition before playing it and this striving led to his soulful interpretation of the works of the classical masters, their violin compositions as well as their chamber music which he cultivated with great zeal and care. In 1821 he toured in Germany, and 1825 in Russia, meeting everywhere with great success. In 1829 he met Paganini once more, quite accidentally at Warsaw. An Italian singing-master there, Soliva, tried by all manner of intrigue to prevent his appearance, that he might afterwards say Lipinski had shunned the comparison with Paganini. The public began to take parts, and the matter developed into a miniature "guerre des Bouffons." Even some of his friends warned Lipinski not to challenge comparison with the "Achilles" of violinists. He simply replied, "but Achilles had a vulnerable heel." Both gave their concert and the matter ended in a long-winded and unedifying press campaign in which the two artists considered it beneath their dignity to take any part. When Paganini was asked whom he regarded as the greatest violinist, he replied: "The second greatest is certainly Lipinski."

Being in the fortunate position that his family circumstances placed him beyond the necessity to earn his living by his art, he returned home after this tour and devoted himself to a prolonged period of serious study. In 1835, however, he started on a tour through Germany, France and England, where on Apr. 25, 1836, he played his Military concerto at a concert of the Philharmonic Society in London. Later in the year he visited Leipzig, where he made the acquaintance of Schumann, who dedicated to him his Carneval, op. 9. He also competed for the vacant post of concertmeister, but this was awarded to David. He then returned home, but soon afterwards started on another tour through Austria and Russia. On July 1, 1839, he became court-concertmeister at Dresden, where he entirely re-organized the Royal chapel, and formed a string quartet to which he devoted a great deal of his energies, and which became famous for its exquisite rendering of the quartets by Haydn, Mozart and Beethoven. In 1860 he was attacked by gout, and although he used repeatedly the waters at Teplitz, this increased in severity so that he had to abandon playing; in 1861 he retired to his estate, Urlow, near Lemberg, where he died.

He was a very remarkable violinist of most original talent. Although he neither had a perfect rapid shake, nor a staccato, yet these shortcomings were more than compensated by his very powerful and singing tone of beautiful quality, to which on the other hand, not unlike Spohr, he sacrificed all the lighter graces in the art of bowing, playing even rapid detached notes with broad and powerful strokes. He had however a remarkable technique in polyphone playing, double stops and chords, and his intonation was of the greatest purity. He wrote a number of concertos, variations, fantasias, etc., among which his effective Military concerto, and his G minor variations are of outstanding merit, although even the former, which for many decades was a universal favourite, is now only used for the purpose of study.

STANISLAUS MACICIOWSKY, b. Warsaw, May 8, 1801. Studied the violin first under a violinist Rozycky, and then under Möser in Berlin; afterwards he took Spohr for his model and became an excellent virtuoso. He toured a great deal and with marked success, especially in London and Manchester. He composed violin pieces of the virtuoso order; a fantasia and a rondo, both with orchestra, are favourably mentioned as showing distinct originality.

ANTON ORLOWSKI, b. Warsaw, ca. 1811. A pupil of Bilawski for violin, and Elsner composition, at the Warsaw Conservatoire, which he left with the 1st prizes for violin and for pianoforte. He devoted himself chiefly to composition and conducting. After visiting Eastern Germany and Paris he went to Rouen, where for a time he was capellmeister at the theatre, and afterwards devoted himself chiefly to teaching.

ADOLPH STAHLKNECHT, b. Warsaw, June 18, 1813; d. Berlin, June 24, 1887. He received his first violin lessons from his father; afterwards he studied under Luge at Breslau and then under Saint-Lubin and Mühlenbruck at Berlin, where he studied also at the Royal Academy. He toured with his brother JULIUS, and in 1844 instituted trio-soirées with him and the pianist Steifensand, whose place was afterwards taken by Löschhorn. He composed 25 string quartets, quintets,

7 symphonies, an opera, church music, songs, etc., only partly pub. at Berlin, Leipzig and Gotha.

STANISLAUS DE KONTSKI, b. Cracow, Oct. 8, 1820. Brother of Apollinaire de Kontski; teacher of the violin in Paris; composed violin and pianoforte pieces of a lighter order.

APOLLINAIRE DE KONTSKI, b. Warsaw, Oct. 23, 1825; d. there, June 29, 1879. A pupil of his brother Charles (b. Sept. 15, 1815; d. Paris, Aug. 27, 1867). He early acquired a remarkable degree of virtuosity, and Paganini, who heard him in Paris, when he was 11 years old, gave him a testimonial in which he ranks him with the most celebrated artists of the time and says that if he continues his studies he will "surpass the most distinguished performers of the age" (*see* Stephen S. Stratton, "Nicolo Paganini," p. 110, from the *Musical World*, June 21, 1838). It has been stated by several biographers that Paganini left his compositions and one of his violins to de Kontski, but it lacks confirmation, as also the statement that Paganini gave him lessons when, on his return from London, he visited Paris for the second time. In 1848 he toured in Germany with phenomenal success, and in 1853 he settled in St. Petersburg as solo violinist to the Tsar. In 1861 he returned to Warsaw, where he founded a Conservatoire under the patronage of the Russian Government, which prospered under his direction. He wrote a number of worthless salon pieces, of which "Le Reveil du Lion" is the most notorious.

ALEXANDER MARTIN, b. Warsaw, 1825; d. there, 1856. The son of a Polish mother and a French father, he became violinist at the Warsaw theatre and a fertile composer. For the violin he wrote a Grand Fantasia with pianoforte, and an Elegy for two violins and violoncello; pieces for violoncello and for oboe, a funeral march for three trumpets and chorus, etc. (played at his funeral); 2 operas remained unfinished, fragments of one were performed and made a deep impression.

HENRY WIENIAWSKY, b. Lublin, July 10, 1835; d. Moscow, Mar. 31, 1880. His father was a doctor of medicine, his mother a sister of the pianist, Ed. Wolff. They recognized the child's early talent and he received his first violin lessons in his sixth year from Paris, the foremost teacher at Lublin. About this time Misca Hauser visited the family and played in the evenings with his mother. The little boy was so fascinated by his playing that he went stealthily from his bed and listened at the door which was left ajar. On Hauser's recommendation the mother took him when he was 8 years old to Massart in Paris, who was so astonished at his talent that he secured his entry into the Conservatoire on Nov. 28, 1843. He became at first a pupil of Clavel, but on Dec. 4, 1844, he joined the class of Massart, where he gained the 1st prize in 1846. It is related as an instance of his unselfish and gentle nature, that on that occasion he was sincerely distressed that he should have carried it off earlier than his older co-student Champenois, who received only the 2nd prize. The news of his success caused the prolongation for several years of his passport by the Polish Minister, to enable him to continue his studies until 1848. In the latter year he made his debut at St. Petersburg with immense success, but returned on Apr. 11, 1849, to Paris, where he entered Colet's class for composition at the Conservatoire; in 1850 he was awarded the 1st prize in this also. He set out immediately after for St. Petersburg again. Three years later he played with his brother Joseph (pianist) at Spa. Fétis, who heard him there, says (Biog. des Musiciens) that, although only a youth of 18, his playing foretold already the high degree of mastership he was to occupy but a few years later. In the following years he toured triumphantly in Belgium, France, England, Holland and Germany. In 1860–72 he was solo violinist to the Tsar of Russia. In the latter year he went with Ant. Rubinstein to America, receiving for his own part £40,000 for the tour. When Rubinstein returned in 1873, he remained until 1874, touring chiefly in California. There he received by cable a request to return to Brussels to take over the duties of Vieuxtemps at the Conservatoire, as the latter had fallen seriously ill. He filled that position from 1875 to 1877, when Vieuxtemps, having partially recovered, returned once more to his post. While he was at the conservatoire Wieniawsky trained many excellent pupils, including Leop. Lichtenberg, who had followed him all the way from San Francisco, and it was hoped that he would definitely fill the position after Vieuxtemps' final retirement. Meanwhile he went to Russia again. In Moscow he was attacked by heart disease—he had for some time already become excessively stout—and died in a hospital, entirely unknown, and without means, in spite of the large sums he had earned. He had been decorated by most of the kings and princes of Middle and Northern Europe. Wieniawsky overcame all difficulties with the greatest ease and gracefulness, his tone combined sweetness with power and he was a poet who sang on his instrument. His higher musicianly qualities showed themselves particularly as a leader of the quartet of the London Monday and Saturday Popular Concerts as well as in his chamber-music soirées with Davidoff at St. Petersburg, and with Brassin (pianoforte) at Brussels. As a composer he stands far above the majority of virtuoso composers; his works are not only brilliant, graceful and original in their passages, but they show poetical inspiration and, especially in the form and orchestral treatment of his concertos, he reveals himself as a musician of a high order, and they, as well as many of his solo pieces, especially the Légende, op. 17, are of lasting value; great favourites are also the Kujawiak, op. 3; Polonaise, op. 4; Mazurkas, op. 12 and 19; Souvenir de Moscou, op. 6; a fantasie on Gounod's Faust used to enjoy great popularity, also Le Carnival Russe, op. 11, and Fantaisie orientale, posthumous; he also wrote three books of studies, "École Moderne," op. 10.

ISIDOR LOTTO, b. Warsaw, Dec. 22, 1840. The son of poor, Jewish parents, who aroused as a violinist in early youth the admiration of all who heard him. When he was 12 he was sent by well-to-do patrons to Paris to study the violin under Massart and composition under Reber. He developed into one of the greatest representatives of the French school, who in some respects even surpassed his compatriot Wieniawski. He overcame the greatest difficulties with an ease as if they were non-existent. His intonation was always perfect, his staccato, double harmonics, etc., absolutely astounding. At the end of his studies in Paris he gave a highly successful concert there and toured in Germany, where he was soon looked upon as one of the greatest virtuosos of his time, and in 1862 was appointed solo violinist and chamber virtuoso to the Grand-Duke of Saxe Weimar. He was given liberal leave for touring and also acted as teacher at the Warsaw Conservatoire, but this strenuous life was detrimental to his constitution. In 1872 he became professor of the violin at the Strassburg Conservatoire. Soon afterwards he contracted enteric fever which for a whole year prevented him from following his profession. After his recovery he took up his position at the Warsaw Conservatoire again till about the end of last century; but later on he was attacked by a mental disease which brought his professional career to a tragic end.

GUSTAV VON FRIEMANN (FREEMAN), b. Lublin, Poland, 1844, of an English father and a Polish mother. His first teacher for the violin was Stanislaus Servaczynsky. From 1862 he studied for four years under Massart at the Paris Conservatoire, where he gained successively the silver and the gold medal and finally the prize of honour: a valuable violin (Bernadel?). After that he toured in Germany, Austria and Hungary with eminent success, and in Darmstadt he was nominated a Grand Ducal chamber virtuoso. Eventually he became teacher of the violin at the Vienna Conservatoire, and later on at the Imperial School of Music at Odessa. He composed solo pieces for violin.

JOHANN CHOMANOVSKI, b. in Poland ca. 1846; d. Paris (?), 1865. Hy. Wieniawski recommended him at the age of 15 to finish his studies of the violin under Massart in Paris, who was also his own teacher. He made rapid progress and became a violinist at the Grand Opera. While playing with equal mastery the concertos by Viotti and Rode and sonatas by Beethoven, he excelled also as chamber-music player. Unfortunately this promising young artist died prematurely.

M. J. NIEDZIELSKI, b. Warsaw, 1851. Pupil of Massart and co-student of Sarasate in Paris. At the age of 7 he appeared in public together with the famous violoncellist Servais. He toured extensively in Europe and America and eventually settled in the latter country. A number of his solo pieces for violin were pub. in New York in and before 1892. His son is a distinguished pianist who has given recitals in London.

TYMOTEUSZ ADAMOVSKI, b. Warsaw, Mar. 24, 1858. A pupil of Massart in Paris. In 1879 he settled in Boston, Mass., where he founded a permanent quartet and a trio. He is also an esteemed conductor and teacher of the violin. His brother JOSEPH became an excellent violoncellist and as such a member of both his quartet and his trio.

STANISLAUS BARCEWICZ, b. Warsaw, Apr. 6, 1858. Son of a post official; in early childhood showed exceptional musical talent. A little toy fiddle was his greatest joy. He soon learned to play, and at the age of 11 he performed de Bériot's 7th concerto before an audience of musical amateurs. He entered the Moscow Conservatoire, where he studied first under Laub, and, when the latter died in 1875, under Hřimaly. In 1877 he left, after gaining the gold medal, and toured in Germany, Norway and Sweden. After a successful concert at Christiania in 1881, the Philharmonic Society there made him an honorary member. In 1885 he became professor of violin at the Warsaw Conservatoire, in 1893 concertmeister of the Opera, and 1911–18 was director of the Imperial Institute for music there. Barcewicz ranks with the foremost virtuosos of the time. He has written various compositions for the violin.

JOSEPH ACHRON, b. Losdseje, Government of Suwalki, May 1, 1866. A violin pupil of Michalowicz and Lotto at Warsaw and, 1899–1904, of von Auer at the St. Petersburg Conservatoire. In 1904 he settled at Berlin, whence he undertook frequent concert tours until 1907. From then to 1910 he devoted chiefly to autodidactic studies in composition. During 1913–16 he was teacher for violin and chamber music at the Music School of the former Imperial Russian Music Society at Charkov. From 1916 to 1918 he served in the Russian army, 1921 he was head of the short-lived master class for violin and chamber music of the Artists' Union, St. Petersburg. From 1922 to 1924 he was mostly in Berlin, and 1925 he went to New York. He has worked with several colleagues to create a Hebrew national art music. He composed: Violin concerto, op. 60; 2 sonatas for violin and pianoforte, pieces for violin and pianoforte, or orchestra; foundations of the violin and bow-technics, chromatic string quartet, op. 26; numerous instrumental and vocal compositions, including operas.

MAX LEWINGER, b. Sulkov, near Cracow, Mar. 17, 1870; d. Dresden, Aug. 31, 1908. Studied the violin first at the Conservatoire at Cracow and Lemberg, where afterwards he played for some time at the theatre. He then gained a scholarship which enabled him to study under Grün at the

Vienna Conservatoire. During 1892–3 he toured as virtuoso. In the latter year he became teacher at the Bukarest Conservatoire and thence went to Helsingfors as concertmeister of the Philharmonic concerts. In the autumn of 1898 he obtained a similar position at the Gewandhaus and the theatre at Leipzig, and in 1898 he succeeded Rappoldi as Royal Court concertmeister at Dresden.

EMIL MLYNARSKI, b. Kibarty, Poland, July 18, 1870. Studied the violin under von Auer at the St. Petersburg Conservatoire. In 1893 he became second conductor of the symphony concert at Warsaw, but in 1894 he went to Odessa, where, until 1897, he was violin teacher at the Music School of the Imperial Russian Musical Society. In the latter year he returned to Warsaw as teacher of the violin at the Conservatoire, and from 1901–5 he was also capellmeister at the Opera and conductor of the Warsaw Philharmonic Society. In 1907 he conducted orchestral concerts with the London Symphony Orchestra and in 1910 he became conductor of the Scottish Orchestra. 1919–22 he was director of the Conservatoire and the Opera in Warsaw. He composed a concerto in d minor for violin and orchestra and a number of solo pieces with pianoforte for violin, some of which have become very popular. He also composed a symphony in F, "Polonia."

JÓZEF OZIMINSKI, b. Warsaw, Dec. 6, 1875. A violin pupil of Stiller and Barcewicz; for theory Noskowski, at the Warsaw Conservatoire. He was 1st violinist from 1901 at the Warsaw Philharmonic Society, and in 1910 became second conductor.

ROBERT POSELT, b. Neu-Sandec, near Cracow, Feb. 17, 1878. A Polish violin virtuoso about whom we only know that he studied at first at the Lemberg Conservatoire, then at Prague under Bennewitz, and finally under Garcin and Marsick in Paris. He started a school for violin-playing at Cracow; afterwards he was teacher of the Conservatoire at Lemberg and, ca. 1928, at Zakopane. He has composed pieces for violin.

BRONISLAV HUBERMANN, b. Czenstochova, Russian Poland, Dec. 19, 1882. He received his first instruction on the violin from Michalowicz, Rosen, and afterwards for three months from Isidor Lotto at Warsaw, where his father was a barrister in very modest circumstances. The parents took him to Berlin to introduce him to Joachim, in which, knowing that master's aversion to prodigies, they succeeded in taking him by surprise, for when Joachim heard the 9-year-old boy play, he was struck by his talent and gave him a recommendation which enabled him to give a number of concerts in various German towns. In Sept., 1892, he played at the International Music Exhibition in Vienna with such success that a second concert was given in the presence of the Emperor Francis Joseph, who presented him with the means to acquire a violin worthy of his talent. Immediately after that he went to Berlin, where he was a pupil of Markees, receiving also some advice from Joachim, whom he admired and took as his model. At the same time he studied secretly under Gregorowitsch, to whose teaching he owes a great deal. In June, 1893, he left Berlin and received still some instructions from Marsick in Paris and of Heermann at Frankfort. He toured all over Middle Europe with considerable success, but it was not until Jan., 1895, when he played at a concert given by Adelina Patti in Vienna, that he created such a sensation that in consequence he gave twelve concerts to crowded houses. His fame soon spread after that and he toured with ever-increasing success all over Europe, Russia and America. Towards the end of Jan., 1896, he played the Brahms concerto in Vienna. The great master, who was present, was so delighted that he promised to write a larger work (fantasia) specially for him, a promise which his death in the following year unfortunately prevented from materializing. Not long after, Hubermann withdrew from the public eye for four years to devote his time to his general and higher musical education, and after that period he resumed his musical tours. In 1909 the Municipality of Genoa honoured him by allowing him to play on Paganini's famous Jos. Guarnerius del Jesu, which since Paganini's death had only been used once by Sivori and once by Kocian, at a concert which he gave for the sufferers from the terrible earthquake of 1908. From 1928 he has made his home in Berlin. His book, "From the Workshop of the Virtuoso," was published in Vienna, 1912.

WACLAW KOCHANSKI, b. Poland, 1884. A pupil of Joachim and Ševčik; lived for some time at Lemberg; for the last few years teacher of violin at Warsaw Conservatoire.

WLADISLAV WAGHALTER, b. Warsaw, Apr. 10, 1885. After receiving his first tuition on the violin at 6 years old, from his father, he became a pupil of Isidor Lotto and progressed so rapidly that he went on a concert tour in Russia at the age of 10. At 14 he resumed his studies under A. Moser and finished them under Joachim in Berlin. He gained the Joachim prize of a violin, and the Mendelssohn prize with his rendering of the Brahms concerto. At the age of 17 he gave his first concert in Berlin, when Joachim conducted the orchestra. In 1905 he deputized as concertmeister in the Stuttgart Court chapel for C. Wendling, who was absent on leave, and was so much admired that when Wendling returned he was offered a parallel post in the chapel. This he declined, to tour in Germany and Austria with great success. In 1912 he was appointed solo violinist and concertmeister at the Berlin Opera. He has all the qualities of an eminent violinist and musician. He founded a permanent string quartet and in conjunction with Hekking, also a pianoforte trio.

MAX WOLFSTAHL, b. Lemberg, 1885. Studied the violin from an early age under his father, a local violinist and teacher; made his first public debut there at the age of 8, and then was sent to Vienna to study under Grün. In 1898 he played there at one of the symphony concerts with marked success, and then he toured in Austria, Hungary, Germany, Russia, Rumania, and Turkey, where he was decorated by the Sultan. On Oct. 18, 1902, he made his London debut at the Crystal Palace.

DAVID MELSA, b. Warsaw, 1893 (?), of Jewish parents. After preliminary gratuitous teaching by violinists at Lodz, who recognized his talent, he received free tuition at the Conservatoire as a pupil of Grudzinski, but in 1905 his father and sister were massacred in a pogrom and he escaped with the mother by fleeing to Berlin, where his co-religionists provided for their wants, and he received a scholarship at the Klindworth-Scharwenka Conservatoire, where he won the prize violin in 1909. The wife of the American ambassador who had become interested in him, raised a subscription to buy him a fine Bergonzi violin dated 1727, and Karl Flesch assisted him in his studies. He made his debut in Berlin before a full house and was hailed by the Press as a young artist of a genuine musical nature. After successful appearances in Berlin he made his debut in the Steinway Hall, London, in Jan., 1913, when especially his performance of Tartini's "Devil's Trill" sonata was praised. "His tone is rich and resonant, his style essentially broad" was the criticism of Gamba in *The Strad*. He has since toured in America, the Continent of Europe, and revisited England with unabated success.

SAMUEL DUSCHKIN, b. Suwalk, Russian Poland, Dec. 13, 1897. A pupil of Rémy at the Paris Conservatoire, and of Kreisler and von Auer. He appeared first in Russia at the age of 9, and toured in America the following year, but returned shortly after, to resume his studies in Europe. At the outbreak of the Great War he enlisted in the British army; on the entrance of America he joined the forces of that country. In 1923 he made his debut as a mature artist with the New York Symphony Orchestra, playing a newly discovered concerto by Boccherini in D major with great success. In June and Nov., 1924, he gave a sonata recital at the Albert Hall in London which proved as successful as his concerts in the provinces. Afterwards he toured in Holland, Germany and France. A recital fixed for Dec. 10, 1925, at the Æolian Hall, London, had to be abandoned as, while in Paris, a few weeks before, he had received a very alluring offer to go immediately to America.

EUGENE POLONASKY. A mid 19th-century violinist who was president and co-founder (?) with the violin-maker Fouquer, of the College of Violinists, and founder of *The Strad* (in 1891).

SIEGMUND FEUERMANN, b. Kolomea, Poland, 1901. Played some songs on the violin in public when he was only 5 years old. His father, who was his first teacher, settled in Vienna in 1909, and towards the end of that year Siegmund became a pupil of Ševčik. In 1911 he made his debut in Vienna and was acclaimed by public and Press alike as well for his virtuosity as for his artistic qualities. Wasielewski in his "Die Violine," etc., justly censures the choice of his programme, including besides works by Corelli, Paganini and Tschaikowsky, the Brahms concerto, a work which requires the understanding of a mature artist, and to which no boy, however talented, can possibly do justice. Feuermann appeared during the following two years in many of the principal towns of Germany,

Austria, Rumania, in London—where in Dec., 1911, he made his debut at a Philharmonic concert with Brahms' concerto, and in Jan., 1912, at a concert by Miss Georgine Kimpton, played the Paganini concerto in D but with moderate success—and also visited Paris. During that time, however, he continued his studies under Ševčik. In the autumn of 1912 he played with success in Vienna; in Jan., 1913, at the Rumanian Court at Bukarest; afterwards he toured in Germany and Austria. In Apr., 1913, he appeared again in Paris, and in the autumn in London. Felix Weingartner was so impressed with his talent that he proposed to tour with him in America.

JASCHA HEIFETZ, b. Vilna, 1901. Began to study the violin under his father Ravin Heifetz and played in Vilna and neighbourhood as a prodigy of 6 or 7 years of age, then became a pupil of von Auer at St. Petersburg. At 9 he played in concerts there. In 1912 he made a most successful debut in Berlin, and after that he toured with unabated success in Germany and Austria until 1917, when the Heifetz family emigrated to America, where he met with popular worship that was almost unparalleled. In the spring of 1920 he made his London debut, when he astounded the musical world by his marvellous and faultless technique, but was declared to be somewhat lacking in poetical and emotional qualities; but this must be taken relatively, and the noble restraint also exercised by Joachim, only means that they are not hung out like a signboard on a shopfront or at an inn. He has since become a familiar figure both in the old and the new world and is now recognized as one of the greatest virtuosos of all times. Apart from his Paganini-like technique, he possesses beauty of tone, absolute purity of intonation and nobility of style.

STEFAN FRENKEL, b. Warsaw, Nov. 8, 1902. A violin pupil at first of his uncle, Moritz Frenkel, a pupil of von Auer, then from 1919 of Ad. Busch, and C. Flesch (composition under Fr. E. Koch) in Berlin. During 1924–7 he was concertmeister in the Philharmonic orchestra at Dresden; since then he has toured successfully as violin virtuoso. He composed a sonata for violin solo, op. 1; suite for 2 violins, op. 3; violin pieces, a quartet for 4 violins, and pianoforte compositions.

# CHAPTER 63
## *Rumania*

EDUARD CANDELLA, b. Jassy, Rumania, June 3, 1841; d. there, Apr. 11, 1923. Son of the violoncellist and director of the Conservatoire, Franz Candella; pupil of Franz Ries in Berlin, 1853–5, then of Alard and Massart in Paris, and in 1860 of Vieuxtemps at Dreieichenhein, near Frankfort a/Main. In 1861 violin teacher at the Jassy Conservatoire, of which he was the director from 1894 to 1901. Composed violin pieces, operas, orchestral fantasies, piano pieces, songs, etc.

FRANZ KNEISEL, b. Bukarest, Jan. 26, 1865; d. New York, Mar. 26, 1926. His father, a native of Olmütz, Austria, and military bandmaster, was his first teacher on the violin; he then entered the Bukarest Conservatoire, where he absolved the whole curriculum and gained the 1st prize for violin-playing before he was 15. In 1879 he entered the Vienna Conservatoire as a pupil of Jac. Grün and Hellmesberger (the latter chiefly for chamber music). He completed his studies there in July, 1882, carrying off the 1st prize for violin-playing again. On Dec. 31 of that year he played Joachim's Hungarian Concerto at a Philharmonic concert, and was immediately appointed Jac. Dont's successor as solo violinist at the Hofburg theatre. In 1884 he became concertmeister of the Bilse orchestra in Berlin, and in the autumn of 1885 he went to Boston, Mass., as concertmeister of the Boston Symphony Orchestra, at the invitation of the conductor Wilhelm Gericke. His beneficial influence soon became manifest in the improvement of the string playing. Kneisel's ambition to form a quartet which should attain the greatest possible perfection was realized by the liberal support of that discriminating patron of music, Col. Higginson, and for thirty-three years this quartet did invaluable service to music in America. There were several changes in the 2nd violin and the violoncello, but the viola remained throughout in the capable hands of Louis Svecenski ; for further particulars about its composition *see* the respective article in Grove's Dictionary and W. W. Cobbett's Encyclopædia of Chamber Music. In 1903 Kneisel, Theodorowicz, Svecenski and A. Schröder resigned from the symphony orchestra to devote themselves entirely to perfecting the ensemble of their quartet. In 1904 they visited London and played at two of the Broadwood concerts in Mar. He married a talented co-student at the Conservatoire, Marianne Thoma, who was a pupil of Grün and Hellmesberger, and who had received a valuable ring from the unfortunate Empress Elizabeth, when playing before her. She was only 17 at the time of their marriage and she gave up her own career to assist that of her husband. Their family life was most happy, but for the untimely loss of their talented pianist-son Robert. Their daughter Victoria is the beautiful wife of Willem Willeke, who succeeded Schröder as the last violoncellist of the quartet; her sister Marianne has formed a quartet of her own, and of the twins, Fred and Frank, the former is a University student and the other a violinist. In 1882 Kneisel led the first performance from manuscript of Brahms' string quintet in F major at the house of the latter's great friend Dr. Billroth, and later he had the wonderful opportunity to play the master's work with the quartet at Brahms' summer retreat at Ischl, where as a rule he refused to hear any music. With his own quartet he toured all over the United States, visiting small towns, engineering camps in the Wild West, coal mines, etc., and awakened in the most uncultured people an interest in music which afterwards became ready for development. In 1905 he was appointed head of the violin department of the New Institute of Musical Art of New York. On the retirement of Schröder in 1907 he was on the point of accepting a conductorship and of, therefore, dissolving the quartet, but was dissuaded by his friends, and the entrance of Julius Röntgen and Willem Willeke brought new life into the combination. In 1917, however, wearied by constant travel, he felt a lack of the necessary freshness to keep up the high standard of the quartet, and he disbanded it after a last public performance on Apr. 3, and a concert, arranged by friends and subscribers, followed by a supper at the Ritz-Carlton Hotel, New York, on Apr. 21, 1917. He said: "I would rather stop now than peter out with only a success d'estime when my bow shakes and I play out of tune." The first concert took place at the Chickering Hall, Boston, Dec. 28, 1885. Kneisel was also an excellent conductor. In his boyhood he had conducted the Bukarest Philharmonic Society, and in the absence of Nikisch he conducted the Boston Symphony Orchestra concerts at the World's Fair in Chicago, 1893, as well as the Worcester, Mass., Festival of 1902 and 1903. After the dissolution of his quartet he devoted himself almost exclusively to teaching, and even at his summer place at Blue Hill, Maine, he had gathered round him some forty pupils. The Universities of Yale (1911) and of Princeton (1915) bestowed upon him the degree of Doctor of Music. He died of peritonitis, following an unexpected, serious operation, deeply lamented by all the great artists who were his friends, and many of whom, including Kreisler, who played an Adagio by Bach, attended the memorial service at the Institute of Musical Art. He ed. the "Kneisel Collection" of violin pieces, composed a book of advanced studies (1910), and only a week before his death completed a cadenza to the Brahms concerto.

GEORG ENESCO (ENESCÜ), b. Liveni, Rumania, Aug. 19, 1882. Studied the violin under Bachrich and Hellmesberger and composition under Rob. Fuchs at the Vienna Conservatoire 1887–93, and from 1894 under Marsick (violin), Massenet and Fauré (composition) at the Paris Conservatoire. In 1897 he awakened an interest in wider circles as a composer of violin sonatas, a string quintet and a "Poème Roumain" for orchestra. Colonne produced also his first orchestral suite (1903) and his first symphony (1906). After that he toured in Europe as a soloist. In 1912 he founded a prize for Rumanian composers, the most important whereof is himself.

## CHAPTER 64

# *Russia*

THE Russians, like all Slavs, are a music-loving people, but, as most of these, practised it until comparatively recent times only in the form of folk and church music. Art music was cultivated only at the Court and by the nobility, who engaged, however, only foreign musicians. The desire to encourage national talent led to the formation in 1772 of the Philharmonic Society of St. Petersburg, which was dissolved in 1851 but resuscitated in 1859 under the title of the "Russian Musical Society," with branch establishments in all the principal towns in Russia. The object of this society was the musical education of native talent at home as well as abroad, and to awaken the sense for good music in wider circles by first-class performances. Of very far-reaching influence was the establishment of the Conservatoires in St. Petersburg in 1862, and Moscow in 1866. Galkin was the first professor at the St. Petersburg Conservatoire. He distinguished himself not only as soloist and conductor but also as a teacher who counted among his pupils such eminent violinists as Lifschütz, Roman, A. Sapelnikov and others. The Moscow Conservatoire has also produced a number of pupils who gained a European reputation.

FRIEDRICH HOFFMANN, b. Novgorod, 1791; d. Frankfort a/M., Apr. 6, 1863. Pupil of Baillot at the Paris Conservatoire, which he entered 1808. In 1811 he was appointed 1st violinist at the Frankfort theatre; 1815 became director of music at Detmold, but in 1820 returned to his former position at Frankfort, where he was also in great request as a teacher and counted Ferd. Hiller among his pupils.

ALEXIS FEODOROVITSCH LWOFF (LVOV), b. Reval, June 6, 1798; d. near Kovno, Dec. 16, 1870. Studied the violin from his seventh year as an amateur, but rose considerably above that status. He received an excellent artistic and general education, and entered the army, in which he rose to the rank of a general, and adjutant to Nicholas II. In that position he was able to do a great deal for the musical life of his country. In 1837 he succeeded his brother Theodor as director of the Imperial Court chapel, for which he wrote a number of compositions, and his activity in connexion with the chapel was also the cause of his essay on old Russian church music (St. Petersburg, 1859). He was known in Russia and Germany as an excellent violinist and chamber-music player, and his permanent quartet in St. Petersburg was famed for its perfect ensemble. He composed a violin concerto, 24 caprices, a fantasia, "Le Duel," for violin and cello, several operas, marches, songs, etc. His only lasting composition is the beautiful Russian anthem (words by Joukowski) written for the unveiling of the Alexander column in St. Petersburg. In 1850 he was attacked by an ear trouble which eventually ended in deafness and caused him to withdraw to his estate at Kovno.

ALEXANDER TARNOWSKI, b. Vilna, 1812. Received his first violin lessons from a local teacher and later became a pupil of Habeneck at the Paris Conservatoire. Afterwards he settled at Clermont-Ferrand as conductor of the Philharmonic Society and teacher of music. He composed fantasias on operatic airs, and romances for the violin.

LEONARD GOLD, b. Odessa, 1818. Was living there, ca. 1880. A pupil of Böhm at the Vienna Conservatoire. After gaining three prizes there he returned to Odessa in 1836, where an opera of his was successfully performed in 1837. In the following year he went on tour, partly for further studies, returning in 1839, when he became 1st violin at the Odessa theatre, which he held until he retired in affluent circumstances.

DOPPLER, b. Kiev, 1819. A pupil of Lipinski at Dresden; settled at Warsaw in 1870 as a virtuoso, teacher and composer. He also wrote violin pieces, mostly in the Salon style.

PRINCE NICOLAUS YOUSSUPOV, b. St. Petersburg, 1827; d. Baden-Baden, Aug. 3, 1891. A pupil of Vieuxtemps and an excellent violinist who had a private orchestra at his palace.

He composed a symphonic concerto for violin with orchestra, a symphony "Gonzalva de Cordova" with violin obbligato, a sonate—caprice for the G string, Adagio dramatique and Rondo, Poème lyrique, and other solo pieces for the violin. He also wrote a book on violin making, "Luthomonographie Historique et Raisonnée," as well as a "History of Music in Russia."

STANISLAV TABOROWSKI, b. Krzemienica, Volhynia, 1830. Removed with his parents to Odessa, where he commenced his musical studies at an early age and afterwards visited the University at St. Petersburg, but decided to embrace music as his profession. After making a successful debut as solo violinist under the patronage of Count Wielhorski and General Rzevuski in the latter city in 1853, he toured in Poland and Southern Russia. He then went to Brussels, where he renewed his studies at the Conservatoire under Léonard for three years. After that he went to St. Petersburg, where he was engaged for some time, thence to Moscow, and in the seventies of the 19th century he toured successfully in Germany.

VASIL VASILEVICH BESEKIRSKY, b. Moscow, Jan. 26, 1835. Studied at the Moscow Conservatoire, made a successful debut in 1850 and soon after became a violinist at the Moscow Opera. In 1858 he took a further course of study for violin under Léonard and for composition under Kameke at Brussels. About this time he performed before Princess Helena of Russia, who was so pleased with his playing that she presented him with a purse of 1,000 roubles which enabled him to continue his studies. In the following year he appeared repeatedly with marked success at Brussels and Paris, and in 1860 he returned to Moscow as concertmeister at the Opera; there he gave concerts and arranged quartet soirées. On his first appearance at St. Petersburg in 1863 he had a most enthusiastic reception. In 1866 he gave four concerts at Madrid, but the journey adversely affected his health and he spent the following winter at Nice, where nevertheless he appeared twelve times in public. In 1867 he returned to Moscow, and in 1868 he had a triumphal success at St. Petersburg and at Leipzig with a concerto of his own composition. This led to an engagement to appear again at the Gewandhaus in 1869, and his success there caused him to obtain a year's leave to tour in Germany, Austria, and to play in Paris again. In 1868 he appeared at the London Philharmonic concerts. He met with a particularly brilliant reception at Prague on Oct. 4, 1869. In 1890 he resigned from his position at the Moscow Opera, but retained his professorship at the Philharmonic Society until 1902. In the following year he went to St. Petersburg as head of the violin and chamber-music classes at the Conservatoire E. Rap-hoph, and as private teacher. On Mar. 14, 1910, he celebrated his sixty years' jubilee as soloist and teacher, when he received marks of esteem and affection from all parts of Europe. He composed works for violin, arrangements and ed. of classical works; cadenzas for classical violin concertos; also Memoirs (St. Petersburg, 1910).

VASSILI BESEKIRSKY, his son, b. Moscow, 1879, is also a fine violinist who has toured in Russia, Germany and Scandinavia (1910–13) and in U.S.A. (1914–16) (Baker).

CARL JOHAN LINDBERG, b. Lemo, Finland, Mar. 8, 1837; d. Stockholm, Dec. 21, 1914. A pupil of Pacius and of Ferd. David at Leipzig and finally of Joachim in Berlin; 1864 violinist at Helsingfors; 1869 at the Royal Opera, Stockholm, where he was as concertmeister 1882 to 1903. He joined Stockholm Conservatoire and in 1897 he received the title of Professor. He composed a large amount of music for teaching purposes. Sigrid Lindberg, his daughter, b. Jan. 5, 1871, is an excellent solo violinist (*see* p. 417).

NICOLAI WLADIMIROWITCH GALKIN, b. St. Petersburg, Dec. 6, 1850; d. there, 1906. A pupil of Kaminski and of L. von Auer at the St. Petersburg Conservatoire, where he studied theory and composition under Johansen and Laroche; continued his studies under Joachim in 1815 in Berlin—where he was at the same time concertmeister in Bilse's orchestra —and 1876 under Sauret in Paris and under Wieniawski at Brussels. About the same time he toured in France, the Netherlands and Germany. In 1877 he became solo violinist at the ballet and in 1895 chief capellmeister at the Alexander theatre in St. Petersburg. In 1880 he became assistant professor to Auer and in 1892 professor for violin at the

Conservatoire. From 1890 he conducted the orchestra and was teacher of the conductor's class there, and from 1892 to 1903 he was director of the symphony concerts at Pavlovsk. He composed some solo pieces for violin, and trained many excellent pupils; among the most prominent are A. Roman, B. Lifschütz, Seligmann and A. Sapelnikov.

ADOLF BRODSKY, b. Taganrog, Southern Russia, Mar. 21, 1851; d. Manchester, Jan. 22, 1929. As a child he delighted in playing folk-tunes on a toy fiddle, and from his fifth to his ninth year he was taught at home by various masters; in spite of the frequent changes, his progress was so remarkable that a rich citizen of Odessa, who heard him at a concert there, provided him with the means to study under Hellmesberger in Vienna from 1860 to 1862 as a private pupil, and from then till 1867 in his class at the Conservatoire. When he left that institution he became 2nd violinist in the famous Hellmesberger quartet, which gave him the best training in that branch of his art. From 1868 to 1870 he was a violinist at the Court Opera and appeared also frequently at concerts as soloist. During 1870–4 he toured all over Russia, as far as Tiflis in the South, and thence to Moscow, where he met Laub, with whom he became very intimate. When Laub died in 1875 Hřimaly succeeded him as first professor of violin at the Conservatoire, and Brodsky took Hřimaly's place as second professor. In 1879 he went to Kiev as conductor of the Symphony concerts. In 1800 he toured in Germany and Austria and thence visited Paris, where he made the acquaintance of Sarasate, who induced him to further studies in the higher technique. In 1881 he gave the first public performance of Tschaikowsky's violin concerto at the concert of the Vienna Philharmonic Society with phenomenal success. After that he visited London, and in the following year he played at the Universal Exhibition at Moscow, where he was hailed with unbounded enthusiasm; then he returned again to Germany where, after playing in various towns, he appeared at Leipzig again in the winter of 1882–3, and met with such success that he was offered, and accepted, the first professorship at the Conservatoire which had become vacant through Schradieck's departure. There he formed a quartet with Nováček, Sitt, and Leopold Grützmacher, which soon acquired a wide reputation; afterwards Hans Becker (son of Jean

399

Becker) became the 2nd violinist, while Nováček took the viola and Jul. Klengel the violoncello. Among the foremost of his pupils at the Conservatoire were, apart from Hans Becker, Felix Berber and A. Fiedemann. In 1891 Walter Damrosch visited Germany to engage first-class instrumentalists for his New York orchestra, and he induced Brodsky to become his leader. Arrived in New York, the latter gave a series of eight chamber concerts, which surpassed all that had been there before. He toured also as soloist with great success in the States. In 1893 he returned to Germany, but after a brief sojourn in Berlin, Sir Charles Hallé engaged him as professor for violin at the Manchester Conservatoire and leader of his orchestra, and when the latter died in 1895 Brodsky succeeded him as director of the Conservatoire. In Manchester he formed again a string quartet with Rawdon Briggs, Simon Speelman and Carl Fuchs, which became far-famed for its accuracy, beauty of tone and above all artistic rendering. Among the most noteworthy of his pupils of that period are A. Catterall, J. Lowsen, Ant. Maaskoff, A. Barker, Lena Kontorowich, etc. Brodsky had a beautiful Jos. Guarnerius violin, which at one time was the instrument of Lafont.

JOSEPH KOTEK, b. Kamenez-Podolsk, Oct. 25, 1855; d. Davos, Jan. 4, 1885. His father was a Bohemian who settled in Russia, his mother a Russian. He was a violin pupil of Ferd. Laub (until 1875) and Hřimaly at the Moscow Conservatoire, which he left in 1877 after gaining the gold medal. He then studied for another year under Joachim at the Berlin High School, where, in 1882, he was appointed teacher for the violin. He composed violin duets with pianoforte accompaniment, solos and studies for the violin.

VICTOR HUSSLA, b. St. Petersburg, Oct. 16, 1857; d. Lisbon, Nov. 14, 1899. Son of a capellmeister; came to Neufchatel in early youth and studied the violin under Hermann and Schradieck at the Leipzig Conservatoire and afterwards under Thomson at Lugano and Nice. In 1887 he became director of the "Real Academia," etc., at Lisbon; in connexion therewith he instituted an orchestral school. He wrote numerous compositions for violin as well as for orchestra, of which three Portuguese rhapsodies and one Portuguese suite have become popular.

OTTO VON TIEDEBÖHL, b. Voronesch, 1863. Toured from 1893 as violin virtuoso and became teacher at the Conservatoire at Tamboi in 1895, and concertmeister at the symphony concerts of the Russian Imperial Music Society there. He then renewed his studies for a time under Gust. Holländer at the Stern Conservatoire in Berlin; afterwards he went on tour again, but a nervous complaint compelled him to abandon all playing. He composed a concerto and a polonaise for violin and orchestra and violin pieces with pianoforte; a larger number of his compositions remained in MS.

DEMETRIUS VLADIMIROVITCH ACHSCHARUMOV, b. Odessa, Sept. 20, 1864; d. there during the Revolution. Pupil of Krassnokutzki at Odessa, Auer in St. Petersburg and J. Dont in Vienna, where he studied composition under Rob. Fuchs. Toured from 1890 as virtuoso. In 1898 he became conductor of the symphony concerts at Poltawa and 1899 director of the newly founded section of the Imperial Russian Music Society.

CHARLES GREGOROWITSCH, b. St. Petersburg, Oct. 25, 1867; of Polish descent. His father, a musical amateur, recognizing his son's early talent, gave him his first lessons and afterwards placed him under Besekirski at Moscow, and from 1882 under Wieniawski, whose last pupil he was. He then studied for a time under Jacque Dont in Vienna and finally under Joachim in Berlin. At the end of his studies he appeared with the greatest success in Paris, Lisbon, Dresden, Leipzig, etc., visited America 1896–7, and made his first appearance in London at a concert of the Philharmonic Society on Nov. 18, 1897, when he met with an enthusiastic reception. Sarasate, although of a totally different school, is said to have counted Gregorowitsch among the first six leading violinists of the time.

MICHEL SICARD, b. Odessa, 1868. Studied at the Kiev music school, with Massart at the Paris Conservatoire, and under Joachim and Bargiel (composition) at the Berlin High School for Music. For some years he was teacher at the Kiev school of the Imperial Russian Music Society; 1894–5 concertmeister in the Colonne orchestra in Paris; afterwards he toured as virtuoso. He composed orchestral and chamber music.

JULIUS CONUS, b. Moscow, 1869. Studied the violin at the Moscow Conservatoire, where he gained the gold medal in 1888, and became teacher there until 1895. He composed a violin concerto and a number of solo pieces with pianoforte. His elder brother GEORG was a teacher of harmony and composition at the same institute, and his younger brother LEO, also a former pupil of that Conservatoire, a pianist who founded a music school in Moscow. Both Julius and Leo were living as teachers in Paris, 1921.

MIECZYSLAV MICHALOWICZ, b. Mielitopol, Taurus, June 17, 1872. A pupil of Barcewicz at Warsaw and von Auer at St. Petersburg. From 1906 violin teacher at the School of Music of the Warsaw Musical Society; in 1916 he received the title of Professor. He counts among his pupils B. Hubermann and Jos. Achron.

ALEXANDER SERGEVITCH PETSCHNIKOV, b. Jelitz, government of Orel, Russia, Jan. 8, 1873. He came to Moscow at a very early age, where a musician, Solotarenko, heard him play and advised to send the 10-year-old boy to the Conservatoire, which a scholarship enabled him to do, and there he studied under Arno Hilf and Hřimaly, leaving it after receiving the gold medal. He then went for some years to Paris, but as the French school was not congenial to his temperament he went to Berlin, where he gave his first concert on Oct. 11, 1895, meeting with so brilliant a reception that he decided to settle there permanently and touring from there in Europe as well as in the United States of America. He possesses a faultless technique and his tone is distinguished more by its velvety quality, roundness and sweetness than by great power. He is the fortunate owner of the beautiful Stradivari which belonged to Ferd. Laub. Petschnikov is famed for his fine interpretation of the works of Bach and Mozart. In 1910 he received in Berlin the title of Royal Professor, and 1913 to 1921 he was teacher at the Royal Academy at Munich. He used to tour with his late wife, LILI, *née* SCHOBER, also an excellent violinist. In 1924 he formed a permanent quartet. Since 1927 he has been teacher at the Stern Conservatoire, Berlin. He and his wife proved very delightful exponents in the art of duet playing about 1912.

ROSA HOCHMANN, b. Proskurov, near Kiev, Mar. 13, 1875. A pupil of Oscar Stock at Kiev, and J. Grün in Vienna. In Nov., 1892, she made her debut there, and was hailed by Hanslick and R. Heuberger as a second Teresa Milanollo. "Individuality, the most beautiful cantilena of all female violinists, breadth of tone, wonderful interpretative powers, and a refined and artistic knowledge of the art of phrasing" are the terms in which R. H. Legge characterizes her playing in *The Strad* of May, 1895. She went on a very success-ful tour in Russia, after appearing in most of the large towns of Eastern Europe. In Vienna she gave a performance of the Goldmark Concerto at one of the Philharmonic concerts under Richter, with quite sensational success.

PRINCE GEORG N. DULOW, b. Moscow, June 4, 1875. Received his first music lessons from his mother, the noted pianist Sograf-Dulova, afterwards pupil of Klammroth, and of Hřimaly at the Moscow Conservatoire, which he left with distinction. During 1897–1901 he was a member of the quartet of the Duke of Mecklenburg, and in 1901 he became professor of violin at the Moscow Conservatoire. Composed violin pieces with pianoforte and with orchestra, studies, technical exercises, and a tutor in 12 books.

M. ZIRELSTEIN. Pupil of Hřimaly at the Moscow Conser-vatoire; concertmeister at Simin's Opera (1875–1910).

MICHAEL ZACHAREWITSCH, b. Osrow, Russia, 1877. The son of a violoncellist, from whom he received his first violin lessons at the age of 10, making such rapid progress that two years later he became a pupil of Ševčik at the Kiev Conservatoire, passing the lowest class. In 1892 he followed his master to Prague, where he continued his studies under him for two more years, and at the final examination he obtained a great success with Joachim's Hungarian concerto, which at a later period secured for him the encomiums and encouragement of the great master. At the end of his studies he went for a short time to Brussels, where he met with a friendly reception and encouragement from Ysaÿe and then made a very suc-cessful debut at Amsterdam. After that he returned for military service to Russia, followed by a year's loss of work caused by "violinist's arm." On his recovery he accepted any small engagements to assist his parents in their straitened circumstances. In 1901 he appeared in Berlin, where his faultless technique, powerful tone, and poetical style were greatly praised and admired, and where he obtained the loan of a fine J. B. Guadagnini, on which he played at his debut in London. He has since appeared there repeatedly and always met with enthusiastic receptions as well as in America, where he toured extensively and at prolonged periods. On the Continent he has met with unqualified success in all the principal towns.

ALEXANDER SCHMULLER, b. Mozyr, Russia, Dec. 5, 1880. A pupil of Ševčik, Hřimaly and von Auer; 1908–14 violin teacher at the Stern Conservatoire, Berlin. After that he went in the same capacity to the Amsterdam Conservatoire. He played a great deal with Max Reger and tours extensively as exponent of modern composers.

JACQUES MALKIN, b. in the Russian government of Mohilev, Dec., 1880. A violin pupil of Friemann, Odessa, and Marsick in Paris. He was for a considerable time viole d'amour player in the Société des Instr. Anciens, founded by Saint-Saëns. Since the end of the Great War he has been principal of the violin class at the Malkin Conservatoire of Music in New York, founded by his brother MANFRED, pianist, with whom (and his brother JOSEPH, violoncellist) he also formed the Malkin trio; their sister, BEATA MALKIN, is an opera singer in Berlin.

EUGEN MICHAELOWITCH GUSIKOV, b. Charkov, 1887. Studied the violin under Hřimaly at the Moscow Conservatoire and under Lucien Capet, Paris. During 1915–18 professor at the Tiflis Conservatoire; toured in Germany in 1822–3, and was appointed in the latter year professor at the Moscow Conservatoire. He is an excellent virtuoso and teacher.

PAUL KOCHANSKI, b. Orol, Russia, 1887. A pupil of Mlynarski at Odessa, whom he followed to Warsaw when the former became director of the Philharmonic orchestra there, and at 14 young Kochanski was appointed concertmeister in that important orchestra. After three years he went to Brussels, where by special favour he was allowed to study at the Conservatoire for three months only, after which he carried off the 1st prize with special distinction. After that he toured all over Europe with the greatest success, receiving many valuable tokens from admirers of his talents, including Sovereigns, Princes, municipalities and university students' associations. In 1906 he appeared with great success in London.

EFREM ZIMBALIST, b. Rostov on the Don, Russia, May 7, 1889. A pupil of his father and, 1901–7, of Auer at the St. Petersburg Conservatoire. In 1907 he made his debut in Berlin with the Brahms concerto, went in the same year to London and 1911 to America. In 1914 he married in London the opera singer Alma Gluck. He composed a suite in the olden style (1911), Slavonic dances for violin and pianoforte, and a musical comedy, "Honeyden" (New Haven, Conn., 1920).

MISCHA ELMAN, b. Talnoi, Kiev, Jan. 21, 1891. The son of a Jewish schoolmaster; studied at first under Fiedemann at the Imperial School of Music, Odessa, where he played the 7th concerto by de Bériot at a school concert in 1899, and attracted the attention of Brodsky, Sarasate, and Auer, under whom he studied at the St. Petersburg Conservatoire from 1901, César Cui being his master in musical theory. On Oct. 14, 1904, he made his debut in Berlin with sensational success, and then he toured all over Germany. On Mar. 21, 1905, he gave his first concert in London with the London Symphony Orchestra, at the Queen's Hall, when he played the Tschaikowsky concerto with such ease and feeling that he fascinated his audience, which was no less charmed with his poetical rendering of Beethoven's Romance in G. Among several encores he played Paganini's Moto Perpetuo with dazzling brilliancy. He has since been touring a great deal in all parts of America as well as in Europe, and counts among the greatest players of our time. He played at first on a small Nicolas Amati, and afterwards on a fine Stradivari dated 1727 (W. W. Cobbett, in Grove). In Oct., 1932, he was once more in London, and again played the Tschaikowsky concerto, as well as sonatas by Handel and Mozart, a tango of his own, and other solo pieces for the British Broadcasting Co., rousing his hearers to the utmost enthusiasm.

LENA KONTOROVITSCH, b. Odessa, 1892. She studied the violin under Fiedemann at the Conservatoire at Odessa, which she entered at the age of 8, and gained the Rubinstein scholarship in the following year. Afterwards she went at Fiedemann's suggestion to Manchester to study for four years under the latter's former master Brodsky, who secured her a scholarship at the Manchester College of Music. During that time she played many times at Manchester and other Lancashire towns with great success, and afterwards she appeared at the Hallé concerts, the Liverpool Philharmonic and at the Winter Gardens at Bournemouth. In 1913 she made her London debut at the Queen's Hall, where she gave a fine rendering of the Brahms concerto with the Shapiro orchestra, which resulted in an invitation to repeat it at the Queen's Hall Symphony Concert in Dec., 1913. She toured at the end of her studies in Russia and also with the Warsaw Philharmonic orchestra in Poland. In June, 1920, she gave a successful recital in London.

PRINCESS LILLY DOLGOROUKY, Russian solo violinist; was in 1892 engaged for a tour of 50 concerts in America at a salary of 250,000 francs, besides expenses for herself and suite of four persons.

CECILIA HANSEN, b. Staniza Kamenska, South Russia, Feb. 17, 1898. A pupil of von Auer at the St. Petersburg Conservatoire. Made her debut as violin virtuoso in 1910; toured in Europe since 1921 and in the United States of America 1923–4. She married the pianist Boris Sacharov.

VIKTOR GRIGORJEWITSCH WALTER, b. Taganrog, 18... A pupil of W. Nemetz and von Auer at St. Petersburg; for many years concertmeister at the Imp. St. Mary's (? Marientheater) theatre there; he was also known as a writer on musical subjects, i.e. "How must one Learn to Play the Violin?" (E. Fr. Naprovonik, St. Petersburg, 1914).

JSSAY BARMAS, b. Odessa. Studied for 5 years at Moscow Conservatoire under Hřimaly and afterwards 3 years under Joachim at Berlin. In 1901 appointed teacher at the Stern Conservatoire, and 1905 first teacher for violin at the Klindworth-Scharroeuka Conservatoire. In touring he gained the reputation of an excellent artist. In 1911 he became Professor. He has written several didactic works and edited all the studies of J. Dont, as well as concertos, etc., by older and newer masters.

ALEXANDER FIEDEMANN, b. Kiev, Oct. 25, 1878. Studied first under Ševčik, then, from the age of 12, under Brodsky at Leipzig. Afterwards he toured successfully in America, also with Mme. Nikisch and then returned, for 14 years, to Odessa as first teacher at the Conservatoire. In 1909 he went in the same capacity to the Stern Conservatoire, where he formed a permanent quartet which soon became favourably known. Among his pupils he counts Mischa Elman, before he went under von Auer, Lena Kontorowitsch and many other notable artists.

BASIL SCHIRINSKI, b. Ekaterinodar, 1901. Pupil of Conus and Krein at the Moscow Conservatoire until 1923, composition under G. Catoire and Nic. Mjaskovsky; since 1923 second violin in the Conservatoire quartet. As a soloist he is an exponent of the modern school, and the first to play the concertos by Prokofieff and by Szymanovski in public. Composed a sonata for violin and pianoforte; sonata for viola and pianoforte; 2 string quartets; suite for orchestra, songs with orchestra and with pianoforte.

BORIS SCHWARZ, b. St. Petersburg, Mar. 26, 1906. Son of the pianist Jos. Schwarz. At the age of 6 he went to a Grammar School (Gymnasium) in Berlin, then he became a violin pupil of A. Fiedemann at the Stern Conservatoire and afterwards of C. Flesch in Berlin, and of M. Hayot and L. Capet in Paris. In 1920 he made his debut at Hanover and has since toured as virtuoso in Germany, Scandinavia, Switzerland, Italy, France, Holland and Poland.

D. KREIN. A pupil of Hřimaly at Moscow; mentioned by Wasielewski without further particulars. He is the son of A. A. or G. A. Krein, and of a Jewish family.

MICHAEL PRESS. A pupil of Hřimaly at the Moscow Conservatoire, as mentioned by Wasielewski.

KOLAKOVSKI. A Russian violinist of merit mentioned by Wasielewski as living ca. 1920 at Kiev or Tiflis.

# CHAPTER 65

## *Scandinavia*

FREDERIK FORKILDSEN WEXSCHALL, b. Copenhagen, Apr. 9, 1798; d. there, Oct. 25, 1845. He began to play the violin very early and played a solo before the Court when he was in his seventh year. He studied successively under Lem, Tienroth, and Möser. In 1811 he became a violinist in the Danish Court chapel. Ca. 1818–19 he toured in France and Germany, and in the latter year he met with Spohr, under whom he studied for some time. In 1835 he was appointed 1st solo violinist in the Royal chapel at Copenhagen. He possessed a brilliant technique combined with a powerful tone of fine quality. Among his numerous pupils he counted for a short period Ole Bull, and also N. W. Gade.

ANDREAS RANDEL, b. Randala parish (Blekinge), Sweden, Oct. 6, 1806; d. Stockholm, Oct. 27, 1864. Supported by the Crown Prince Oscar of Sweden, he studied, 1821–28 at the Paris Conservatoire, violin under Baillot and composition under Cherubini. On his return he became a violinist in the Royal chapel and teacher at the Conservatoire where, 1859, he received the title of professor, and in 1861 he became also first concertmeister in the chapel. He was one of the first to introduce the Swedish folk-tune element into his music for plays. He composed also violin concertos, fantasias on folk songs, quartets, and choruses for male voices. He was chiefly famed, however, for his romances, which were widely popular.

JOHANNES FREDERIK FRÖHLICH, b. Copenhagen, 1806; d. there (?), 1860. A pupil of Claus Schall, Copenhagen. He appears to have toured abroad from 1829 to 1831, and was appointed concertmeister and capellmeister in the Danish Court chapel in 1835. In 1844 he retired on account of a nervous complaint. He was one of the best violinists and quartet players of his time.

OLE BORNEMANN BULL, b. Bergen, Feb. 5, 1810; d. at his villa, Lysöen, near Bergen, Aug. 17, 1880. The art of Ole Bull cannot be measured by ordinary standards and has been adversely criticized and accused of charlatanry by those who did so; yet the fact remains that he was a phenomenal figure, unrivalled in his own particular way. His art reflects the grand but rugged spirit of his native country, and he could touch the hearts of men as well as dazzle them by his prodigious technique. It was the latter as well as the lack of systematic training plus the low popular taste that led him to indulge in those tricks which, while not belonging to the domain of legitimate musical art, delighted the crowd and brought him a golden harvest. He was in this respect a counterpart of Paganini. As in the case of nearly all great artists, he showed an early love for music, which found ample food in the musical home where frequent quartet practices were held. His uncle Jens, who noticed his talent, presented him with a lemon-yellow fiddle when he was but 5 years old, and to the surprise of all he soon learnt to play. A good amateur violinist, Paulsen, a Dane, who played in his father's quartet, gave him some instruction, and before long he was able to take Paulsen's place when the latter was absent. At the age of 9 he played 1st violin in the band of a small amateur orchestra in which his father was interested, and in 1822 he received his first systematic lessons from Lundholm, a Swede, who had been a pupil of Baillot. His father had intended him for the Church and sent him to the University of Christiania, but although he managed to scrape through the B.A. examination, he spent most of his time in practising the violin, and for a time conducted a Philharmonic Dramatic Society at Christiania. In May, 1829, he went, against his father's wish, to Cassel with the intention to study under Spohr; but met with a cold reception and returned in a somewhat despondent frame of mind. When he came to Christiania, however, he was vociferously cheered by his friends, who compelled him to conduct once more at the above society. In 1831 he went to Paris, where he met with several adventures told in the biography by his widow. One of these was fraught with important consequences. All his possessions, including his violin, had been stolen from him, and in utter despair he threw himself into the Seine.   He was saved, however, and a wealthy lady of rank who happened to be passing, was so struck with his resemblance to her late son that she adopted him temporarily, provided him with means and gave him a Guarnerius violin.   In that year he met also his first wife, Alexandrine Felicie Villeminot, at the house of her grandmother who had nursed him through a long and serious illness.   The chief object of his sojourn in Paris was to hear Paganini and to adopt his style.   In 1832 he gave a concert in Paris under the patronage of the Duke of Montebello and afterwards toured with varying success in Switzerland and in Italy.   At Naples his Guarnerius was stolen, and he had to pay a large sum for an Amati.   In 1835 he revisited Paris, where in the following year he was married and also made the personal acquaintance of Paganini.   Soon afterwards he started on a tour through England, Belgium, Spain, Germany and Russia, and returned with a modest fortune to Norway.   In 1838 he toured again in Germany and met with a friendly reception from Spohr at Cassel.   The latter gives his opinion of him at that time to the following effect: "His double stopping and chord playing and the surety of the left hand are admirable, but, like Paganini, he sacrifices to his acrobatics too many of the nobler things of the instrument.   His tone, with the thin strings he uses, is bad, and with an almost flat bridge he can use the A and D strings only in the lower positions and *pp*.   That makes his playing, when he cannot show off his fireworks, rather monotonous.   We noticed this in two Mozart quartets which he played at my house.   He plays however with great feeling, but not with refined taste."   In Berlin the press was merciless in its criticism.   He extended his tour to Vienna and Budapest, where he purchased a Stradivari violin inlaid with ebony and ivory ornaments, dated 1687.   The tone of this beautiful instrument was only moderate.   In 1843 he went to America, where he travelled all over the States and gave 200 concerts which brought him fame and substantial reward.   In Dec., 1845, he rejoined his family in Paris, and in the following year he toured in France.   In 1847 he went to Algiers and returned via Spain, where he was received with great honours and decorated with the Order of Carlos III, set in diamonds. In 1848 he went via Paris and Brussels to Norway, where he attempted to found a national theatre but failed on account of differences with the authorities. The attempt cost him a considerable part of his fortune. In 1852 he went again to America, where he toured with Adelina Patti and the pianist Strakosch, and purchased large tracts of land in Pennsylvania for the establishment of a Norwegian colony; but the agent sold him land for which he had no title, and Bull lost every penny of the money. He continued his tour right into South America where, in the neighbourhood of Panama, he was again robbed of his baggage and his violin. He remained there in the endeavour to retrieve his property and was attacked by yellow fever, from which however he slowly recovered, and when he returned to Philadelphia he learned of the loss of his Norwegian colony. In New York he gave a series of successful concerts and in 1857 he returned to Bergen, where he interested himself again for the National theatre, but with little success. In 1885 he went to Germany and in 1862 to Paris. During 1863–7 he toured again in Germany, Poland and Russia, and during that period he acquired in Moscow an Amati as well as a Joseph Guarnerius violin. In Nov., 1867, he went to America for the third time, where he made the acquaintance of the lady who in 1870 became his second wife. She survived him and as Sarah C. Bull wrote his biography. The marriage took place in Norway, and in 1872 he made a fourth journey to America, but returned in the following spring to his country house on the island of Lysö. From there he undertook a further number of concert tours, including one to Egypt in 1876; but gradually withdrew from public life, working among others on a tutor for the violin based upon his own experiences. One of the features in his concerts was the playing of melodies in full four-part harmony. It was for this purpose that he had the arching of his bridge lowered till it became almost flat, as mentioned by Spohr (*see* p. 410). He also used a very long and heavy bow. One of his most precious violins was a very perfect specimen of Gasparo da Salo's art with a beautiful head in place of the scroll— said to have been carved by Benvenuto Cellini. His numerous compositions are of the virtuoso kind; the best are his fantasias on Norwegian airs.

HOLGER SIMON PAULLI, b. Copenhagen, Feb. 22, 1810; d. there, Dec. 23, 1891. A violin pupil first of Klaus Schall, then of Wexschall; entered the Royal chapel in 1828 as violinist, then became ballet trainer, 1849 concertmeister and 1861 capellmeister. In 1866 he was co-founder and one of the directors of the Royal Conservatoire; 1865–70 conductor of the orchestral concerts of the Musical Union; 1872–77 also conductor of the (St.) Cecilia Union. He also conducted the first performances of Wagner's Lohengrin (1870), Meistersingers (1872) and Tannhäuser (1875) at Copenhagen. He composed studies for violin, a Singspiel, an overture, ballets and songs.

EDUARD HELSTED, b. Copenhagen, Dec. 8, 1816; d. there, 1900. In 1838 violinist in the Royal chapel; 1863 concertmeister; from 1869 only teacher at the Conservatoire. Between 1840 and 1850 he wrote several ballets and incidental music. He was a personal friend of Schumann.

SIEGFRIED SALOMON, b. Tonderen, Denmark, ca. 1818; d. Stockholm, July 22, 1899. His father, a merchant and good amateur violinist, gave him his first lessons on the violin; from his twelfth year he had various violin teachers at Copenhagen and Weise and Siboni for composition. A Government scholarship enabled him to travel in Germany. At Dessau, where he was engaged in the theatre orchestra, he continued his theoretical studies under Fr. Schneider. In 1841 he went to Dresden to perfect himself on the violin under Lipinski. Returning to Denmark, he lectured on musical theory. He then wrote several successful operas and toured as a virtuoso in Germany, Russia and the Netherlands. He lived alternately at Brussels and some of the Rhenish towns, and married in Holland in 1850 the eminent singer Henrietta Nissen, whom in 1859 he followed to Russia. After her death at Harzburg in 1879 he settled at Stockholm. He composed a Romance for violin and pianoforte (Hamburg, Schuberth) and other violin pieces, operas, overtures and songs.

WALDEMAR TOFTE, b. Copenhagen, Oct. 21, 1832. Pupil of Joachim and Spohr. In 1863 solo violinist in Danish Court Chapel, and from 1866 eminent teacher at Copenhagen Conservatoire.

CHRISTIAN FREDERICK SCHIÖRRING, b. Aarhus, Feb. 10, 1837; d. Copenhagen, Dec. 20, 1893. He became violinist in the

Royal chapel, Copenhagen, in 1858, and solo violinist in 1870. He was an excellent chamber-music player and composer for his instrument.

JOSEPH DENTE, b. Stockholm, Jan. 23, 1838; d. there, May 24, 1905. Studied the violin under d'Aubert at Stockholm and Léonard at Brussels, and composition under Winge and Franz Berwald. In 1853, violinist in the Stockholm Court chapel; 1861 chorus master at the Opera there; 1868 concert-meister. In 1870 he became an M.A. He composed a violin concerto, a romance for violin and pianoforte; symphony in d minor (awarded prize in Berlin, 1888); concert overture; an operetta, songs, etc. In 1872 he was vice-capellmeister; 1882–1903 teacher of composition and orchestration at the Conservatoire; 1809–91 conductor of the symphony concerts of the Opera orchestra.

CHRISTIAN FREDERIK HILMER, b. Copenhagen, Feb. 13, 1845; d. there, 1901. Till 1874 pupil of the chamber musician Schjörring, then of Lauterbach at Dresden and finally of Joachim in Berlin. By 1872 he had become a violinist in the Royal chapel at Copenhagen, and after completing his studies he returned to that position and lived there also as a virtuoso, leader of a quartet and teacher.

ANTON PLUM SVENDSEN, b. Copenhagen, June 23, 1846. Pupil of Fritz Schramm and W. Tofte, studied afterwards in Paris and Berlin; then violinist, and, 1895–1910, concert-meister in the Royal chapel, Copenhagen. In 1904 he was teacher at the Royal Conservatoire, and 1915 chairman of the committee there.

AMANDA RÖNTGEN, *née* MAIER, b. Landskrona, Feb. 19, 1853; d. Amsterdam, July 15, 1894. Wife of Julius Röntgen. Studied the violin at the Stockholm Conservatoire 1869–72; afterwards under Engelbert Röntgen at Leipzig. Excellent violinist. A violin sonata of her composition was published 1877 by the Stockholm Musical Art Society.

LARS JOHAN ZETTERQUIST, b. Tveta (Province Värmland), Sweden, Mar. 25, 1860. After studies at the Royal Conservatoire in Stockholm, 1875–78, and with Léonard in Paris, 1878–80, he joined the Royal Orchestra in Stockholm, 1882, was concert-master there 1886–1914, first concert-master in the Stockholm Symphony Orchestra, 1915–27, and director of music at several Swedish military bands during 1886–97. He was professor at the Royal Academy of Music in Stockholm, 1903–27, and has achieved a wide reputation as solo-violinist. Since 1927 he has lived at Arvika in Värmland, where he is a teacher at the National School of Music (Folkloga musikskolan i Arvika).

JOHAN HALVORSEN, b. Drammen, Norway, Mar. 15, 1864. Studied the violin under Lindberg, and theory under Nordquist at the Stockholm Conservatoire. In 1887 was concertmeister at the "Harmony" at Bergen; after renewed studies under Brodsky at Leipzig he toured as virtuoso; was for some time leader at the Aberdeen Philharmonic Society; then for three years teacher at the Helsingfors Conservatoire. After that he studied composition under Albert Becker in Berlin, followed by another course of violin studies under César Thomson at Liège. During 1893–9 he was conductor of the Harmony symphony concerts, and at the theatre at Bergen, then became capellmeister at the National theatre at Oslö, where he also conducted the symphony concerts and did much meritorious work with regard to musical life in Norway. He married a niece of Edw. Grieg. He composed a violin concerto, 3 suites for violin and pianoforte; sarabande with variations for violin and viola; violin pieces; 2 symphonies; 2 Norwegian rhapsodies; 9 orchestral suites; ancient dances for the Hardanger fiddle; coronation cantata; incidental music to various dramas; songs, etc. His early work, "March of the Bojars", has acquired universal popularity.

HJALMAR VON DAMECK, b. Copenhagen, Mar. 24, 1864; d. Berlin, Dec. 30, 1927. Pupil at the Leipzig Conservatoire 1879–82, of Schradieck and F. Hermann for violin and W. Rust for theory; afterwards he studied for some time under H. Petri. During 1882–92 he was 1st violinist in the Gewandhaus and theatre orchestra and, 1888–92, he was also a member of the Gewandhaus quartet. In the latter year he went to Barmen as concertmeister, and in 1902 he went to New York as teacher at the German Conservatorium, and from 1904 also at the College of Music. In 1910 he went to Berlin, where, from 1911 to 1917, he was teacher at the Stern Conservatoire. He edited a number of works by older masters.

TOR AULIN, b. Stockholm, Sept. 10, 1866; d. there, Mar. 11, 1914. Studied the violin at first at the Stockholm Conservatoire, then under E. Sauret in Berlin, where Ph. Scharwenka was his master for composition. From 1889 to 1902 he was concertmeister at the Stockholm Opera. In the latter year he founded, and became conductor of the Concert Union there, and in 1909 he was appointed conductor of the Gothenburg Symphony Orchestra, also director of the Philharmonic Society and leader of the Chamber Music Union at Stockholm until the time of his death. As soloist he toured with great success in Scandinavia, Finland, Russia and Germany. He was an excellent chamber-music player and founded a permanent quartet in 1887, with which he toured successfully in Sweden, Norway, and Denmark. He composed 3 violin concertos, 1 orchestral suite, violin and pianoforte sonata in d minor, op. 12, and a number of solo pieces, some of which are still very popular with violin virtuosos, as well as with amateurs.

FREDERIK SCHNEDLER-PETERSEN, b. Rudkjöbing, Feb. 16, 1867. During 1885–8 a pupil of Tofte (violin), Gade and J. P. E. Hartmann (composition) at the Copenhagen Conservatoire, and, 1888–92, of Joachim at the Berlin Hochschule, and studied during the winter 1892 in Paris. From 1897 he was violinist at the Copenhagen Tivoli orchestra; 1898 to 1901 and again 1904–5 capellmeister at Marienlyst, in between at Sommerlyst, 1905 to 1909 at Åbo (Finland), then again at Copenhagen where, since 1912, he has been conductor of the town concerts. He also tours occasionally as conductor.

JOHANNES CHRISTIAN FREDERIK SCHIÖRRING, b. Copenhagen, Jan. 10, 1869. Studied the violin there first under N. Hansen, then under his father, Christian Fred. Schiörring, and for three years under Tofte at the Royal Conservatoire. From 1890 to 1892 he was violin teacher at Bedford, and at the same time, 1890–1, leader under Aug. Manns at Glasgow. In 1892 he returned to Copenhagen, became, 1893, violinist, 1917 concertmeister in the Royal Chapel there, and from 1910 also teacher at the Royal Conservatoire. In 1894 and again in 1899–1900 he renewed his studies under K. Haliř and under Joachim at the Berlin High School of Music, played in the Philharmonic Orchestra under Nikisch, and took part in its tour to Russia in May, 1899. In 1907 he visited Paris, and in 1912 he travelled in Germany and Austria for the sake of further improvement of his art.

FRIDA SCHYTTE, b. Copenhagen, Mar. 31, 1871. A pupil of F. Stockmarr, W. Tofte and of Massart and Berthelier at the Paris Conservatoire. Made her debut at Copenhagen, 1889. Since then she has toured most successfully under the professional name of FRIEDA SCOTTA. She was married to the late Fr. A. von Kaulbach, the well-known painter at Munich. In Feb. and Mar., 1893, she gave some very successful concerts in Berlin, and played with great success at Mrs. Henschel's concerts in London during the season of 1894.

J. RICHARD OHLSSON, b. Stockholm, Mar. 9, 1874. Violin pupil at the Royal Conservatoire, Stockholm, and in 1896 at the Royal Academy of Music, London (also composition). In 1915 he was a member of the Royal Academy of Music, Stockholm. Has composed concert pieces for violin and orchestra, also other pieces for do. do.; 3 string quartets.

PEDER MÖLLER, b. Brönderslev (Denmark), Feb. 28, 1877. Studied in Copenhagen and Paris. Concert-master du Jardin d'acclim. Returned 1910 to Copenhagen, where he became a member of the Royal Orchestra and Professor at the Conservatoire. He is an excellent private teacher, is member of the Adler-Jensen trio and is often heard in Denmark and abroad.

MAJA BANG, b. Tromsö, Norway, Apr. 24, 1877. Studied the violin first at the Leipzig Conservatoire, then under Marteau at Geneva, and finally under Auer at St. Petersburg. She made a successful debut in 1900 at Oslö, where she opened a school of music. In 1919 she became a violin teacher at Auer's Academy, New York, and in 1922 she married Baron Hoehn there. She wrote a tutor for violin in 6 books (1922).

HAKON SCHMEDES, b. Gjentofte, Oct. 31, 1877. A violin pupil of Ysaÿe; lived, 1896–1900, in Berlin; 1902 at Brussels; till 1904 in Paris; 1904–5 at Boston, Mass.; since then at Copenhagen. Toured chiefly as virtuoso, visiting also Spain and Russia. Composed violin pieces, pianoforte pieces, songs, an operetta, and the music to a play.

OLE BORNEMANN BULL

APOLLINAIRE DE KONTSKI

WILLY BURMESTER

FELIX BERBER

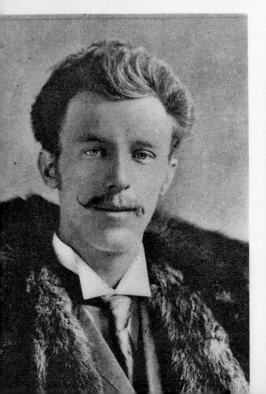

BROR OLAV JULIUS RUTHSTRÖM, b. Sundswall, Sweden, Dec. 30, 1877. From 1894 to 1899 pupil at the Stockholm Conservatoire and 1901–3 pupil of Joachim at the Berlin High School of Music where he became leader of the school orchestra. During 1907–9 he was concertmeister in the Philharmonic orchestra at Gothenburg; since 1912 violin teacher at the Stockholm Royal Conservatoire, where in 1926 he became first teacher of violin; he is also leader of a permanent string quartet. He wrote, "Mechanism of Passage Playing," 1914; "The Art of Bowing," 1921; "Studies in Double Stopping," 1924; and a tutor for the violin, 1928 (all in Swedish).

SULO HURSTINEN, b. Helsingfors, Dec. 1, 1881. Pupil of Ševčik at Prague and Halíř in Berlin. Was for a short time teacher at the Reval Conservatoire, since then at the Conservatoire at Helsingfors. Tours also as virtuoso. He composed, edited and arranged pieces for violin, composed orchestral pieces and wrote a violin tutor.

SIGRID LINDBERG. Daughter of concertmeister C. J. Lindberg; professor of violin at the Stockholm Conservatoire, where Sigrid studied and received a violin scholarship for the Paris Conservatoire, and at the end of her studies she made a very successful debut at the Pierrefonds Jubilee in 1893.

GUNNA BREUNING-STORM, b. Copenhagen, Jan. 25, 1891. A violin pupil of Prof. Anton Svendsen there and of H. Marteau in Berlin. Royal Court violinist and leader of the Breuning Bache Quartet. During 1918–23 she was teacher at the Royal Conservatoire, Copenhagen.

NILS GREVILLIUS, b. Stockholm, Mar. 7, 1893. A violin pupil of Book at the Stockholm Conservatoire, studied afterwards at the Sondershausen Conservatoire. During 1911–14 he was 1st violinist in the Royal chapel and at the Opera, Stockholm; 1914–20 second conductor at the Konsertföreningen. After that he made studies in conducting in various countries and devoted himself entirely to that art. After touring as a conductor he became engaged in that capacity at the Stockholm Opera (Royal Orchestra).

CHARLES BARKEL, b. Stugun (Province Jämtland, Sweden), Feb. 6, 1898. Having passed through the Royal Academy of Music in Stockholm, he went under Professor Carl Flesch, Berlin, partly as his private pupil, partly in the master-class at the Königl. Hochschule für Musik in Berlin. Since his debut, 1918, Barkel is considered to be the foremost violinist of Sweden. He has given recitals abroad with greatest success, and for several years has been first concert-master (primario) and first solo-violinist at the Stockholm Symphony Orchestra. He is also known as an eminent chamber-music player, especially through the Barkel-quartet, founded by him and recognized as the very first ensemble of Scandinavia. He has done much private teaching, and since 1925 has been Professor at the Royal Academy of Music in Stockholm. His execution is characterized by technical mastery, an exceedingly beautiful, full tone together with an extraordinary capacity for musical interpretation.

H. PAULLI. A living Danish violinist, son of H. S. Paulli (?), of whom we have no further particulars.

# CHAPTER 66

# *Spain*

JESUS MONASTERIO Y AGUEROS, b. Potes, province of Santander, Spain, Mar. 21, 1836; d. Santander, Sept. 28, 1903. Appeared as a prodigy at the theatre del Principe in June, 1845. From 1849 to 1851 he was a pupil of de Bériot at the Brussels Conservatoire; 1856 professor of violin, and, 1894, director of the Madrid Conservatoire, also solo violinist in the Royal chapel and the Royal chamber music; 1869–76 also conductor of the concert society (new Orquesta Sinfonica). He toured with great success in Germany and France. He composed a violin concerto; fantasia on Spanish folk-songs for violin and orchestra; Adios à la Alhambra for violin and pianoforte which formerly enjoyed great popularity; 20 concert studies for violin which, since 1878, have been in constant use at the Brussels Conservatoire, and some orchestral works.

PABLO MARTIN MELITON SARASATE Y NAVASCUES, b. Pampelona, Spain, Mar. 10, 1844; d. Biarritz, Sept. 21, 1908. He received his first violin lessons from his father, an Artillery bandmaster, at the age of 5. Afterwards he studied under Manuel Rodriguez at Madrid, where, at the age of 10, he performed at the Court, and was presented by Queen Isabella with a Stradivari violin as well as the means to continue his studies in Paris. There he studied from 1856 to 1859 at the Conservatoire under Alard. In 1857 he gained the 1st prize for violin-playing; it was a violin which, having been lent to a member of the orchestra, perished in the fire which destroyed the Opera. It was replaced by the Government, who had a new one made which was inscribed and dated 1874. Alard was so delighted with the success of his pupil that he asked him what he would like for a present; to his surprise the boy answered without a moment's hesitation, "A box of tin soldiers." A Mme Lassabatlin had taken a great fancy to him, she had taken him into her house and supervised his studies; Rossini also received him frequently at his house and gave him much encouragement. After the death of his benefactress in 1859 he began to tour in Spain, then in Italy and Austria. In Germany he joined forces with Max Bruch, who was then a pianist, at the beginning of his career. Bruch afterwards dedicated to him his second violin concerto in D, in the performance of which Sarasate was unrivalled. The two artists toured together all over Germany with immense success. It is stated that Sarasate visited England in 1861 (B. Henderson, *The Strad*, Mar. 1907), but little notice was then apparently taken of him in this country, while his fame grew apace on the Continent. Ella brought him over once more in 1874 to lead a series of Chamber concerts at the Musical Union, together with Papini, but this was not in his line and he soon resigned his part of the arrangement. In 1876 he met Otto Goldschmidt at Frankfort a/M., who became his faithful accompanist, friend and secretary. About that time Sarasate toured with Pauline Lucca, and Otto Neitzel, who also toured with him for some time about the end of last century; afterwards he toured with that excellent pianist, Berthe Marx, as his accompanist. He had a wonderful technique of the left hand as well as of the bow, over which he had a most perfect command, executing the most difficult bowings with such ease and grace that their difficulty was no longer apparent. His tone was limpid, sweet and pure, and unrivalled in its fascinating beauty, while his intonation was absolutely faultless. His rendering of the Bach solo sonatas was unique in the clearness with which he brought out the parts in polyphone movements with the absence of the slightest roughness, and if they did not reach the monumental grandeur of Joachim's playing thereof, they were entrancing to listen to. A work which he resuscitated, and which appeared as if specially written to show off the strong points of his technique was Raff's "Fée d'amour," which frequently figured in his programmes. He played many classical works with taste and understanding, but brilliant virtuoso music was his forte, and in the playing of his own compositions he was inimitable. Ysaÿe said: "Sarasate has taught us all to play in tune." Flesch, who relates this, adds: "The great Spanish artist might in a way be

called the boundary between the old and the new school."
Apart from the Stradivari of 1724, presented to him by
Queen Isabella, he possessed another priceless specimen of
that master's art dated 1713 (*see* Hill's "A. Stradivari"). He
also had a collection of valuable bows, but he generally used
one by Vuillaume. He received many high orders of knighthood from various European sovereigns, and he was also an
honorary professor of the Madrid Conservatoire, although he
never devoted himself to teaching, and the constant change of
place, which his career implied, would in any case not have
been favourable for that, even if he had been inclined for it.
His death was quite unexpected; there is little doubt that he
was poisoned.

CAYETANO GAITO, b. Buenos Aires (?), 1852. An Argen-
tinian violinist (Head or founder of Gaito Institute), father of
CONSTANTINO GAITO, composer and principal of the above
institute.

ENRIQUE FERNANDEZ ARBOS, b. Madrid, Dec. 23, 1863.
Studied the violin under Monasterio at Madrid, Vieuxtemps
at Brussels, and Joachim at Berlin. Although a brilliant virtuoso he follows the serious vein of Joachim in his art. For
a short time he was concertmeister of the Berlin Philharmonic
orchestra, then successively teacher at the Hamburg and the
Madrid Conservatoires. From 1891 to 1904 he was professor
of violin at the Royal College of Music, London; then professor at the Madrid Royal Conservatoire and concertmeister
in the Royal Court chapel. For several years he had a permanent trio with the pianist Carlos Sobrino and A. Rubio the
violoncellist. Although all three were then residing in London they performed chiefly at the Court at Madrid. Arbos
has composed violin pieces, a pianoforte trio and an operetta.
He also orchestrated Albeniz's suite "Iberia," and made a
new ed. of the works of Vieuxtemps.

ANTONIO FERNANDEZ BORDAS, b. Orense, Jan. 12, 1870.
Studied concurrently law and music at Madrid; became a
Doctor of Law in 1893, and soon after devoted himself
entirely to music, and studied the violin under Monasterio
at Madrid and in Germany. He has toured extensively as
virtuoso and on his return to Madrid he became deputy for his
master, Don Jesus de Monasterio, as concertmeister in the

Royal chapel, and first teacher of violin at the Royal Conservatorio de Musica. He devoted himself almost exclusively to teaching, and eventually succeeded F. Breton as director of the above institute. He is one of the foremost Spanish violinists and excels in chamber-music playing.

JOSÉ GOMEZ, b. Barcelona, 1875. He received his first instruction in violin-playing from José Miro; three years later he entered the Conservatoire as a pupil of Domingo Sanchez. After touring for some time studied once more for two years at Naples under a Bohemian, Eusebio Dworzak. After several successful appearances at Malta he came to London, where he played before the King and members of the Royal family and appeared with great success at London and provincial concerts. He became also a teacher at the Royal College of Music.

JUAN MANEN, b. Barcelona, Mar. 14, 1883. His father, a merchant and musical amateur, instructed him in pianoforte and violin-playing from the age of three and a half years. He made quick progress in both, but showed a predilection for the violin and received further instruction thereon from Clemente Ibarguren, a pupil of Alard. He soon acquired a degree of virtuosity which enabled him to undertake successful, extensive tours as a prodigy. In the course of his travels he heard and came into personal contact with many eminent violinists and further improved his technique by dint of keen observation and hard practising. He also began the study of musical theory and composition without a master, yet attained to a high degree of perfection. His style, tone and technique are said to resemble in many respects those of Sarasate, and in Manen the virtuoso element is also very pronounced. He made his debut in London in 1910 in Evelyn Suart's concert in the Bechstein Hall and on Apr. 20, 1912, played at the Queen's Hall, when the sweetness of his tone, combined with the ease and grace in overcoming technical difficulties, were greatly praised. Compositions of his began to appear from 1899, but he acknowledges none written before 1907; these are marked by the letter A before the opus number. Pub. are: 2 violin concertos; variations on a theme by Tartini for violin and orchestra; suite for pianoforte and violin with orchestra; "Juventus" concerto grosso for 2 violins and orchestra; little Spanish suite for violin and pianoforte; violin pieces, op. 33; an ed. of Paganini's works, transcriptions from chamber-music works; pianoforte concerto; 3 operas; a symphonic drama; symphonic poem; songs, etc. The Conservatoires of Barcelona and Valencia conferred upon him the honorary professorship.

JULIO FRANCES. A 20th-century Spanish violinist; pupil of Ysaÿe; teacher of violin at Royal Conservatoire and concertmeister at the Royal Opera, Madrid. He founded the Quarteto Frances, is conductor of a choral society, and leader of the orchestra de Cuerda. Composed orchestral suites and pieces, and a Balada for solo voices, chorus and orchestra.

EDUARDO TOLDRA, b. Villanueva y Geltru (Barcelona). A pupil of Nicolau, Millet, and Morero, founder of the quartet Renaixement. An excellent Catalonian violinist and composer. He wrote 6 sonnets for violin and pianoforte; orchestral works and numerous songs, some of which appeared in a rich collection of Catalonian songs, "Les nostres Cançons," with some by his masters and other Catalonian song composers.

# CHAPTER 67

## Switzerland

CAROLINE KRÄHMER, *née* SCHLEICHER, b. Stockach, on Lake Constance, Dec. 17, 1794. The daughter of a military bandmaster who became afterwards a member of the Ducal chapel at Stuttgart. Caroline and her elder sister there received instruction in violin-playing from the Court musician Baumiller, and at the age of 9 her father taught Caroline the clarinet. They both made rapid progress and after a time the father resigned his position at the Court and toured with them in the Tyrols and in Switzerland. At Zürich they found a permanent engagement for the concerts of the musical society and remained there for several years. Then they went to the town of Baden, where they played at the theatre and the church, and where Caroline, apart from playing the violin and the clarinet, sometimes conducted the orchestra. After a time they toured again, and at Augsburg Caroline heard P. Rode, whose playing impressed her so much that it greatly influenced her progress. At Karlsruhe (1819) Caroline perfected herself under Fesca, taking lessons in composition from Danzi and also studied the pianoforte. After two years she went on tour again, arriving in Vienna in Feb., 1822, where she met with an enthusiastic reception in the double rôle of violinist and clarinetist at her concerts in the theatres on the Wien and at the Kärnthner Thor. It was about this time that she met and married J. E. Krähmer, 1st oboist at the Imperial theatre. A sonatina for clarinet and pianoforte of her composition was pub. at that time by Leidesdorf.

JACOB ZEUGHEER, b. Zürich, 1805; d. Liverpool, June 15, 1865. An excellent violinist, pupil of Wassermann at Zürich and Fränzl at Munich. In 1824 he formed a string quartet with J. Wex (afterwards Anton Popp), 2nd violin,

Carl Baader, viola, Jos. Lidel, violoncello, which toured under the pseudonym of "Gebrüder Herrmann" in Western Europe with great success until 1830. In 1831 he became conductor of the Gentlemen's Concert at Manchester, and 1838 took a similar position at the Liverpool Philharmonic Society, where he remained to the end, having high reputation as a teacher.

FRIEDRICH HEGAR, b. Basle, Oct. 11, 1841. A pupil of Ferd. David, 1857–61, at the Leipzig Conservatoire. After concluding his studies, for a short period, concertmeister in Bilse's orchestra, Berlin; then he went successively to Baden-Baden and Paris, and was for some time director of music at Gebweiler in the Alsace. In 1863–5 he was concertmeister at Zürich, where he became conductor of the subscription concerts in 1865 of the Tonhallen orchestra in 1868, and director of the newly founded Conservatoire in 1876. From 1875 to 1877, and again from 1886 to 1887, he was conductor of the Male Choir and took a great interest in choral societies and singing in schools. In recognition of his merit in the musical life of Switzerland, the University of Zürich bestowed upon him the honorary degree of Dr.Phil. in 1889. He composed a violin concerto in D major, a violoncello concerto, a string quartet; an oratorio and very effective songs, etc., for male chorus.

KARL JAHN, b. Berne, Aug. 29, 1846. Received his first instruction in violin-playing, while studying theology, from music director Edele, and continued under concertmeister G. Brassin, studying composition under Ad. Reichel. In 1870 he resolved to devote himself entirely to music and entered the Berlin High School, studying first under de Ahna, then under Joachim. When Brassin left Berne, Jahn succeeded him as concertmeister, first teacher of violin at the Conservatoire and leader of a string quartet. In these positions he was still active ca. 1920, although he had given up solo playing for some time on account of advancing age.

KARL COURVOISIER, b. Basle, Nov. 12, 1846. Was destined for a commercial career, but persisted in following his bent for music and entered the Leipzig Conservatoire in 1867 as a pupil of Ferd. David and Röntgen, and finished his studies under Joachim in Berlin 1869–70. In 1871 he was violinist at the Thalia Theatre at Frankfort a/M., but soon afterwards became conductor, studying singing at the same time under

G. Barth. In 1875 he was conductor of the Municipal orchestra at Düsseldorf, but in the following year he devoted himself exclusively to teaching and the conducting of vocal societies. In 1885 he settled at Liverpool, chiefly as singing-master. He wrote a tutor for the violin, and "Technics of Violin Playing" (*The Strad* Library) for students. He composed a symphony and 2 concert overtures.

GUSTAV KÖCKERT, b. Geneva, Oct. 27, 1861. Dr.Phil. and a violin pupil of César Thomson at Liège; lives at Geneva as teacher of the violin. He wrote "Rational Violin Technics" (1904, etc.), which has found a wide circulation.

CARL MARKEES, b. Chur, Feb. 10, 1865; d. Berlin, Dec. 4, 1826. Began the study of the violin in his boyhood, but his father had destined him for a mercantile career, and himself wavered between that of a scientist and that of a musician, but finally decided in favour of the latter, and in 1881 went to Berlin to study at the High School, first under E. Wirth and then under Joachim. In 1884 he joined the Philharmonic orchestra there, but left this in 1886. In 1889 he was appointed teacher at the High School, receiving later on the title of Royal Professor. He counts among his many successful pupils B. Hubermann, Gust. Havemann, Leonora Jackson, etc. He is praised both as soloist and chamber-music player and as such was a member of the Kruse quartet and afterwards of the Haliř quartet. As a soloist he toured successfully in Germany, Switzerland, Italy and Turkey. He wrote "Contributions to technical studies for the violin."

ANNA HEGNER, b. Basle, Mar. 1, 1881. A pupil of Stichle and H. Heermann; 1904–8 violin teacher at the Hoch Conservatoire, Frankfort a/M. During 1908–12 she led a string quartet she had formed at Freiburg i/B.; since then she has lived at Basle. Her brother is the pianist, OTTO HEGNER, with whom she made her London debut in 1893; in 1923 she gave concerts at the Queen's Hall.

LOUIS NICOLE, b. Geneva 18... After preliminary studies at Geneva he became a violin pupil of Schradieck, and afterwards of Röntgen and for composition of Jadassohn and Reinecke at the Leipzig Conservatoire. Reinecke took a personal interest in him, invited him to his house and opened up in him a deeper understanding for Mozart. In 1881 he went to Paris, where for a year he studied composition under Henri Littolf. In 1882 he came to London and began his career as a soloist, but an accident laid him up for two years, and had to relinquish the strenuous practice required for concert work. At that juncture he received an invitation to go to Athens to reorganize Musical teaching there, in which his studies of philosophy and medicine at the University of Leipzig stood him in good stead. He remained there for six years, during which time he also deciphered, translated and harmonized the ancient Hymns to Apollo, then newly discovered at Delphi. Later, in London, he was one of the first to introduce Goby Eberhardt's method of violin teaching, and also introduced important reforms at the College of Violinists, which he became chairman of the Board. He lives now in retirement in Geneva.

FRITZ HIRT, b. Lucerne, Aug. 10, 1888. His first teachers were Jos. Lipa and W. Alsen at Lucerne. During 1902–4 he was a pupil of Brun, Hegar and Kempter at the Zürich Conservatoire; 1904–6 of Ševčik at Prague, and 1906–8 he was in Berlin. From 1908 to 1910 he was concertmeister in the Concertverein orchestra at Munich; 1911 was in London; 1912–14 at Heidelberg. By 1915 he was head of the violin classes at the Basle Conservatoire, concertmeister of the Allgemeine Musik Gesellschaft (Symphony concerts) and founder and leader of the Basle String Quartet.

WALTHER GEISER, b. Zofingen, May 16, 1897. Entered the Basle Conservatoire in 1917 as violin pupil of Fritz Hirt; composition, of Suter; afterwards of Bram Eldering at Cologne, and of Busoni in Berlin. Since 1924 teacher of violin and chamber-music playing at the Basle Conservatoire. Has composed a suite for violin and pianoforte, op. 10; 2 string quartets, op. 3 and op. 6; string trio, op. 8; an overture for pianoforte; flute and vocal compositions.

SILVIO FLORESCO. Living ca. 1920 at Berne, Switzerland; took out a patent for the improvement of modern violins.

L. V. LAAR. A pupil of H. Marteau at Geneva.

H. BLUME. A pupil of H. Marteau at Geneva.

# CHAPTER 68

## *Turkey*

CHEVALIER AUGUST VON ADELBURG, b. Constantinople, Nov. 1, 1830; d. Vienna, Oct. 20, 1873. He was intended for the diplomatic service, but his love for the violin supervened and he studied under Mayseder 1850–4. He toured in the 'sixties of the last century with eminent success and was greatly admired for the power and beauty of his tone. His compositions, described as of distinct merit, consist of violin concertos, sonatas, and studies, 3 operas, string quartets, etc. He also wrote a critique of Liszt's "Die Musik der Zigeuner" (1859). A mental affliction brought his life to an untimely end.

HAIG GUDENIAN, b. Cæsarea, Asia Minor, May 19, 1886. An Armenian violinist. He lived in Constantinople until 1904, when he went to Brussels. There he studied under César Thomson, Matthieu and Crickboom, and afterwards continued his studies at Prague under Ševčík (violin) and Novák (composition). Then he travelled in the East and in the Balkans, studying and collecting traditional native tunes. To facilitate the use of Eastern modes, especially in double stopping, he employs various tunings, which allow of the frequent use of open strings. He combines a considerable technique of the left hand and the bow with purity of intonation. He uses a rather flat bridge, wire first string (or first and second) and a light and rather short bow. On a visit to America in 1918 he married Miss Katherine Lowe, a distinguished pianist, with whom he had toured in the United States, and in England, where he appeared at many public and private concerts, and in June, 1925, he gave a concert in London, with the Queen's Hall orchestra, conducted by Sir Henry Wood, when, as usual, he played his own compositions, including a kind of Fantasia illustrative of scenes from the Rubáiyát by Omar

Khayyám. The majority of his compositions are descriptive of various objects in nature, one of his favourite themes being a bird singing in a tree, in which he employs natural and artificial harmonics with great skill. He has a fertile imagination, Oriental in character, and his performances partake largely of improvisation. His tone is sweet, sympathetic and carrying, but not powerful.

ROSA EHRLICH, b. Constantinople, 1896, of Galician parents. Her mother, a talented violinist, did not live to see her daughter's success; her father was a conductor. Showing early talent for the violin she was sent to Budapest Conservatoire. At the age of 7 she made her successful debut in Vienna, and in the third year of her studies at the Conservatoire she was a pupil of Hubay. At the end of that time a series of concerts were arranged for her at Constantinople, Cairo, and other towns in the East, which proved very successful. In 1907 she became a pupil of Ševčik at Prague where in 1909 she was awarded a diploma, and then toured again in Southern Austria and Turkey, after which she followed her master to Vienna, where he had taken over the violin class at the Meisterschule. In 1912 she gained the diploma and two prizes, one of which was bestowed as a special mark of favour by Ševčik. She visited London with her master, and other of his pupils, in Dec., 1911, when she attracted a good deal of attention. At the end of her studies she toured in Austria and Germany, and in Dec., 1912, she played the Bruch G minor concerto at a concert of the German Gesangverein (London) and other London and provincial concerts with great success.

CHAPTER 69

# United States and South America

FRANCISCO DE SÁ NORONHA, b. Vienna do Castello, Feb. 24, 1820; d. Rio de Janeiro, Jan. 23, 1881. Celebrated as a violin virtuoso and composer; was entirely self-taught. His operas, operettas, vaudevilles, etc., were performed in Portugal and Brazil, and his violin fantasias, caprices, etc., were very popular.

GEORGE F. BRISTOW, b. New York, Dec. 19, 1825; d. there, Dec. 13, 1898. Appeared in public successfully as a violinist and pianist, but his chief claim lies in his merit as a composer in almost all branches of music. Jullien produced his symphonies, which met with a very good reception. He was teacher of singing at New York State schools.

ISAAC BARRET POZNANSKI, b. Charleston, South Carolina, U.S.A., Dec. 11, 1839; d. London, Aug., 1896. The son of the Rev. Gustavus Poznanski, of Polish extraction and a pupil of P. Bassvecchi, a Charleston violinist, from the age of 8, and from 1858 to 1859 of Vieuxtemps in Paris. In the summer he followed his master to Frankfort a/M. and there, as well as at Darmstadt and other German towns, he appeared with success as a soloist. During the American Civil War his supplies from home were cut off, but fortunately he was meanwhile engaged as 1st violinist at the Opéra-Comique in Paris, where he also obtained a number of pupils, and toured successfully with his brother Joseph, a talented pianist, in Southern France. After the war the brothers returned to America and gave successful concerts in New York, and later Isaac toured throughout the States, during which period he gave 2 concerts for the benefit of the poor of Charleston, the City Council, in recognition thereof, presenting him with a silver cup in Apr., 1866. Afterwards he settled down as a teacher in New York and subsequently became director of the

Illinois Conservatoire of Music. In 1879 (according to others in 1881) he returned to Europe and settled in London, where he was highly esteemed as a teacher at the London College of Violinists. He composed a large number of solo pieces for the violin, and wrote an excellent instruction book, "Violine und Bogen," which, by means of illustrations, shows the correct and faulty positions in violin-playing.

GUSTAV DANNREUTHER, b. Cincinnati, July 21, 1853; d. New York, Dec. 19, 1923. A pupil of Joachim and de Ahna at the Berlin High School of Music, 1871–3. Resided in London until 1877, when he went to Boston, Mass., as violinist in the Symphony orchestra. In 1884 he founded the Beethoven—now Dannreuther—quartet. During 1886–9 he was leader of the Symphony and the Oratorio societies. From 1907 he was teacher at the Vassar College. He pub. scale and chord studies for violin. His brother was the famous pianist Edw. Dannreuther.

EMIL MOLLENHAUER, b. Brooklyn, New York, Aug. 4, 1855. Son and pupil of Friedr. Mollenhauer. In 1871 violinist in the Thomas and afterwards in the Damrosch orchestras; 1884–8 concertmeister in the Boston Symphony Orchestra. Then capellmeister successively of the Germania Orchestra, the Boston Festival Orchestra; 1899 of the Boston Handel and Haydn Society, and in 1915 also of the Brooklyn Choral Society.

SAM FRANKO, b. New Orleans, La., Jan. 20, 1857. A violin pupil of Blecha at Breslau, then of de Ahna in Berlin. He made his debut at Breslau at the age of 10, and two years later at New York; returned to Berlin, where he resumed his studies, 1876–8—first under de Ahna, then under Joachim, studying composition under A. Hollander; 1878–80 he completed his studies under Vieuxtemps and Léonard in Paris. In 1780 he became violinist in the Thomas orchestra, New York, where, 1887–90, he held the post of concertmeister. From 1891 to 1897 he was viola player in the New York Philharmonic Orchestra. In 1883–4 he toured as leader with the Boston Mendelssohn Quintet Club in the United States and Canada. During 1893–1901 he gave chamber concerts with his own combination in New York, where in 1894 he founded the American Symphony Orchestra and also gave concerts of ancient music (17th and 18th centuries). The latter he continued in Berlin, 1910–14, and there he became teacher of the violin master class and conductor of the orchestra at the Stern Conservatoire. At the end of 1914 he returned to New York, where he continued the concerts of ancient music and also instituted chamber concerts and operetta performances in 1919–20. He ed. pieces of the old masters for violin as well as a number of their orchestral compositions (concerti grossi). He is still (1929) active as teacher in New York.

GEORGE LEHMANN, b. New York, July 31, 1865. A pupil of Schradieck and Hermann (violin), Lammers (harmony), Jadassohn (composition and fugue) at the Leipzig Conservatoire, 1880–3. In 1883 he won the Helbig prize with Joachim's Hungarian concerto, then went to Berlin, where he studied one season under Joachim. Afterwards he formed the Lehmann quartet and with that and as soloist he toured till 1893. During 1886–9 he was leader of the Cleveland, Ohio, Symphony Orchestra; 1889–92 he toured in Europe; 1892–3 he gave 20 concerts with his quartet at Denver, Colorado; 1899 he was living at New York as soloist, teacher, writer and critic on the periodical *Musical America*. He wrote "True Principles of the Art of Violin Playing" (New York, 1899).

DAVID MANNES, b. New York, Feb. 16, 1866. Studied the violin first in New York, then under de Ahna and Halíř at the Berlin High School of Music, and finally under Ysaÿe at Brussels. In 1891 he became violinist, and 1898–1912 concertmeister in the New York Symphony Orchestra and leader of a string quartet. In 1904 he founded the Symphony Club, of which he was the leader; in 1912 founded the music school settlement for coloured people, and, 1916, he opened a music school of his own. He married Clara, daughter of Leop. Damrosch, an excellent pianist.

MAURICE DENGREMONT, b. Rio de Janeiro, Mar. 19, 1866; d. Buenos Aires, Aug., 1893. He toured all over Europe as a violinist prodigy in 1877 and the following years and was acclaimed with enthusiasm. After a few years he returned to South America, and nothing more was heard of him in Europe.

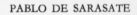

PABLO DE SARASATE

GEORG PHILIPP TELEMANN
By kindness of Prof. O. E. Deutsch.

MAX BENDIX, b. Detroit, U.S.A., Mar. 28, 1866. A pupil of Jacobsohn; appeared as soloist at Philadelphia and with Damrosch orchestra in New York; concertmeister in Germania orchestra, also in Thomas orchestra (1886–96). Founded the Bendix quartet; from 1909 to 1915 he was teacher and soloist in New York and Chicago; no later particulars.

CECIL BURLEIGH, b. Wyoming, New York, Apr. 17, 1866. A pupil of Witek, Grünberg, and Sauret. He is an eminent violinist, professor of violin at the Wisconsin Conservatoire, and has composed 2 violin concertos (one on an American-Indian melody), 2 violin sonatas with pianoforte (based on sacred subjects), a large number of violin pieces with pianoforte.

MAUD POWELL, b. Peru, Illinois, Aug. 22, 1868; d. Uniontown (Pa.), Jan. 8, 1820. A pupil of William Lewis, Chicago; of Schradieck, Hermann, Reckendorf and Richter at the Leipzig Conservatoire 1880–1, of Chas. Dancla at Paris, and 1883–4 of Joachim and Jacobsohn at the Berlin High School of Music. Toured in England in 1882 and made her debut in New York in 1884 under Th. Thomas; 1885 she played Bach's A min. concerto at the Berlin Philharmonic Society with great success. In 1892 she went on an extensive tour in Europe with the New York Arion under Frank van der Stucken. In 1894 she formed a permanent quartet. After then she was a frequent visitor to London, where in 1904 she married a Mr. Godfrey Turner and in 1905 made her permanent home at New York.

NETTY CARPENTER, b. New York, 186?. She made her debut there as a child prodigy, leading a Haydn quartet, and showing, apart from remarkable technical facility, excellent musicianship, which decided her parents to send her to Paris, where she studied at the Conservatoire, gaining the 1st prize in July, 1884. She made her debut at London Promenade concerts in 1882, but it was her reappearance at these concerts in Sept., 1884, that definitely established her reputation as a finished artist. After that she toured all over Great Britain in the company of Sims Reeves. Later in the year she played at Monte Carlo and at Pasdeloup concerts in Paris. She continued to tour on the Continent, where she played also at most of the Courts of the ruling Princes. In

1891 she married the violoncellist LEO STERN. They toured together for some time with great success, but in 1898 the marriage was dissolved and Mme Carpenter resumed touring under her maiden name. In 1892 she visited Northern England and Scotland with the Harrison Company.

THEODORE SPIERING, b. St. Louis, Sept. 5, 1871; d. Munich, Aug. 11, 1925. At first he was a pupil of his father, 1886–8 of Schradieck at Cincinnati, 1888–92 of Joachim at the Berlin High School of Music, and for composition as private pupil of G. Vierling. During 1892–6 he was third concert-meister in the Thomas orchestra at Chicago, where in 1893 he formed a string quartet, of which he was the leader for twelve years; 1898–9 he was teacher at the Chicago Conservatoire; 1899–1902 he conducted a violin school of his own; 1902–5 he was one of the directors of the Chicago Musical College, and also orchestral and opera conductor. From 1905 to 1909 he was teacher at the Stern Conservatoire, and in 1909 he became concertmeister of the New York Philharmonic Society under Mahler. When the latter fell ill in 1911 he took his place for the rest of the season, after which he returned again to Berlin. In 1914 he went again to New York, where until 1916 he was teacher at the New York College of Music and conductor of the Women's Orchestral Club at Brooklyn. From 1917 he toured again as virtuoso. He composed violin studies, op. 4, pianoforte pieces and songs.

PAUL LISTEMANN, b. Boston, Oct. 24, 1871. Son of Bernhard Listemann and pupil of his uncle Fritz as well as of his father. He joined the Listemann quartet and the Listemann Concert Co. in 1888. After touring with these for two years he went to Leipzig, studied under Brodsky and A. Hilf from 1890 to 1893, and completed his studies under Joachim in Berlin 1893–5. Then he returned and was leader of the Pittsburg, Pa., orchestra till 1896, when he took the same position in the American Orchestra of New York; afterwards he toured in the States with the "Redpath Grand Concert Co." His brother, FRANZ LISTEMANN, is a distinguished violoncellist.

AMADEO VON DER HOYA, b. New York, Mar. 13, 1874; d. Linz, Austria, Apr. 4, 1922. A pupil of Kotek, Kruse,

Joachim, Sauret and Halíř for violin; G. Kogel and E. E. Taubert for theory. Toured as virtuoso, then became conductor of the New York Symphony Orchestra. During 1894–6 concertmeister at the Court opera, Weimar, as successor of Halíř. From 1901 he was concertmeister at Linz. He wrote "The Foundations of the Violin Technics" (containing new and revolutionary ideas on the subject), "Modern Studies in the Positions of the Violin," and "Study Breviary" (1919).

FRANCIS MACMILLEN, b. Marietta, O., Oct. 14, 1885. Pupil of Bernhard Listemann at Chicago from early childhood; 1895–9 pupil of Markees and Joachim in Berlin; 1900–2 of César Thomson at Brussels, where he gained two prizes, and afterwards of Flesch and of Auer in St. Petersburg. In 1903 he appeared successfully in Brussels and London, and 1906 with the New York Symphony Society. He played Brahms, d'Erlanger and Mozart E flat concertos at Queen's Hall, Nov. 2, 1906. Since then he has toured in the United States and in Europe (1911–14). He has composed a number of violin solo pieces and arrangements, pub. Carl Fischer.

ALBERT SPALDING, b. Chicago, Ill., Aug., 1888. Studied the violin until 1902 at the Bologna Conservatoire, then under Lefort in Paris, where he made his debut in 1905, after which he toured in Europe. He made his first appearance in America at a concert of the New York Symphony Society in 1908 and was the soloist in that society's first European tour in 1920. In 1917–19 he served in the American Army in France and Italy. After the War he toured again in Europe and America. In 1922 he was the first American to play at the Paris Conservatoire concerts, and in 1923 he was a member of the jury awarding the violin prize at that institute. In 1925 he gave a successful concert with orchestra at the Queen's Hall, London. He has composed for the violin: many solo pieces and transcriptions, a suite in C major, with pianoforte, pub.; two concertos and a sonata with pianoforte, still MSS.; also a string quartet, pianoforte pieces and songs.

FLORIZEL VON REUTER, b. Davenport, U.S.A., 1891, of a German father who died seven months before his birth and a mother of mixed Scottish and French blood, who carefully watched and guided his musical propensities, which showed themselves very early. At the age of a little over 2 he had the gift of absolute pitch and could read music, and at the age of 3 he began to play on a quarter-size violin under his mother's tuition. At 4 he received lessons from a professional teacher and at 5 he played concertos by de Bériot, Viotti, Rode, Kreutzer, Spohr, etc., with wonderful perfection. About that period he studied for some time under Ysaÿe, who was greatly attracted by his manifest gifts and pronounced him "the most marvellous genius I have ever heard." After that he studied for some time under Marteau at the Geneva Conservatoire where, in June, 1901, he obtained the first diploma as the youngest pupil to whom this had ever been granted. On that occasion he played the concertos by Mendelssohn and Vieuxtemps, No. 1, Bach's solo sonatas, Paganini's 24 caprices, and 12 études by various composers. After that he toured all over the Continent, and on July 16, 1900, he made his debut at the old St. James's Hall, an enthusiastic and full account of which is given in *The Strad*, vol. xv, No. 172, where J. Broadhouse speaks also of his talent as pianist, composer and conductor. The most astounding part of his musicianship at that early age was his artistic maturity. He played the Tschaikowsky and Paganini D major concertos not only with the faultless technique of a great master but also with that musical insight which we only expect from eminent artists of a riper age. He has fulfilled all the great expectations which he awakened at that time, and he is now touring all over America and Europe as one of the greatest masters of his instrument. During the War he was for some time director of the Zürich Academy of Music, but at the end of it he settled in Germany, where his "Guide to Violin Music" was pub. in Berlin, 1926. He has composed 2 books of Rumanian dances and other pieces for violin and pianoforte and for violin alone, an activity which he has cultivated largely of late. He also ed. Paganini's Caprices, and compiled a suite from the Caprices by Locatelli. He composed, moreover, 3 operas and a number of orchestral works.

SASCHA CULBERTSON, b. Dec. 29, 1893, where, authorities differ, some say in Galicia, some in America. His mother was Russian and he lived in early childhood in the Carpathian mountains, then in the Caucasus, and gipsy and

Cossack music exercised an early influence on his mind. Showing an early love for the violin, he received lessons from the member of a Cossack band. From the age of 9 he studied the instrument for two years at the Conservatoire of Rostoi on the Don, and from 1905 to 1908 under Ševčik at Prague, where he made his debut in 1906. In 1908 he appeared in Vienna. He also played in London with great success.

YEHUDI MENHUIN, b. New York, Jan. 22, 1917. As his parents were very musical but too poor to afford a nurse, they took him with them when they went to a concert from the time he was 14 months old, and he showed signs of evident enjoyment. From the age of 3 he began to play the violin and six months later he became a pupil of Persinger. At the age of 6 he made his public debut at San Francisco before an audience of 12,000 people, and created a sensation. After then his parents received tempting offers from all parts of the world for his appearance, but they restricted his public performances to about two a year. He made his London debut at the Queen's Hall on Monday, Nov. 4, 1929, when he played the Brahms concerto with orchestra, conducted by Fritz Busch. His success was such that when he gave a recital, playing the César Frank sonata, Bruch's Scottish Fantasia, Bach's Chaconne, etc., at the Albert Hall, Nov. 10, the huge place was filled. He is the fortunate possessor of a beautiful Grancino dated 1733, and a very fine Stradivari dated 1695, both gifts of wealthy admirers. Menhuin has devoted three hours to practice each morning, with recreation in the afternoon as other boys of his age, tennis and the cinema being his favourite amusement, especially the films of Charlie Chaplin, who is a very great personal friend of his. With regard to his playing, let it be said that not only is his technique and beauty of tone astounding even at a time when prodigies with a Paganini-like power of handling their instrument are no longer solitary phenomena, but his intellectual grasp of the big works he has attempted, promise to place him with the greatest masters of the violin. Of his playing at the Albert Hall, London, Nov. 21, 1932, *The Times* said, "His playing has a singularly musical quality; always beautifully smooth, and his execution is of masterly ease."

RUGGIERO RICCI, b. San Francisco, of Italian parents, July 24, 1920.  Pupil of Miss B. Lackey and Persinger.  Gained gold medal in contest at age of 6, Weil scholarship in 1926 and 1927.  In 1928 he gave his first public recital in San Francisco, and soon after appeared at New York with Manhattan Orchestra, where he played the Mendelssohn Concerto, Mozart Concerto and Vieuxtemps' Fantasia Appassionata, when the New York *Telegraph* described him as "the greatest genius of our time in the world of interpretative music."  In Nov., 1932, he played with the London Symphony Orchestra with great success.

# List of Abbreviations

| | |
|---|---|
| Apell (Apel) . . . . | *Gallerie der vorzüglichsten Tonkünstler, etc.,* Cassel, 1806. |
| B.B. . . . . . . . | Berlin State Library. |
| B.Br. . . . . . | Breslau Town Library. |
| B.c. . . . . . . . | Basso Continuo. |
| B. and H. . . . . | Breitkopf and Härtel, Leipzig. |
| B.M. . . . . . . | Munich State Library. |
| Beckmann (G.) . . . | *Das Violinspiel.* |
| Berlin Th. . . . . | Therlemeier Collection in Joachimsthal Library. |
| Bologna . . . . . | Library of the Liceo Musicale. |
| Bouwst. . . . . . | Bouwsteene, *Tijdschrift der Vereeniging van Nord Nederlands Muzickgschiedenis.* |
| Brenet (Mich.) . . . | *Les Concert en France.* |
| Brit. Mus. . . . . | British Museum. |
| B. Wagner . . . . | Wagner Library. |
| Caffi, 1, 2 . . . . | *Storia . . . di San Marco*, Venice, 1854–5. |
| Castil Blaze . . . . | *Chapelle Musique des Rois de France*, 1832. |
| cemb. . . . . . . | Clavicembalo. |
| Clarke—*see* Mason Clarke. | |
| Davey (Hy.) . . . . | *History of English Music*, 1895. |
| Dlabacz (J. J.) . . . | *Allgemeines historisches Künstlerlexikon für Böhmen*, Prag, 1815. |
| Dörffel (Alfr.), I . . . | Führer durch die Musikalische Welt. |
| ,,      ,,      II . . | *Geschichte der Gewandhauskonzerte.* |
| Eitner (Rob.) . . . | *Quellenlexikon.* |
| ,,      ,,      I . . | *Musikalische Sammelwerke des 16 und 17 Jahrhunderts.* |
| Exempl. . . . . . | Exemplar—copy. |
| Forkel (Joh. Nich.) . . | *Musikalischer Almanach*, 1782, 3, 4, 9. |
| | *Kritische Bibliothek*, Gotha, 1778–9. |
| Fürstenau (Moritz) . . | *Beiträge zur Geschichte der Kgl. Sächsischen Musik-Kapelle . . .*, Dresden, 1849. |
| Gaspari (G.), I . . | *Ragguagli sulla capella . . . S. Petronio.* |
| ,,      ,,      II . . | *La Musica in Bologna.* |
| ,,      ,,      III . . | *Ragguagli biografici, etc.*, Modena. |
| Gerber (E. L.), I . . | *Historisch biographisches Lexikon*, 1790. |
| ,,      ,,      II . . | *Neues Historisch biographisches Lexikon*, 1812–14. |
| Grillet (L.) . . . . | *Les Ancêtres du Violon.* |
| Hanslick (Ed.) . . . | *Geschichte des Conzertwesens in Wien*, 1869. |
| harps. . . . . . | Harpsichord. |

# List of Abbreviations

| | |
|---|---|
| Hawkins (Sir John) . . | *History of Music.* |
| Hosaeus (W.) . . . | *Fr. Wm. Rust, etc.,* Dessau, 1882. |
| Israel (Karl) . . . . | *Frankfurter Concert Chronik,* 1713–80, Frankfort a/M., 1876. |
| Köchel (Dr. L. von), I . | *Die Kaiserliche Hof. Musikkapelle in Wien von 1543–1867.* |
| ,, ,, II . | Joh. Jos. Fux, *Wien,* 1872. |
| La Borde (B. de) . . | *Essai sur la Musique.* |
| Laurencie . . . . | L. de La Laurencie, *L'Ecole Française de Violon,* Paris, 1922. |
| Ledebur (K. von) . . | *Tonkünstler Lexikon Berlins,* Berlin, 1861. |
| Liepm. . . . . . | Leo Liepmanssohn, Auction Catalogues. |
| Lipowski(y) . . . . | Lipowsky, F. J., *Baierisches Musik Lexikon,* 1811. |
| Lowinski (Alb.) . . . | *Les Musiciens Polonais, etc.,* Paris, 1857. |
| Lpz. Ztg. . . . . | *Allgemeine Musik Zeitung,* Leipzig, 1798–1848 and later. |
| Lucchini (Luigi) . . . | *Cenni Storici sui più celebri Musicisti Cremonesi ...,* Casalmaggiore, 1887. |
| M.f.M. . . . . . | *Monatshefte für Musikgeschichte.* |
| Marpurg (Fr. Wm.) . . | *Historisch Kritische Beiträge ...,* Berlin, 1758–78. |
| Marschalk (Baron E. von) | *Bamberger Hofmusik,* Bamberg, 1885. |
| Mason Clarke . . . | *Dictionary of Fiddlers,* London, 1895. |
| Mattheson (J.) . . . | *Grundlage einer Ehrenpforte,* Hamburg, 1740. |
| Mendel . . . . . | H. Mendel and A. Reissmann, *Musikalisches Konversations Lexikon,* Berlin, 1880–2. |
| Musikfr. . . . . . | Library of the Gesellschaft der Musikfreunde, Vienna. |
| Nagel (W.) . . . . | *Annalen der Englischen Hofmusik.* |
| Opel (J. O.) . . . | *Neue Mitteilungen ... Weissenfels Querfurter Musiker ... im 17, 18 Jahrhunderts.* |
| Peregrinus (Joh.) . . | *Geschichte der Salzburger Domsänger Knaben,* Salzburg, 1889. |
| Pohl, 1, 2 . . . . | *Mozart und Haydn in London,* Wien, 1867. |
| ,, 3, 4 . . . . | *Joseph Haydn,* Leipzig, 1882 (incomplete). |
| Pougin (A.) . . . . | *Le Violon, etc.,* Paris, 1924. |
| R.A.M. . . . . . | Royal Academy of Music, London. |
| R.C.M. . . . . . | Royal College of Music, London. |
| Schering (A.) . . . | *Geschichte des Jnstrumental Konzerts,* Leipzig, 1905. |
| Schilling (G.) . . . | *Universallexikon der Tonkunst.* |
| Schneider (L. and H.) . | *Geschichte der Oper, etc., zu Berlin,* 1852. |
| Sittard (Jos.), I . . . | *Geschichte der Musik und des Concertwesens in Hamburg,* Altona, 1890. |
| ,, ,, II, III . | *Zur Geschichte der Musik und des Teaters am Württemberger Hofe,* 1890–1. |
| Spitta (Phil.) . . . . | *Joh. Seb. Bach,* 2 vols., 1873–80. |
| Str. ⎫ Straeten ⎭ . . . . | { E. van der Straeten, *La Musique aux Pays-Bas,* Brussels, 1867–88. |

# List of Abbreviations

| | | |
|---|---|---|
| Tebaldini (Giov.) | . . | *L'Archivo musicale della Capella Antoniana in Padova*, Padova, 1895. |
| Thayer (A. W.) | . . . | *L. van Beethoven*, Berlin, 1866–79. |
| Thomas (G. S.) | . . . | *Die Grossherzogliche Hofkapelle ... Cassel, 1806*, Darmstadt, 1859. |
| v. | . . . . . . | Violin. |
| Viertelj. | . . . . . | *Vierteljahrsschrift für Musikwissenschaft*, Leipzig, 1855–94. |
| Walther (J. G.) | . . . | *Musik Lexikon.* |
| Wki. | . . . . . | J. von Wasielewski, *Die Violine, etc.*, Leipzig, 1920. |

# Biographical Index

## INCLUDING REFERENCES TO INSTRUMENTS AND HISTORY

### A

Abaco, Evaristo Felice Dall', i, 152
Abegg, Dominik, ii, 93
Abel, Aug., Jun., i, 312
Abel, C. F., i, 28
Abel, Leop. Aug., sen., i, 312
Abel, Louis, ii, 269
Abel, Ludwig, ii, 250
Achron, Joseph, ii, 386
Achscharumov, Demetrius Vladimirovitch, ii, 401
Adam, i, 95
Adam, Jos., i, 187
Adamovski, Tymoteusz, ii, 385
Adelburg, Chevalier August von, ii, 428
Adson, John, i, 63
Agrell, Johann Joachim, i, 305
Agricola, Martin, Musica deudsch, i, 8
Agus, J. F., ii, 66
Agus, Joseph (Giuseppe), ii, 66
Ahna, Heinrich Karl Hermann, De, ii, 119
Alard, Delphin Jean, ii, 180
Alay, Mauro, ii, 75
Alber, Johann, i, 110
Alber, Paul, i, 110
Albergati, Count Pirro Capacelli, i, 161
Alberghi, ii, 64
Alberghi, Paolo, ii, 64
Alberti, Gius. Matteo, i, 162
Alberti, Jean Mathieu, i, 162
Albertini, Ignazio, i, 164
Albicastro, Henrico (Weissenburg, Heinrich), i, 119

Albinoni, Tommaso, i, 151
Albinus, tuning of fiddle, i, 26
Albrecht, Zachäus Wm., i, 327
Alday, L'Aîné, i, 270
Alday, Le Jeune, i, 270
Aldrovandini, Giuseppe Antonio Vincenzo, i, 171
Alexandre, Charles Guillaume, i, 292
Alfonso del Violino, i, 164
Alghisi, Paris Franc, i, 147
Alleaumes, Moritz, i, 298
Almeri, Andrea Roberti Degli, ii, 64
Almeyda, Carlo, Francesco, ii, 92
Althaus, Basil, ii, 303
Altmuetter, Matthias (Altmitter), i, 191
Amati, Andreas, i, 31, 40, 41, 44
Ambreville, Mich. Aug. D', i, 283
Ambrose de Myllan (see Lupo)
Ambrosio, Alfredo, D', ii, 363
Anderle, Franz Joseph, i, 217
Andrea, Giovanni D', i, 39
Andriel, Ant., i, 95
Andries, Jean, i, 207
Anet, Bapt., i, 237
Angelini, Bernardo, ii, 71
Angelis, Bernardo de, detto Bernarduccio, ii, 13
Angermayr, Joh. Ign., i, 208
Angropoli, Nicolo, ii, 18
Anicot, i, 292
Anolgio, ii, 45
Ansaldi, Francesco, ii, 72
Antgarten, Arnold, i, 305
Anthony, Evangeline, ii, 310
Antoine, Heinrich (called Crux), i, 365
Antonii, Pietro, Degli, i, 132

443

# Biographical Index

## L

Laar, L. V., ii, 427

Laar, Peter van (surnamed Bomboccio), i, 172

Labadens, i, 297

Labarre, Louis Julien Castels, De, i, 279

Labeo Notker, bow shown in his translation of Psalms, i, 17

Labitzki, August, ii, 154

Labitzki, Joseph, ii, 153

Labitzki, Wilhelm, ii, 154

Labitzki, Tony, ii, 154

Lacroix, Antoine, i, 266

Lacy, Michael Rophino, ii, 297

Ladurner, (née Mussier de Gondreville—prof. name Mlle De La Gonchère), i, 298

Lafont, Charles Philippe, i, 290

Lagarde, i, 283

Lahoussaye, Pierre, i, 252

Lalo, Edouard Victoire Antoine, ii, 184

Lalouette, Jean François, i, 85

Lamberti (L' Aîné), i, 204

Lamolinary, Jean (Lamoninary), i, 247

Lamotte, Franz (Lamotta), i, 188

Lamoureux, Charles, ii, 186

Lampugnani, Giov. Bat., ii, 16

Lancez, i, 296

Landsberg, Herrad von, Hortus deliciarum, i, 6, 14

Lanfranco, Giov. Maria, Scintille di musica, i, 9, 38

Lang, Adolph, ii, 240

Lang, Hermann, ii, 285

Lange, Hermann François, De, i, 199

Langhans, Fr. Wilhelm, ii, 247

Langley, Beatrice (Mrs. Basil Tozer), ii, 307

Lanzoni, ii, 72

Lasserne, L., i, 263

Lates, James, i, 412

Laub, Ferdinand, ii, 156

Laurenti, Bartolomeo Girolamo (Geronimo), i, 131

Laurenti, Girolamo Nicolo, i, 171

Laurenti, Pier Paolo, i, 171

Lauterbach, Johann Christoph, ii, 246

Lavotta, Johann, i, 416

Law, Mary, ii, 318

Lazarin, i, 85

Leblanc, i, 265

Lebrun, Félicité, i, 288

Leclair, Antoine, Remi (called Le Cadet), i, 239

Leclair, Jean Benoit, 1, 242

Leclair, Jean Marie (L' Aîné), i, 237

Leclair, Pierre, i, 241

Lederer, Joseph, ii, 287

Ledger lines, avoided by older composers, i, 78

Le Duc, Simon (L'Aine), i, 261

Le Duc, Pierre, i, 266

Leenders, Maurice Gerard Hubert, ii, 369

Lefèvre, Théodore, i, 268

Le Fevre, Jacob, i, 317

Léger, i, 85

Legrenzi, Giovanni, i, 129

Lehmann, George, ii, 432

Lehner, Eugen (Léner), ii, 339

Lehneiss Anton, Junior, i, 360

Lehneiss, Karl Matthias, Senior, i, 360

Lehritter, i, 391

Lejeune, Claude (Claudin), i, 79

Lejeune, Henri, i, 38, 84

Lejeune, Michel, i, 84

Lemière, L'Aîné, i, 265

Lemire, Germain François, ii, 77

Lem, Peter, ii, 88

Lenton, John, i, 68

Léonard, Hubert, ii, 137

Leoni, Giovanni Antonio, i, 134

Lepeintre, Auguste, i, 89

Leriche, Jean Baptiste, i, 296

Levey, Richard Michael, ii, 298

Lewinger, Max, ii, 386

Liber, Anton Joseph, i, 327

Liber, Regalis, Westminster Abbey, i, 8

Limido, Estafano, i, 131

Linarol, family, i, 31, 42

459

Strauss, Johann (the father), ii, 112
Strauss, Johann, ii, 112
Strauss, Joseph, ii, 105
Strauss, Joseph (the younger), ii, 112
Striggio, Alessandro, i, 124
Strinasacchi, Regina, ii, 59
Strobach, Franz, i, 217
Strobach, Joseph, i, 217
Strube, Gustav, ii, 283
Strungk, Nicolaus Adam, i, 102
Struss, Fritz, ii, 266
Strzosky, Manswet, i, 225
Stulichi, Antonio, ii, 75
Such, Henry, ii, 305
Suk, Josef, ii, 168
Suonata (Sonata), i, 47
Svendsen, Anton Plum, ii, 413
Symphonia Platonis, title page described, i, 33
Székely, Zoltán, ii, 339
Szeprio, Giuseppe, Count Contin de Castel, ii, 356
Szigeti, Joseph, ii, 338

**T**

TABLATURE FOR VIOLIN, i, 37
Taborowski, Stanislav, ii, 397
Tagliacozzo, Riccardo, ii, 364
Tagliaferry Liberati Il Conte Germano, i, 147
Täglichsbeck, Thomas, ii, 214
Taglietti, Giulio, i, 146
Taglietti, Luigi, i, 146
Tagnani, ii, 34
Taillasson, Gaillard (called Mathalin), i, 82
Taille (tenor violin), 177 *et seq.*
Talich, Vaclav, ii, 290
Tanner, Edmund, i, 72
Tarade, Theodor Jean, i, 265
Tarnowski, Alexander, ii, 396
Tartini, Giuseppe, ii, 5
Tartini, Giuseppe, and the bow, i, 22
Tasca, Mme (Tosca), ii, 42
Taschengeige, Kit, i, 9
Tauber von Tauberfurt, Karl, Baron, von, i, 385
Tauschmann, Ambrosius, i, 346
Telmányi, Emil, ii, 338

Tempia, Stefano, ii, 356
Teniers, Guillaume Albert, i, 202
Terby, François, ii, 136
Terby, Joseph, i, 205
Terby, Joseph (son), ii, 135
Tessarini, Carlo, ii, 4
Tessaro, Agostino, i, 125
Testori, Carlo Giovanni, ii, 18
Teyber, Matthäus, i, 187
Thieme, Clemens, i, 100
Thieriot, Paul, i, 384
Theodorus of Cesarea, archpriest, i, 15
Thibaud, Jacques, ii, 193
Thistleton, Frank, ii, 322
Thomson, César, ii, 144
Thomas, Tessie, ii, 318
Thompson, Peter, i, 406
Thrandorf, i, 396
Thrane, Waldemar, ii, 89
Thurn and Taxis, Prince Alexander Ferdinand of, i, 329
Tibaldi, Giovanni Battista, ii, 15
Tiedeböhl, Otto von, ii, 401
Tieffenbrucker, W., Lyra da gamba, i, 58
Tiemer, Joseph, i, 198
Tietz, August Ferdinand, i, 191
Tietz, Ludwig, i, 375
Tietze, Joseph, i, 360
Tile, Antonio, ii, 42
Tilmant, Theodore Alexandre, ii, 176
Timner, Christian, ii, 372
Tingri, Jean Nicholas Célestin, ii, 139
Tinti, Salvadore, ii, 37
Tintoretto, lyra in picture, i, 31
Todeschini, Francesco, i, 134
Toeschi, Alessandro, ii, 27
Toeschi, Carlo Giuseppe, ii, 27
Toeschi, Carlo Teodoro Giov. Batt., ii, 28
Toeschi family (real name Toesca della Castella Monte), ii, 27
Toeschi, Giovanni Battista, ii, 28
Tofte, Waldemar, ii, 412
Tolbeque, Auguste Joseph, ii, 131
Tolbeque, Charles Joseph, ii, 132
Tolbeque, Jean Baptiste, ii, 131
Toldra, Eduardo, ii, 423
Tomasini, ii, 356

# Biographical Index

Weist-Hill, Ferdinand, ii, 321
Wenck, August Heinrich, i, 391
Wendel, Ernst, ii, 287
Wendling, Carl, ii, 286
Wendling, Karl, J., i, 362
Werner, Justus, i, 310
Wéry, Nicolas Lambert, i, 206
Wessely, Hans, ii, 124
Wessely, Johann, i, 229
Westerhoff, C. W., i, 395
Westhoff, Johann Paul von, i, 111
Wexschall, Frederik Forkildsen, ii, 408
Wheeler, Paul, i, 62
Wichtl, Georg, ii, 219
Wichtl, Rudolph, ii, 219
Wieck, Alwin, ii, 233
Wiedemann, Justus Bernhard, i, 306
Wiele, Adolf, ii, 209
Wieniawsky, Henry, ii, 382
Wietrowetz, Gabriele, ii, 126
Wilhelmj, Adolf, ii, 263
Wilhelmj, August Emil Daniel Friedrich Victor, ii, 261
Willmann, Johann Ignaz, i, 192
Willmann, Karl, i, 395
Willmann, Olaf, ii, 89
Wipplinger, Paul Carl, ii, 235
Wirth, Emanuel, ii, 158
Witek, Anton, ii, 168
Wittenberg, F. J., ii, 81
Wliceck, Carl, i, 233
Wodiczka, Joseph, i, 321
Wodiczka, T., i, 191
Wodiczka, T., i, 321
Wodiczka, Wenzel, i, 321
Woldemar, Michel, i, 264
Wolff, Heinrich, ii, 228
Wolf, Adolf Friedrich (Wolff), i, 349
Wolfgang, Pater, i, 355
Wolf, Johannes, ii, 373
Wolf, Ludwig, i, 385
Wölfi (Wölfi Schneiderhahn), ii, 130
Wolfstahl, Max, ii, 389
Wollaneck, Anton, i, 229
Wollgandt, Edgar, ii, 289
Wood, Haydn, ii, 307
Woodcock, Thomas, i, 406
Wranitzky, Anton (Wraniczky), i, 190
Wranitzky, Paul (Wraniczley), i, 190

## X

Ximenes, Antonio, ii, 91
Ximenes, Nicolas, ii, 91

## Y

Yaniewicz, Felix, ii, 82
Young, Talbot, i, 73
Young, William, i, 66
Yussupov, Prince Nicolaus, ii, 396
Ysaÿe, Eugène, ii, 144

## Z

Zacconi, Prattica di Musica, i, 39
Zacharewitsch, Michael, ii, 403
Zajic, Florian, ii, 163
Zander, Johann David, ii, 89
Zanetti, Gasparo, i, 132
Zanetti, Girolamo, i, 133
Zanetto, Peregrino, viola, i, 39
Zani, Andrea, ii, 24
Zannetti, Francesco, ii, 37
Zanni, Giovanni, ii, 63
Zavateri, Lorenzo Gaetano, ii, 22
Zebell, ii, 220
Zeising, Heinrich Christian, i, 326
Zeller, Georg Bernhard Leopold, i, 322
Zetterquist, Lars Johan, ii, 413
Zeugheer, Jacob, ii, 424
Zich, Franz, i, 379
Ziegler, Joseph, i, 188
Zimbalist, Efrem, ii, 405
Zimmer, Albert Jacques, ii, 148
Zimmermann, August, ii, 224
Zimmermann, Louis, ii, 375
Zinkeisen, Konrad Ludwig Dietrich, i, 381
Zipoli, real name of Corrette, i, 91
Zirelstein, M., ii, 403
Zsolt, Nándor, ii, 337
Zuber, Gregor, i, 107
Zuccari, Carlo, ii, 43
Zucchi, Giacomo, ii, 75
Zyka, Anton, i, 232
Zyka, Ferdinand, i, 233
Zyka, Franz, i, 232
Zyka, Josef, i, 232
Zyka, Joseph B., i, 233

Printed in Great Britain by
Butler & Tanner Ltd., Frome and London
F7.5.833